The
Wenner-Gren
Foundation

For Anthropological Research, Inc.

Property in Question

WENNER-GREN INTERNATIONAL SYMPOSIUM SERIES

. . . .

Series Editor: Richard G. Fox, President, Wenner-Gren Foundation for Anthropological Research, New York.

ISSN: 1475-536X

Since its inception in 1941, the Wenner-Gren Foundation has convened more than 125 international symposia on pressing issues in anthropology. Wenner-Gren International symposia recognize no boundaries—intellectual, national, or subdisciplinary. These symposia affirm the worth of anthropology and its capacity to address the nature of humankind from a great variety of perspectives. They make new links to related disciplines, such as law, history, and ethnomusicology, and revivify old links, as between archaeology and sociocultural anthropology, for example. Each symposium brings together participants from around the world, for a week-long engagement with a specific issue, but only after intensive planning of the topic and format over the previous 18 months.

In fulfilling its mission to build a world community of anthropologists and to support basic research in anthropology, the Foundation now extends its distinctive and productive pattern of pre-symposium planning to the preparation and publication of the resulting volumes. Never before has the Foundation taken responsibility for publishing the papers from its international symposia. By initiating this series, the Foundation wishes to ensure timely publication, wide distribution, and high production standards. The President of the Foundation serves as the series editor, and the symposium organizers edit the individual volumes.

Some landmark volumes from the past are: *Man's Role in Changing the Face of the Earth* in 1956 (William L. Thomas); *Man the Hunter* in 1968 (Irven DeVore and Richard B. Lee); *Cloth and Human Experience* in 1989 (Jane Schneider and Annette Weiner); and *Tools, Language, and Cognition in Human Evolution* in 1993 (Kathleen Gibson and Tim Ingold). Reports on recent symposia can be found on the foundation's website, *www.wennergren.org*, and inquiries should be addressed to *president@wennergren.org*.

The Wenner-Gren Foundation
For Anthropological Research, Inc.

Property in Question

Value Transformation in the Global Economy

Edited by

KATHERINE VERDERY AND CAROLINE HUMPHREY

Oxford · New York

English edition
First published in 2004 by
Berg
Editorial offices:
1st Floor, Angel Court, St Clements Street, Oxford, OX4 1AW, UK
175 Fifth Avenue, New York, NY 10010, USA

Berg is the imprint of Oxford International Publishers Ltd.

Library of Congress Cataloging-in-Publication Data

Property in question : value transformation in the global economy /
[editors] Katherine Verdery and Caroline Humphrey.—English ed.
        p. cm.—(Wenner-Gren international symposium series, ISSN
1475-536X)
        ISBN 1-85973-882-6 (cloth)—ISBN 1-85973-887-7 (pbk.)
   1. Property—Philosophy. I. Verdery, Katherine. II. Humphrey,
Caroline. III. Series: Wenner-Gren international series.

HB701.P738 2004
330.1'7—dc22

                                                        2004003079

British Library Cataloguing-in-Publication Data

A catalogue record for this book is available from the British Library.

ISBN 1 85973 882 6 (Cloth)
         1 85973 887 7 (Paper)

Typeset by JS Typesetting Ltd, Wellingborough, Northants.
Printed in the United Kingdom by Biddles Ltd, King's Lynn.

www.bergpublishers.com

For Jane Collier and Marilyn Strathern
Exemplars

Contents

Acknowledgments

This volume emerged from a conference that took place in April 2001 in Ronda, Spain, with the support of the Wenner-Gren Foundation for Anthropological Research. Its instigator was Sydel Silverman, president of Wenner-Gren from 1987 to 1999, who invited the two editors to propose a conference for the foundation's program. Of the themes we proposed, the one selected was "Changing Property Relations at the Turn of the Millennium." We express our deep thanks to Sydel for encouraging the conference (as well as our regret that she was unable to attend it), and to the foundation for making it possible.

In her stead we were fortunate to work with the foundation's new head, Richard Fox, whose guidance – both logistical and intellectual – was essential to the event's success. This was Dick's first conference and he gave it his all, from helping us draft the call for papers to participating in the conference discussions to advising us on the final manuscript. We are in his debt for his many contributions.

Wenner-Gren symposia are a conference organizer's paradise: the foundation does all the work of setting up and ensuring that it runs smoothly. The person most responsible for our having such a wonderful meeting was Laurie Obbink, veteran of many such symposia, who has a gift for being present wherever something needs to be resolved. Her good sense and great personal warmth were indispensable to making the event a pleasure for us all.

To our participants, as well, we are grateful for that outcome. Both editors found this the most congenial group of brilliant people we had ever conferenced with. If a goal of any conference is to come away with a changed and enlarged perception of the intellectual issues at stake, this one succeeded superbly, and our participants were the reason. Beyond this, however, they created an atmosphere of fun; we all had a great time together. We thank Bill Maurer for suggesting some colleagues unknown to us who proved especially stimulating additions.

Finally, our symposium was greatly enriched by the presence of four people who do not appear in the volume: Jane Collier, Chris Hann, Annelise Riles, and Marilyn Strathern. Through their comments on the papers and in discussion, their conference summaries, and their correspondence with us afterward about our introduction, they helped us to keep the central issues clearly in focus. All symposia should be so fortunate in their discussants.

The theme of this volume is of vital importance not just in the contemporary world, but particularly to the editors, both of whom work in Eastern Europe and the former Soviet Union. Because property held a very specific place in socialism's political economy, transforming socialism necessarily put property front and center. As we began to educate ourselves in it, however, we saw that new property arrangements in postsocialist contexts were but a subset of broader transformations involving property worldwide. Our objectives for the conference, then, included exploring the emergence of new property forms and using that exploration to reconsider what, exactly, "property" is – and perhaps to develop a new definition of it. During our discussions, however, it emerged that new property forms make apparent a multiplicity of possible conceptualizations of property, rather than leading us to a single new definition. We therefore came to see our task as to explore the very idea of property itself, as something that works in manifold ways in the contemporary world.

List of Contributors

Catherine Alexander, Goldsmiths College, University of London
Michael F. Brown, Williams College
Cori Hayden, University of California, Berkeley
Caroline Humphrey, University of Cambridge
Bill Maurer, University of California, Irvine
Bronwyn Parry, Queen Mary College, University of London
Elizabeth Povinelli, University of Chicago
Arvind Rajagopal, New York University
Carol M. Rose, Yale University
Michael Rowlands, University College London
Suzana Sawyer, University of California, Davis
Anthony Seeger, University of California, Los Angeles
David Sneath, University of Cambridge
Katherine Verdery, University of Michigan

Introduction: Raising Questions about Property

Caroline Humphrey and Katherine Verdery

There is nothing which so generally strikes the imagination, and engages the affections of mankind, as the right of property; or that sole and despotic dominion which one man claims and exercises over the external things of the world, in total exclusion of the right of any other individual in the universe.

(William Blackstone, *Commentaries*, Book II)

Property is nothing but a basis of expectation . . . There is no image, no painting, no visible trait, which can express the relation that constitutes property. It is not material, it is metaphysical: it is a mere conception of the mind.

(Jeremy Bentham, *Theory of Legislation*)

What is property, and how can we most fruitfully think about it? These questions animated the planning of the conference from which this volume derives. As is evident from the two epigraphs, they are not new questions. The context in which we are asking them, however, differs substantially from that of Bentham or Blackstone, and therefore the answers will necessarily differ as well, for property – like other "native concepts" essential to the self-understanding of Euro-American societies ("race," "nation," "market," and so on) – is a protean idea that changes with the times. So, then, does its definition, which even within our own scholarly and legal tradition has been variously understood as things, as relations of persons to things, as person-person relations mediated through things, and as a bundle of abstract rights.[1] Questioning

1

property is especially warranted at the turn of the millennium, with the upending of socialist property regimes in so many countries and the appearance across the world of objects newly designated as property, from software to body parts. We might see these phenomena as aspects of a broader global transformation, in which new areas are incorporated into the capitalist economic circuits for which property is so fundamental a concept.

Perhaps, however, looking for a new definition is not the most fruitful way to think about property; that is the position taken in most of these chapters. Instead, they use ethnographic material to examine the *concept* of property as held in different societies – a concept that has great power in the world – as itself an ethnographic object. This angle of vision sets the present volume apart from other books that have appeared on property, many of which take property for granted without problematizing it.[2] Most of our chapters, by contrast, problematize the notion of property in some way. They ask, for example, how "property" comes to be the label under which certain kinds of phenomena are arrayed; how the concept enters into political argument, such as in native land-claims cases; how the "persons" or "things" of a property relation come to be understood as persons and things; how its real-world effects emerge from the ways in which property itself is constituted as real; what it entails as a native concept or category, replete with its own native "theories;" and what consequences those property theories have. Asking these questions, then, the chapters reflect back upon the concept of property. Rather than looking for a better definition of it, we ask how this concept works, who uses it, for what purposes, and with what effects.

Let us dwell for a moment on this last point. As a Western native category, property acts powerfully in the contemporary world. While its conceptual content varies from case to case (and discipline to discipline), it contains its own implicit theories, which endow it with ideological effects. If we begin by viewing property as first of all a form or category of thought and speech, we note that it appears more in some circumstances than in others. The term itself seems to gain purchase in the sixteenth century, although in retrospect we find much earlier a variety of terms and phenomena that came to be called "property."[3] Each time there is some upheaval in how "property" works in the world – as was true beginning in about the 1980s (when, as we discuss later, the balance of public and private property began to be questioned and new objects such as information came to be defined as "property") – there is a resurgence of talk about it. One task, then, is to understand

what sort of work a property concept is doing when it seems to acquire
new amplitude. We might begin this by examining property's implicit
theories, as seen in Euro-American property ideas, since this is where
the concept that is now so resonant internationally originated. Following this exploration, our introduction will comment on the papers in
the volume.

The Work of Property

From early political thought onward, for instance, some sort of property
concept was central to thinking about a whole nexus of themes: civil
government, forms of economy, gender, morality, individuality/
personhood, work, entitlement, conquest. Political theorists have
clarified many of the stakes in earlier writings (see, e.g., Dunn 1996;
Macpherson 1962; McClure 1996; Pocock 1985; Tully 1993; Waldron
1988), particularly emphasizing the economic and the political ones.
To begin with, talk about property was part of the justification for
private ownership. Most economists understand property as a means
of regulating access to scarce resources by assigning persons rights in
them relative to other persons, a premise common to many political
and legal scholars as well.[4] This economistic view assumes that when
resources are scarce, assigning property rights is a good way of figuring
out how to get those resources and keep others out. Once we do that,
once we create property rights and deliver them to people, the economists' property ideology says that those people will have an incentive
to work well and to use assets efficiently, disciplined by the market (see
Rose, chapter 12 of this volume).

A second ideological element is the connection of property with
liberal democracy. John Pocock has observed that this connection has
two distinct roots, one based in natural law (the tradition of Locke) and
the other in civic virtue (the classical tradition revived by Harrington).
Pocock sees the present-day struggle between the heirs of these traditions as a struggle to define the lineage of liberalism (1985: chapters 3
and 6). Here John Locke is a pivotal figure. He theorized property as a
particular relation between state and citizens, a form of subjection to
which property entitlements were central. In his work as well as
subsequent political theory, this became a connection between democracy and property: the property-owning citizen is the responsible
subject of a democratic polity.

Much though Locke is credited with providing an economic justification for private property, reinterpretations of his thought have proposed

that his concern in thinking about property was rather to investigate the nature of political power and the moral justifications for opposing it. He was also justifying European conquest of the New World on the argument that Europeans could exploit the Americas more effectively than the native peoples because Europeans would create private property in land and improve it, something the natives did not do. In so arguing, he was also justifying conquest especially by the English rather than the French, for the former developed agriculture whereas the latter merely traded in furs (Tully 1993: chapter 5). (Rarely noted is Locke's own role in these colonizations, which included writing the Carolina land laws as well as an agricultural venture in the Carolinas that fell victim to the fur trade [ibid., 142–5].) The colonial context continued to keep property very much a live concern in both theory and practice. Following the unsuccessful attempt to exploit India through commercial companies, for example, the British undertook to colonize it directly, justifying that as necessary for the protection of persons and property. Suddenly property became a fundamental justification for government in practice, not just in the theoretical formulations of thinkers such as Harrington, Locke, or Hobbes.

Locke's most signal contribution may have been that he *naturalized* property, by seeing it as present in the state of nature, prior to government – unlike other thinkers (Hobbes, Rousseau) who saw it as a reason for and consequence of creating government. For Locke, property is always-already there, becoming a problem only with the development of a money economy, at which point men must make government so as to regulate people's use of already-existing property. These observations show that Locke is a critical source of the native theory linking property, prosperity, and democratic practice.

Together with the work of helping to clarify either people's access to resources or values (the economistic view) or the foundations of government and civil society (political theory), talk about property was a means of establishing the grounds for a specific form of appropriation, one premised on land, individuals, civil society/government, and plow agriculture (Pocock 1992). In the writings of nineteenth-century evolutionists such as Lewis Henry Morgan (1985 [1877]), property was what distinguished "civilized man" from the "primitives." During that same time, arguments about the merits of private as opposed to common property also entered into politically charged debates about the origins and forms of landholding. Is collective property a "barbarian deformation" of a "natural" law of private property? scholars asked. Thinkers such as Numa Denis Fustel de Coulanges (1980 [1864]) and

Sir Henry Maine (1986 [1861]) argued these matters partly in the idiom of "Germanic" vs. "Roman/French" modes of existence and of scholarship. As Paolo Grossi explains (1981), in these disputes "French" stood for private and "German" for common property, as well as for different models of the civilized subject. Beneath the surface was the challenge German historicism posed to reigning English doctrines such as utilitarianism, by suggesting that all institutions are historically relative and human nature therefore changeable. "Property" was the idiom for these momentous arguments.

It retained this role in the work of post-evolutionist anthropologists in the twentieth century, who wrote of property to show that "natives" (who were found to have it) were sufficiently civilized to warrant the respect of their colonial masters (Lowie 1928; Speck 1915; see Nadasdy 2002: 250) and could administer aspects of justice themselves (Gluckman 1943,1965). These works and other arguments for the "universality of property" (Hallowell 1955) would later be important in fostering indigenous land claims (Nadasdy 2003). We should not forget a final kind of work that property talk did in the twentieth century: following upon nineteenth-century uses of it in opposition to socialists, it became a central weapon in the Cold War and in American anti-communism. This made it especially potent in the politics around the collapse of the Soviet empire in 1989–91, with results that Alexander, Sneath, and Verdery describe in their chapters here. These chapters discuss, for Kazakhstan, Mongolia, and Romania respectively, the consequences of transforming collectivist property regimes through introducing "private property."

What further kinds of work has talk about property accomplished at various times? One is its hint of morality – something we see clearly from Locke's using interchangeably the words "property" and "propriety."[5] What is the proper relation of people to each other with respect to things? How should property claims be judged? Linked to this moral or normative aspect is yet another piece of the native theory implicit in Western property concepts: it emphasizes "rights" or entitlements and sees the subjects of property relations as inherently *rights-bearing*; hence the prevailing language of "property rights." A final pseudo-theoretical element is that if property involves persons, things, and their relations – the standard anthropological conception – then those "persons" and "things" are clearly bounded, have integrity, and are easily recognizable as separate kinds of entities. This conception, to which we return below, limits the applicability of Western property theory, as we can see in this chapter 8 of volume from Povinelli's discussion of aboriginal land claims.

Questioning Property Ideology

These thoughts on the work that the "property" concept accomplishes suggest some questions concerning how we might think about property somewhat differently. One issue concerns the problematic assumptions of the language of "rights" so prevalent in Euro-American property discourse. Scholars in political theory and legal philosophy have subjected this language to critical scrutiny (e.g., Glendon 1991; Mamdani 2000; Williams 1991), objecting to the premise that rights can be universal and revealing the kinds of persons and subjects that rights talk assumes.[6] To avoid such assumptions without jettisoning the notion that *some* sort of entitlement often enters into conflicts over property, it may be preferable to use the language of claims, liabilities, or debts (as Verdery does). Most of the chapters in this volume use the word "rights" only in a general social sense, rather than in the sense of property law.

Other questions revolve around the notions of "person" and "thing" (or "subject" and "object") inherent in a view of property as relations among persons by means of, or with respect to, things. This conception presupposes an unproblematic distinction between persons and things – that is, it assumes an object-relations view of the world; yet to generalize such a conception is ill-advised. Although it has long underpinned the worldview of modern Euro-American societies, it faced serious challenge with the sudden eruption of intellectual property claims in the late twentieth century, partly as a result of new technologies capable of "mining" resources hitherto not considered as such – for example, body parts (wombs, cell lines, organs for transplant, etc.). As any fan of *Star Trek* knows, the distinction between person and thing is also being eroded with the development of intelligence in machines and the incorporation of thing-like elements such as computer chips into bodies, trends exemplified fictionally in the "persons" of Mr. Data and the Borg.

We can go further, questioning the very notions of "person," "thing," and "relation." Standard property theory assumes that persons are bounded units consistent through time, but what if/when they're not? Especially influential in raising this question has been the work of Marilyn Strathern (e.g., 1984, 1988), who posits that her Mt. Hageners are not bounded units but "dividuals," partible assemblages of the multiple social relations in which they participate. Their elements can be decomposed (as in mortuary ceremonies) without any assumption that they *should* be whole, as the Western "individual" is assumed to be. They are like nodes in a network, or something like a railway station, through which people, wealth, creativity, and other things pass. This is a far cry from standard conceptions of "person" in Euro-American settings.

Questions comparable to Strathern's have emerged in post-structuralist analyses of the "death of the subject," which drop the assumption that personal identity is stable or continuous. And similar ideas about the person appear as well in the work of some psychologists, whose research failed to discover consistency of personality across contexts (e.g., Mischel and Shoda 2000). Collier suggests that what creates the notion of the stable and bounded person is the development of landed property, followed by the creation of censuses, naming practices, and cadastres that fixed people to territory.[7] Complementing this is Pocock's suggestion that when commerce began to overtake land as a source of wealth in England and with the development of paper money, there emerged a notion of the commercial personality as driven by ungovernable passions, as flighty, as feminized and unstable (Pocock 1985: 111–15). Works such as these serve to historicize the notion of the bounded person, contributing further to our questioning its relation to property.

A fascinating by-product of this questioning of the bounded unity of persons relates to the theme of cultural property, raised in the chapters by Brown, Rowlands, and Povinelli in this volume. Anthropologists such as Myers (1989), Weiner (1992), and Humphrey (2002) have raised the possibility that "persons" may appear to be unitary through a process of projecting personal or group identity onto things that symbolize immortality (a variant of Collier's and Pocock's arguments). That is, positing certain things as unitary enables the appearance of unity for the persons to whom the things are linked; Weiner argues that to maintain this unity requires withholding some things while giving other things away. The concept of "cultural property" rests precisely on this premise – a homology between the oneness of the group or "people" and certain kinds of objects in which they see their identity as residing. (See Brown's argument on cultural integrity and Rowlands's discussion of lost cultural artifacts here.) As Povinelli and Rowlands show, such ideas also become the basis for a "politics of recognition" in which marginal groups make property claims so as to improve their situations or seek redress, using a tool – the property concept – that dominant groups provide.[8]

If we call into question the unity of "persons" then we must reassess the entire nexus of "persons-things-relations" central to the most prevalent way of understanding property. What is a "thing"? Is it possible that things may *consist of* assemblages of social relations rather than *antedating* those relations, as Alexander's chapter on Kazakhstan indicates? Wherein lies the thingness of a gene sequence or other forms of bio-information now subject to "prospecting" (see the chapters by Hayden and Parry)? As we see in Sawyer's chapter detailing how prospectors define oil as "property" by denying local social and ecological relations, sometimes the most interesting aspect of a property analysis is figuring out what the "thing" is, seeing how it is "made." This sort of question disappears if we think of property as only about rights, for then, as Hallowell contended, the nature or thingness of the thing doesn't matter, only the rights established to it (1955: 242). Yet emergent property forms compel a new attention to the nature of the "things" of property, raising questions about how to conceptualize it. We return to this point below.

Even the idea of "relations" can be problematized, as in Alexander's and Sneath's chapters, both of which discuss the problematic emergence of social links in the postsocialist environment. What kinds of relations does a property analysis include? Overwhelmingly, because the tendency has been to presume that persons and things are recognizable and separate, establishing a property relation means overcoming while affirming that separateness: some persons are united with the thing as against other persons, who are excluded from it. But how about "relations" of consubstantiality, as in Sneath's or Povinelli's chapters concerning Mongolia and Australia, in which persons and things are not seen as clearly bounded and separate but as participating in one another? Is that a "property relation"? And don't all these questions discourage us about the continuing utility of a property conception based on the "persons-things-relations" nexus? At the least, we should tailor our use of it to situations in which the presumed identifiability, unity, and separation of persons and things obtain ethnographically.

"New" Property Forms?

We suggested that flurries of property talk and (re)definition are likely to accompany changes in how property operates. Since 1990 a large number of publications attests to the fact that after a period of neglect, the topic of property has come newly into vogue in anthropology and other social sciences (see Hann 1998). This surge of interest comes at a time of reorganization in the global capitalist economy and, accompanying that, a wholesale transformation of values, as information begins to surpass land or manufacturing as the number-one basis for accumulating wealth. When the values being appropriated change, so too does their form. In particular, their materiality loses importance. Although it was once thought that the political individual needed a material anchor (Pocock 1985: 111), now the objects of many property rights are not material in form – and even when they are, it is not the material form that counts but the information contained in it (see Parry's chapter).

Information poses special and interesting problems for thinking about property, for the technologies of the "information age" make it abundant rather than scarce. One way of trying to capture information is to create intellectual property rights in it, which will make it scarce. Precisely this insight encourages us to wonder at the economistic assumption that scarcity is a basis of property rights – a view presupposing that resources are "naturally" scarce a priori, rather than being *made* scarce only within a given system of values and power relations.[9] Doesn't the scarcity postulate naturalize something – scarcity – we should instead problematize? If property is a way of organizing access to resources, as economists think, does it sometimes do so by *creating* scarcity? With this possibility in mind, analysis should not posit scarcity as a condition of creating property rights but, rather, make the relation of scarcity to property a question, as does Rajagopal in his chapter on public space in an Indian city. Rose, in this volume, offers yet another critique of scarcity arguments.

Focusing on information's abundance relates to contemporary theories about signification. An example is Foucault's proposing, in "What Is an Author?," the concept of the author-*function*, in which the notion of "author" serves as a device to control the proliferation of meaning. Compare this with Derrida's thoughts on the abundance of signification, with authors unable to control the readings to which they are subject, and to postmodern concepts of "floating signifiers," freed from referents. Attempts to tie down meanings or usages often take the form of trade-mark legislation; other means include reworking the notions of "creativity" and "genius." These notions are invoked in intellectual property claims on signification. For example, in deciding intellectual property cases about bioprospecting, legal arguments use the notion of "creativity" in order to answer the question, "who 'MADE' the cell line?," so as to determine who will profit from allowing others to use it (see Gold 1996). Perhaps the ongoing utility of "creativity" and "genius" as grounds for intellectual property claims is somehow related to their being the most individualizing justifications available for carving into public domains.

The proliferation of intellectual property claims beginning in the late twentieth century is sometimes seen as part of a wider process of "enclosing the commons" or a "massive intellectual land grab" (Aoki 1996, Boyle 1996). Taking resources once felt to be either public goods or freely available to all through open-access property regimes, the process involves establishing ways to exclude others from them, as Rajagopal vividly describes in his chapter on traders in Mumbai. Thus, abundant signification ceases to be a commons – is fenced off – even as *air* and *water* have become scarce objects of trading. Although we have long had examples of conflict over rights to water that might prepare us for its commodification, air is another matter. We hear of proposals to institute shares in air as a way to equalize life chances in developed/developing worlds: heavy polluters will have to buy air shares from those in less developed countries, thereby providing them with sources of revenue based precisely in their underdevelopment. One now has to own one's pollution and can then sell it to someone else (see, e.g., Rose, this volume; von Benda-Beckmann 1995).

Because these practices ultimately individualize, they participate in a trend toward the erosion – or at least reconceptualization – of the public domain. The "public" has come to be construed, sometimes, as meaning "audience" (Lury 1993), or as a "general interest" in commerce, an interest furthered paradoxically, as Gold (1996) and Radin (1993) point out, through intellectual property-rights decisions that privilege individuals over any concept of the public domain. As was evident in the celebrated case of Moore vs. the University of California (California 1990), in which Moore unsuccessfully sued the UCLA hospital for a share in the expected revenues from a new cell line created from his excised spleen, the individuals favored are those who promote commerce – the doctors who developed the cell line – rather than those who might claim the original cells as "theirs." In this volume, Hayden and Parry offer nuanced and original analyses of the "public domain" in relation to the risks and rewards associated with commerce in biological materials.

Research Directions

From the examples of these chapters, what should research into property in the twenty-first century look like? First, our authors employ a variety of conceptions of property, rather than shoe-horning themselves into a single one. We believe this variety is part of how best to think anthropologically about property. Although all seek to avoid conflating "property" with "thing" (as in "land is property") and to take a relational view in their analyses, some emphasize property as a concept performing ideological work, others as a symbol, others as person-person relations through things, others as processes of appropriation; some combine more than one of these. The word "property" appears more in some chapters than in others, as does an explicit effort to theorize it. Some of the authors (e.g., Rose) question standard assumptions; others (Maurer) engage in a much more radical deconstruction of customary understandings about property, using new property forms so as to lay bare aspects of property that were previously more hidden.

Second, the chapters suggest that we should question the *language* of property, problematizing uses of it rather than assuming those uses have a clearly understood single meaning or referent. An important matter for ethnographic inquiry into property should be, When is property language used? – that is, when is a conflict or phenomenon called a matter of property, rather than something else? Who uses that language, in what contexts? What social processes does it accompany? The chapters here find it associated with processes of individualization, commodification, the narrowing of "property" to mean ownership – and we find it an especially effective instrument for these purposes. This kind of inquiry shows us property language used as an instrument in political struggle, ranging from cases as varied as the cultural property claims in Brown's chapter to the conflicts between the music industry and "folk music" in Seeger's to the aboriginal land claims in Povinelli's.

A third question our approach raises is whether, given the "native theories" embedded in the property concept, we want to continue to use the word as an analytical instrument at all. Isn't it preferable to abandon a term so heavily populated with common-sense meanings as to be analytically useless? In her closing comments at the conference, Marilyn Strathern suggested instead that we "disappear" property, offering our descriptions and analyses without worrying what these say about the meaning of property, or whether the events they describe are really about property, or how we might redefine property, and so forth (see also Gold 1996). This might indeed be the best route, just as renouncing use of the words "nationalism" and "ethnicity" might improve our thinking about those equally loaded terms. There are circumstances, however, in which it is important to keep the word anyway. As mentioned above, for instance, Frank Speck and Max Gluckman wrote about "property" in their work on Algonkian and African peoples earlier in the 1900s, so as to challenge colonizers' evolutionist assumptions about those peoples. For comparably political reasons, the chapters here that deal with postsocialist transformation find it necessary to talk about "property," since that was the paradigm encompassing the phenomena Alexander, Verdery, and Sneath discuss. Property was the idiom used by international organizations, which made economic assistance conditional on changes in property rights; it was used as well by local and national politicians, wanting either aid from abroad or electoral capital, since anyone seen to resist creating private property might be accused of being "communists." Likewise, students of cultural property and of native land claims perforce employ the concept of property (Brown, Rowlands, Povinelli). But other chapters in this volume find that language confining and proceed with minimal reference to it.

A related and obvious point is that students of property should try to discover whether the people under study *have* a property concept and what it amounts to. What terms do they use, with what meanings, and in what circumstances? How do they talk about what we might think of as a property matter? Just because someone refers to "my land" does not mean that he or she is talking about private ownership; he or she might as well be referring to land over which he or she has only use rights but for which those rights are sufficient for him or her to think of the land as "his" or "hers" (cf. Vysokovskii 1993, Humphrey 2002). More subtly, amid much talk of "my land" the ethnographer might hear villagers also using a word better translated as "mastery" than as "ownership." Further investigation might reveal a conception rooted not in notions of "self" or "belonging" that underlie the English words "property" (Latin *proprius*) and "owning" (German *eigen*) but rather in quite different concepts of dominion or lordship (see Verdery, this volume and 2003 [chapter 4]). Other notions we might loosely translate as property could be better seen as forms of *custodianship* or of *knowing* (Sneath, this volume; Anderson 1998, Nadasdy 2003). In these latter cases, we might decide that to use the term property would confuse rather than illuminate the issues.

Finally, a number of these chapters touch in one way or another on the question of value, central to any property relation of persons and things: no one wants to establish social relationships with respect to things of no value. A significant feature of life at the turn of the millennium, however, has been thorough-going changes in what is considered to have value, and thus in the kinds of things subject to property interest. The question of value and its transformation is readily seen in the postsocialist cases, where the process of privatization raises thorny problems of how to establish the market value of a state-owned firm, as well as of how that relates to the value it represented in the socialist period and to other contextual values being stripped away as firms become private property. Alexander's chapter on how decollectivization proceeded in Kazakhstan offers a particularly sensitive discussion of this issue. She shows that value may be a quality not of single objects but of networks of things and institutions, such that value can be lost by disembedding things from their previous networks. In addition to her chapter, those by Sneath and Verdery speak to the question of how things go from being values to being valueless, junk, or waste – with or without change in ownership – simply because the surrounding conditions have changed. These cases are part of the larger set of processes of commodification, in which money values are assigned to things previously thought immune to them. The chapters by Parry on transacted body parts and Seeger on copyright in music reveal the complexities of trying to determine these commodity values, as well as of ascertaining the owners to whom they might apply.

The matter of values and how they are established or contested through property conflicts appears in other variants as well. In examples very different from the ones just cited, Hayden's, Parry's, Sawyer's, and Rowlands's chapters all touch in various ways on the problem of appropriate compensation (often to native peoples) when local knowledge, biological materials, oil, or land have entered into broader circuits of capital accumulation. What kinds of returns or reparations should these people receive? The question is tricky, for as Hayden and Parry point out, "compensation" in bioprospecting is about the *promise* of a return in some distant future – a concept difficult to explain to those expecting it and difficult to calculate for those who will supposedly pay it. Here, compensation means simple payment, a kind of disguised "rental" of knowledge or substances. More commonly, however, it implies redress or reparations for an injustice. When "compensation" means redress, Povinelli suggests (2002), it implies a moment of *consent*, which must be elicited – and that is part of what the notion of compensating does: it makes a taking seem consensual. This point illuminates the other chapters on this theme, in that the notion of agreement underlying the term "compensation" fits not just the bioprospecting cases but also Seeger's discussion of folk music. Those takings, too, will have to become contracts, in which one party has almost no idea of the long-term potential gains it might expect. In all such cases, putting a monetary value on possible returns to be gained or losses suffered can mean pushing aside other kinds of value attributed to the goods in question, while contributing further to the ever-greater narrowing of "value" to budgetary or commodity terms.

Major Themes

We have grouped the chapters in the volume according to four rubrics, though readers should bear in mind that all of the chapters are rich in ideas and therefore frequently crosscut any simple categorization.

"The 'Things' of Property"

One aim of this volume is to question the standard anthropological view of property as social relations among persons by means of things. Some of the chapters accomplish this by asking about the effects of "propertizing" new kinds of things, such as body parts, gene sequences, musical fragments, and culture. For example, Bronwyn Parry, in chapter 1, asks how property relations have changed as new technology changes the form of the things in question – specifically, the way industries such as the pharmaceutical and medical industries have moved from collecting whole specimens to banking them in the form of information (what she calls "derivatives"). What effects does this have on the kinds of transactions and claims to which digitized life forms can be subject? In addition to showing how these technologies permit vast increases in the speed with which these life forms can be commercialized (and profits thus increased) by rental arrangements she calls "pay-per-view," she also points to wholly new spatial and temporal patterns that such virtualization permits.

Michael F. Brown, in chapter 2, takes the question of the "things" of property in a different direction, exploring some of the dilemmas attendant on treating culture or heritage as property. Like Parry's and Hayden's chapters, his touches on the matter of indigenous rights, although from a different angle. *Can* culture be property? How, and to whose benefit? How can native peoples use property ideas to protect what they perceive to be sacred symbols or objects, and what do they lose in the process? Concerned not only to present the arguments for and against treating culture as property, Brown also suggests how specific indigenous groups' claims to cultural property might be productively negotiated in particular cases.

In chapter 3, Anthony Seeger touches on comparable questions. He focuses not on bio-information but rather on new forms of the commodification of music, based in "sampling" techniques that permit "stealing" the creations found in both folk traditions and other musical forms. His example differs from those of Parry, Hayden, and Brown in that music has been subject to property claims via copyright for at least two centuries, whereas most of those other examples involve items that hitherto had not been treated as commodities. What's new in the case of sampling is that the "creativity" grounds for copyright are being applied to smaller and smaller units, barely recognizable (if at all) as the creation of someone else. In the domain of folk creations, by contrast, copyright protection is deemed unnecessary since these are collective products rather than individual creations. The music industry can thus commodify these musical forms with no recompense to the communities that made them.

Suzana Sawyer's chapter 4 also addresses the question of the "things" of property but from yet another angle. In her discussion of ARCO's oil operations in the Ecuadorian Amazon, she asks how ARCO seeks to constitute oil as a "thing" of property in ways that emphasize its sublime qualities, drawing attention away from its sticky, viscous nature as well as from the equally "sticky" social relations the company is disrupting. Like the other chapters, hers insists that the "thingness" of oil – as well as of other property objects – is a cultural and not a "natural" product. By contrast, ARCO emphasizes the placement of oil in a special habitat once called a jungle but now transformed into a "rainforest," an entirely natural setting into which ARCO enters with great care for the environment, even while wreaking havoc on the lives of different groups with which it comes into contact.

Risk, Value, and Liability

Cori Hayden's chapter 5, on bioprospecting in Mexico, takes the intellectual property questions of the above chapters in a different direction, by asking about the "publics" constituted for new property forms. Hayden focuses on the confrontation of private-sector legal agreements with the rights of indigenous communities. In the case she explores, the contracts for benefit-sharing between drug companies and local communities in Chiapas were fairly soon cancelled as too risky, after political activists effectively accused firms and universities of "biopiracy." Hayden argues that the episode was nevertheless productive – not in fact of benefits shared, but of a range of new instrumental taxonomies for rights in resources. The crucial move was when companies declared an extraordinary range of resources as "in the public domain" (and thus not classified as communal or indigenous property): microbes on government land, medicinal plants sold at markets, petri dishes in university laboratories, weeds on the roadside, or knowledge published in anthropologists' articles. Hayden thus further argues that a key effect of bioprospecting, along with the generation of new objects of property, is the simultaneous construction of various kinds of "publics" – public domains and accountabilities. Inherent in this process is not just the explosive issue of who will become the beneficiaries of the new international politics of biodiversity entrepreneurship, but also how the risks and liabilities are to be created and distributed (cf. the chapters by Alexander, Verdery, and Maurer). Declaring a resource "public" is a way of evading a potential political risk. But, as Hayden also shows, it does not always work, for activists, academics, and NGOs call up notions of "publics" too – public rights and domains opposed to those of the bioprospectors (cf. Rowlands's chapter 9). Hayden shows that in a climate of shifting locations for "property," it is important to consider not just privatization but processes of public-ization as well.

Katherine Verdery's chapter on restitution of property rights in rural Transylvania also deals with questions of risk and obligation, inter-twined with the question of value. She explores the unexpected loss of value of farming land when collective farms were divided up and parceled out to individual families and small groups. Observing that "private property" does not just involve "rights" considered as positive assets, she shows that it also brings with it risk, obligation, and liability. The liabilities of property such as land, suddenly shifted from the state onto the shoulders of individuals, dramatically decrease its value, at least in the short term. The language of "rights" so prevalent in writing on property only serves to obscure the extent to which we need to think in different terms, such as the *obligations* of ownership. Rights termin-ology creates only one kind of person, who has or does not have rights. De-emphasizing such language helps to reveal more clearly the different kinds of persons that property restitution creates: the efficient "masters of the land" on the one hand, and those ground down by account-ability, risk, and debt on the other.

David Sneath's chapter 7 on privatization in Mongolia continues Verdery's theme of exploring the diverse cultural understandings of property that privatization programs aim to homogenize, and he too brings in notions of risk and liability. The Mongols did not have any one term that can be confidently translated as "property" (especially not "private property"), but rather a range of combinable terms expressing variations of mastery, custodianship, and use. Sneath shows how these were embedded in what he calls the "sociotechnical system" of Mongolian mobile pastoralism. The basic contours of this system were maintained, in one form or another, not only throughout the Qing Dynasty (1644–1911) but also during the socialist period. In the 1990s, however, the Mongols set about creating private property according to international advice. Not only did this atomize what had been an integrated system, thus serving to create great differentiation between the wealthy and the great majority of impoverished pastoralists, but it created a political impasse too. Successive postsocialist governments have tangled with the issue of whether (and how) to acknowledge the Mongols' cultural practices of past eras.

Cultural Recognition

A dilemma similar to the postsocialist cases is explored by Elizabeth Povinelli (chapter 8) in her discussion of Australia and indigenous land rights, but she treats it using a different frame, one of "cultural recognition." There also, a colonial private-property regime was superimposed on practices that, just as in Verdery's and Sneath's cases, lacked any equivalent to legal property. Access to and use of land were constituted within complex social and spiritual linkages between people and territorially delimited places, through ties that did not have an abstract existence but were activated within social gatherings and rituals. What happens when the concept of "property" is extended into such situations? Although the Australian government had resolved to recognize and incorporate "other forms" into their notion of "property," Povinelli shows that it was forced – because it assumed property as a legal category – to employ a specific mode of discursive regulation to implement it. In response, Aboriginal Australians were required to "live up to" this mode in making claims, in other words to reconceptualize their social bonds in the particular forms specified in the legal discourse.

Povinelli's chapter shows the contortions people may be forced into, to prove both that they deserve to own land because they have retained a strong indigenous culture and that this culture does not clash with larger national values. In chapter 9, by contrast, Michael Rowlands addresses the more general issue of what it is that is being recognized when culture is refigured as property. If what is recognized is grievance, this entails acknowledging that rights to ownership are something claimed as the outcome of a certain kind of shared memory, and a willingness to redress ignorance and silence on the part of the dominant. If, on the other hand, what is recognized is authenticity, a quite different discourse is entailed, one involving assumptions about where creativity and identity lie and about how assimilation policies erase authentic distinctiveness. The new politics of recognition encompasses and to a great extent dissolves such differences by creating a nexus of "cultural property" ideas embedded in neoliberal discourse.

With Arvind Rajagopal's chapter 10, however, we are faced with a telling example of the limits of such discourse. Media representations invoke rights to a particular culture or a way of life, confronting other aggressive definitions such as that of a middle-class idea of public space. Categorizing urban roads as public space enables the circulation of images of the street hawkers of Mumbai as dirty and disordered, "encroaching" into common territory. The media reorder perceptions and precipitate new ways of seeing and thinking. Such images (as with other forms of intellectual property) are characterized by plenty rather than scarcity, but this very fact undermines their effectiveness in relation to political action. The Pheriwalas (street hawkers) thus symbolize the struggling entrepreneur essential to urban life and at the same time are tied to images of their "selfish" appropriation of public space. Nationwide television broadcasting has recognized, e.g., in advertising, certain redoubtable Pheriwala values (cheekiness, toughness) while nonetheless confirming the illegitimacy of this way of life. And in fact, Pheriwalas are frequently cleared off the streets.

Critiques of Property

Beginning in the late twentieth century there has been a general move throughout the world to reduce or dissolve communal and collective forms of property in favor of "private property." The chapters in this volume describe this shift in many different arenas, from the replacement of the collectively managed Mongolian steppes by individually "owned" pastures, to the transformation of the once-public city street of Mumbai into a cleansed area from which certain citizens were debarred. The increased legitimacy of "private property" is widely associated with the advance of capitalism in its various guises and with the spread of neoliberal discourse into new settings. But are we now reaching the end of the road? Several of the chapters in this volume advance critiques of the assumptions about "property" embedded in such frameworks; we close the volume with three that do so the most comprehensively.

The first set of chapters questioned the nature of the "things" of property. Catherine Alexander, in chapter 11, broadens that concern to question *all* the elements of the standard definition of property as relations among persons with respect to things or values. In privatization, it is often difficult to know what the "thing" is, what count as "persons" and "relations," and how value is assessed? For instance, when the very same privatized factory in Kazakhstan can change its property status overnight, from state-owned to joint stock and finally to open stock property, we are forced to ask whether it is "the factory" that is being transformed, or the nexus of social relations it consists of at any one time. The implication of this insight, Alexander argues, is that we have to rethink value too. Value cannot be just a quality of material objects in relation to prices, but is created in an entire agglomeration of political and social institutions. When these fall apart, that value is lost, even when the object remains materially unchanged. People are bewildered by this loss – or "theft," as they call it. In Alexander's words, "The theft that is talked about here indicates a loss of social relations," and this loss in turn transforms the social persons who had been constituted by those relations. By the end of her argument, we are considerably less sure than we were about what is meant by "thing," "person," "relation," and "value" – and this puts the standard notion of property into serious jeopardy.

Carol Rose's chapter 12 offers a very different kind of critique, exploring the idea of the "property regime," the dominant set of shared understandings about property in a given political economy. Unlike in most of the other chapters, Rose does not use ethnographic data to question the categories of property thinking but rather summarizes a wide literature in law and economics, in order to challenge some of the premises of a Western economistic view of property. Whereas this view would posit that scarcity produces private-property regimes, which enable more efficient uses of resources and thus the creation of wealth, Rose examines several circumstances in which that does not occur. Private property is arrayed against the wide-open "commons" on the one hand and against statist forms of property on the other. Contrary to the assumptions of liberal economists, Rose argues that there may be "good" forms of commons in some circumstances, and that state-created entitlements can also be beneficial. She considers in particular how we might analyze "tradable environmental allowances," such as trade in sulfur dioxide emissions. Enthusiastically received by environmentalists in some quarters on the grounds that they substitute private property for governmental control, such trade cannot be understood, Rose argues, outside the political forces and the clout that enable monitoring.

Bill Maurer's chapter 13 asks two important questions related to the issues opened up by Rose. The first is whether the emergence of a set of new objects of proprietary concern (internet banking products, electronic commerce transactions, and web-based offshore finance services) destabilizes the regulatory frameworks established to control capitalist economies fundamentally rooted in the nation state. Does the apparently a-spatial nature of these new property objects require us to think again about fundamental ideas, such as the relation between property and taxation? If so, Maurer's second question concerns whether the moral orders in which property is instituted may also be destabilized. Cyberspatial property, he argues, points up the contours and limits of both the liberal theory of property and certain established critiques of it, such as that found in Marxism. We need to reconsider, Maurer suggests, our very conceptual apparatus of critique. Indeed in his chapter, the premises of critique, and the analytical form itself, become the ethnographic object.

In the spirit of these chapters, we conclude our Introduction not by offering a generic definition of property but by pointing to modes of approach we have employed. Property can be seen variously as sets of relations, as a powerful political symbol, as processes of appropriation, and perhaps most important, as a historically contingent Western "native category" that has strong effects in the world. The vivid ethnography in these chapters makes clear how complex is the "object" status of many property objects. If we add the idea that persons (as "owners") may themselves be conceived culturally in various ways (see Strathern 1988) and that these ways may change historically, we see how complex is the seemingly simple concept of property as sets of relations. To clarify the political and institutional frameworks that are often "disappeared" in discussions of property, the idea of the "property regime" is fruitful. With new property objects – such as body parts, toxic emissions, or items in cyberspace – that seem to escape such regimes, our contributors seek innovative ways of conceptualizing the processes by which those are formed as "property" and the consequences of how that happens. In addition, several of our chapters show how, with privatization, the mistake was to see a historically contingent private-property form as universal, natural, and neutral. Privatization thus rested on an ideological premise that, in turn, led to invoking property as a political symbol. A similar process is shown in the literature both on native land claims and on cultural recognition, as peoples to whom such a concept was not indigenous nonetheless found that using it enabled them to make substantial claims on the polities that incorporated them. In all these ways we see "property" at work, revealed more clearly for our having placed it in question.

Acknowledgments

For their help in formulating the ideas in this introduction we are grateful to Marilyn Strathern, Jane Collier, Richard Fox, Chris Hann, Paul Nadasdy, Elizabeth Emma Ferry, and the paper-givers at the conference.

Notes

1. Legal scholar Thomas Grey suggests that these different understandings reflected the different "realities" of property at different times and places. The nineteenth-century definition of property as things, for example, as exemplified in the writings of Blackstone, was close to the reality of the time, when wealth was based on thing-like forms (or, in different words, when profits were made primarily from establishing ownership rights to material objects – land and manufactured commodities – and their disposition). The emphasis on things had an ideological function as well, aiming to depart from the conception of property – as webs of relations among persons – that was characteristic of the feudal period they were leaving behind. "Property conceived as the control of a piece of the material world by a single individual meant freedom and equality of status" (Grey 1980:73–74). By the mid-twentieth century, however, Grey suggests that processes internal to capitalist development had undermined property as both a concept and an institution, as the "objects" of property claims were, increasingly, intangibles (such as ideas and techniques); the definition that suits these new forms of entitlement emphasizes property as a bundle of abstract rights (ibid., 75–6).

2. A small sample of these titles would include the following books: Boyle 1996; Brown 2003; Brush and Starobinsky 1996; Coombe 1998; Cultural Survival 1996; Fine-Dare 2002; Hann 1998; Lury 1993; Ostrom 1990; Radin 1993; Rose 1994; Ziff and Rao 1997. An excellent discussion of contemporary property issues is found in Frow (1997).

3. Aristotle described property using words such as *oikos* (things that belong to the household head), *ktesis* (obtaining [possessions]), and *chremata* (things used, or goods, or money) (see *Politics*, Book 1, chapters 3 ff.). He uses these

terms without, however, understanding "property" as an institution, or writing as if there were such a thing as a "property owner." (Thanks to Anthony Long for these observations.)

4. See, for instance, Demsetz 1967; Ostrom 1990; Rose 1994.

5. An excellent discussion of property and propriety in Locke is McClure 1996, Part I.

6. There are also strong counter-objections to the attacks on "rights-talk," coming particularly from people in critical race and feminist legal studies. Their position is that "rights-talk" has been very important to left-out groups in asserting themselves as persons and political actors. (Thanks to Carol Rose for this observation.)

7. Personal communication. She observes that before landed property, we have many ethnographic examples of "soul loss," "dividuals," and other conceptions of the person that do not imagine it as bounded and stable.

8. We note parenthetically that although claims based in cultural property or the politics of recognition are aired in the name of "diversity," international procedures for producing and justifying cultural property (such as UN Conventions) have homogenizing effects: they create similar cultural bureaucracies worldwide, generalize certain definitions of "owning," draw people into using legal procedures and categories, and entrap them in agendas set elsewhere.

9. Skeptics might want to look at Marshall Sahlins's essay (1972) on "the original affluent society," which raises doubts that scarcity is always present.

References

Anderson, David G. 1998. "Property as a way of knowing on Evenki lands in Arctic Siberia." In *Property relations: Renewing the anthropological tradition.* Edited by C. M. Hann, 64–84. Cambridge: Cambridge University Press.

Aoki, Keith. 1996. "(Intellectual) property and sovereignty: Notes toward a cultural geography of authorship." *Stanford Law Review* 48: 1292–1355.

Boyle, James. 1996. *Shamans, software, and spleens: Law and the construction of the information society.* Cambridge, MA: Harvard University Press.

Brown, Michael F. 2003. *Who owns native culture?* Cambridge, MA: Harvard University Press.

Brush, Stephen B., and Doreen Stabinsky (eds.). 1996. *Valuing local knowledge: Indigenous people and intellectual property rights.* Washington, D.C.: Island Press.

California, State of. 1990. "Moore vs. The Regents of the University of California." 793 *Pacific Reporter*, 2d series, 479–523.

Coombe, Rosemary. 1998. *The cultural life of intellectual properties: Authorship, appropriation, and the law.* Durham, NC: Duke University Press.

Cultural Survival. 1996. "Genes, people, and property: Furor erupts over genetic research on indigenous groups." *Cultural Survival Quarterly,* special issue, 20: 22–57.

Demsetz, Harold. 1967. "Toward a Theory of Property Rights." *American Economic Review* 57: 347–59.

Dunn, John. 1996. *The political thought of John Locke: An historical account of the argument of the "Two Treatises of Government."* Cambridge: Cambridge University Press.

Fine-Dare, Kathleen S. 2002. *Grave injustice: The American Indian repatriation movement and NAGPRA.* Lincoln, NB: University of Nebraska Press.

Frow, John. 1997. *Time and commodity culture: Essays in cultural theory and postmodernity.* Oxford: Clarendon.

Fustel de Coulanges, Numa Denis. 1980 [1864]. *The ancient city.* Baltimore: Johns Hopkins University Press.

Glendon, Mary Ann. 1991. *Rights talk: The impoverishment of political discourse.* New York: Free Press.

Gluckman, Max. 1943. *Essays on Lozi land and royal property.* Rhodes-Livingstone Institute.

——. 1965. *The ideas in Barotse jurisprudence.* New Haven: Yale University Press.

Gold, E. Richard. 1996. *Body parts: Property rights and the ownership of human biological materials.* Washington, D.C.: Georgetown University Press.

Grey, Thomas C. 1980. "The disintegration of property." In *Property.* Edited by J. Roland Pennock and John W. Chapman, 69–85. New York: New York University Press.

Grossi, Paolo. 1981. *An alternative to private property: Collective property in the juridical consciousness of the nineteenth century.* Chicago: University of Chicago Press.

Hallowell, A. Irving. 1955. "The nature and function of property as a social institution." In *Culture and experience.* Philadelphia: University of Pennsylvania Press.

Hann, C. M. 1998. "Introduction: The embeddedness of property." In *Property relations: Renewing the anthropological tradition.* Edited by C. M. Hann, 1–47. Cambridge: Cambridge University Press.

Humphrey, Caroline. 2002. "Rituals of death as a context for understanding personal property in socialist Mongolia." *Journal of the Royal Anthropological Institute* (N.S.) 8(1), March: 65–87.

Lowie, Robert. 1928. "Incorporeal property in primitive society." *Yale Law Journal* 37: 551–63.

Lury, Celia. 1993. *Cultural rights: Technology, legality, and personality.* London, New York: Routledge.

Macpherson, C. B. 1962. *The political theory of possessive individualism: Hobbes to Locke.* Oxford and New York: Oxford University Press.

Maine, Henry Sumner. 1986. *Ancient Law.* Tucson: University of Arizona Press.

Malinowski, Bronislaw. 1935. *Coral gardens and their magic.* London: Allen & Unwin.

Mamdani, Mahmood, ed. 2000. *Beyond rights talk and culture talk: Comparative essays on the politics of rights and culture.* New York: St. Martin's.

McClure, Kirstie. 1996. *Judging rights: Lockean politics and the limits of consent.* Ithaca, NY: Cornell University Press.

Mischel, W., and Y. Shoda. 2000. "A cognitive-affective system theory of personality: Reconceptualizing situations, dispositions, dynamics, and invariance in personality structure," In *Motivational science: Social and personality perspectives.* Edited by E. Tory Higgins and Arie W. Kruglanski, 150–76. Philadelphia, PA: Psychology Press/Taylor & Francis.

Morgan, Lewis Henry. 1985 [1877]. *Ancient society.* Tucson: University of Arizona Press.

Myers, Fred. 1989. "Burning the truck and holding the country." In *We are here: Politics of aboriginal land tenure.* Edited by Edwin N. Wilmsen, 15–42. Berkeley: University of California Press.

Nadasdy, Paul. 2002. "Property and aboriginal land claims in the Canadian Subarctic: Some theoretical considerations." *American Anthropologist* 104(1): 247–61.

———. 2003. *Hunters and bureaucrats: Power, knowledge, and aboriginal-state relations in the Southwest Yukon.* Vancouver: University of British Columbia Press.

Ostrom, Elinor. 1990. *Governing the commons: The evolution of institutions for collective action.* Cambridge: Cambridge University Press.

Pocock, J. G. A. 1985. *Virtue, commerce, and history.* Cambridge: Cambridge University Press.

———. 1992. "Tengata Whenua and Enlightenment anthropology." *New Zealand Journal of History* 26: 28–53.

Povinelli, Elizabeth A. 2002. *The cunning of recognition: Indigenous alterities and the making of Australian multiculturalism.* Durham, NC: Duke University Press.

Radin, Margaret Jane. 1993. *Reinterpreting property*. Chicago: University of Chicago Press.

Rose, Carol M. 1994. *Property and persuasion: Essays on the history, theory, and rhetoric of ownership*. Boulder, CO: Westview.

Sahlins, Marshall D. 1972. "The original affluent society," In *Stone Age economics*. Chicago: Aldine Atherton.

Speck, Frank G. 1915. "The family hunting band as the basis of Algonkian social organization." *American Anthropologist* 17: 289–305.

Strathern, Marilyn. 1984. "Subject or object? Women and the circulation of valuables in Highland New Guinea." In *Women and property, women as property*. Edited by Renée Hirschon, 158–75. London: Croom Helm; New York: St. Martin's.

——. 1988. *The gender of the gift: Problems with women and problems with society in Melanesia*. Berkeley: University of California Press.

Tully, James. 1993. *An approach to political philosophy: Locke in contexts*. Cambridge: Cambridge University Press.

Verdery, Katherine. 2003. *The vanishing hectare: Property and value in postsocialist Transylvania*. Ithaca NY: Cornell University Press.

von Benda-Beckmann, Keebet. 1995. "Private ownership of air shares: An appropriate way of letting the poor profit from the global natural resource base?" *Proceedings of the Commission on Folk Law and Legal Pluralism*. 10th Annual Congress, Legon, Ghana.

Vysokovskii, Aleksandr. 1993. "Will domesticity return?," In *Russian housing in the modern age: Design and social history*, Edited by William Craft Brumfield and Blair A. Ruble, 271–308.

Waldron, Jeremy. 1988. *The right to private property*. Oxford: Clarendon.

Weiner, Annette. 1992. *Inalienable possessions: The paradox of keeping-while-giving*. Berkeley and Los Angeles: University of California Press.

Williams, Patricia J. 1991. *The alchemy of race and rights*. Cambridge, MA: Harvard University Press.

Ziff, Bruce, and Pratima V. Rao (eds.). 1997. *Borrowed power: Essays on cultural appropriation*. New Brunswick NJ: Rutgers University Press.

Part I

The "Things" of Property

Bodily Transactions: Regulating a new Space of Flows in "Bio-information"

Bronwyn Parry

There is a series of issues relating to property, technology, bodies, materiality, and transactional behavior to which I restlessly return, again and again, rather like a dog with an unfinished bone. Although the substantive basis of my empirical work concerns the commodification of bodies and bodily parts (both human and non-human), the theoretical concerns that inform this work have, I suspect, some resonances for those interested in the commodification of different, but I would argue related, resources: music, published works, finance, computer software and the like. I am particularly interested in exploring the question of how property relations are reworked as a consequence of the (changing) form or constitution of the "thing" in question: that is to say, how changes in the form or constitution of an object can create new regimes of commodification, new modes of transaction, and a concomitant acceleration of trade and exchange; and with them, a series of challenges for existing property rights regimes.

In this chapter, I draw on my recent empirical work on bioprospecting and my current and forthcoming work on the commodification of human derivatives in order to explore the proposition that changes in the form or composition of biological materials (notably their translation from a corporeal to an informational state) are altering the way such materials are made subject to commercial transactions, and how they are understood and administered in law as commodities and forms of property to which particular rights may obtain. The chapter is organized in four parts. In the first, I begin by exploring how technological innovations are transforming the way in which biological materials are understood, used, and valued as commodities in the life-sciences industry. In the second, I consider a series of questions that revolve around spatial relations. As a geographer, I am particularly interested to investigate how our ability to render biological materials in progressively less corporeal and more informational forms has acted to improve the transmissibility of such resources, and in the process, facilitated the creation of a new global commodities market in genetic and bio-chemical "information."

In the third section, I examine the effect that these developments are having on the traditional dynamics of biological resource exploitation, and in the fourth, their implications for property relations. Many forms of existing property rights are predicated on the nature of the "thing" in question – for example, the question of whether materials may be copyrighted or patented rests on differences in their materiality and means of production. When materials are transmuted from one form to another it is no longer immediately evident to which property regime (if any) they rightfully belong. While some protocols have been introduced to regulate this new resource economy in "bio-information," it is by no means clear that they are adequate to the task of effectively or justly governing these new forms of trade and exchange. Evidence suggests that we have yet to fully come to terms with either the existence of this new economy in bio-information or with our own role as commodities within that economy. My hope is that this paper might alert us to such issues, to stimulate debate and promote a further and wider discussion of these matters.

Collecting Biology: Transformations and Transmissibility

Two activities that have garnered considerable publicity in recent times – the collection and patenting of plant, animal, and human genetic materials, and the collection and unauthorized use of human tissues (as revealed in the Alder Hey body parts scandal in Britain[1]) – promote the conception that the collection and commodification of human and non-human biological materials are somehow new practices, when, in fact, they have a very long history. They have been evidenced over time in the collection, breeding, exchange, and sale of both animate and inanimate biological materials – dried fish, seedlings, grain crops, cows, and even whole persons during the era of slavery. Despite this, a collective sense is now emerging that the covetous demands of a newly burgeoning life-sciences industry might well engender an entirely new phase in the history of the collection and commodification of biological resources. This intuition is a valid one. A new phase is emerging, distinguished, I would argue, by collecting practices and transactional behaviors that remain qualitatively different from any that have previously been witnessed in this domain.

The impetus for this new phase has been primarily technological. Extraordinarily rapid biotechnological advances that began in the 1970s have progressively transformed the capacity to remake life by re-engineering the constituent elements of existing organisms. An apparent but little-researched consequence of this development is the impetus that it has provided for the creation of a new resource economy, or market, in these constituent parts. Since the early 1980s, demand for biological materials has escalated rapidly as the agricultural, pharmaceutical, and cosmetics industries have become increasingly biotechnology dependent. This demand, which is primarily for novel materials that might form the bases of new patentable products, could not be adequately met by "mining" existing stores of collected materials. Consequently, the 1990s witnessed the institution of a multiplicity of new biological collection programs.

This "historic revival of interest in collecting" (Boyd and Paul 1995:91) peaked in the years from 1985–1995 but remains ongoing. Studies undertaken by Darrell Posey, GRAIN, and Acción Ecólogica have revealed that over 200 different US-based organizations and institutions began new biological collection programs in these years (Laird and ten Kate 1999), a fact confirmed by my own research into the organization and operation of the bioprospecting industry (Parry 2001; 2004). Although the scale and scope of these new collecting activities has not been rivaled since colonial times, the nature of the collection process has since undergone substantial change. Technological advances have transformed the way in which biological materials are understood and valued as commodities, and this, in turn, is fundamentally altering the spatial and temporal dynamics of biological resource exploitation and associated transactional behaviors.

As I have noted elsewhere (Parry 2001), breeders interested in reproducing organisms in their existent form, or alternatively, in gaining access to traits such as pest-resistance that might be introduced into other varieties have long collected exotic species from various parts of the world. These transactions have traditionally taken place within certain biological, geographical, and temporal parameters. The reproduction of either whole organisms or specific traits has historically required the acquisition of whole organisms capable of self-reproduction (e.g., living beings with reproductive organs or seeds capable of self-regeneration).[2] Different traits could be combined but only between related species. Moreover, the transmission of traits could be effected only through the interbreeding of whole plants or animals, processes that were constrained by the need for proximity and certain fixed timescales of gestation. The utility of the collected specimens as a source of reproducible material only lasted as long as their reproductive capabilities remained intact. This required that they be maintained as living specimens or breeding populations in appropriate natural or artificial environments.

These parameters have now all but collapsed and with them the traditional paradigm that has governed the nature and scale of transmission of genetic and biochemical material. Collectors still covet such materials; however, they now have the capability to extract them from minute samples of plant, animal, or human tissue. It has, of course, long been possible to preserve samples of tissue – in alcohol for example. However, the genetic and biochemical materials embodied in these samples have been irrevocably damaged by immersion in fixative and are no longer reproducible. Improvements in cryogenic storage technologies, cell preservation, and tissue-biopsying techniques have since transformed this archiving process. Cryogenically stored tissues, blood samples, and cell lines retain the key genetic and biochemical properties of the whole organism, and as little as a few micrograms of material drawn from them is now sufficient to act as a "starter" for artificial processes of replication and modification. These samples of genetic and biochemical material may also offer breeders, chemists, and researchers information about the structure or function of the organism that is crucial to their research endeavors; and this information may now also be rendered in new artifactual forms. DNA can now be extracted from minute samples of tissue and sequenced and the sequences stored on genomic databases. Alternatively, bodies may be dissected and scanned to create new electronic archives of three-dimensional digitalized images such as those created by the Visible Human Project.[3]

All of these new artifacts – whether corporeal or informational in form – are set to play a central role in re-writing the dynamics of biological exploitation, as they have the ability to act as "proxies" that can effectively "stand in for" or "represent" whole living organisms in their absence. Of course, these proxies do not act as effective substitutes in all circumstances: for example if you mean to collect trees for timber or firewood, a three-milligram sample of the tree material would not serve you well, equally if you are seeking tissue for transplantation, a scan or image of the organ will not suffice. However, if what is sought is a replicable, living form of genetic material, a viable source of biochemical extracts, or genetic or biochemical information, then these proxies may well prove to be *fungible* for whole organisms – in that, as the definition suggests, they may serve for, or be replaced by, another answering to the same definition when an individual specimen is not meant.

One of the most significant – and I would argue intended – consequences of translating biological materials from a corporeal to an informational state is to make them more mobile and hence more amenable to circulation. Whole organisms are cumbersome, they are demanding to transport and to store, and they require considerable space to maintain them, particularly if they are to retain their reproductive capabilities and, hence, their viability as sources of replicable material. When translated into new forms, biological materials become infinitely more *transmissible*. Tissue samples for example, are more easily collected, circulated, concentrated, and recirculated than are whole organisms.

These impacts are even more pronounced when biological materials are translated into wholly informational forms – for example, when extracted DNA is sequenced and notated onto databases, or when it is enframed by digital imaging technologies. When in a wholly informational form, valuable genetic resources can be circulated instantaneously via technologies such as the Internet. Scanned images and sequences can be down- and uploaded in seconds, copied, and circulated to hundreds of recipients instantaneously. Transactions suddenly have the capacity to reach phenomenal speeds. These new technologies are not, of course, only acting to reduce the amount of biological material necessary for processes of replication, modification, or identification; they are simultaneously extending the temporal limits of the viability of these materials. Improvements in storage techniques in cryopreservation and in bio-informatics are ensuring that genetic resources – whether in a corporeal or informational form – remain available for use now, and for many hundreds of years into the future.

A "Space of Flows": The Emergence of a New Resource Economy in Bio-information

These developments are combining to transform the traditional dynamics of biological resource exploitation. Until recently, pharmaceutical companies interested in securing ongoing supplies of genetic or biochemical materials found it necessary to mount collection programs in the field. However, technological developments are now releasing corporations from their dependence on *in situ* collecting. The acquisition of genetic or biochemical materials is still necessary, but the collection of whole organisms is not. Commercial bio-prospectors (who are employed to collect on behalf of scientific institutions and corporations) are increasingly aware that tissue samples drawn from existing *ex situ* collections held by botanical or zoological gardens, agricultural institutes, public research centers, and other like institutions may also provide genetic or biochemical material capable of being reproduced in the laboratory using plant cell culture, PCR, or synthesization.[4]

Many such collections of tissue samples have been created over the past decade. The US National Cancer Institute (NCI), for example, instituted collecting programs in over 40 countries in the years from 1985–95, amassing a collection of 50,000 tissue samples and in excess of 114,000 different biochemical extracts. This collection is now housed in a dedicated repository in Frederick, Maryland, in 28 double-decker walk-in cryogenic storage freezers. Other similar-sized libraries of tissue samples and extracts are held by large corporations such as Merck, Smith Kline Beecham, Bristol Myers Squibb, and Pfizer, and by smaller pharmaceutical companies. For example, California's Shaman Pharmaceuticals (now Shaman Botanicals) has amassed a substantial collection of materials from bio-prospecting expeditions they conducted in Peru and Ecuador in the 1990s. Many other academic and scientific research centers also hold well-characterized collections of material of increasing interest to the life-sciences industry.

Samples of human tissue are now also being collected and used in novel ways. Over the past decade similar institutions – the US National Institutes of Health and private corporations such as Incyte Pharmaceuticals, Amgen, and Sequana Therapeutics – have begun to collect blood and tissue samples from remote communities in Kosrae (Micronesia), Tristan Da Cunha, and Papua New Guinea, with the intention of developing proprietary treatments for specific maladies based on the identification and modification of "disease genes." Blood samples and skin scrapings taken in the field have been transported back to the US and there transformed into valuable collections of cell lines and sequenced DNA. Some of these collected materials have since translated into purely digital or "bio-informatic" forms. Sequences of DNA have been notated onto computers to create new databases of genomic information such as Incyte Pharmaceuticals' LifeSeq Database, which now contains over 5.8 million DNA sequences derived from samples of human tissue. The database, reputedly the largest in the world, also contains some 120,000 gene transcripts, 60,000 of which are not available anywhere else (Incyte 1999).

Consumers of biological materials (in the life sciences industry at least) are now often less interested in whole organisms than they are in the genetic or biochemical information embodied in those organisms. Archived collections of biological derivatives of various kinds provide increasingly important points of supply for this bio-information. As I have suggested here, when biological materials are translated into these partially decorporealized or wholly informational forms, they become infinitely more transmissible and amenable to circulation, trade, and exchange. A nascent resource economy and a new "space of flows" in bio-information are being created as a consequence.[5] This new trade is characterized by a particular set of transactional behaviors that warrant closer inspection.

Transacting Bio-information

As economists have famously noted, information is a peculiar commodity in that it can be given away and yet still owned. Consequently, popular forms of commodity exchange for informational products are rental, licensing, and pay-per-view. If we consider that new markets are being created for the informational content of biological material, it should not come as any great surprise to discover that their operation is characterized by similar kinds of transactions. For example, evidence from my empirical research suggests that we are seeing the emergence of companies that intend to specialize in creating and then renting out "libraries" of genetic and bio-chemical materials and genomic information. Each operates on the premise that collected libraries of material – whether corporeal or informational – constitute a resource that can be utilized and reutilized by a number of interested parties. Each consumer may be looking for different types of information and, as a consequence, the same material may be recirculated a number of times before becoming exhausted.

Two examples serve to illustrate the point. The NCI currently lends material from its repository to researchers (public and corporate) interested in testing them for efficacy against various disease states. They currently make only a nominal charge for this service, although they could charge commercial rates for access. If a company finds a promising lead, the NCI then directs them to the original supplier of the material (usually a developing country or community), leaving it up to these two parties to arrive at a mutually satisfactory agreement on appropriate compensation. The NCI has chosen to play no role in these negotiations.

Other, privately run, organizations are employing the same principle but are charging companies on a strictly commercial "pay-per-view" basis. Rather than loaning the material, they rent it out repeatedly – circulating it over and over again as a commodity that interested parties will pay to inspect but not keep. The Knowledge Recovery Foundation (KRF) and Pharmacognetics, two US-based brokerages, are both engaged in this practice. The KRF has undertaken its own collection programs in China and Peru and intends to rent out samples from the library of extracts that it has created from this collected material, to any interested individual or company. Pharmacognetics acts as a brokerage or clearing-house, renting out collected botanical samples to researchers working in the agricultural, pharmaceuticals, and cosmetics industries. Neil Belson, the president of Pharmacognetics, explained to me how these "rental" or "pay-per-view" transactions occur. N.B.: "You don't have to sell them the samples – you basically license them out for experimental purposes only . . . [B.P.]. Is this what I would call rental? N.B.: Exactly, rent it and then if they find something interesting they can work with you on doing something more with that sample . . . The agreement would say that for x dollars you are getting the right to test this material and to have first right to negotiate further collaboration with us if you find something of interest. That's how it would work."

Similar modes of transaction are evident in exchanges involving information derived from human genetic material. Bill Neirmann of the American Type Culture Collection explained to me how their collaborator, Smith Kline Beecham, intends to control access to their newly created genomic database: "They [SKB] are basically looking at establishing sequences of human genes and they're setting up this huge database of these kinds of gene sequences. And so what they are doing is licensing people to search it for things – to pay money to look. And as part of the agreement, you can look, you can find things, you can commercialize it, but Smith Kline gets first right of negotiation with you on commercial arrangements."

The amount of money that may be generated through pay-per-view of genetic databases is substantial. In February 2000 Incyte announced that they had signed access agreements with Pfizer Inc, Eli Lilly & Co., AstraZeneca, and other major drug manufacturers giving these firms access to their database of genetic information and data-management software tools. More significantly, the company announced its intention to fully exploit the informational aspects of their products by creating a new Internet Strategy that is designed to enable researchers (both corporate and academic) to tap into the database on-line from their home institutions, wherever they may be. In announcing the decision, the company's director revealed that the total life-science research budget of US academic institutions alone amounts to $18 billion dollars, about twice that of the global pharmaceutical industry. He noted that the company expects to capture a sizable portion of this budget in return for access to their databases. In the wake of this announcement Wall Street analysts raised their 12-month price target estimates for Incyte Inc. from $235 to $374 per share, an increase in value of some 60 percent (Incyte, 1999).

John Barton (1997: 55), an international expert on intellectual property rights and genetic resources, has suggested that these developments have serious implications. As he has confirmed, "Biotechnologists are increasingly likely to look to global genomic databases rather than to the underlying organisms from which the information is derived." He notes, significantly, that "the export (e.g., over the Internet) of a gene sequence from a nation is now the operational equivalent of the export of the organism containing the gene sequence," warning that there is consequently every possibility that "genetic resource issues may, in fact, soon be outflanked by genomic information issues."

Property Relations: Property-in-the-Body?

These developments raise important questions regarding property relations. How does the valuation that attaches to biological materials change as they are translated from a corporeal to an informational form? If property rights are vested in biological materials as things that are understood and constituted as corporeal bodies, what happens to those rights when the things themselves becomes de-corporealized and exist only in an informational form? Which, if any, might be the most appropriate mechanism for protecting material that exists in an "interstitial" state? Extracted DNA, for example, might be understood as a type of embodied information, in that it contains genetic information capable of being read, sequenced, and notated onto a database. While containing this information, it nonetheless remains part of an organism and is thus subject to the laws that extend to "real property" – unless, of course, it is drawn from a human body, in which case it is not subject to those laws, as property rights do not currently extend to "property in the body" – in theory at least.

The property regimes that apply to informational resources and to "real property" differ from one another, as what they seek to protect is qualitatively different. The transactions that characterize the exchange of each reflect this – while also pointing up the complexities associated with determining how these entities might be known and administered in law. Biological materials have traditionally been bought and sold outright. "Ownership" in this context was usually absolute, providing the purchaser with the right to exercise the maximum degree of formalized control or dominion over the acquired resource. A different set of property relations attaches to the exchange and trade of information. As I noted earlier, information is a curious commodity in that it may be given away and yet still owned. For this reason it is clearly difficult to exercise complete dominion over information-based products such as books, films, or computer games. The information on which they are based may be readily transmitted and replicated without any apparent loss to the original owner.

As executives working in the music and computer-software industries have discovered, regulating the dissemination and unlicensed copying of informational works is a particularly complex task. The most common form of property protection for works likely to be printed, transmitted, or broadcast is copyright law. The principal aim of copyright law is to enable authors to protect their creative works from unlicensed reproduction by others. Maps, musical works, architectural designs, computer software, and motion pictures may all be copyrighted. The difficulties that regulators have experienced in tracking the unlicensed reproduction and sampling of such works have been greatly exacerbated by the introduction of satellite telecommunications and new digital technologies, which have combined to facilitate their rapid circulation and reproduction.

As practitioners of information technology law have suggested (Reed 1996), new informational technologies are particularly significant as they have the effect, to use their words, of "de-materializing" products such as books or films, which previously enjoyed only a "hard-copy" existence. Works that were once distributed as prints, disks, cassettes, films, or in other physical forms can now be transmitted in an electronic or digitalized form via the Internet. Such works, I would argue, have not become completely "de-materialized" but have, rather, taken on a new materiality. Computers, modems, servers, etc. remain material objects that are produced out of, and embedded in, a distinct set of social, cultural, and economic relations that variously restrict or promote access to new digitalized resources. However, I agree absolutely that this process of "radical re-materialization" – the ability to translate prints or films, etc. to a digital format – does affect profoundly the dynamics of transmissibility, radically accelerating the speed with which such materials can be distributed and consumed.

The ability to translate these materials into digitally coded information – a sequence of binary numbers – introduces a further complication for regulators: the ability to create *exact copies* rather than close replicas of these works. As media analyst Andy Johnson-Laird (1995: 4) has suggested, "digitized information can be copied quickly, easily and cheaply and the copy *is quite literally* every bit as good as the original. Add to that the notion that by standing on an electronic street corner, millions of passers-by can make identical copies for themselves in an instant and it is easy to see why the Internet, both physically and psychologically, is on a collision course with conventional copyright law." Infringement problems are myriad but include: the unlicensed reproduction of software and other digitized material created for electronic computer networks; copying original materials, such as photographs, onto the internet and transmitting them without authorization; excerpting coded sequences from particular software programs, such as elements of computer games, and using them to create other programs; and downloading copyrighted material from the net for use in other formats, such as pamphlets or magazines, again without permission. As Simon (1996: 33) concludes, one of the effects of the digital age is to make physical copies of an author's work less valuable. Such processes reveal that it is not the form of the work but *the transmissible content of the work* that is most valuable and hence, most needing protection and/or compensation.

Alternative forms of property rights and regulations have emerged for governing exchanges of information that recognize the inherent transience of "ownership" in information. Rather than focusing on forms of absolute ownership, rights are given to access information for specified periods of time. For example, licensing protects an individual's right to exclusive, but temporally limited, access to a body of information. Equally, royalties are a mechanism designed to ensure that producers of creative, information-based works receive a payment each time the work or a substantial part of that work is used commercially.

Valuable and replicable genetic and biochemical material and information can now be drawn from cryogenically stored tissue samples and biochemical extracts, from cell lines, from extracted DNA, and from coded sequences of DNA stored on a database. This genetic and biochemical material and information can now also be copied, modified, sampled, recombined, and recirculated with relative ease. It could be argued that just as processes of de-materialization have undermined attempts to keep track of the successive uses that are made of copyrighted information, so processes of de-corporealization are also destined to derail attempts to regulate the successive uses that are made of these "bio-informational" resources.

The property relations that characterize trade in biological materials have not traditionally had to take account of such dynamics. Until very recently, collectors have bought specimens outright on a strict "fee-per-sample" basis. The amount paid per sample or specimen varies, but ranges from between $50 and $200 dollars per kilo of collected material. The difficulty with this compensatory regime is that it presumes a cycle of consumption and resupply. It operates on the principle that the recipient of the resource will be provided with an initial supply of material, for which they will pay a fixed amount, but that they will in time consume that material and return for a further supply, at which point the supplier will secure further income and/or the opportunity to renegotiate existing contracts on more favorable terms.[6]

However, the creation of new technologies that now enable companies to extract, store, and then replicate collected materials over both space and time, and the creation of new networks of trade and exchange that provide alternative sources of supply for such materials, are obviating the need for re-collection. A number of principled actors within the bioprospecting industry have recognized that biological materials are, in effect, now being used *successively* as informational resources rather than simply consumed as material resources. They suggest, therefore, that in order for processes of exploitation to be equitable, a royalty should be paid to suppliers of collected biological materials whenever they are used as the basis of a commercial product, even in instances when the product is ultimately produced by replicating, modifying, or synthesizing elements derived from the original material.

The decision to include a royalty payment among compensatory measures is a development of the greatest significance, one that represents a sea-change in the way in which biological materials are both understood and valued as resources. For although Plant Breeders' Rights have provided protection for the successive uses that are made of whole organisms, this is the first occasion in the history of natural-resource governance that a provision has been made to compensate for the successive uses that are made of the genetic and biochemical components of those organisms. It is particularly significant that the mechanism adopted to meet this requirement (the royalty) is conventionally used to compensate for the successive uses that are made of other types of information-based works such as literary and musical compositions and computer software. This perhaps suggests, as I noted above, that as with these other works, what is of greatest value and requiring the most protection in biological materials or "works" is no longer necessarily the form of the work but the transmissible content of that work.

Although based on similar principles to copyright regulations, the rate of royalty that is paid to the suppliers of genetic materials rarely rivals those paid to authors. The creators of software packages, authors, and musicians would expect to receive something on the order of 10–15 percent royalty of net profit on the successive uses that are made of their works. The industry standard rate of royalty offered to the suppliers of genetic materials is 1–2 percent for a sample of biological material and 3–5 percent for a prepared extract. Some consider this appropriate, arguing that no creative act of authorship is involved in supplying samples of genetic or biochemical material. While this is true of materials collected at random, it can be argued that establishing the efficacy of particular materials as medicaments through generations of experimentation involves many inventive or creative steps and that the royalty rates paid for these highly characterized materials to community groups should, therefore, rival those paid to other authors. In either case, royalties are paid in recognition of the fact that the bio-informational resources embodied in tissue samples are now likely to be extracted, stored, and used successively over space and time. Without a system of royalty payments, suppliers will be compensated only once – and at a proportionally small level – for the resources that will form the foundation of many future products developed by the life-sciences industry.

Although the introduction of these royalty mechanisms implies the creation of a just and equitable regime for the governance of trade in bio-information and biological derivatives, some serious questions surround their efficacy. Royalties offer considerable potential rewards, but in order for that potential to be realized, three interrelated conditions must be met. First, the collected sample must form the basis of a marketable drug. Second, companies or organizations must *acknowledge* that a collected sample of material has formed the basis of a marketable drug. Third, it must be possible to distinguish the collected sample of material from any others of which the drug is comprised, and, most importantly, it must be possible to identify and locate the supplier of that sample of material over space or time. It is clearly impossible to pay a royalty unless it is possible to determine to whom that royalty should be paid. For this to occur it is essential that each successive user of the collected material be prepared, and able, to establish the provenance of the material they are using. Several factors – the transmissibility, manipulability, and replicability of these resources – act to complicate this process.

As I have illustrated, collected materials are now subject to myriad processes of modification, synthesization, or replication, circulated to and utilized by a variety of different recipients, cryogenically stored and subject to similar processes of transfer and manipulation over space and time. The complexities of tracing the circulation and consumption of the bio-informational resources that are derived from these materials *over space* are evident at a number of different scales: transnationally, nationally, and even microscopically. Companies now collect in many countries, and it may well be impossible for any source country to prove retrospectively that the material that formed the basis of a successful drug was in fact sourced from within their borders. It has always been difficult for governments to control the illegal export of biological specimens, but never more so than it is now that the most valuable components of such organisms – the genetic or biochemical materials embodied within them – can be conveyed in either a partially or wholly de-corporealized state. Where border officials once had to search for whole organisms or collections of organisms, they find that they must now detect the illegal export of a few milligrams of material.

Replicable quantities of genetic and biochemical material can now also be secured through the illicit "re-mining" of existing scientific and academic collections. Although these ex situ collections are also comprised of materials collected in developing countries, they were created before the introduction of the Biodiversity Convention and, consequently, are not subject to benefit-sharing agreements. Samples that are drawn from such collections may be circulated to a variety of users with complete immunity. There is no obligation to monitor where these materials go or how they are subsequently used. With the introduction of techniques such as gene splicing and combinatorial chemistry, it has become even more difficult to trace the trajectory of particular gene fragments and molecular compounds as they are manipulated, combined, sampled, copied, and recombined, even within the relatively confined space of the laboratory.

The difficulties associated with tracking the movement and use of such samples over space are now compounded by those associated with tracing how archived materials are used over time. The question of how to compensate suppliers for the prospective use of collections that are being created now and cryogenically stored for future use still awaits effective resolution. As Henry Shands, director of Genetic Resources at the United States Department of Agriculture, confirms: "That's one of the real problems that people haven't addressed because things can sit in a gene bank for a hundred years and of course that exceeds the lifetime of the corporate history – there is no history left then unless it's recorded on a database. By that time the whole intellectual property rights (IPR) structure will have changed and you'll probably have a whole new set of issues – that might not be such a bad thing!"

These developments raise serious questions about whether existing property rights regimes are capable of regulating transactions that are "suspended:" where the first part of the transaction – the collection of the sample from which the bio-information is derived – occurs at one point in time, but where the use of the material and the associated payment of compensation in the form of royalty is delayed for, perhaps, many hundreds of years. To whom would such royalties be paid? How would suitable recipients be identified? What types of use would attract a compensatory payment and what wouldn't? Inequitable and unjust practices are, after all, already emerging, particularly in relation to this last question.

While providing samples of genetic or biochemical material is not generally considered to constitute an inventive act, modifying them to form new products is, and patents are given on this basis. Combining sequenced DNA to form new databases of information is also construed in IPR law as a creative act, and databases are frequently copyrighted. Those creators who wish their databases to be freely available to the general public for non-commercial use effectively exempt those users from the infringement of their copyright that occurs when they access these materials. However, creators who wish to profit by selling access to their databases charge a fee each time the information stored on the database is accessed. Although the sequence information that forms the substantive basis of such databases is usually drawn from collected samples of genetic and biochemical material, royalties derived from these applied uses of the collected materials are not shared with those countries and communities that supply them. Any licenses or fees that consumers pay to access the databases are paid directly and exclusively to the *creators of the database.*

Until recently, there has been limited debate about the commercialization of human materials. This is because it is often assumed that such commercialization cannot, or will not, occur. The human body and bodily parts have historically been construed as "exceptional" in that it has not been considered morally or ethically desirable or acceptable to extend property rights to them, and this is reflected in legislation.[7] For example, although laws in many countries permit the donation of body parts, most expressly outlaw the sale of body parts. Munzer (1997: 26) suggests that it is "morally objectionable to participate in a market for body parts as (say) a broker or buyer, if by doing so one offends the dignity of oneself or others." Radin (1993: 17) concurs, stating, "My present view is that many of our personal endowments and capacities associated with the body stubbornly resist conventional descriptions as property." However, interestingly, she also notes that as matter such as blood and organs becomes constructed as what she terms "severable fungible commodities," objections to markets in organs and blood "will be even harder to make out on personhood grounds." To follow Radin's argument to its logical conclusion, it would seem that feelings of disassociation and a concomitant willingness to objectify and commodify human biological materials might well increase as they are translated from a corporeal to a fully informational state.

Munzer (1997: 28), drawing on Kantian arguments about offences to human dignity, notes, significantly, that the core of Kant's protest is his objection to "the sale of any part that is *integral* to the normal biological functioning of that person" (my emphasis). This privileging of context is key, in my view: when biological material or information remains embodied within the person, it is considered inalienable; however, when decontextualized, or to consider it another way, progressively decorporealized, it is more readily commodified.

Munzer goes on to suggest (p. 29) that it is important to "distinguish between isolated sales and frequent exchanges in a market," arguing that the latter pose a graver risk to the dignity of many individuals and suggesting, rightly, that the creation of a formal market for human biological commodities could transform attitudes that human beings have to themselves and others. Discussions about the desirability (or otherwise) of creating new commodity markets or resource economies in human biological materials continue apace but risk being outmoded by the fact that the commercialization of human biological materials is, in reality, well advanced. The collection of samples of human biological material – tissue and blood samples – has been systematically undertaken for some time. This collected material has been used, as I have illustrated here, to create cell lines and sequenced human DNA databases that have been the subject of commercial transactions. Nonetheless, the fiction of human exceptionalism has been carefully maintained, perhaps precisely because the translation of the material from a corporeal to an informational state allows it to be.

However, a recent development must surely now result in an irrevocable and final erosion of this fancy. On April 9, 2000, and with remarkably little fanfare, the Human Genome Organization (HUGO 2000) announced that they were recommending that royalty-based benefit sharing agreements be applied to human as well as non-human genetic research. The need for the introduction of such a regime was particularly important, they noted, as many new products, including vaccines and drugs for common diseases, are now based on human genetic research, and as much governmental and non-profit research in these areas is being commercialized and taken over by private industry. They recommend, consequently, that profit-making entities dedicate a percentage (e.g., 1–3 percent) of their annual net profit to healthcare infrastructure or to humanitarian efforts that benefit those who have donated their materials.

As they note, "A benefit is a good that contributes to the well-being of an individual or group [and is therefore] not identical with profit in the monetary or economic sense." While this is right in principle, it is difficult to construe the disbursement of royalties in this context as anything other than a profit-sharing mechanism. Whatever squeamishness is evidenced in our collective inability or unwillingness to understand this as a financial transaction ought to be overcome. This burgeoning new resource economy in both human and non-human biological derivatives and information is now well established, and it would be foolish to suggest otherwise. Whether or not we morally endorse this new trade, it is important that we acknowledge its character. Without this recognition, it will be impossible to develop appropriate and effective regimes adequate to the task of regulating access to and use of property in, *and out of,* the body.

Conclusion

Biological materials are undergoing a fundamental transformation induced by profound technological changes. The genetic and biochemical materials and information that exist in biological materials are now available in a variety of highly transmissible and easily replicable forms – as cryogenically stored tissue samples, cell lines, extracted and even sequenced DNA. These new technological artifacts are of great interest to commercial collectors and to researchers working in the life-sciences industry, as they may effectively substitute for whole organisms that are too cumbersome or awkward to obtain. New resource economies in biological derivatives and information are being created as a consequence.

Unfortunately, existing property regimes have proven inadequate to this task of regulating this new trade in bio-information. Although suppliers of genetic and biochemical materials are entitled to receive monetary compensation for the successive commercial uses that are made of their donated materials, they often do not receive any share of the profits that accrue from these uses – especially in circumstances where the material has been translated into a more elusive informational form. Compensation is also not paid when the collected genetic materials are of human origin, even though they are clearly being employed as raw materials in what is proving to be a most lucrative new industry. The Human Genome Organization's recent attempt to "map" the existing benefit-sharing regimes that were devised to regulate commercial uses of non-human genetic materials over onto transactions involving human tissues is to be applauded in my view, if for no other reason than because it forces us to interrogate closely on what basis we have made, and seek to maintain, a distinction between the commodification of human and non-human biological materials.

Many issues that relate to the commercialization of both human and non-human forms of bio-information remain unresolved – they demand to be the focus of a collective societal debate, one which is unlikely to take place, however, unless there is first a much wider recognition and acceptance of the existence and nature of this very profitable new resource economy. As we enter a new millennium in which the remaking of life forms (our own included) will be one of our principal economic enterprises, it will become ever more important to address how, and in what ways, we wish to remake existing property law and relations so that they might better reflect new understandings of property in bodies and in information, as well as the increasingly complex relationship between the two.

Acknowledgments

I would like to thank the Wenner-Gren Foundation for giving me the opportunity to attend the symposium and my colleagues there for making it such a valuable and enjoyable experience. I would also like to thank the three referees who gave helpful suggestions when review-ing an earlier draft of this chapter.

Notes

1. It was revealed in 1999 that thousands of organs and tissues of children who had been patients at the Alder Hey Children's Hospital in Liverpool, UK, had been removed and retained, post-mortem, for use in bio-medical research without the knowledge or consent of parents.

2. One early exception to this is grafting.

3. Begun in 1995 by the US National Library of Medicine, and the US National Institutes of Health, this project involved dissecting and scanning two donated corpses to create a 23-CD-ROM digital archive of three-dimensional, interactive images of the body now available for the purposes of diagnostic modeling, surgical planning, and visual pedagogy.

4. PCR – Polymerase Chain Reaction – is a revolutionary technique for generating unlimited copies of any fragment of DNA, in order to produce enough DNA to be adequately tested.

5. A term used by the sociologist Manuel Castells (1989) to describe the new spaces created by movement or circulation of information, people, and commodities in an increasingly inter-connected world.

6. One important historical exception to this generality is evident in the practice of "renting" stud bulls and the like for the sole purpose of interbreed-ing. Although it would be anachronistic to construe this as a deliberate renting of "genetic information," the practice anticipates current more dedicated activities of this type in important and interesting ways.

7. Interestingly and significantly, exceptions in law have been made for abandoned bodily *waste products*: urine, nail clippings, shorn hair, etc. and for what Radin might call *severable* bodily products: blood, gametes, and sperm.

References

Barton, John. 1997. "The Biodiversity Convention and the Flow of Scientific Information." In *Global genetic resources: Access, ownership, and intellectual property rights*. Edited by K. E. Hoagland and A. Y. Ross-man, 51–6. Washington, D.C: Association of Systematics Research Publishers.

Boyd, M. and K. Paul. 1995. "Some practical considerations and applications of the National Cancer Institute in-vitro anticancer drug discovery screen." *Drug Development Research* 34: 91–109.

Castells, Manuel. 1989. *The informational city: Information technology, economic restructuring, and the urban regional process*. Oxford: Blackwell.

HUGO. 2000. Press release statement on benefit sharing regimes. http://www.hugo-international.org/hugo/benefit.html

Incyte press release, November 22, 1999, PRNewswire.

Johnson-Laird, Andrew. 1995. "Exploring the information superhighway: The good, The bad and the ugly." Paper presented at the Electronic Information Law Institute Meeting San Francisco, March 2–3.

Laird, Sarah and Kerry ten Kate. 1999. *Commercial uses of biodiversity*. London: Earthscan.

Munzer, Steven. 1997. "Human dignity and property rights in human body parts. In *Property problems: From genes to pension funds*. Edited by J. W. Harris, 25–38. London: Kluwer Law International.

Parry, Bronwyn. 2001. "The fate of the collections: Social justice and the annexation of plant genetic resources." In *People, plants and justice*. Edited by C. Zerner, 374–401. New York: Columbia University Press.

———. 2004. "Trading the genome: investigating the commodification of bio-information." New York: Columbia University Press (Forthcoming).

Radin, Margaret. 1993. *Re-interpreting property*. Chicago: University of Chicago Press.

Reed, Chris (ed.). 1996. *Computer law*. London: Blackstone Press.

Simon, E. 1996. "Innovation and intellectual property protection: The software industry perspective." *The Columbia Journal of World Business* 31: 31–7.

Heritage as Property

Michael F. Brown

> Ownership gathers things momentarily to a point by locating them in the owner, halting endless dissemination, effecting an identity.
>
> (Strathern 1996: 30).

Frontiers tend to be disordered and troublesome places. Where concepts of property are concerned, a particularly unruly frontier lies at the crossroads of ethnic nationalism and control over the disposition of knowledge in its multiple forms: artistic, spiritual, and technological. The dramatic dematerializations facilitated by new digital and genetic technologies have made information hard to regulate. In societies whose social organization relies on elements of secrecy, loss of control over the movement of information is deeply threatening. Add to this the injustice of powerful corporations reaping profits from indigenous music, art, biological knowledge – even the genetic code of isolated communities – and one has a recipe for anxiety and anger. (See chapters by Hayden, Parry, Rowlands, and Seeger, this volume.)

Public discussion of these issues is taking place on several fronts. Social scientists are forging analytical links between Western knowledge practices and broader questions of intercultural exchange. Legal codes such as the Native American Graves Protection and Repatriation Act (NAGPRA) of 1990, implemented in the United States, have provoked dramatic policy changes in museums, archives, and other public repositories. International organizations are struggling to formulate protocols for the protection of "heritage," the term increasingly used to encompass native cultures as well as the biological species and geographical locations to which (at least in the minds of international lawyers) they are ineluctably tied (Daes 1998).[1] As is often the case with newly contested domains, debate about heritage protection darts from one metaphor to another. Some indigenous advocates argue that "control over one's culture" should be considered a basic human right. Others appeal to a supposed right of cultural privacy.[2] Nevertheless, most policy forums addressing the disposition of indigenous knowledge gravitate to the language of property.

In the United States, Canada, Australia, and other settler democracies, legislation dealing with cultural ownership thus far has focused primarily on the disposition of human skeletal remains and objects of religious significance. The success of repatriation policies has shifted attention to the realm of the intangible and led to calls for the "repatriation of information." But here matters quickly become vexed, raising knotty questions. To what extent, if any, do ideas submit to a logic of ownership? What kinds of regulatory structures must be deployed to maintain the level of control that would make such ownership possible? Should anthropology abandon its relativizing impulse in favor of the transcultural categories that some experts believe are necessary to protect indigenous heritage? Might there be an escape from what Marilyn Strathern (1999: 134) sees as the inevitable link, at least in the modern context, between issues of identity and matters of property?

To begin to answer these questions, I first consider recent efforts to reconceptualize cultural heritage as a set of things and practices subject to principles of group ownership – in effect, as a form of property, although the identification of culture with property may be emphatically denied by proponents of such protection schemes. I then explore some of the paradoxes of the expansive vision of heritage protection that seems to be gaining ground in international circles. Finally, I sketch an alternative vision of how the integrity and dignity of indigenous societies might be defended without capitulating to the inexorable, commodifying logic of the culture-as-property perspective.

Culture Materialized

One would be hard pressed to find a term more frequently used and, in anthropology at least, more widely disputed than culture. In the interests of sidestepping the definitional quagmire, I am content to rely on the conventional anthropological vision of culture as an abstraction or analytical place-holder for shared behavioral patterns, values, social practices, forms of artistic expression, and technologies. It hardly matters whether this formulation is good or bad because the culture concept was long ago expropriated by non-anthropologists, and anthropology's continuing debate about its utility has had little impact on how it is used in the world at large.[3]

Popular definitions of culture share several characteristics. Culture is, or is fast becoming, a synonym for society, such that one can be said to "belong to a culture" or be "a member of a culture," assertions that most anthropologists would reject. Culture, in other words, is seen as bounded and isomorphic with a specific community. It has also become entangled with the rise of ethnic nationalism, leading to demands that groups be granted "cultural sovereignty" to complement the political sovereignty they seek or sometimes already possess.[4] The notion that culture is concrete, circumscribed, and amenable to control by deliberate policy is impossibly far from the Boasian view of culture that proved so influential in North American anthropology.

As popular notions of culture become more reified, the knowledge, codes, and genres that underlie culture have, contrariwise, grown increasingly slippery and immaterial, a transformation facilitated by technologies that can instantly strip content from context. The disembedding of information from its original matrix has led to a wave of list-making – essentially an effort to block decontextualization by inventorying cultural content. The much-cited UN Draft Declaration on the Rights of Indigenous Peoples (1994) is essentially an enumeration of what constitutes culture and how it should be protected.[5] Likewise the attempt by a consortium of Apache tribes to identify their chief cultural resources. "Cultural property," Apache leaders declare, "includes all cultural items and all images, text, ceremonies, music, songs, stories, symbols, beliefs, customs, ideas, and other physical and spiritual objects and concepts inalienably linked to the history and culture of one or more Apache tribes" (Inter-Apache Summit on Repatriation 1995: 3). The formulation of such lists is a primordial act of will that defines the ethnic nation. Lists etch boundaries between what is possessed and what is not in a world of permeable borders.

Indigenous peoples, of course, are not alone in worrying about the integrity of their cultural heritage. One can see a similar impulse in the efforts of the Académie Française to maintain the purity of the French language or the policies implemented by Canada to defend itself from cultural influences emanating from the United States. Until recently, the principal goal has been to slow the introduction of alien cultural elements from elsewhere. Today it is flows in the opposite direction – from within a minority community to the surrounding mass society – that garner the most attention. The perceived violation of boundaries about which indigenous leaders complain threatens the distinction between sacred and profane, which in Durkheimian fashion also implicates the Us and the Not-Us. Resources must be inventoried to protect them from theft; the sacred must be catalogued to protect it from contamination.

Boundary-setting has practical as well as symbolic implications. In the United States, growing acceptance of Native American sovereignty has created new sources of economic power for enterprising tribes. The rise of the Indian gaming industry is the most obvious example, but this is only the leading edge of innovative, strategic uses of the autonomous political space enjoyed by Indian nations.

Familiar examples of identity's material value can be found in the art world. Molly H. Mullin's study of the Santa Fe Indian Market (Mullin 2001) shows how a major venue for the appraisal and sale of Native American art has codified questions of identity to guarantee authenticity. Similar issues preoccupy the art market in Australia. In 1997 it was revealed that an established Australian artist, Elizabeth Durack, had for some years created a series of paintings under the Aboriginal pseudonym "Eddie Burrup" – paintings that had begun to attract favorable attention from museums and galleries. Durack created a persona for Burrup that included explanatory texts written in colloquial Aboriginal style. The news that Burrup was an invention of a white woman evoked predictable expressions of outrage, including the claim that the goal of Durack's hoax was to reinvigorate her career by exploiting the strong contemporary market for Aboriginal art. More sympathetic observers suggested that Durack, who died in 2000 at the age of 84, felt compelled to create Eddie Burrup to give expression to a lifetime of deep involvement with Aboriginal people and their way of experiencing the Australian landscape. The controversy foregrounded the fragility of the link between the value of indigenous art and the authenticity of its creator. Under these conditions, Simon Harrison (1999) argues convincingly, identity becomes a scarce resource.[6]

The emergence of what Michael Rowlands (this volume) calls the "heritage industry" is expressed in a different way by the rise of lawsuits in which native populations seek damages for "cultural loss," typically associated with environmental disasters such as the 1989 Exxon Valdez oil spill in Alaska. Because scholars have long argued that property is as much about relationships as about things, damage to the social relationships central to culture can logically be equated with property losses (Kirsch 2001). The apparently growing acceptance of this argument in judicial and policy circles attests to the reification of culture and its increasing identification with property.

Cultural Property, Intellectual Property, or Something Else?

 Advocates for the protection of indigenous heritage today deploy the term "cultural property," once applied to items of national patrimony plundered in wartime or looted from archaeological sites, to encompass all manifestations of an individual culture, both material and intangible. The expression works adequately as a general cover term, but it is burdened with awkward implications when subjected to close scrutiny. Some of these have been reviewed by Peter H. Welsh (1997: 13), who observes that the meaning of property varies so greatly among societies that persistent use of the word may, as he puts it, "extend the influence of Euroamerican values in the guise of supporting a return to traditionalism." He proposes instead that many questions falling under the rubric of cultural property would be better framed as conflicts over "inalienable possessions," invoking a concept first developed by Annette Weiner (1992). Weiner defined inalienable possessions as sacred or cosmologically ordained elements of a group's identity that are circulated within the group, largely between generations, to reproduce itself in a social sense. Inalienable possessions, according to Weiner (ibid.: 37), encompass such things as "myths, genealogies, ancestral names, songs, and the knowledge of dances intrinsic to a group's identity." These contrast with exchange goods that circulate reciprocally between groups.

 In the concept of inalienable possessions Welsh finds a suppleness that cultural property lacks. Cultural property implies a concern with origins, titles, and lines of demarcation that may not be appropriate when applied to the intangibles of heritage. The idea of inalienable possessions, in contrast, foregrounds the constructed quality of meaning and its links to social well-being. "Understanding the reasons for attachment to possession," he observes, "has less to do with understanding the source of rights than with understanding the consequences of loss" (Welsh 1997: 16).

 Welsh's proposal has undeniable virtues. It shifts the focus from economic questions to matters of community survival and human dignity. Its flexibility allows for adaptive changes in the roster of elements that a group defines as essential. Yet these advantages come at a cost. If the inventory of supposedly inalienable possessions is subject to constant change, how are surrounding groups to know what is off limits to them amid today's cacophony of media voices and images? If we define the holder of inalienable possessions as communities rather than cultures, who determines what constitutes a community? The latter is more than a theoretical point. Indigenous peoples are marrying out of their own ethnic groups at historically high rates, making it ever more difficult to determine who belongs to what group and which of these groups qualify as aboriginal.

The idea of inalienable possessions is itself problematic, as critics of Weiner's work have insisted (see for example Friedman 1995). Heritage protection has become a *cause célèbre* because so many elements of indigenous cultures have proved eminently alienable. A strategically placed DAT recorder, a video camera – even a simple notebook or a visit to the public library – can send abstracted elements of a group's heritage into the world at large. It is not clear that much can be done to slow these flows of information short of draconian state intervention.

Moreover, some of what is claimed today as cultural property has never before been "possessed" in Weiner's sense of the term. Obvious examples include rare and commercially valuable blood factors or genes found in isolated human populations. One struggles to see how such resources, the existence of which has been known to humanity for only a decade or two, qualify as inalienable possessions sacred to a group's identity. Nearly as ambiguous is the standing of traditional ecological knowledge (TEK). Although elements of TEK doubtless satisfy Weiner's requirement that inalienable possessions provide "cosmological authentication," much of TEK is so implicit, so much a part of a people's way of being in the world, that it resists claims of conscious ownership. Given these conundrums, there is reason to doubt that the concept of inalienable possessions can supplant other idioms for the assertion of control over a group's intangible resources.

By far the most influential model for regulating claims to the intangible is provided by intellectual property law. The Western intellectual property rights (IPR) tradition is often characterized by indigenous critics as an ontological aberration of the Occidental mind. Nevertheless, analogies to IPR are found in many aboriginal societies. Early in the twentieth century, Robert Lowie (1920: 235–43) offered a host of compelling examples of what he labeled "incorporeal property" among tribal peoples who see stories, dances, myths, magical rites, or even dreams as the exclusive property of individuals.[7] The ethnographic record contains many other examples of transferable, personal rights in information that bear a striking resemblance to Western copyright.

Still, one is on firm ground when emphasizing the contrast between the individualistic core of Western IPR law and the collective ownership characteristic of most folkloric productions. Hence the importance of Australian case law that has gradually recognized community rights and responsibilities in the work of Aboriginal artists.[8] Awaiting determination is this principle's outer limit. To what extent, if any, does the principle apply to indigenous artists who live in urban areas? And what about people of mixed heritage? Presumably those who claim indigenous identity must answer to their communities in a social sense, but is this something that can be enshrined in law?[9]

A difficulty of Western intellectual property law is that its mercantile and utilitarian principles are hard to reconcile with the moral concerns of native nations. Copyright and patent law has emerged as an untidy, negotiated arrangement involving multiple tradeoffs. It acknowledges the legitimacy of a creator's desire to be rewarded for inventiveness and intellectual labor but balances this against the need for society as a whole to make use of innovation to move forward. Admittedly, the utilitarianism that underlies the existing intellectual property system has not proved completely successful even on its own terms. Many IPR experts argue convincingly that current patent and copyright practices do more to inhibit innovation than promote it. Supporting evidence of this claim can be found in the arena of biotechnology, where the awarding of patents on overlapping gene fragments is already creating obstacles to research. Advances in biotechnology have undermined the boundaries necessary for property law to operate efficiently (Heller 1999), just as digital technologies challenge the barriers that maintain cultural distinctiveness.

Equally problematic are limits on the life of copyrights and patents. From the time Western intellectual property laws were put in place, patents and copyrights have been designed to expire. Although copyrights and patents arguably qualify as property, they differ from other forms of property in their statutory impermanence, an impermanence reflecting a calculus of social utility that weighs individual incentives against the needs of society. This makes sense if the creator is a person or commercial entity that has a limited lifespan, but the notion that control over elements of culture should expire is unacceptable to advocates of indigenous rights. (See Anthony Seeger, this volume, with particular reference to rights in sacred music.) Most proposals for modifying existing intellectual property law to accommodate indigenous societies dance around the sensitive question of time limits, but one may reasonably infer that native peoples are generally opposed to termination of their rights after some arbitrary period. This may explain growing interest in the utility of trademark practices, an element of the IPR system that lacks a statutory life span.[10]

Trademark laws protect symbols and signs that give a distinct identity to a product's manufacturer. As long as a trademark holder defends a registered mark from infringement, the mark is protected in perpetuity. The permanent character of trademarks and official insignia (symbols identified with non-profit organizations and government agencies) is proving attractive to indigenous groups. Early in 2000 it was announced that the Snuneymuxw First Nation, a small Coastal Salish-speaking tribe whose lands are located on Vancouver Island and adjacent islands in British Columbia, had secured protection for examples of rock art that the community insists were created by its ancestors (Tanner 2000). Although the petroglyphs are located in a provincial park visited by thousands each year, they have now been registered as official insignia of the Snuneymuxw. This makes it illegal for manufacturers to reproduce them without permission on tee-shirts, stationery, or postcards. The Snuneymuxw goal in seeking protected status for the images is not to defend their commercial use but rather to insure universal *non-use* – that is, to prevent anyone, including other native groups, from using the sacred petroglyph designs for any purpose that the Snuneymuxw deem inappropriate. New Zealand appears to be moving toward a legal framework in which applications for trademark registration of any "word, symbol, sound, or smell" thought to have originated among the Maori will have to be screened for appropriateness by a Maori consultative body (Janke 1998: 143).

In an effort to find a concept that adapts intellectual property law to the expressed desire of ethnic communities to control elements of heritage that are currently unprotected, the legal scholar Susan Scafidi (2001) proposes the invention of a new legal category, "cultural products." These would consist of anything derived from "ongoing expression and development of community symbols and practices" (ibid.: 814). Unlike the creations protected by copyright and patent law, cultural products would not have to demonstrate novelty, nor would their authorship necessarily be of concern. Among the examples she offers is the institution of Kwanzaa, now an important set of annual rituals for many African Americans. Kwanzaa is usually described as the creation of a specific individual, Maulana Karenga, a professor of African-American Studies, but it can now be said to belong to the entire African-American community. Scafidi apparently believes that African Americans should be given the legal power to control the diffusion of Kwanzaa and to protect it from unwanted appropriation or misuse. Moving beyond questions of heritage protection, she suggests that communities have an opportunity – perhaps even an obligation – to circulate carefully selected cultural products among consumers in the wider marketplace. "A source community with little social standing or political influence, or even one to which the majority culture may be hostile, might advance its cause by feeding, clothing, instructing, or entertaining the general public with distinctive cultural products" (Scafidi 2001: 839).

Although Scafidi's proposals are thoughtful and original, they would entail the creation of a staggeringly complex framework of regulations. These are likely to generate new inequities. The statutory regulation of product authenticity offers a simple example. In the United States, the Indian Arts and Crafts Act of 1990, which built on similar legislation dating to the 1930s, protects the authenticity of Native American art by prohibiting the sale of products falsely claiming to be made by American Indians or Alaska Natives. Far from being universally appreciated by Indian artists, however, this law is deeply resented by some who, owing to the vagaries of tribal membership rules, are prevented from identifying their work as Native American (Sheffield 1997; Hapiuk 2001).

Scafidi and others who support the idea of using new variations of intellectual property law to protect indigenous heritage rarely mention IPR's tenuous moral standing at the grass-roots level. Discussion with ordinary citizens in the United States quickly reveals that they find aspects of IPR law illogical and even an affront to everyday morality. I vividly recall the bafflement expressed by my undergraduate students when in a lecture I mentioned that Home Depot holds a trademark on the color orange. (More precisely, Home Depot has been awarded a monopoly on commercial use of a particular shade of orange in the promotion of tools, home-improvement products, and related hardware.) "That's crazy," one responded. "How can a company own a color?" The moral ambiguity of intellectual property law is nowhere better illustrated than by the explosive growth of file-sharing technologies that facilitate the fee-free (and illegal) transfer of copyrighted music. On a daily basis, millions of citizens demonstrate their indifference to the intellectual property rights of media corporations. Although industry's efforts to stem the tide of file-sharing have punished a few rogue companies and individuals, the technology has thus far managed to stay ahead of enforcement efforts. My point is that unlike the theft of material goods, which all but a few radicals and anarchists regard as reprehensible, the unlawful use of intellectual property is less burdened with moral weight for most citizens. Such moral ambiguity does not bode well for efforts to establish an enforceable principle that ethnic groups "own" their histories, languages, or art styles.[11]

The many difficulties of using intellectual property law, or modifications of it, to protect indigenous heritage has led to a search for entirely different approaches. One is to graft heritage protection onto existing human-rights protocols (Coombe 1998). The move toward human rights has several attractions. The global human-rights system occupies a moral high ground on which those seeking to protect indigenous cultural rights can add their own edifice of advocacy. But this strategy entails risks. Whatever power human-rights protocols possess comes from their transparency. Murder, torture, and the right of habeas corpus are readily understood by people everywhere. Once human-rights thinking wades into waters as muddy as "culture," "heritage," and "knowledge," we face the possibility that the legitimacy of all human-rights standards might be undermined.

Influential figures in the indigenous-rights movement have concluded that heritage protection will only succeed if it is based on new *sui generis* safeguards that apply to entire cultures. In the language of taxonomics, they advocate lumping rather than splitting.[12] Erica-Irene Daes, author of the UN's much-cited report *Protection of the Heritage of Indigenous People* (1997: 3), eloquently makes the case for lumping. "Indigenous peoples," she writes, "regard all products of the human mind and heart as interrelated, and as flowing from the same source: the relationships between the people and their land, their kinship with other living creatures that share the land, and with the spirit world." Discounting the romanticism of such rhetoric, redolent as it is with hints of New Age holism, we are left with the claim that indigenous lifeways can be protected only through rigorous quarantine of the entire context of a people's heritage, from land to philosophical concepts and everything in between. In drawing an impregnable wall around culture, however, we end up with something thoroughly property-like in its essence, exhibiting such key attributes of property as responsibility, identity, rights of control or disposition, and a "distribution of social entitlements" (Hann 1998: 7). The UN report authored by Erica-Irene Daes insists that heritage is not property but a "bundle of relationships." In light of the powerful current of scholarly thought that defines property itself as a bundle of relationships, we find ourselves stranded in a circular argument without exit.

Advocates of comprehensive regulation also seem indifferent to the negative political effects of their supposedly benign commodification of culture. Universalist strategies, especially those that would reduce cultural property to a matter of fundamental rights, may have the perverse effect of stopping rather than promoting dialogue between groups. The political philosopher John Gray (2000: 116–117; see also Glendon 1991) declares that "the adversarial practice of rights has obscured the permanent necessity of political negotiations and compromise." "If we seek a settlement of divisive issues that is legitimate and stable," Gray concludes, "we have no alternative to the long haul of politics." In multi-ethnic states, that means a process characterized by strategic compromise rather than a focus on absolute, non-negotiable rights.

One wonders how citizens will be able to talk to one another when key symbols of national history have been redefined as the exclusive property of Maoris, Native Americans, Aboriginal Australians, and other ethnic communities. The jointness of shared historical experience tends to get lost in proposals for comprehensive control of key cultural symbols and forms of expression (Munro 1994). Consider an obvious example. Navajo weavers are admired for their skilled craftsmanship and impeccable sense of design. But the rugs for which they are justly famous are a medium that emerged from the Spanish colonial period. Navajos acquired knowledge of weaving from Pueblo Indians who took refuge among them after the Pueblo Revolt in the late seventeenth century. The wool from which the rugs are woven comes from sheep introduced by Europeans. It is well known that Anglo-American traders often provided basic designs and color schemes that individual weavers embellished and made their own. In an important sense, then, Navajo weaving is the product of a cultural conjunction: mercantile and aesthetic, European and indigenous. This is not to question the authorship of individual weavers – or, if you prefer, the cultural community to whose creativity they give expression. It is only to note that at a fundamental level Navajos cannot claim absolute ownership of the Navajo rug as an art form. It evolved in collaboration with other Indian peoples and Hispanic and Anglo-American settlers as part of their shared historical encounter.

The movement toward legal protection of intangible heritage offers rewarding vistas for connoisseurs of irony. To defend their cultures from commodification, indigenous leaders deploy Western idioms of property in their protests and communiqués. In the name of protecting diversity, international lawyers – whom the legal scholar Martin Chanock (1998: 59) labels "the quintessential centralists and uniformisers" – draft protocols that wedge cultural differences into standardized categories. To solve problems created or sharply intensified by globalization, advocates for indigenous rights demand global solutions, leading to a situation in which proposals to conserve the cultural heritage of indigenous peoples from the Arctic scarcely differ from those advanced in defense of Native Amazonians. Most of these plans, however well intentioned, have a powerful tendency to flatten difference in the interests of procedural uniformity.

Other Paths

Are there alternatives to the apparently inexorable transformation of heritage into property? To imagine other ways of helping indigenous peoples to maintain the integrity and vitality of their cultures we must first acknowledge that totalizing, legalistic approaches are incompatible with the diversity of values they claim to promote. The powerful norming and rationalizing currents of formal law cannot readily accommodate the situation-specific negotiations required to ensure the dignity of indigenous cultural life in pluralist states. Although broadly framed rights policies are useful instruments for bringing contending parties to the negotiating table, every additional degree of specificity increases the likelihood that laws will produce unintended harm, especially when confronting the complex, dynamic quality of living cultures.

A different solution lies in strategic use of the diverse resources of civil society. Usually defined as the complex web of interlocking private and commercial associations standing between the individual and the state, civil society encompasses organizational nodes defined by shared religious, fraternal, occupational, political, and mercantile interests.[13] Globalization has internationalized civil society. In the following discussion, then, it should be understood that I refer both to local-level groups of the smallest scale and to powerful, highly organized advocacy groups (i.e., large NGOs) and transnational corporations. These organizations of different scales form an interlocking social ecology that also encompasses indigenous organizations and quasi-governmental bodies such as the United Nations.

To the extent that property concepts are at issue, universalist approaches either push toward the complete commodification of culture or deny that property concepts are appropriate at all. In fact, it is obvious that the spectrum of indigenous cultural productions encompasses things that are property-like in their essence – for instance, closely guarded technical knowledge of medicinal plants – as well as practices and concerns remote from property. The pursuit of indigenous agendas in each of these distinct spheres offers better prospects for introducing creative alternatives to present practice than does a top-down regulatory approach. A review of local-level cultural-rights negotiations strongly suggests that face-to-face encounters of people who are neighbors, who share even to a limited extent the overlapping allegiances characteristic of civil society, create a context in which indigenous concepts of property may spread, virus-like, into negotiated arrangements with institutions and ultimately the state.

The advantages of letting heritage-protection reforms work themselves out in diverse venues are both substantive and tactical. On the tactical front, they provide opportunities for non-natives to hear other perspectives first-hand and to reassure themselves that they are ceding rights and resources for a worthwhile purpose. The power of voluntarism in changing hearts and minds in majoritarian societies should not be underestimated. In substantive terms, the solutions that emerge from local-level negotiations are more likely to be tailored to the relevant circumstances, increasing their prospects for success.

Decentralized, non-regulatory approaches to heritage protection are regarded skeptically by the many legal scholars who hold that social conflicts between parties of unequal political power are rarely settled without the influence, direct or implied, of formal law. The threat of invoking the power of law forces adversaries to negotiate. This perspective is evident in the assertion of Susan Scafidi (2001: 826) that, where cultural property issues are concerned, "without a legal structure there can be no framework for discussion of meaning and normative use, dispute resolution, or even recognition of conflicting values."

It is undeniable that positive social change often takes place, as the saying goes, in the shadow of the law. Supporting evidence can be found in such domains as civil rights and environmental protection. Where indigenous heritage is at issue, however, the argument conveniently ignores the inherent risks of legalism and the long history of high-minded but ultimately destructive regulation of indigenous societies by settler governments. Nor does it take sufficient account of the positive change already effected by the implementation of NAGPRA in the United States and the Aboriginal and Torres Strait Islander Heritage Protection Act in Australia. Although these statutes say little or nothing about the disposition of intangible expressions of culture, they have led to the creation of institutional review boards and advisory committees on which indigenous people are conspicuously represented. Closer engagement with indigenous perspectives has prompted museums and archives to revise policies that reach far beyond the scope of existing law.

A case from California serves to illustrate the latter point. California State University, Chico, was bequeathed the substantial ethnographic collection of Dorothy Morehead Hill, a local anthropologist who died in 1998. During her long career, Hill amassed thousands of photographic images and hundreds of taped interviews of local Indians, mostly from Wintun, Maidu, and Pomo communities. By all accounts, the collection is of great value, both to anthropology and to California Indians, because it documents stories and practices that are threatened with extinction. It may also prove useful in land-claims litigation and the protection of sacred sites. Yet some of this information is considered sensitive and proprietary by Indian people. Among the most controversial items are photographs of religious rituals that today are closed to the public.

Out of respect for Dorothy Morehead Hill's long and cordial relations with the region's Indians and the university's own interest in maintaining a positive image, the collection's overseers have established an advisory committee that represents the donor's family, the university, and local Indian tribes. The committee, with the help of knowledgeable Indian people, is systematically reviewing the collection to determine which items should be available to researchers and which should be subject to restricted access. Far from creating a new arena of conflict, joint management of the collection has been portrayed by Native American leaders as a welcome opportunity to build trust between the university and local tribes (March 2002).[14]

No law specifically requires the university to take tribal concerns into account. The positive response thus far seems to be driven by a combination of public-relations acumen and the obligation of a public institution to attend to community concerns about its resources and programs. Of course, nothing guarantees that the advisory process will satisfy everyone. At other archives and museums in the United States, requests that collections be closed to women or members of specific ethnic groups have been rejected on the grounds that such practices violate state and federal laws prohibiting discrimination. Repositories are also obliged to respect the donor's preferences when these are compatible with relevant laws and policies. The result may be a series of awkward half-measures that make no one completely happy. They will almost certainly fail to satisfy the UN's demand that "each indigenous community . . . retain permanent control over all elements of its own heritage" (Daes 1997: 4). Compromise solutions are rarely elegant, yet they may be the best outcome when irreconcilable values collide. Unconstrained by statute, they can readily change to reflect improving relations between indigenous communities and national societies.

In the context of a spirited debate about whether a people owns its culture, Manuela Carneiro Da Cunha (Strathern *et al.* 1998: 115) insists that treating knowledge as property is the best and perhaps only way for indigenous peoples "to define, to represent, to keep or to dispose of" their heritage. Unfortunately, the suppleness of thought that allows anthropologists to move comfortably between the literal and figurative meanings of ownership may not be characteristic of those whose job it is to turn such sentiments into implementable law. Law has its own implacable logic, and it may unfold in ways that are difficult to foresee or to control. There is clearly much to be done to reform dominant property concepts, as well as ideas about the public domain, so that they are less prejudicial to indigenous interests. But if modernity has shown anything, it is that highly rationalistic legal frameworks presided over by mandarins and bureaucrats often work against the interests of the poor, the marginal – indeed, all those outside the boundaries of elite occupational networks. Contemplating the prospect of endless litigation in defense of cultural elements newly defined as property, one is reminded of the Mexican saying, "May you have a lawsuit in which you are sure you are right." It is invoked not as a blessing, I'm told, but as a curse.

Acknowledgments

This chapter benefited from the critical intelligence of all the participants in the Ronda symposium, especially the organizers, and from the support of the Wenner-Gren Foundation, which made our conversations possible. I also recognize my continuing debt to three institutions – Williams College, the National Endowment for the Humanities, and the Institute for Advanced Study – that provided financial support crucial to the timely completion of this research.

Notes

1. In this discussion I avoid the expression "cultural appropriation" except when quoting the work of others. The phrase is now so burdened with opprobrium and at the same time so inconsistently applied that it has been rendered nearly useless for assessments of cultural flows. It should be obvious – and obviously deplorable – that these flows are sometimes divisive or hurtful, and that they may take place in the context of uneven power relations. But talk about cultural appropriation has become a convenient way to assert a moral

stance while sidestepping tough questions about the ethical ambiguities of intercultural exchange.

2. For an assessment of the potential utility and limitations of a principle of cultural privacy, see Brown 2003: 27–42. A provocative essay by George Marcus (1998) explores the arguments for using censorship to guarantee indigenous control over the transmission of proprietary or secret knowledge.

3. The literature on this issue is vast. Useful sources include Brumann 1999, Fox and King 2002, and Kuper 1999.

4. For a concise argument in support of the emerging concept of cultural sovereignty in the American Indian context, see Coffey and Tsosie 2001.

5. The full text of the Draft Declaration on the Rights of Indigenous Peoples (E/CN.4/Sub.2/1994/2/Add.1) can be accessed at the Human Rights Library of the University of Minnesota <www1.umn.edu/humanrts/instree/declra.htm> (accessed 13 September 2001).

6. On the Durack/Burrup relationship, see Smith 1997, an article that touched off an avalanche of commentary in the Australian press. On the general problem of authenticity and value in Australian art, key sources are Myers 1995 and 2003. I am grateful to Fred Myers for granting me access to chapters of his 2003 book prior to its publication.

7. I owe thanks to James A. Boon for bringing Lowie's observations to my attention.

8. For specific examples see, among many others, Golvan 1992 and Janke 1998.

9. Although published legal scholarship seems mostly to favor the expanded use of intellectual property law to protect indigenous cultural property, a few scholars of law have voiced more skeptical assessments. See for example Farley 1997 and Sunder 2000.

10. Space limitations prevent me from considering the subject of moral rights, another area of intellectual property law in which time limitations do not apply. Some experts on indigenous heritage-protection view the moral-rights framework as potentially useful because of its permanence and inalienability. But moral rights are poorly developed in the copyright laws of some nations – notably, the United States. As the legal scholar Paul Goldstein (1994: 166–171) points out, moral rights may be antagonistic to the interests of the public by limiting the scope of fair use, possibly including the use of copyrighted material for free-speech purposes.

11. A national survey commissioned by the New Jersey Institute of Technology in 2003 found that although 55 percent of respondents aged 18–34 agreed that file-sharing of copyrighted music qualifies as theft, 54 percent of them felt that such illegal traffic should not be restricted. The survey obtained similar responses from this age cohort when they were questioned about the illegal copying of copyrighted software. For details, see Carlson 2003: A27.

12. Posey and Dutfield (1996) propose that indigenous heritage can be protected through the concept of "traditional resource rights." Suffice it to say that this approach is promising but seems to offer few avenues for dealing with the rights of deterritorialized groups or people of mixed heritage.

13. Other participants in the Wenner-Gren conference in Ronda urged me to substitute the Foucauldian term "governmentality" for "civil society" on the grounds that the latter has become too freighted with ancillary connotations to be useful. After considerable reflection, however, I have concluded that civil society is preferable for my purposes because of its greater familiarity and clear identification with non-state, non-legislative groups and institutions.

14· Steve Santos, an employee of CSU-Chico and also Tribal Chairman of the Mechoopda Indians of Chico Ranchería, reports that progress in assessing the Hill Collection has been slowed by several factors, including a state budget crisis that has made it difficult to obtain funds to reimburse Indian consultants for travel to Chico to examine the collection's photographs, tapes, and textual materials. Nevertheless, he is generally optimistic about the program's prospects for creating a platform from which the university can reach out to the region's Native American community. Santos noted with particular approval the university's immediate repatriation of an interview tape identified by Dorothy Hill as a recording that should be heard only by members of a specific California tribe (Steve C. Santos, telephone interview, 20 June 2003).

References

Brown, Michael F. 2003. *Who owns native culture?* Cambridge, MA: Harvard University Press.

Brumann, Christoph.1999. "Writing for culture: Why a successful concept should not be discarded." *Current Anthropology* 40 (Supplement): S1–27.

Carlson, Scott. 2003. "Poll finds that most young people believe file sharing is wrong." *Chronicle of Higher Education*, 4 July 2003, A27.

Chanock, Martin. 1998. "Globalisation: culture: property." In *Cultural heritage: Values and rights*. Edited by George Couvalis, Helen Macdonald, and Cheryl Simpson, 47–60. Proceedings of the 1996 International Conference on Cultural Heritage. Adelaide, S.A.: Centre for Applied Philosophy, Flinders University.

Coffey, Wallace, and Rebecca Tsosie. 2001. "Rethinking the tribal sovereignty doctrine: Cultural sovereignty and the collective future of Indian nations." *Stanford Law and Policy Review* 12: 191–221.

Coombe, Rosemary J. 1998. "Intellectual property, human rights, and sovereignty: New dilemmas in international law posed by the recognition of indigenous knowledge and the conservation of biodiversity." *Indiana Journal of Global Legal Studies* 6: 59–115.

Daes, Erica-Irene. 1997. *Protection of the heritage of indigenous people*, United Nations, Office of the High Commissioner for Human Rights no. E.97.XIV.3. Geneva: United Nations. Sub-Commission on Prevention of Discrimination and Protection of Minorities, 45th session E/CN.4/Sub.2/1993/28. 30.

———. 1998. Some observations and current developments on the protection of the intellectual property rights of indigenous peoples. Opening address presented at the WIPO Roundtable on Intellectual Property and Indigenous Peoples, Geneva.

Farley, Christine Haight. 1997. "Protecting folklore of indigenous peoples: Is intellectual property the answer?" *Connecticut Law Review* 30(1): 1–57.

Fox, Richard G., and Barbara J. King (eds.). 2002. *Anthropology beyond culture*. Oxford: Berg.

Friedman, Jonathan. 1995. "The paradox of keeping-while-giving." *Pacific Studies* 18: 118–27.

Glendon, Mary Ann. 1991. *Rights talk: The impoverishment of political discourse*. New York: Free Press.

Goldstein, Paul. 1994. *Copyright's highway: The law and lore of copyright from Gutenberg to the Celestial Jukebox*. New York: Hill and Wang.

Golvan, Colin. 1992. "Aboriginal art and the protection of indigenous cultural rights." *European Intellectual Property Review* 14: 227–32.

Gray, John. 2000. *Two faces of liberalism*. New York: The New Press.

Hann, C. M. 1998. "Introduction: The embeddedness of property." In *Property relations: Renewing the anthropological tradition*. Edited by C. M. Hann, 1–47. Cambridge: Cambridge University Press.

Hapiuk, William J., Jr. 2001. "Of kitsch and kachinas: A critical analysis of the Indian Arts and Crafts Act of 1990." *Stanford Law Review* 53: 1009–75.

Harrison, Simon. 1999. "Identity as a scarce resource." *Social Anthropology* 7:239–51.

Heller, Michael A. 1999. "The boundaries of private property." *Yale Law Journal* 108: 1163–1223.

Inter-Apache Summit on Repatriation. 1995. Inter-Apache policy on repatriation and the protection of Apache cultures, 8 pp. Manuscript in possession of author.

Janke, Terri. 1998. *Our culture: our future: Report on Australian indigenous cultural and intellectual property rights*. Surrey Hills, N.S.W.: Michael Frankel and Company.

Kirsch, Stuart. 2001. "Lost worlds: Environmental disaster, 'cultural loss,' and the law." *Current Anthropology*, 42: 167–98.

Kuper, Adam. 1999. *Culture: The anthropologists' account*. Cambridge, MA: Harvard University Press.

Lowie, Robert H. 1920. *Primitive society*. New York: Boni and Liveright.

March, Taran. 2002. "A Legacy in Trust: The Dorothy Morehead Hill Collection." *Chico Statements*, Spring 2002, <www.csuchico.edu/pub/cs/spring_02/legacy_in_trust.html>, accessed 9 June 2003, n.p.

Marcus, George E. 1998. "Censorship in the heart of difference: Cultural property, indigenous peoples' movements, and challenges to Western liberal thought." In *Censorship and silencing: Practices of cultural regulation*. Edited by Robert C. Post, 221–42. Los Angeles, CA: Getty Research Institute for the History of Art and Humanities.

Mullin, Molly H. 2001. *Culture in the marketplace: Gender, art, and value in the American Southwest*. Durham, NC: Duke University Press.

Munro, Doug. 1994. "Who 'owns' Pacific history?" *The Journal of Pacific History* 29: 232–7.

Myers, Fred R. 1995. "Representing culture: The production of discourse(s) for Aboriginal acrylic paintings." In *The traffic in culture: Refiguring art and anthropology*. Edited by George E. Marcus and Fred R. Myers, 55–95. Berkeley.: University of California Press.

——. 2003. *Painting culture: The making of an Aboriginal fine art*. Durham, NC: Duke University Press.

Posey, Darrell A., and Graham Dutfield. 1996. *Beyond intellectual property: Toward traditional resource rights for indigenous peoples and local communities*. Ottawa: International Development Research Centre.

Scafidi, Susan. 2001. "Intellectual property and cultural products." *Boston University Law Review* 81: 793–842.

Sheffield, Gail K. 1997. *The arbitrary Indian: The Indian Arts and Crafts Act of 1990*. Norman, OK: University of Oklahoma Press.

Smith, Robert. 1997. "The incarnations of Eddie Burrup." *Art Monthly Australia* 97: 4–5.

Strathern, Marilyn. 1996. "Potential property: Intellectual rights and property in persons." *Social Anthropology* 4: 17–32.

——. 1999. *Property, substance and effect: Anthropological essays on persons and things*. London: Athlone.

Strathern, Marilyn, Manuela Carneiro da Cunha, Philippe Descola, Carlos Alberto Afonso, and Penelope Harvey. 1998. "Exploitable knowledge belongs to the creators of it: A debate." *Social Anthropology* 6: 109–26.

Sunder, Madhavi. 2000. "Intellectual property and identity politics: Playing with *Fire.*" *Journal of Gender, Race, and Justice* 4: 69–98.

Tanner, Adrienne. 2000. "Image problem." *The Province* (Vancouver, B.C.), 13 February 2000, A22–3.

Weiner, Annette B. 1992. *Inalienable possessions: The paradox of keeping-while-giving.* Berkeley: University of California Press.

Welsh, Peter H. 1997. "The power of possessions: The case against property." *Museum Anthropology* 21: 12–18.

The Selective Protection of Musical Ideas: The "Creations" and the Dispossessed

Anthony Seeger

The expansion of market capitalism into the realm of "intangible property" is clearly found in music, where publishing companies established control of musical ideas in the eighteenth century and have attempted to keep those ideas from returning to the public domain ever since. Copyright law owes much to philosophical concepts of individualism and to a particular economic formation. The "traditional" or "folk" music of the rural, poor, non-literate, populations is not protected under most copyright legislation. Technological changes in the way sounds are recorded, stored, and transmitted have challenged some of the ownership customs of earlier centuries, and concerns of communities and nations whose patrimony is largely "traditional" and thus exploitable are forcing changes in international legislation. In this chapter I review current practice relating to intellectual property and the global music industry. In addition, I discuss international copyright laws as they have been applied to music, the reaction to current practices on the part of many nation states in Africa, UNESCO, and WIPO, and the implications of this for an anthropological understanding of property.

Conflict over the ownership of music has been much in the news, thanks to the tremendous popularity of Napster and other Internet music-exchange programs among popular-music enthusiasts, and to the conflicts over music sampling. Castigation, litigation, prophecies of the death of an old industry and the dawning of a new age, and the dramatic consolidation of yet another global industry obscure an important fact: conflict over the ownership of music has a long history. Some of the best historical scholarship on music has been completed as expert testimony for court cases; some of the most shameful denials of rights were perpetuated in the nineteenth century; some important lessons can be learned by looking backward as well as prophesying forward.

This is not to say there have not been some important changes in the perception of music as property over the past century. The digitization of sounds and the possibilities of rapid transfer over the Internet are transforming the entertainment industry in ways paralleled by "bio-information" described by Bronwyn Parry elsewhere in this volume. These changes raise many of the issues floated in the volume's Introduction. But while music sampling and Napster could not have been envisioned before the arrival of Internet with bandwidth, eighteenth- and nineteenth-century inventions led to major reformulations long ago, and ideas from the Enlightenment, applied with the certainty stemming from evolutionism and colonialism, reveal the gnarled (not to say rotten) ancient roots of many contemporary issues.

Property in American Music

My training in social anthropology was the most important asset I brought to my new job in 1988, when I was hired as the Curator and Director of a famous record company that had recently been acquired by the Smithsonian Institution. It gave me an immediate grasp of the reality that music is not just sound – though of course it is also sound. Music is also a web of rights and obligations that both establish relationships among people and organizations and are also an expression of those relationships. Social relationships – the famous networking of the US entertainment industry – are felt to be tremendously important by all parties, but at some point they find (somewhat) direct expression in contracts, permissions, and the like. These contracts have become more and more complicated over the years as new possibilities have emerged, and where the balance between corporations and artists has shifted somewhat more to the artists' advantage. It was precisely my anthropological training, along with the practical need to run a record company and my extensive fieldwork in a non-literate indigenous community in the Amazon, that led me to investigate the intellectual-property issues of recorded sound.

Sounds are a peculiar kind of "property." They were ephemeral before the invention of the audio recorder in 1877, and sound recordings were only recognized in US copyright law about one hundred years later.

Rights in Music in the United States

1. Rights over the composition (the most established form of rights)
   a. rights over the text
   b. rights over the melody

2. Rights over the performance (the sounds)
   a. performing artists's rights
   b. producer's rights
   c. rights of the recording engineer, mastering engineer, etc.

3. All these rights are held for (relatively) limited terms, then the work enters the public domain

4. Rights may be licensed, permanently transferred, or denied if the work is seen as "work for hire"

Figure 3.1. A list of some of the rights held over musical productions in 2001

Printed music – hymnals, song books and sheet music – has long been governed by the same regulations as other printed materials. For convenience, Figure 3.1 outlines some of the rights held in music and how they were handled in the recording industry through the year 2000, when a great push toward internet downloads began to transform the earlier patterns.

A composition (I will be using "songs" as an example for most of this paper) is not necessarily produced by a single person – it may have various creators, each of whom is recognized. This is different from many printed publications, where a single copyright holder prevails. The composer(s) of the sounds may not be the author(s) of the text, and the performer(s) of the composition may not be either of those. More than one person may compose a work. A number of people may be involved (and credited) in the production of the sounds themselves in addition to the principal performer, including additional performers, engineers, producers, and so forth. Information about these different actors in the realization of a recording must be provided in the printed materials that accompany recordings (but the financial arrangements are not public). Most of the collection and distribution of royalties is handled by large collection companies, music-publishing companies, and recording companies (which are today the principal owners of music-publishing companies).

Laws and regulations protecting "compositions" are much older and more elaborate than those covering recorded performances fixed on audio recordings. Printed music has a much longer history, dating back to the 1500s, when international copyright law developed based on concessions to English and French printers' guilds. In England, exclusive right to make copies was granted to printers partly as a mechanism for ensuring state-sponsored censorship and eventually evolved into exclusive licenses to enable publishers to recover the investment of publishing during a limited period of time.[1] The 1909 revision of the US copyright code paid a great deal of attention to print publication and practically ignored the fledgling recording industry. Only after 1972 were the actual sounds on a recording protected by US law (as opposed to local anti-piracy laws), in legislation passed in 1974 (possibly stimulated by the fear of the temptation to copy sounds onto the newly emerging audio cassette format). The reason for ignoring recorded performances for so long was the power and influence of print publishers in earlier centuries. Music publishing flourished – especially with hymn books, singing-school books, and sheet music – prior to the appearance of sound publications on wax cylinder and disc in the late nineteenth and early twentieth centuries.

Like most copyright, the copyright on music gives exclusive right to publish (or control) the composition for a fixed period of time. It also covers only "new works" – above all, works having an identifiable composer. It does not protect or make arrangements for payment for the use of "traditional" materials, or "folklore," unless a specific person can be indicated as the creator. Folklore and compositions whose copyright has expired are in the "public domain," a pool of musical ideas that may be used and arranged freely. In many countries, the public domain specifically includes "folklore" and collective or anonymous compositions and prevents them from being copyrightable. Hayden's chapter in this volume contains a useful discussion of the notion of the public domain, in relation to intellectual-property rights in bioprospecting.

To concretize the rights situation briefly, consider an example. Woody Guthrie (an author and songwriter who inspired, among others, Pete Seeger, Bob Dylan, and Bruce Springsteen) wrote a song about a woman labor organizer, called "Union Maid." He set the lyrics to a lively old fiddle tune widely known as "Redwing." Because "Redwing" was an old song, he did not need to be concerned about any individual's rights to the melody. When he sang the song, he was the writer and performer (the famous "singer-songwriter"). However, other groups also sang

"Union Maid." Then the composition rights and the performer's rights were separated, and both could be expected to receive royalties.

When a popular group called the Weavers performed "Union Maid" in the 1950s, they controlled the rights to the performance (or rather, the record company with whom they had a contract owned the actual sounds of the performance) but Woody Guthrie controlled the composition. Like most songwriters, Woody Guthrie turned over the administration of his rights to a music-publishing company. Even though little sheet music is published these days, music-publishing companies can be large and powerful organizations, and they have undergone the same kind of consolidation that has occurred in other parts of the entertainment industry over the past thirty years. Publishing companies act as agents of a composer to authorize use of his or her compositions and to collect money for the use of the composition. Woody Guthrie signed over virtually all of his songs to The Richmond Organization (TRO), which acts as his agent (now the agent for his estate) in all matters pertaining to the use of the song "Union Maid." When another artist performs the song on a recording, TRO must approve and license the use. There is a "statutory rate" or pre-established rate that is the highest a publishing company can charge for an audio recording (now about 8 cents per song per copy sold of the recording). The publishing company also must authorize any printing of the song in song books, sheet music, or text books (to cite common uses), or its use in film sound tracks or advertising. There is no standard "statutory rate" for such uses, and each use must be negotiated with TRO by those who wish to use the composition. This time-consuming and expensive process has often made it impossible for scholars publishing in small presses to obtain the permissions they would need to have, so as to publish their books with the most appropriate examples. Woody Guthrie's designated publishing company ensures that permissions are asked, that royalties are paid, and (in earlier days) that copyrights were renewed in a timely fashion (something no longer necessary).[2] It receives money from central collecting agencies like the Harry Fox Agency and BMI, and also from record companies, songbook publishers, and other licensed users.

One of the ways existing copyright concepts have been challenged by the digitization of sound is in the use of small sound samples (sampling) to create new works. In this case a composer or disc jockey might take just a fragment of a song, or the sonority of a particular voice, and use that to create something new. First started by rap musicians and DJs, sampling raised difficult legal questions, for the unit was no longer an entire song or melody, but a small fragment of one (see Sanjek 1996).

In the United States, the songwriter's rights have long been the best protected. This is a legacy of the long history of the print publishing industry and the power of the music publishing industry from the mid-eighteenth century on. By the late nineteenth century, music-publishing companies were large and well funded, and they benefited from the tremendous expansion of music performance in middle-class homes. The terms of music copyright were similar to those of other printed creations. The revisions of the copyright laws in 1974 and 2000 further extended the rights of music-publishing companies, but addressed few of the other aspects of musical performance.

Copyright laws in different countries have different provisions for music (although GATT is forcing some standardization). These regulations protect the compositions for different periods of time and collect money in different ways and for different parties in the musical creative process. In the United States, only music publishers receive money for radio play; artists and record labels do not. In Europe record labels receive money for radio play, which they are supposed to share with artists.[3] The United States works hard to protect its own interests and tends to oppose any regulations that impose payments to artists, or threaten to require payment for works in the public domain (both employed in some other countries). Add to these regulations the current inequities in the collection and disbursement of royalties, and you have a system with many critics, but also some very large profitable businesses, and a music industry whose better-paid and more famous members benefit most from its provisions.

What's the Problem with Music Copyright?

There are at least five problems with the current legislation regarding music. These are not original observations on my part, but reflect points made in countless discussions, publications, and literature reviews that have appeared over the years. Most of the problems stem from a single cause: the application of a single, European-created, commerce-driven standard to all forms of music, in all societies, in all nations. The five are: (1) Laws require all music to be treated as a commodity. (2) They protect only new works, not "works of folklore" or traditional music. (3) They ignore existing local concepts of ownership and control, imposing a single standard. (4) Although the laws are international, they are fundamentally based on European Enlightenment ideas of the

individual and romantic ideas of creation. (5) Legislation, encouraged
by parties with financial interests in the outcome, has tended toward
a steady extension of the time period for control and a diminishing
definition of "public domain" and "fair use." I discuss these individually, below.

1   Copyright legislation assumes that all music is a commodity and
in so doing transforms any music that was not so intended into a
commodity. It assumes that all music should be subject to the limited-
term exclusive right to exploit it, and then move into the public
domain. While that may be true for some music, it is certainly not true
of all music. Even where local ideas of music ownership are quite clear,
they may have nothing to do with commodification. For example, a
secret and sacred chant may not be considered a commodity by those
who hold it sacred. It is neither bought nor sold, but rather revealed
and maintained accessible to a limited group within the society. Yet it
may be commodified by other people who record it, after which it will
inevitably enter the public domain for free use. Rights to music are also
not everywhere considered limited-term. If a clan "owns" a song, the
clan may be presumed to own that song from generation to generation,
not simply for 28, 56, or 70 years after the death of the "composer."
The commodity model, imposed on all musical performances by
copyright law, transforms those sounds, designs, and dances into
something they were not.

Here is another concrete example. For the Suyá Indians, in Mato
Grosso, Brazil (among whom I have worked since 1971, see Seeger 1981,
1987), there is no such thing as a human "composer." All songs are
either "revealed" through direct contact between human spirits and
animals, from whom the human spirits learn new songs, or through
appropriation from another human (not completely human, as they
are not Suyá) community. One of the songs they sing today was
originally sung by a jaguar. It was overheard and remembered by a man
whose spirit was living with the jaguars, and he taught it to the rest of
the community. One of the moieties sang it for the first time more than
75 years ago. It is still sung today. According to the Suyá, the "master"
(kandé, which I have also translated as "owner/controller") of the song
is the moiety whose members sang it the first time. The other moiety
must ask the controlling moiety's permission in order for the whole
community to sing it. However the song's creator is the jaguar (when I
wanted a clearer translation of one such song they said, "Only the
jaguars know, go ask them if you want"). The rights situation grows

more complex when you add a researcher with a tape recorder, an archive, an ethnographic recording, and requests to license songs from that recording for feature films. By Brazilian law this song was "traditional" and difficult to protect.[4] How does one defend the rights of a collectivity? How does one define a jaguar as an individual author? What is the lifetime of a jaguar (does it matter)? And since the song is revealed and ultimately religious, what is the lifetime of a God? The Suyá would not agree that any of those is 75 years.

2   Copyright legislation, based on the concept of an individual creator, protects only "new works." Collective works and "expressions of folklore," as the Suyá example given above would be characterized, are specifically excluded. This is clearly an expression of the bias of the literate, urban, commercial sectors of society as against the rural, traditional, "backward" and possibly exchange-based communities. Just as the rural agricultural commons were enclosed and became private property, so rural intellectual property was declared to be in the public domain, and therefore exploitable by urban, literate, publishing, creators.

3   The legislation ignores local concepts of ownership and control, and imposes a single standard. European and American copyright laws generally exclude from copyright all "traditional" materials, or "expressions of folklore." This means that even when traditional artists and their communities consider their works to be "property," they are denied the kinds of payment for their creations that individual "creators" receive. Not only does this discriminate against the traditional in favor of the newly developed, it also tends to discriminate against industrializing countries at the expense of the industrialized. A number of African countries have been particularly active in their attempts to retain control over the "traditional" materials of the communities in their country. Some nations, including Ghana and Bolivia, have instituted a "paid public domain" arrangement, whereby those who use public domain material from their countries are required to take out licenses and pay licensing fees to the nation for that material. These funds are then supposed to be used to support folklore and traditional arts.[5] This kind of legislation will probably be applied increasingly by "content-provider" countries in the future.

Although a system of paid public domain combined with unlimited-term control over traditional music has its attractions, Michael Brown (1998, and this volume) highlights some of the theoretical and practical difficulties such a system could engender. While he raises many extremely salient points, the failure of legislation to address these issues also has implications for the artists and for the future of their art forms.[6] I see no reason why legislation could not be devised that provided some benefit and/or protection to most of those who are now completely unprotected, and whose "property" is not deemed "ownable."

4   The international laws being imposed through GATT on most of the world are based on European ideas of the individual, property, and creativity that grew out of the Enlightenment. Copyright laws tend to apply European definitions of "creativity" and "property" to an area of human endeavor that earlier had a variety of definitions. Nor could the European definition of rights be expected to anticipate major transformations in the world economy. The legislators did not foresee the significance of the traditional performing arts themselves, the impact of tourism, and the money that could be made from folklore and traditional arts in future centuries. Nor were their formulations suitable for an era that has seen the end of colonialism and the disappearance of social Darwinism as a coherent model of human societies.

5   Legislation, encouraged by parties with financial interests in the outcome, has steadily expanded the time period for which a creative work is protected, and has diminished the definition of public domain and fair use (the latter is found in US legislation). The term stipulated in the US Constitution is for a period of 14 years plus an additional 14 years. By 1909 this had become 28 years and an additional 28 years. In 1974 this was lengthened to the creator's lifetime plus fifty years, and in the 1990s lengthened again to the creator's lifetime plus 70 years. Since the average life span has also increased during this period, individuals' rights in their creations (or more likely the rights of a company that controls the rights) have been vastly extended. This means less material is available in the public domain, which is itself being encroached upon in other ways (see McCann 2002).

Recent Developments: The Internet Challenge

Over the past several years, the increasing bandwidth of Internet connections and inexpensive high-capacity removable digital storage devices have made the transmission of music (and video) on the Internet a reality – one that has threatened to clog campus computer systems on the one hand, and that has led to a great deal of debate about the future of the music industry on the other.[7] While some companies have specialized in providing music downloads that pay both artists' and composers' royalties, other software has been developed that requires neither. First MP3.COM and later Napster and other musical download software made it possible for computer users to download music without paying anything for it.

On the other side of the ledger, many companies that control rights to music are making more money than they used to from licensing and other income. In one Swedish recording company the proportion of income from sales of physical products and income from non-tangible rights (such as licensing) inverted between 1990 and 2002. In 1990, 65 percent of its income came from sales of product and 35 percent from rights management; in 2002, 65 percent of its income came from rights management and 35 percent from product sales. This example demonstrates the importance of intangible property to recording companies, and how much they have at stake in the on-line music business (Krister Malm, lecture at UCLA, October 2002).

Napster and MP3 represent a clear case where a new technology has set off a complex review of issues of ownership, just remuneration to artists and composers, and the limits of fair use. But it is important to remember that this is not the first time in the past 100 years that such things have happened. The music industry reacted strongly to the appearance of radio (1920s), jukeboxes (1930s), and the audio cassette recorder (1970s), but certain changes in payments and regulations were made and the industry continued to grow. The recording industry blocked the widespread use of DAT (digital audio tape) recorders by consumers because of the same fears – although it has not done the same with the CD-R (recordable CD), probably because those are used to store all kinds of data, not just music. The shrillness of the debate today implies that this is the first time these issues have arisen, but it is not. It is only the first time they have arisen in this particular way.

Yet the perceived threat to recording companies is real. In early 2003 most of the major recording companies were laying off workers and up for sale. Many users of the Internet argue that all information should be free.

What will happen now? The economic and political power of the entertainment industry is a formidable obstacle to a significant realignment of rights that might accompany the technological changes. The RIAA (Record Industry Association of America) and other industry groups are developing their own digital download systems which will observe copyright laws. Thomas Streeter, examining the history of intellectual property and US broadcasting, suggests that Liberal intentions have tended to create bureaucratic solutions to intellectual property that mimic the market but are not market-driven. He writes, "In the day-to-day workings of the television industry, the concepts of ownership, property, and copyright have become increasingly residual categories, supplanted by considerations of efficiency, fairness, and the overall functionality of the system" (Streeter 1996: 318). It is quite possible that a similar bureaucratic solution, mandated by a Federal agency, and implemented in the interest of "efficiency, fairness, and functionality" will be used to resolve the current dispute over intellectual property and music. On the other hand, they may already have lost too much control over these materials to avoid major changes.

What is Property Becoming in the New Global Political Economy?

Any discussion of the direction in which the concepts of property are moving in the twenty-first century must take into account political and economic power and influence. Large corporations and nations whose exports rely on tight control of intellectual property are insisting on broader and more extended legislation, as well as new definitions of property in order to apply old laws to new things – like the sound quality of a voice, or a very short melodic sample. Relations among people through property are thus being controlled by powerful vested interests. These are represented in the United States by the vast entertainment and software industries, which have even influenced US foreign policy – for example, toward the People's Republic of China – the way other major industries have influenced policies in Central America and the Middle East.

The phrase "global economy" does not simply mean that all parts of the world are linked to one another economically. It also involves relationships of power and inequality. To a certain extent these replicate the colonial relationships of preceding centuries. The "rich Northern" countries take content that is not recognized as property (folk music and biological specimens, for example) in the "poorer Southern" countries of origin, then "improve" it in some way that also turns it into legally recognized property that can be commodified. The "improved" product is then sold back to the poorer "Southern" country, and income is derived from the improvement. While many industrializing nations whose traditions form the basis of popular music have protested this kind of cultural exploitation, legislation that might change it is still far away.

The music industry is a very technology-sensitive industry, and has been since the invention of the earliest printed music (Chanan 1994). Every change in technology has led to major changes in the industry, with associated bankruptcies, layoffs, and opportunities. The digitization of music and the new ways of distributing it are once again changing the industry – and also the ideas about who owns what in music.

When sound becomes digitized, its manipulation and transfer become far easier than they were in the analog era. This has led to the emergence of a vast amount of judicial case law on recorded sound. When a person's voice is digitally manipulated to sound differently, is it still his or her voice? Who owns the hybrid? What is the minimum musical idea for which credit (and payments) must be given? How are royalties divided when dozens or even hundreds of separately authored sounds are mixed into something that is at once entirely new and yet made up of existing copyrighted pieces? These interesting questions, which make for fascinating speculation in university classrooms, will probably be decided in the courts, enriching some people and criminalizing others.

The new technologies also deliver the means of producing and distributing music into the hands of individuals, and eliminate the relative monopoly on both of them that music publishers have enjoyed for centuries. Musicians can create their own masters in their home studios and distribute them without a recording and distribution company. Free file sharing makes music available without having to pay manufacturing, distribution, royalty, or profits. In the 1990s and the early part of the first decade of the twenty-first century this has reshaped the industry. It has made "pirates" out of millions who don't consider themselves such and led to recriminations and threats from the industry to their products' most avid consumers. If an existing form of property becomes uncontrollable by its "owner" is it then no longer property? Major corporations are pitting themselves against the consumer psychology that lies at the heart of the capitalist market system: supply, demand, and getting the best product for the lowest price.

One could argue that it was a technology (printing) that transformed music by commodifying it. Perhaps another technological development will so alter the way music is produced and experienced that it will transform the experience and lead to the commodification of some *other* aspect of music. Live performance may become the backbone of the music industry, as (legal) sales of product decline. Computers may eventually be linked in one huge sing-along, in which files are shared, altered, and re-sent, and recorded sound occupies (or intrudes into, or liberates) more hours of our lives than ever. Or they may not.

Whatever happens, the process will be a very interesting one to observe, and should be watched carefully by anthropologists studying the way humans relate to one another through the things that, in turn, define them.

Notes

1. See John Feather's fascinating article on "From Rights to Copy to Copyright: The Recognition of Authors' Rights in English Law and Practice in the Sixteenth and Seventeenth Centuries" (Feather 1994).

2. TRO goes beyond granting permissions and collecting money. It has requested retractions from authors or publishers who write that the melodies of some of Guthrie's songs are "traditional folk songs" and it has required that statements Woody Guthrie himself made about "stealing good musical ideas" be removed from the text of publications that also want to cite lyrics controlled by TRO. This is justified as "protecting the author's copyright." TRO is probably not unusual in this respect.

3. In the fledgling internet distribution collection plan being undertaken by the Recording Industry Association of America (RIAA), this one-sided collection is being balanced by allocating some of the money collected from digital distribution to record companies and (at the artists' request – since they often don't trust their record companies) allocating separate funds to artists for the playback of digital radio.

4. I had an advisory printed on the back of the LP record the Suyá and I co-produced in 1981 that said, "This disc was made with the knowledge and approval of the Suyá. The songs are artistic productions of this society. The author's rights will be delivered to them and should be paid: the inappropriate use of these songs is prohibited not only by law but also by moral force, against the exploitation of these artists" (Seeger 1982, LP rear cover).

5. These funds do not go back to the performers or traditional artists, however, and thus the way the paid public domain has been instituted has not resolved the problem of the economic marginalization of traditional artists.

6. In response to questions about how to preserve "traditional" and non-commercial arts, I regularly suggest "pay the artists." Only when artists are paid is there an incentive for younger artists to apprentice themselves or otherwise learn their art forms. While prestige and social capital are nice, unless they can be transformed into a living wage it is difficult for an artist to have disciples.

7. *Billboard Magazine* has covered this subject extensively, as has the popular press. Principal actors on the side of the recording industry include the Recording Industry Association of America (RIAA) and certain musical groups.

References

Brown, Michael F. 1998. "Can Culture be Copyrighted?" *Current Anthropology* 39(2): 193–222.

Chanan, Michael. 1994. *Musica Practica: The Social Practice of Western Music from Gregorian Chant to Postmodernism.* London: Verso.

Feather, John. 1994. "From Author's Rights in Copies to Copyright: The Recognition of Authors' Rights in English Law and Practice in the Sixteenth and Seventeenth Centuries." In *The Construction of Authorship: Textual Appropriation in Law and Literature,* Martha Woodman and Peter Jaszi (eds.), 191–210. Chapel Hill, NC: Duke University Press.

McCann, Anthony. 2002. "Beyond the Commons: The Expansion of the Irish Music Rights Organisation, The Elimination of Uncertainty, the Politics of Enclosure." Unpublished Ph.D. Dissertation, University of Limerick.

Sanjek, David. 1996. "'Don't Have to DJ No More': Sampling and the 'Autonomous' Creator." In *The Construction of Authorship: Textual Appropriation in Law and Literature,* Martha Woodman and Peter Jaszi (eds.), 343–60. Chapel Hill, NC: Duke University Press.

Seeger, Anthony. 1981. *Nature and Society in Central Brazil: The Suyá Indians of Mato Grosso.* Cambridge, MA: Harvard University Press.

——. e a comunidade Suyá. 1982. *A Arte Vocal dos Suyá.* Long-playing 33.3 rpm record and liner notes. São João del Rei: Tacape 007.

——. 1987. *Why Suyá Sing: A Musical Anthropology of an Amazonian People.* Cambridge: Cambridge University Press. Accompanied by audio cassette of examples of speech and song.

——. 1992. Ethnomusicology and Music Law. *Ethnomusicology* 36(3): 345–60.

——. 1996. "Ethnomusicologists, Archives, Professional Organizations, and the Shifting Ethics of Intellectual Property." *Yearbook for Traditional Music* 28: 87–105.

——. 2001. "Intellectual Property and Audio Visual Archives and Collections." In *Folk Heritage Collections in Crisis*, 36–47. Washington DC: Council on Library and Information Resources, May 2001. Also available on-line.

Streeter, Thomas. 1996. "Copyright and the Bureaucratization of Property." In *The Construction of Authorship: Textual Appropriation in Law and Literature*. Edited by Martha Woodman and Peter Jaszi, 303–26. Chapel Hill, NC: Duke University Press.

Suggested Website

A very well considered and broad selection of links to other sites of interest in the field of intellectual property, compiled by Anthony McCann.

http://www.beyondthecommons.com/additionalresources.html

Crude Properties: The Sublime and Slime of Oil Operations in the Ecuadorian Amazon

Suzana Sawyer

Sublime: vt 2: (a) to elevate or exalt especially in dignity or honor; (b) to render finer (as in purity or excellence); (c) to convert (something inferior) into something of higher worth. vi: to pass directly from the solid to the vapor state.

Sublime: adj. 1: (a) lofty, grand, or exalted in thought, expression, or manner (b) of outstanding spiritual, intellectual, or moral worth (c) tending to inspire awe usually because of elevated quality or transcendent excellence

Merriam-Webster's Collegiate Dictionary, Ninth Edition.

In late 1999, the Atlantic Richfield Company (ARCO) published a coffee-table picture book commemorating its oil operations in the Upper Amazonian rainforest.[1] Entitled *The Villano Project: Preserving the Effort in Words and Pictures*, ARCO's book documents the technological wonders that ARCO Oriente, Inc. (ARCO's subsidiary in Ecuador) conceived in designing and constructing the infrastructure needed to discover, develop, and pump petroleum out of the Upper Amazon. "Ecuador's rainforests," the book notes, "rank among the world's most biologically diverse regions" (1999: 8). And it was ARCO's concern for protecting this "incredibly rich environment" that spurred its geophysicists and engineers to harness their "technological ingenuity" and build innovative oil operations with only a "minimal footprint" in the rainforest.

The Villano Project is a photo gallery, and the more I leafed through its pages the more intrigued I became. It is filled with vibrant and compelling images that convey the sights, sounds, and smells of the rainforest in Pastaza – Ecuador's central Amazonian province where both ARCO and I have worked since 1988: ARCO as an oil company and I as a cultural anthropologist. Aerial photographs of a mantle of lush forest throughout the book mirror those gracing innumerable contemporary volumes on the rainforest's dazzling biodiversity (Myers 1984; Terborgh 1999; Prance 1982; Wilson 1988, 1996, 1999). Pictures of towering trees shrouded in morning mist almost seem to beckon to the musings of natural scientists on the tropics' untold mysteries (cf. Humboldt 1819–1829; Grosse 1860–1862; Wallace 1853; Darwin 1832). Images of languid rivers enveloped in green foliage call to mind the serene, awe-inspiring tropics painted by the masters over the centuries (Heade 1868; Church 1859; La Farge 1891; Rousseau 1910).[2] And the photo spreads of tree frogs and Hercules beetles echo the injunction of systematists to discover, index, and conserve the forest's cacophony of life (Linnaeus 1735; Wilson 1984, 1996, 1999; Terborgh 1999).

Interspersed in ARCO's book among these pictures of biological wonders are pictures of technological wonders: the heavy equipment, the sophisticated technology, the elaborate infrastructure, and the crucial labor-power necessary to construct oil operations in the neotropics. *The Villano Project* chronicles ARCO's engineering acrobatics for meeting the challenges that the Upper Amazon posed with its rugged terrain and intense rainfall, focusing on the company's heroic efforts to preserve this fragile ecosystem. Given the massive materials and machinery needed to stabilize a well site, build a drilling platform, drill 2-mile-deep oil wells, and construct a pipeline in a region vexed by unstable soils and geological faults, this was no easy feat. ARCO's message, however, rings clear: oil development and environmental preservation can go hand in hand.

So what, one might ask, does this have to do with property? Broadly speaking, anthropological thought has come to define property as a relation between social persons by means of things. Placed squarely in the realm of the social, property is neither a "thing" nor the relationship between a person and a thing. Rather, it encompasses the connections among differently situated social beings that create, and are created by, notions of rights in and benefits to things. This conceptualization of property tends, however unwittingly, to leave the "thing" itself outside culture – making it seem natural, as it were, transparent and self-evident. In this chapter, I would like to suggest that the "thing" (even when it includes "nature") is very much a cultural construction and that the particular way the "thing" is constructed has effects. In the context which I explore (one heavily steeped in unequal relations of power), how the "thing" itself is created serves to reify certain rights claims while circumscribing others and the language through which they can be voiced.

In pursuing these thoughts, I borrow two metaphors – the sublime and the slime – that both Bill Maurer (2000) in his brilliant work on globalization and Rod Giblett (1996) in his iconoclastic work on landscape deploy. In the oil operations described above, what is the place of the sublime in producing the nature of the "thing"? What are the consequences of this production for shaping property relations among variously situated natural and artificial persons?[3] And how might we rethink both questions through desublimation – by contemplating unstable slime? As Giblett suggests, "the formula that 'all that is solid melts into air' under the 'etherealising project of modernity,' borrows the chemical metaphor of sublimation – the transformations from a solid to a gaseous state ... without considering its obverse, desublimation – the transformation from solid to sticky, oozing liquid" (Maurer 2000: 672 commenting on Giblett 1996: 25). Sublimation is haunted, following Giblett, by its murky, mucky other; "slime is the secret of the sublime" (Sofoulis 1988, in Giblett 1996: 27).

With respect to ARCO, I would like to suggest that by construing the "thing" to which it has rights as being "oil activity in the *rainforest*," the corporation performed an act of sublimation; it enabled the company to convert something foul into something pure, something crudely material into something transcendent. Similarly, I would like to suggest that scholars of property who assume the unproblematic thingness of a "thing" are likewise enabling a sublimation. More productive may be mucking through the unruly slime of a "thing's" constitution and what that constitution does. Viscous, slippery movements haunt and taunt both the sublime of the rainforest and the sublime of oil work within it, allowing us to consider how sublimation vaporizes the social relations that produce things.

Rather than the story of multinational capital raping the earth and pillaging third-world resources, ARCO's book tells the tale of rational science and enlightened capitalism joining forces to save the day. And indeed, ARCO's operations are (ecologically and technologically speaking) among the cleanest operations in the oil industry south of the equator. But, my research with the oldest and largest indigenous organization in Pastaza (OPIP, *Organización de Pueblos Indígenas de*

Pastaza – founded in 1978 and representing 15,000 people) tells me that the *Villano Project* offers a skewed picture of the politics of petroleum in the province. What fascinates and disturbs me is how compelling, yet distorted, ARCO's story is.

Without doubt, glossy aerial photos in the *Villano Project* do capture what biological science christens the rainforest's astonishing profusion of life. But that was not what captured Marco (a savvy indigenous leader) as we viewed the forest from above. In late August 2000, I flew to ARCO's operations with Marco and Leonardo, two indigenous leaders and long-time friends. As our Cesna circled the company's operations, Marco craned his neck to point out how ARCO's pipeline cut through his grandmother's old *chacra* (agricultural plots) and present-day *purina* (distant cultivated zones). Pictures of the forest steeped in mist do evoke the fantasies of imperial science. But this was not what had moved Leonardo as he pointed through the morning fog ten years earlier to a 20-foot burning gas flare. It was July 1990, and I was on my first tour of areas in the northern Ecuadorian Amazon devastated by 25 years of oil contamination. Similarly, pictures of rivers indeed resonate with those produced by Euroamerican artistic sensibilities, but they were antithetical to Sonia's concerns. In November 1993, I accompanied Sonia and her neighbor as they traced the flow of oil in a small river near their homes back to its source – a 500-gallon diesel tank that had fallen from the sky as it was being transported by helicopter to ARCO's well site. The image that sticks in my mind's eye is of a film of oil collecting around Sonia's legs as she stood in a shallow stream. And although pictures of a cacophony of creatures excite the systematist's desire to name and claim, this is only one of multiple forest sounds. What echoes more starkly in my head is the roar of ARCO and military helicopters circling an indigenous protest at Villano in December 1994. The roar drowned out the critters and any possibility for a natural order of things.

Like all picture books, ARCO's is made up of photographs carefully selected to portray a particular image: in this case, the company's capacity to produce crude oil heroically in a fragile ecology. Creating such an image is not an innocent act. Instead, ARCO's picture book – along with its corporate rhetoric and its practices – subtly constructed the "thing" of property relations to which it was bound, indeed, to which it bound itself. The multinational corporation did not simply acquire rights to explore for and extract crude oil. It acquired these rights in the *rainforest*. By situating its oil operations in the "rainforest," ARCO conferred new rights and responsibility on itself – rights of property that served to sanction, even champion, the company's activities in the Ecuadorian Amazon. In making a messy business clean and green, ARCO's biotechnical calculus was sublime. The company projected itself as a model global citizen whom the Ecuadorian Ministry of Energy and Mines and the World Bank have praised and sought to replicate. Disturbingly, the act of sublimation – elevating its oil operations through a discourse of environmentalism and technological rationality – vaporized the company's own less than honorable acts that negated the rights of property among OPIP indígenas and solidified new subjectivities among other indígenas. ARCO disappeared the power relations in which it was imbricated, narrowed the focus of its own responsibilities, and delegitimized the majority of local people while simultaneously legitimizing a minority. Mucking through the unruly slime of the sublime places in question supposed transcendence.

The Sublime Nature of Things

Among the scenes which are impressed on my mind, none exceed in sublimity the primeval forests undefaced by the hand of man . . . . The land is one great, wild, untidy, luxuriant hothouse, made by nature herself.

(Charles Darwin, 1832)

The image on the front cover of ARCO's picture book offers a grand, aerial view of a wet tropical forest that sweeps around the book's bounded edge and spills across its back (see Figure 4.1). The forest is dense and vibrant. It appears teeming with life as it undulates across the landscape as far as the eye can see. In the center of the photograph is the Villano well site – submerged in the forested "green sea" yet towering as a technological wonder. Below the well site bold print announces: "The Villano Project" – a citadel of progress in the midst of pure nature. The well site itself is compact and contained – encompassing only four hectares (ten acres) and housing up to a hundred workers. Yet, most impressively, this icon of late-industrial capitalism has neither destroyed its luxuriant natural surroundings nor apparently interfered in ecological processes. ARCO's 210-foot oil rig stands alongside majestic trees bursting with biodiversity. Technological progress and primeval nature happily coexist. The only humans in sight are the speck-sized individuals at the base of the Villano oil rig. And the only artifact of a human presence is the well site itself. In the center

Figure 4.1. Reproduced with permission of BP America Inc.

of the book's back cover, a rainbow arches through the sky, plunging into the forest. Both the well site and the rainbow point to untold riches: the black gold (oil) lodged deep below the forest and the green gold (biodiversity) housed within it.

The angle of the photograph offers a god's-eye view; it projects grandeur and transparent vision. This is the view that ARCO invites the reader/consumer to share. Extracting crude oil from the rainforest is no easy task. Only 100 miles a bit further to the north where I witnessed my first crude waste pit, oil operations by other companies in the Upper Amazon have led to extensive and devastating industrial contamination (CESR 1993; Kimerling 1993; Switkes 1995; Sawyer 2001, 2002). Yet, ARCO appears to have succeeded where others have not. *Deus ex machina*: like the god in a Greek drama who appears to resolve an intractable dilemma, ARCO has performed the sublime. In the struggle between the global need for hydrocarbon fuels and the global need to save biodiversity, the "Villano Project" transcends the crisis and inspires awe. Darwin's words upon seeing the Brazilian tropical forests capture ARCO's operations all the more: "wonder, astonishment & sublime devotion, fill & elevate the mind" (cited in Wilson 1988: 10).

Biodiversity defines the essence of the space of ARCO's operations – a space known today as the "rainforest," yet known only a few decades ago as the "jungle." This distinction is significant. The "jungle" is the realm of treachery and decay, lugubrious and insalubrious.[4] The "rainforest" is the realm of wonder and exuberance, imaginative and generative. A relatively recent cultural artifact, the "rainforest" emerged with the environmental movement in the late 1970s. It gained further scholarly and popular understanding as a place teeming with life forms in the mid-1980s, when a group of eminent biologists coined the term "biodiversity." Gathered together under the auspices of the US National Academy of Science, these scientists turned the moist tropical forest – the ecosystem "richest in species" yet "greatest in danger" – into the poster child of biodiversity (Wilson 1988: 3). As E. O. Wilson, the grandpapa of the biodiversity concept, proclaims, rainforests hold their own special mystique: "the species diversity of the rainforest borders on the legendary" (Wilson 1988: 9). Apocalyptic concerns warn that habitat destruction will annihilate legions of unknown, unclassified, untallied species and place "humanity" on the brink of an "extinction spasm" (Myers 1988: 28). With a fervor amounting to a conservation crusade, the high priests of conservation biology created a sacred site – the "rainforest" – and proselytized about the urgent need "to index, use, and above all else preserve" the "untold biological diversity" within it (Wilson 1988: 3).[5] They encourage "responsible stewardship" among all world citizens to protect and preserve this "planetary patrimony."[6]

The god's-eye view on the *Villano Project* cover is precisely the perspective needed for responsible stewardship. "Good stewardship," Maurer reminds us, "entails responsibilities," and responsibility entails rights (2000: 679). It is the particular quality of the rights and responsibilities that ARCO acquired by being "an exemplary steward" that is of interest here (ARCO 1999: 10). As told in ARCO's origin story, the corporation signed an agreement with the Ecuadorian government to explore for and exploit hydrocarbons from an oil concession (Block 10) in 1988. Inaccessible by road, the 200,000-hectare concessionary block was located in the "primary" or "virgin rainforest," that realm unde-faced by the hand of man (ARCO 1999: 8). In 1989, ARCO's seismic exploration identified potential oil deposits and, in 1992, the company discovered an oil field with "excellent reservoir characteristics" (ARCO 1999: 10).[7] A second exploratory well in 1993 "confirmed the discovery"

and the fact "that the Villano field could be a commercial success."
There were, however, concerns in developing this newly found asset.
First, because the field was located in a "highly sensitive environment,"
its development would require "extraordinary measures." Second, a
"number of incidents" (i.e. the obstruction of oil operations) at various
petroleum installations in Ecuador made ARCO "uneasy about developing the Villano discovery." And third, "protests at [ARCO] headquarters
in Los Angeles" over the company's operations in the Ecuadorian
rainforest further compelled the company to think twice. U.S. executives agreed to give the go-ahead, however, if they had "assurance that
a development plan could be created [that would] protect the environment." In 1994, such a plan was developed, though its "implementation
was delayed" due to protracted negotiations with the Ecuadorian state
over the construction of a pipeline. In 1997, ARCO signed an agreement
with the state to develop the oil field that led eventually to the Villano
Project.[8]

According to the high priests of conservation biology, the rainforest
– the "oldest ecosystem on the planet" – is the source of ancient wisdom
and hope for the future, a "virtual powerhouse of evolution" (Myers
1988: 72). E. O. Wilson muses: over the course of "the 150 million years
since its origin, the principally dicotyledonous flora has . . . evolved to
grow thick and tall" – that is, to be the moist tropical forests of today
(1988: 9). Similarly, Myers writes that the forests of "Amazonia probably
appear much the same now as they did aeons ago" (1984: 11). Tropical
ecologists consider the Ecuadorian Amazon, in particular, to be one of
the world's few "evolutionary nurseries," one of those warm, moist
refuge zones that incubated speciation during the Pleistocene and
whose staggering endemic species diversity was the womb from which
the forest emerged as the glaciers retreated to their poles.[9] Sir Walter
Raleigh (1614) equated the "Tropicks" with "the Paradise of Eden."
Darwin called it a "luxuriant hothouse," the site of creation and
procreation. E. O. Wilson in turn has called it "our Eden, progenitrix,
and sibyl," the eternal spring from which prophecy and promise well
(1984: 12). The rainforest embodies a procreative vessel and comes to
stand for evolution *her*self.

At first glance ARCO's story seems straightforward, even honorable.
ARCO is a corporation that has long prided itself on being environmentally responsible.[10] A quick glance at the corporation's Annual
Reports and Environmental, Health, and Safety Reports underscores the
centrality of a green image in ARCO's self-representations. Since Block
10 was situated in such a unique, cherished, sensitive environment,

ARCO could only proceed in good conscience once the right "techno-logical ingenuity" was devised to protect the rainforest's ecology. But two assumptions underlie this appeal for technological magic to protect a magical place: first, ARCO had to label all "incidents" and "protests" as *environmental* and second it had to see the "rainforest" in strictly biological and geophysical terms. Once this was affirmed, ARCO invoked the science of tropical ecology in its picture book, its environ-mental impact studies, and its corporate rhetoric to define the space of its operations and the urgent need for ecological preservation and protection. The "rainforest equals biodiversity" thesis entitled ARCO to explore for and exploit hydrocarbon resources so long as it did so in an ecologically responsible way and acted as a good steward. Not only does science sublimate nature, it also sublimates all activity done in its name: that is, all operations enacted to preserve the rainforest's integrity for the benefit of you and me.

Importantly, the aerial view image on the cover of ARCO's book also captures the vantage point that Haraway calls the "god-trick" – that ability "to see everywhere from nowhere" (1988: 577). The image mirrors science's claim to transparency and to profess truths from a purportedly neutral and unmarked stance. This is similarly the perspect-ive of the video ARCO produced for the workers on the Villano Project. In the opening shots the camera pans over a mist-shrouded mantle of forest, while the narrator whispers of the rain forest's untold evolution-ary treasures – "the Ecuadorian Amazon is one of the world's most biologically diverse regions" – and exotic pan-pipes play hauntingly in the background. Furthermore, it is the perspective of ARCO's "site map" (see Figure 4.2). The map depicts Ecuador, a handful of cities, the TransAndean pipeline, Block 10 (ARCO's oil concession), and the pipeline that connects it to the company's processing facilities and the TransAndean pipeline. ARCO's map is disconnected. There is no relief to indicate the country's geological terrain or geopolitical context. What we see are simply ARCO's operations. The oil concession itself is displaced from its sociocultural and political-economic context. It is superimposed on an unmarked and unclaimed space filled only with "pristine rainforest."

Extracting a place from its lived context is a crucial maneuver for claiming authorship and authority over that space. Denying a locale its historical and cultural specificity was a central strategy in many colonial ventures (Cosgrove and Daniels 1988; Harley 1990; Sawyer and Agrawal 2000). In the case of the Villano Project, ARCO has removed the forest from its Upper Amazonian context and repositioned it within

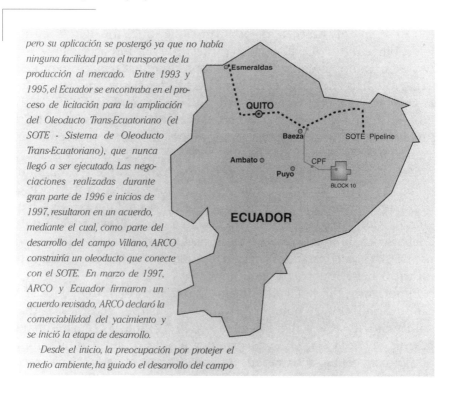

pero su aplicación se postergó ya que no había ninguna facilidad para el transporte de la producción al mercado. Entre 1993 y 1995, el Ecuador se encontraba en el proceso de licitación para la ampliación del Oleoducto Trans-Ecuatoriano (el SOTE - Sistema de Oleoducto Trans-Ecuatoriano), que nunca llegó a ser ejecutado. Las negociaciones realizadas durante gran parte de 1996 e inicios de 1997, resultaron en un acuerdo, mediante el cual, como parte del desarrollo del campo Villano, ARCO construiría un oleoducto que conecte con el SOTE. En marzo de 1997, ARCO y Ecuador firmaron un acuerdo revisado, ARCO declaró la comerciabilidad del yacimiento y se inició la etapa de desarrollo.

Desde el inicio, la preocupación por protejer el medio ambiente, ha guiado el desarrollo del campo

Figure 4.2. Reproduced with permission.

the unmarked and unquestioned context of sublime nature – the domain of conservation biology and an enlightened global society. As McClintock reminds us, "[t]he poetics of male authorship" implicit in the project of naming is not simply "a poetics of creativity" but simultaneously a politics "of possession and control over . . . posterity" and propriety (McClintock 1995: 103).[11] The idea that Pastaza's rainforest expanse is "primary" or "pristine" grants the illusion that the forest is a place untouched by humans and hence a space with no competing claims. Marco's grandmother's claim over the area she cultivates as her *chacra* and *purina*, or Sonia's claims to what type of activity should take place in her ancestral home, have no place here. This image of the rainforest deflects attention away from politically charged questions of rights, resources, and property regimes by substituting other ones.

The "pristine" rainforest of the Villano Project is anything but pristine. Today, approximately 20,000 indigenous people (Kichwa, Achaur, Shiwiar, Zapara) live in Pastaza province and approximately

12,000–15,000 live in the forested region.[12] Furthermore, the tropical forests we know today are hardly the result of uninterrupted evolutionary processes. Throughout history, people have played an integral role in actually creating what may appear to many as the untouched rainforest. Archaeologists suggest that humans lived in the area we understand today as Amazonia long before the forest even existed (Denevan 2001; Roosevelt 1989, 1997; Prance 1982).[13] Only 10,000 years ago, the Amazon was largely a savanna. As the forest spread throughout the basin with a shift toward warmer and wetter climes in the Holocene, many scholars suggest that people were part and parcel of that spread. Thus, rather than being a sublime order of evolution, Amazonia is perhaps better understood as the muddled impure order of embodied cultural and historical processes. What lowland Kichwa Indians call *jatun sacha* (the big forest) is very much a human environment where people living in multiple homes spread across the landscape shape the species content, distribution, and diversity of the forest, through planting, transplanting, and selectively managing different vegetation (cf. Balée 1994, 1998; Descola 1994; Posey and Balée 1989). Moreover, during the past five centuries the Upper Amazon has witnessed multiple shifts and transformations among an array of peoples connected to extractive activities: gold from Spanish colonialism to the present, chinchona and sarsaparrilla in the seventeenth and eighteenth centuries, rubber during the late nineteenth and early twentieth centuries, and petroleum exploration since the 1920s (Hvalkof 2000; Naranjo 1987; Oberem 1980; Oberem and Moreno 1995; Taylor and Landázuri 1994; Whitten 1976). Royal Dutch Shell, which worked in the "jungles" of Pastaza province from the 1930s to 1950, drilled the first Villano oil well in 1949. In short, humans have not been absent from this forested landscape and it is anything but pristine. Sublimation obscures the very social relations that have produced it.

The Slimy Social of Things

> For Sartre, the slimy . . . does not permit the stasis of western 'man-made' structures . . . The slimy upsets the solidities of the positions of master and possessor.
>
> (Giblett 1996)

The centerpiece chapter in ARCO's picture book is entitled the "Invisible Pipeline." Rather than a god's-eye view, the photograph offers an

Figure 4.3. Reproduced with permission of BP America Inc.

intimate, penetrating perspective of a pipeline as it slinks through the
rainforest, as round and smooth and silent as a snake (see Figure 4.3).
The picture's brilliance and detail seem to capture nature's truth. Far
from being an industrial eyesore, the pipeline appears downright
natural. Its curves and bends mirror the contours of the terrain, allowing
the pipeline to meld into the landscape. The scene in the photograph
is peaceful, vaguely idyllic, and even contemplative, beckoning the
viewer to follow the trail as it slips into the distance out of view. This
is the sublime of the vanishing point, the trick of transporting the
viewer into the fantasy of the image. There are no signs of bulldozers
uprooting, gashing, or trampling the fragile rainforest. And while much
labor (over 500 workers for eight months) went into building the
pipeline (as other photos in the chapter show), all the pictures of the
completed pipeline mirror that above. Once the work is complete there
is not a human in sight. The pipeline invisibly evaporates into sublime
nature.

Snaking its way through a green tunnel, ARCO's "invisible pipeline"
carries crude oil from the well site *in* the rainforest to ARCO's processing
facilities *outside* the forest. The book's second map helps locate the
pipeline in relation to both (see Figure 4.4). To the right we see the

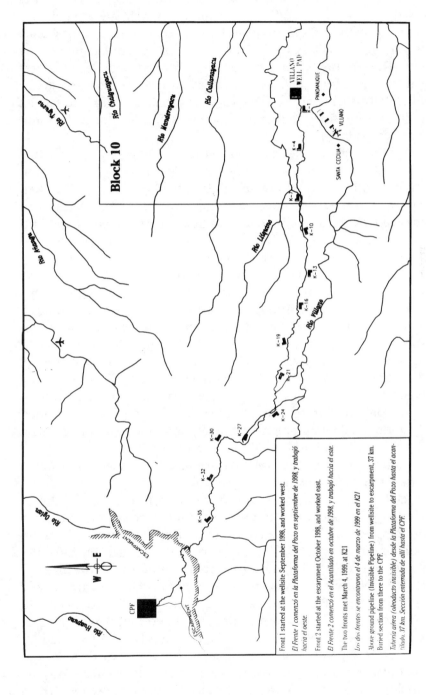

Figure 4.4. Reproduced with permission.

northwestern corner of ARCO's oil concession, Block 10. The clearly marked "Villano Well Pad" is the company's well site. The airstrip indicates a nearby military installation. Two communities (Santa Cecilia and Pandanuque) along the Villano River represent indigenous settlements. The "invisible pipeline" stretches westward from the well site for 37 km, gaining 1,000 feet in elevation until it reaches ARCO's Central Processing Facility up an escarpment to the left. Small rectangles paralleling the pipeline mark the site of safety shutoff-valves and helicopter landing pads.

This is the first pipeline anywhere in the Upper Amazon (an area that includes the eastern lowlands of Ecuador, Colombia, Peru, Bolivia) to be built without a road. In the northern Ecuadorian Amazon (as well as elsewhere) oil roads have encouraged poor mestizo farmers to homestead the forest and timber and agrobusiness to deforest it. Without doubt ARCO's decision not to build roads for its heavy industrial activity mitigates against Pastaza forests being further degraded.

But the distinction between "in" and "out" of the forest is not so sharp or easily defined. "In" or "out," it is all the same biogeography. The area above the escarpment is full of lush vegetation, though substantial portions of it have been transformed into a patchwork of pasture and agriculture along with forest. Similarly, Villano is a patchwork landscape. The area around the military base is largely pasture, and a handful of mestizo colonists have also homesteaded in the region.[14] Granted, deforestation is not as great in Villano as it is above the escarpment. But both areas are shifting landscapes – in which intervention and reforestation continually appear. One is not sublimely "pristine" while the other is slimily "tainted." Remember, even the dense forest through which the invisible pipeline snakes is very much an artifact of human use and manipulation.

Proclaiming itself an eco-saint *in* the rain forest – the realm of biodiversity and sublime nature – allowed ARCO to gloss over the fact that ecology was not its main concern *outside* the rainforest – the realm of human intervention. ARCO spent five million dollars on 230 miles of transit infrastructure in the area purportedly "outside" the forest. It built and reinforced roads and retrofitted bridges to carry heavy equipment to the Processing Facility. Furthermore, the company did build a road along the length of its second and longer pipeline that carries processed crude oil from the Processing Facility to Ecuador's TransAndean Pipeline. All of these entailed massive earthworks and ecological disruption. Furthermore, regardless of how sophisticated the technology, oil is a messy business in which the earth's secretions (crude oil, brimy fluids, and sludge) ooze and mix with industrial discharge (solvents and drilling muds) in always potentially volatile ways.

What I find more troubling, however, about ARCO's "invisible pipeline" is its ability to both sublimate its own materiality and vaporize the social relations that constituted it. Like the aerial photo and site map, the unpeopled pipeline implies that the area in which ARCO works is a space of sublime nature. Not only is the region presented (as in Figure 4.4) as if it were devoid of any social history, but there are also no signs of competing claims in it. The two communities located near ARCO's well site offer some inkling that people live in the area, but they are never mentioned in the text. ARCO's own operations (the boundaries of Block 10 and the pipeline itself) are the only markings on the detailed map that have a social character. But, the area of ARCO's oil operations is very much a lived and contested landscape. Thousands of indigenous peoples – mostly lowland Kichwa – live in the province and hundreds live, manage, and use resources in the area directly surrounding ARCO's well site and pipeline. ARCO has figured prominently in creating conflict among them.

When a multinational petroleum corporation acquires an oil concession in Ecuador, it obtains rights to search for and to exploit oil. It does not own the land where it works, nor does it own the crude oil it extracts. It only possesses rights to exploit petroleum and to a handsome percentage of the extracted crude as payment for its services.[15] At the time that ARCO began its exploratory activities in 1988, none of the lowland Indians living in Pastaza's forested zones held legal title to their lands. Indeed, the state had repeatedly denied indigenous attempts beginning in the late 1970s to legalize their claimed ancestral lands. ARCO knew that although there was indigenous opposition to its operations, Indians could not legally prohibit oil development. According to the constitution, all subterranean resources – of which petroleum is the most coveted – belong solely to the Ecuadorian state, and the state guarantees the unimpeded production of petroleum with military backing if necessary.[16] But the company also knew, from past experience, that indigenous people could interrupt ARCO's oil activities. Within months of ARCO's beginning its seismic exploration in 1989, communities belonging to the most representative indigenous organization in the province, OPIP (*Organización de Pueblos Indígenas de Pastaza*), detained corporate and state officials in the rainforest for 12 days in an effort to stop exploratory activity and gain legal title to their lands. The OPIP-led action halted ARCO's operation for one year. This interruption, like others to follow, cost the company money.

ARCO reasoned that the best way to secure the company's operations was to build alliances with communities that might be receptive to oil development. Once such a community was identified, ARCO helped it gain legal title to its surrounding lands and then sited its oil well there. The company believed that if a community gained legal title as a result of ARCO's intercession, and if ARCO gave it gifts, then the company's oil operations would be safe and proceed unhindered. Pandanuque was such a community. In early 1991, ARCO personnel strategically intervened to secure the legal titling of 10,569 hectares in Pandanuque's name. ARCO drilled its Villano exploratory wells on this land.[17] At the time, Pandanuque was made up of a cluster of houses scattered among planted forest whose residents (estimated at 50 people) lacked the material and cultural capital necessary to pressure the state into giving them land title. Yet, through crucial corporate persuasion, the community that ARCO most needed to have acquiesce in its oil operations received communal legal title to surrounding lands without delay.

At the very moment ARCO sublimated its technological achievements, its social and political activity was mired in sticky, viscous power relations. The company orchestrated the isolated titling of the land that it needed to control and played a key role in creating and exacerbating division among the lowland Indians. Following the practices of every transnational petroleum corporation working in the Ecuadorian Amazon, ARCO bestowed gifts and small "development" projects on the communities surrounding its work site. When the company began developing the Villano oil field, ARCO gave Pandanuque and Santa Cecilia an array of material objects – ranging from candies to blankets, from school supplies to a one-room school house, from airplane rides to high school scholarships – as compensation for letting the company complete its work. For ARCO – a corporation that invested $370 million to explore and exploit oil in Block 10 – these were incidental gestures. For a marginalized indigenous community, these gifts were near monumental. In conjunction with the rhetoric of ARCO's community-relations employees, the corporation's gifts became, for indigenous recipients, talismans of progress and fetishes of modernity.

A leader from the Villano area put it this way as we chatted one afternoon on the streets of the provincial center: "We in Pandanuque, we want to work. We have contracts with la compañía. We want to work for a living. We want to develop. If OPIP had its way, we would be naked and barefoot." Raul was taller than most Kichwa Indians. He looked handsome in his slick new hair cut and shiny new shoes. "You know," he continued as he leaned against ARCO's Chevy Trooper, "la compañía says that Villano will soon be 'Ecuador's new petroleum capital,' and that land in Villano is ours – we own it and control it." More than simple compensation, these gifts – be they candies or contract – seeped into and transformed a local senses of self, property, and propriety. ARCO's field employees were instrumental in fabricating illusions of imminent betterment for Pandanuque residents: that oil operations would raise Villano hamlets out of their poverty and transport them to the land of progress. ARCO had discovered black gold, and Raul, along with others from Pandanuque, were sitting on the jackpot at the end of the rainbow.

In order for Pandanuque to take charge of its good fortune, ARCO personnel encouraged its residents to form their own indigenous organization, which the company supported financially through the pretense of contracts. Thus was born an anti-OPIP and pro-ARCO indigenous organization: ASODIRA (*Associacíon de Desarrollo Indígena Region Amazónica*). Since ARCO had experienced fierce OPIP opposition to its oil operations, the existence of an anti-OPIP indigenous representative body served the company well. ARCO needed docile and compliant people near its exploratory wells to ensure that its oil operations proceeded unimpeded; ASODIRA filled this role. Pandanuque residents treated their newly titled land as their exclusive property and threatened violent retaliation against anyone who sought to intervene in what they deemed to be their affairs.

But the notion that one small community could control oil activity within an arbitrarily delineated land block was for many Pastaza Indians absurd. Their sense of land and land use did not subscribe to the assumptions of private property. One morning, while I helped her weed her chacra, Sonia's mother explained, "Those *runaguna* [referring to Kichwa Indians in Pandanuque], they are few. We are many. And a few people cannot permit that *la cumpañía* enter there as it pleases. They think that the *sacha* (forest) is theirs, but it is ours too. Because we might leave from here in one or two days, live for a month there, and return later. Our life is not only here. Our life is not only in one place. Thus our ancestors left us. Thus we will leave our children."

In general, indigenous people throughout Pastaza Province live in and manage multiple forest zones that may be great distances apart, crossing river systems and ecological niches (Guzman 1997; Reeves 1988; Whitten 1976, 1985). Furthermore, in general, different groups have different rights over different resources in the same area. Historically layered overlapping privileges precluded a cluster of people from having exclusive rights over a large region. Pandanuque was founded in the late 1970s when a handful of Kichwa families moved to the area; in the eyes of most Indians that was hardly long enough to have sole rights over much of anything other than what one planted. According to most OPIP-affiliated indígenas, the community members that formed Pandanuque could not determine the fate of petroleum development for the close to 15,000 indigenous people who lived in Pastaza's rainforest. In their minds, the indigenous individuals near ARCO's oil wells did not own the land on which they lived, in the way one owns private property. Nor did they have inalienable rights over it. Land was a relation, not a commodity. Authority over it was the effect of social relations wrought over time, not a "right" of inalienable ownership; and control over activities within land was contingent on the concerns of others, not an act of individual will. Such indigenous understandings, however, were far from immutable. Through ARCO's intercession and its alliances with the state, ASODIRA leaders began to think of and treat their land as private property, and concomitantly to imagine their own identity differently.

To ARCO's surprise, in 1992 the state adjudicated legal title to over one million hectares of the remaining indigenous claimed lands in Pastaza. An array of historical conjunctures led to this unprecedented land titling, for 1992 was a big year in the Americas. In the global arena, the transnational continental campaign against the quincentennary celebration of the "discovery" of the New World, and the United Nations conference on environment and development in Rio de Janeiro, piqued global awareness of indigenous rights and the preservation of the rainforest. OPIP channeled these concerns at the national level and orchestrated a two-week trek in which 2,000 indigenous people marched from the Pastaza rainforest to the President's Palace in Quito (Ecuador's capital) demanding legal title to their ancestral territory (Sawyer 1997, 2004; Whitten 1997). With the help of national and international pressure from indigenous rights and environmental groups, OPIP succeeded in its demand for legal communal title.

It would, of course, have been easier for ARCO if Pandanuque Indians were the only ones with legal rights to rainforest land in Pastaza. But while the company could not prevent further land titling, ARCO could intervene in *how* more land titles were granted. OPIP specifically demanded that the state adjudicate land on the basis of indigenous "nationalities" – dividing the one million hectares of Pastaza land into the "traditional" territories of Kichwa, Achuar, Shiwiar, and Zapara Nationalities. In consultation with ARCO and the Ministry of Energy and Mines, however, the state adjudicated the newly titled one million hectares into 19 separate segments. These arbitrarily defined land segments created 19 new juridical divisions that had no relation to actual land-use practices or authority structures on the ground. OPIP insisted that these state-defined divisions be ignored; for the most part, this has been the case since indígenas move widely throughout the region and land divisions have never been marked on the landscape. Yet in a few instances – Pandanuque being the most prominent – distinct individuals living within an arbitrarily defined land segment have come to treat this land as private property. This redefined sense of self and property has greatly exacerbated conflict in the region, especially in relation to oil activity.

By sublimating its oil operations – by making sure that they did not alter the biophysical processes in the rainforest – ARCO diverted public attention away from the sucking, viscous matrix through which its operations affected and transformed local people's lives. A biophysical focus compelled the company to deny its own practices that actually heightened tensions, conflicts, and inequalities among indigenous groups. Making invisible its own hand in creating social divisions in Pastaza gave the impression that conflict between indigenous peoples was natural. This was a case of chaotic, irrational Indians fighting among themselves, a matter about which the company could do nothing. If ethnic conflicts had created such an unruly mass, then the corporation could easily dismiss indigenous protest and delegitimize indigenous claims that were founded in the sticky, intractable moral and political problematics surrounding resource extraction. Furthermore, indigenous unruliness was cause for ARCO to militarize its operations and protect them from any sabotage that might hurt the fragile rainforest environment.

Crude Properties

Braun notes that "the authority of corporate capital today is related in important ways to historical practices of imagining, representing, and purifying 'natural' landscapes" (1997:27). In this chapter, I have suggested that the way ARCO imagined the terrain of its operations significantly affected its rights, responsibilities, and legitimacy to explore for and exploit petroleum in Ecuador. How the "thing" to which ARCO had rights was created shaped the relations of property in the Upper Amazon. Buttressed by the authority and truth claims of conservation biology, ARCO proclaimed the area of its operations as the "rainforest" – that fragile luxuriant hothouse of biodiversity and sublime nature. Committing itself to produce petroleum in this realm, then, entailed certain rights and responsibilities that ARCO valiantly took on. Through diligence and ingenuity, the corporation developed the cleanest and greenest oil operations under the equatorial sun. ARCO turned technologically sophisticated and environmentally sensitive oil development into a noble act. In appealing to a global discourse on environmentalism, ARCO's oil operations were transformed; the crude metamorphosed into the sublime.

Nature is far from natural. Landscapes are far from transparent. How and why they become imagined the way they are has particular effects – effects that shape relations of property. That is because a landscape is not simply a self-evident physical space: it is a conceptual space that carries with it moral significance (cf. Arnold 1996; Cronon 1995; Slater 1995, 2001, 2003; Stepan 2000). Over the past two decades, conservation biology has heavily defined the moral significance of rainforests. This moral significance, in turn, helps justify what types of activity can occur within it. It sublimates – and consequently authorizes and legitimizes – particular practices like green oil operations. One might say, perhaps, that the era of overt conquest has become enveloped by the era of management. Part of that management is the constitutions of the *things* of property relations. In this case, the thing-ness of property relations served both to vaporize the social relations that produced it *and* to normalize the profoundly unequal social, political, and economic terrain on which such relations took place.

In 1994, ARCO established a forum called the Technical Environmental Committee to demonstrate its concern for local indigenous peoples. The Committee was made up of what the corporation called "the stakeholders of Block 10": representatives of ARCO, the Ministry of Energy and Mines, and three indigenous organizations (OPIP, ASODIRA, and a small evangelical group). The forum focused on defining the technologies needed to preserve biodiversity in the rainforest: i.e., the size and location of well sites, the pipeline route, the processing facility, and the technology for building all. OPIP leaders found that the Committee was the space where the company and the government recognized their legitimacy as leaders. However, in order to be heard, Indians were forced to address only issues ARCO, and not they, termed their "common ground" – that is, a shared concern for the biodiversity of the rainforest. ARCO thus effectively circumscribed discussion. The result was to grant indigenous leaders a space in which to "mouth," rather than a forum in which to speak. OPIP's primary concerns were only about the rainforest in a broad social (not narrow biotechnical) sense.

In fall 2000, Ecuador signed loan agreements with the World Bank and the International Monetary Fund, totaling nearly $2 billion. The loans were part of strategies to modernize the country. With oil revenues comprising nearly half of the state's budget and providing significant monies for paying the foreign debt, the oil sector was of key concern. However, given that Ecuador's petroleum reserves lie in the Upper Amazon and that the global force of environmentalism has influenced even the World Bank, the Bank found in ARCO a savior. It hailed ARCO's operations as the standard that all new oil companies working in the Ecuadorian rainforest should emulate. And it committed hundreds of thousands of dollars to establishing tripartite negotiating fora along the lines of ARCO's Committee. In the postcolonial empires of neoliberalism, the environment, like democracy, is sublime. All activities done in the name of encouraging, sustaining, and preserving it are enshrined.

Property, as an analytical concept, helps sort out the maneuvers of power at work in ARCO's oil operations. If we understand property to be the relations that materialize things into this world, then it is absolutely crucial to examine the thing-ness around which property relations coalesce. This is perhaps even more the case as late capitalism stretches into the twenty-first century. What one observes in the case of ARCO is that even in an industry as crude and material as oil, outright ownership is not necessary or even desirable for production. ARCO did not overtly claim any property in the conventional sense; it did not claim rights of control over land or petroleum. Rather, it was a service company that explored for and extracted crude. Its services were paid for in barrels of oil. As regimes of production in transnational capitalism transform to allow for greater flexibility, mobility, and profitability, the attachments, responsibilities, and liabilities that accompany overt property relations may be less and less desirable. The effect may well be a disappearing of overt property from many processes of accumulation.

Property as an analytical concept may serve us well precisely in uncovering how things materialize and what their particular materialization does – especially when they are otherwise disappeared. In the case of ARCO, the ability of the corporation to authorize and legitimize its operations hung on the particular way it couched the service it offered: exploring for and exploiting oil in the *rainforest*. The care and precision with which the corporation devised clean and green operations in the rainforest – that seemingly most primeval and edenic space on earth – served to exalt its oil operations beyond reproach. In large part, ARCO was able to do this, building on two decades of Western conservation biology, by isolating the rainforest as a purely biophysical realm that its corporate scientific and technological prowess would protect. It thereby created itself as a new moral, ethically upright subject at the service of enlightened global society. Presenting the rain forest as exclusively a natural realm bursting with biodiversity precluded, however, understanding it as a social environment filled with messy human relations. By presenting the thing-ness of the property relations to which it was connected as a realm of absolute and exquisite nature, ARCO disavowed any duties, responsibilities, and accountability to the people that populate the rainforest. In the process, it erased local people and obliterated their voices except when articulated through the sacrosanct language of nature.

Given this, the name of ARCO's project is curious. "Villano" is the name of the river near the corporation's well site.[18] Similarly, "Villano" has come to define a small yet distinct region ever since multinational capitalism and the Ecuadorian military set up shop there in the mid-1940s. The Royal Dutch Shell Company named the oil well it drilled in the area Villano-1; today, the tapped well can be found a mere quarter-hour walk from ARCO's well site. The Ecuadorian military named the installation it built to protect and facilitate Shell's operations the "Villano Outpost"; today, the small army base sits across the river near ARCO's well site. Consequently, while it makes sense that ARCO named its project "Villano," the name is ironic. "Villano" is an antiquated term for "villain" in Spanish. A villain is the bad guy, one whose rights of property are not legitimate. For many local peoples, ARCO is as slimy as a villain.

Acknowledgments

I thank Katherine Verdery and Caroline Humphrey for inviting me to the Wenner-Gren conference and for their fabulous comments. Similarly, I am very grateful to Marilyn Strathern, Jane Collier, Bill Maurer, Cori Hayden, Chris Hann, and all the conference participants for their stimulating comments in strengthening this chapter. Thanks also to Jake Kosek for generously tutoring me in the language of property early on.

Notes

1. I thank Teresa Velasquez, my research assistant and dear friend, for sending me ARCO's book soon after it was published.

2. Examples of nineteenth-century paintings of the tropics include Martin Johnson Heade's *South American River* (1868), Frederic E. Church's *The Heart of the Andes* (1859), John La Farge's *Afterglow, Tautira River, Tahiti* (1891), and Henri Rousseau's *The Dream* (1910).

3. I thank Bill Maurer for introducing me to Giblett.

4. Imagery of the "jungle" has a long history in Western novels: Joseph Conrad's *Heart of Darkness* (1902), Sir Arthur Conan Doyle's *Lost World* (1912), Norman Mailer's *The Naked and the Dead* (1948). For films see: *Tarzan of the Apes* (1918), *The Lost World* (1925), *Aguirre: The Wrath of God* (1972), and *Apocalypse Now* (1979).

5. Janzen goes a step further and ordains "[b]iologists, tropical ecology's clergymen," as "the representatives of the natural world," "in charge of the future of tropical ecology" (1986: 396, 306). Mimicking colonial predecessors, biodiversity experts have appropriated Nature as global and simultaneously appointed themselves her keeper: scientists sought "to generalize, predict, and ultimately control . . . the *Amazon* of input from nature" (Soulé, 1988: 466, emphasis added).

6. The term is Myers's (1984).

7. ARCO, *Villano Project*, 10. ARCO's first exploratory well in Block 10 was at a site called "Moretechocha" approximately thirty miles south of the Villano area. The next two exploratory wells were at Villano. The Villano oil reservoir contained 700,000 barrels of 21 degree API oil – i.e., good light oil.

8. Negotiations were protracted due to the 1995 Amazonian war between Ecuador and Peru, disagreements about how to build a pipeline from Villano to Ecuador's main TransAndean pipeline, and how to expand the carrying capacity of the TransAndean pipeline.

9. This is understood in conservation biology as the "refugia theory of speciation." See Prance (1982) for an elaboration of this theory.

10. See ARCO annual reports from the mid-1970s onward.

11. In conjuring up a sense of the "naturalist's trance, the hunter's trance" Wilson writes of his first journey to Surinam in 1961: "I imagined richness and order as an intensity of light . . . I imagined that this place and all its treasures were mine alone and might be so forever in memory" (1984: 6–7).

12. Archaeological research and early colonial accounts suggest that the population in the Amazon Basin was substantially denser at and before the Spanish invasion. Contrary to popular thought lowland Kichwa are not highland Kichwa who migrated to the Upper Amazon. Most scholars believe

that lowland Kichwa have lived in the rainforest region for thousands of years (Guzmán Gallegos, 1997; Reeves1988; Whitten, 1976, 1985). Achuar also live in the southern part of the province, and Shiwiar and Zaparo Indians inhabit the area near the Peruvian border.

13. For a discussion of the effects of climatic changes on Amazonia during the late Pleistocene and early Holocene, see Prance (1982).

14. After the 1981 border war between Ecuador and Peru, the Ecuadorian government encouraged individuals to colonize the Villano area. Colono households were given private title to 50 hectares of land. There are six to eight colono households in Villano.

15. Legal contracts between multinational oil companies and the Ecuadorian state have varied over the years. ARCO's arrangement was a "risk-service contract."

16. Ecuadorian Constitution Art. 46. As defined by the National Security Law (Art. 50) and the Hydrocarbon Law (Art. 6 and 8), petroleum is a national-security resource of strategic importance and its production must be guaranteed by military action.

17. Similar processes took place in Moretecocha, the site of ARCO's first exploratory well in Block 10 (Sawyer 2004).

18. The Villano River flows into the Curraray River, which flows into the Napo, a tributary of the upper reaches of the Amazon River.

References

ARCO. 1999. *The Villano Project: Preserving the effort in words and pictures.* Quito: Imprenta Mariscal.

Arnold, David. 1996. *The problem of nature: Environment, culture, and European expansion.* London: Blackwell. Atlantic Richfield Company.

Balée, William. 1994. *Footprints of the forest : Ka'apor ethnobotany – the historical ecology of plant utilization by an Amazonian people.* New York: Columbia University Press.

Balée, William (ed.). 1998. *Advances in historical ecology.* New York: Columbia University Press.

Braun, Bruce. 1997. "Buried epistemologies: The politics of nature in (post)colonial British Columbia." *Annals of the Association of American Geographers* 87: 3–31.

CESR (Center for Economic and Social Rights). 1994. *Rights violations in the Ecuadorian Amazon: The human consequences of oil development.* New York: Center for Economic and Social Rights.

Cosgrove, Daniel and Stephen Daniels. 1988. *The iconography of land-scape: Essays on the symbolic represention, design and use of past environments.* Cambridge: Cambridge University Press.

Cronon, William. 1995. *Uncommon ground: Rethinking the human place in nature*. New York: W.W. Norton.

Darwin, Charles. 1993 [1832]. *The origin of the species by means of natural selection, or, The preservation of favored races In the struggle for life*. New York: Modern Library.

Denevan, William M. 2001. *Cultivated landscapes of Native Amazonia and the Andes: triumph over the soil*. Oxford: Oxford University Press.

Descola, Philippe. 1994. *In the society of nature: A native ecology in Amazonia*, transl. by Nora Scott. Cambridge: Cambridge University Press.

Ehrlich, Paul. 1988. "The Loss of Diversity: Causes and Consequences." In *Biodiversity*. Edited by E. O. Wilson. Washington, D.C.: National Academy Press.

Giblett, Rod. 1996. *Postmodern wetlands: Culture, history, ecology*. Edinburgh: Edinburg University Press.

Grosse, Phillip H. 1860–1862. *The romance of natural history*. New York: Sheldon.

Guzmán Gallegos, María Antonieta. 1997. *Para que la yuca beba nuestra sangre*. Quito: Abya Yala.

Haraway, Donna. 1988. "Situated knowledges: The science question in feminism and the privilege of partial perspective." *Feminist Studies* 14: 575–99.

Harley, J. B. 1990. "Cartography, Ethics, and Social Theory." *Cartographia* 27: 1–23.

Humboldt, Alexander von, and Aime Bonpland. 1819–1829. *Personal narratives of travels to the equinoctial regions of the new continent during the years 1799–1804*. London: Longman.

Hvalkof, Soren. 2000. "Outrage in rubber and oil: Extractivism, indigenous peoples, and justice in the Upper Amazon." In *People, plants, and justice*. Edited by Charles Zerner. New York: Columbia University Press.

Janzen, Daniel. 1983. *Costa Rican natural history*. Chicago: University of Chicago Press.

——. 1986. "The future of tropical ecology." *Annual Review of Ecological Systematics* 17: 305–24.

Kimerling, Judith. 1993. *Crudo Amazónico*. Quito: Abya Yala.

Linnaeus, Carl. 1964 [1735]. *Systema Naturae*. New York: Stechert Hafner.

Maurer, Bill. 2000. "A fish story: Rethinking globalization on Virgin Gorda." *American Ethnologist* 27: 670–701.

McClintock, Anne. 1995. *Imperial leather: Race, gender, and sexuality in the colonial contest*. New York: Routledge.

Myers, Norman. 1984. *Primary source*. New York: W. W. Norton.

——. 1988. "Tropical forests and their species: Going, going . . .?" In *Biodiversity*. Edited by E. O. Wilson. Washington, D.C.: National Academy Press.

Naranjo, Marcelo. 1987. *Etnohistoria de la zona central del alto Amazonas, siglos XVI–XVIII*. Urbana: University of Illinois.

Oberem, Udo. 1980. *Los Quijos, historia de la transculturación de un grupo indígena en el Oriente Ecuatoriano*. Otavalo, Ecuador: Instituto Otavaleño de Antropología.

Oberem, Udo and Y. Segundo Moreno. 1995. *Contribución a la etnohistoria ecuatoriana*. Otavalo, Ecuador: Instituto Otavaleño de Antropología and Quito: Ediciones del Banco Central del Ecuador.

Posey, Darrel and William Balée (eds.). 1989. *Resource management in Amazonia: Indigenous and folk strategies*. New York: New York Botanical Garden.

Prance, G. 1982. *Biological diversity in the tropics*. New York: Columbia University Press.

Reeves, Elizabeth. 1988. *Los Quichuas del Curaray: el proceso de formación de la identidad*. Quito: Abya Yala.

Roosevelt, Anna. 1989. "Resource management in Amazonia before the conquest: Beyond ethnographic projection." In *Resource management in Amazonia: Indigenous and folk strategies*. Edited by Darrell Posey and William Balée, 1–21. New York: New York Botanical Garden.

——. 1997. "Paleoindian cave dwellers in the Amazon: The peopling of the Americas." *Science* 272: 373–84.

Sawyer, Suzana. 1997. "The 1992 Indian mobilization in lowland Ecuador." *Latin American Perspectives* 93: 67–84.

——. 2001. "Fictions of sovereignty: Of prosthetic petro-capitalism, neoliberal states, and phantom-like citizens in Ecuador." *Journal of Latin American Anthropology* 6: 156–97.

——. 2002. "Bobbittizing Texaco: Dis-membering corporate capital and re-membering the nation in Ecuador." *Cultural Anthropology* 17: 150–80.

——. 2004. *Crude chronicles: Indigenous politics, multinational oil, and neoliberalism in Ecuador*. Durham, NC: Duke University Press.

Sawyer, Suzana, and Arun Agrawal. 2000. "Environmental orientalisms." *Cultural Critique* 45: 71–108.

Slater, Candace. 1995. "Amazonian as Edenic narrative." In *Uncommon ground: Rethinking the human place in nature*. Edited by William Cronon. New York: W. W. Norton.

——. 2001. *Entangled Edens*. Berkeley: University of California Press.

—— (ed.). 2003. *In search of the rain forest*. Durham, NC: Duke University Press.

Soulé, Michael. 1988. "Mind in the Biosphere: Mind of the Biosphere." In *Biodiversity*. Edited by E. O. Wilson, 465–9. Washington, D.C.: National Academy Press.

Stepan, Nancy. 2000. *Picturing tropical nature*. Ithaca: Cornell University Press.

Switkes, Glen. 1995. "Texaco: The peoples vs Texaco." *NACLA* 38(2) (September/October): 6–10.

Taylor, Anne Christine, and Cristóbal Landázuri.1994. *Conquista de la región Jivaro, 1550-1650: relación documental*. Quito: Marke, Ifea, Abya-Yala.

Terborgh, John. 1999. *Requiem for nature*. Washington, D.C.: Island Press.

Wallace, Alfred Russel. 1853. *A narrative of travels on the Amazon and Rio Negro*. London: Reeves.

Whitten, Norman. 1976. *Sacha Runa: Ethnicity and adaptation of Ecuadorian jungle Quichua*. Urbana: University of Illinois Press.

——. 1985. *Siguanga Runa: The other side of development in Amazonian Ecuador*. Urbana: University of Illinois Press.

——. 1997. "Return of the Yumbo: The indigenous Caminata from Amazonia to Andean Quito." *American Ethnologist* 24: 355–91.

Wilson, Edward O. 1984. *Biophilia*. Cambridge, MA: Harvard University Press.

——. 1988. "The Current State of Biological Diversity." In *Biodiversity*. Edited by E. O. Wilson, 10. Washington, D.C.: National Academy Press.

——. (ed.). 1988. *Biodiversity*. Washington, D.C.: National Academy Press.

——. 1996. *In search of nature*. Washington, D.C.: Island Press.

——. 1999. *Biological diversity: the oldest human heritage*. Albany, NY: New York State Museum.

Part II

Property, Value, and Liability

Prospecting's Publics

Cori Hayden

From controversies over patenting "indigenous DNA" to the development of biotechnologically engineered seeds and genetically modified foods, the end of the twentieth century and beginning of the twenty-first have seen a stunning intensification in transformations of life forms and life processes into property. This, in turn, has given new dimensions to longstanding social conflicts. In Chiapas, Mexico, during the late 1990s, the intersection of new modes of property- and wealth-production with deeply sedimented conflicts over land tenure, sovereignties, and indigenous rights took some vivid turns. Chiapas is the site of the ongoing Zapatista uprising, an armed indigenous movement which made its debut on the international stage on 1 January 1994: the day the North American Free Trade Agreement took effect. Drawing attention to the effects of neoliberalism on indigenous communities, the Zapatistas have continued to make both an armed and a political case for democratization in Mexico and for indigenous sovereignty, political as well as territorial. At the center of the "low-intensity" conflict have been government and military efforts to control indigenous lands, on and under which reside some rather potent economic resources: tropical hardwoods, petroleum, and minerals.

In 1998, as the uprising continued to simmer, two US academic researchers attempted to institute a "bioprospecting" agreement in the Mayan highlands of Chiapas. With funds from a US government prospecting program, University of Georgia ethnobiologists Brent and Elois Ann Berlin began negotiations with Tzeltal and Tzotzil communities over a new form of biotech-mediated trade. Their goal was to send plants and microbes from these communities to a Welsh biotechnology firm (Molecular Nature, Inc.), in exchange for promises of a portion of future royalties, which would come back to participants in the form of community development funds. Together with a Mexican research institute, ECOSUR, the Berlins established an NGO in Chiapas (PROMAYA) that was to help manage the distribution of royalties to participating communities.

This was precisely the kind of arrangement warranted by the 1992 UN Convention on Biological Diversity – a multilateral accord that has served as an important focal point for powerful changes in the north-south traffic in biological resources. In the name of sustainable development as well as redistributive justice, the CBD mandated that drug and biotechnology companies share economic benefits with source nations and/or communities, if they desire continued access to southern resources. In its binding power, it is a fragile mandate indeed: the United States, home to many such companies, has not ratified the Convention, and UN treaties in general are not known for their enforcement power. Nonetheless, the CBD has created a structure and idiom of expectation which has had important effects on international conceptions of the rights and obligations that come with plants, microbes, and other bio-resources (see Reid et al. 1993).

In the CBD's name and sometimes, as we shall see, in its stead, myriad prospecting agreements of the type proposed by the Berlins in Chiapas have taken shape in Mexico and across the southern hemisphere since the mid-1990s. Through these contracts and the controversies surrounding them, the CBDs benefit-sharing mandate is constantly in the making – as well as in the un-making. In fact, while many prospecting collaborations have been up and running in Mexico for over a decade, the so-called "Maya ICBG" program barely got off the ground before it was brought to its knees by concerted opposition from a potent coalition of actors decrying "biopiracy in Chiapas" (see RAFI 1999a, 1999b). Mexico City-based intellectuals, international and Mexican NGOs, and an organization of traditional healers and midwives in Chiapas (COMPITCH) argued that the negotiating process for this exchange was neither fair nor transparent, and that the regulatory conditions do not exist in Mexico for ensuring that such exchanges transpire with anything resembling legitimacy. Under the weight of these arguments, which notched into powerful international activist sympathies toward the question of indigenous rights in Chiapas, the sponsoring bodies in Mexico and the United States withdrew their support from the project. The Maya ICBG was canceled in 2001.[1]

For many drug companies and universities with a wary eye on the new, multilateral ethic of "equitable returns," the demise of the Maya ICBG is precisely the kind of political "disaster" which they desperately hope to avoid as they confront the prospect of setting up benefit-sharing collaborations. It is not difficult, indeed, to imagine the many things that "went wrong" with the Maya ICBG project – not least, that its US leaders were seeking access to biological resources in the middle of what is effectively a war zone, in which indigenous control over land and resources is at the very center of the conflict. But for many prospecting institutions and companies, the demise of the Maya ICBG merely confirms a slightly cynical argument that has permeated the world of benefit-sharing since its inception: that entering into prospecting collaborations with indigenous communities is a hopelessly and inherently "risky" enterprise.[2]

It is this allegation of risk, and most pointedly some of its ancillary effects, which structure my concerns in this chapter. The CBD's fragile incitement to share has, it turns out, been remarkably generative, though not of royalties, products, and benefits shared. To date, none of the high-profile prospecting projects initiated across Latin America and parts of Africa in the early 1990s has produced any drugs or – therefore – royalties paid to southern participants. But one of the things that it *has* helped generate, I would argue, are some remarkably instrumental taxonomies of rights-in-resources that overlay longstanding struggles over definitions of nature, value, and nation. Most pointedly, declaring themselves daunted by the prospect of negotiating benefit-sharing contracts with indigenous peoples, many companies, Latin American biodiversity policy officials, and university researchers have stated a clear preference for screening resources considered "safely in the public domain." This public domain is populated by a remarkable array of inhabitants. Microbes on government-protected lands and medicinal plants sold in urban markets, weeds on the sides of the road and knowledge published in anthropologists' articles, petri dishes in private university laboratories and vines growing in their friends' backyards – these are just some of the "public" sites that Latin American researchers are activating in agreements I have been tracking. What allows researchers to identify this assortment of sites, some of which are indeed private property, as effectively public? Their denomination as such takes shape against what they are not: it's not the "private" that is other, here, but the *ejidal*, the communal, the indigenous – and a host of national histories that give these categories particular weight and shape.

While much critical activist and scholarly commentary on bioprospecting hinges on the question of privatization, and rightly so,[3] I want to address the crucial concerns of access, entitlements, and exclusions through an idiom other than that of privatization per se. The "safe" collecting zones just listed impel me to think about an accompanying concern, one which we might call public-ization: the construction of various kinds of "publics" – public domains, public spheres, public accountabilities – as among the key effects of bioprospecting practice. These publics are crucial resources which prospecting participants *and* critics invoke, materialize, and contest in their efforts to define the limits and obligations of contemporary resource appropriation.

Much of the work of producing prospecting's publics comes to us in the practice of scientific collection itself. One of the aspects of bioprospecting that most intrigues me as an anthropologist of science is the way that academic plant-collecting practices, with their own long-standing complexities, rationales, and socialities, are saddled with new kinds of accountabilities. In a context in which plant collection comes tied to benefit-sharing provisions, these practices, and their practitioners, are being asked to do new kinds of political and social work: routine or "merely" disciplinary decisions about where and what to collect become inextricably laced with the explosive questions of who shall become the "beneficiaries" of a new international politics of biodiversity entrepreneurialism, and on what basis. Mainstream sociology of science has long placed a premium on the idea that knowledge and natural artifacts are teeming with social interests and relations (Latour 1987 and 1993). Bioprospecting contracts make this argument almost all too literal, requiring in fact that plant researchers now identify the relations and interests that come with collected plants, so that they may properly compensate them. If, in science studies, natural artifacts are always social artifacts (that is, they always come chock-full of webs of interests), then, in the practice and debates over bioprospecting, plants come with their publics in some distinctly explicit ways.

The animation of prospecting's publics points us to ways in which science studies might productively mingle with a reinvigorated anthropology of property relations. The key question for prospecting practitioners and critics alike is, *who* shall be entitled to rights in resources that are being made subject to new regimes of value-production? And yet, as contributors to this volume show so vividly, there is a great deal to be gained in paying anthropological attention not just to the "goods'" of property – rights and entitlements – but also to the creation and distribution of the "bads" – risks and liabilities (Verdery, Alexander, and Maurer, this volume).

In this light, we might do well to ask not just how potential rights are being constructed in the context of prospecting disputes, but also anticipated or feared liabilities. In the language provided to us by science studies, I want to explore here how the material properties, even the very nature, of artefacts such as plants or microbes, are increasingly understood with reference to the projected liabilities, entanglements, and political solutions that they "contain" or avoid (see also Parry, this volume). Researchers designate certain resources and places as *inherently public* in their attempts to make explicit and thus evade the presumed liabilities found in a nature that comes newly laden with potential stakeholders and political conflict.[4]

For all of this, we shall see that such designations and inscriptions are not always as robust as their practitioners might like. Despite their best efforts, the publics invoked by university researchers to cordon off unruly (indigenous) politics from their samples and collecting sites aren't always up to the task. In Mexico and internationally, activists, academics, and NGOs call up notions of publics too – public rights, domains, and accountabilities – in their increasing opposition to bioprospecting's contentious modes of inclusion and exclusion. In the face of some of these challenges, researchers' invocation of safe collecting spaces have proven fragile indeed.

The remainder of this chapter sketches some of the practices through which compensation-oriented relationships and histories are actively written into biological resources – and right back out of them again. We cannot ask these questions without thinking about how public domains and spheres are made active, as sites of refuge and risk. I begin with a brief discussion of some theoretical and regulatory domains which must guide our understanding of publicness. I then move on to discuss two different efforts in Mexico to prospect in public. Throughout, my goal in arguing that publicness is an open question is not to deconstruct it. Rather, I want to show the public in action.

Public Spheres and Analytical Domains

In social theory and legal studies, discussions of the public are often directed into two channels: the public domain in the juridical sense of that which stands outside private property relations and thus offers "open access;" and the public sphere in the Habermasian sense of a space of political debate and participation in liberal democratic process (Habermas 1989). Bioprospecting is one of many arenas in which these "publics" mix promiscuously. In conflicts over prospecting in Mexico (as elsewhere), property-inflected questions of dominion have everything to do with shifting and highly contentious debates over democratic process, sovereignty, and governance.

In theoretical terms, one of the central meeting points between Habermasian theories of the public sphere and juridical treatments of the public domain is the invocation of public-ness as a space of non-commodified purity – of open access, of the absence of private property, of free flows. This is a point with much purchase in biodiversity politics. Many critics of bioprospecting pose the creation and protection of public domains as a crucial oppositional strategy: that is, as a way to counter increasing corporate control over crop and medicinal resources, and to protect indigenous knowledges and resources against the kind of privatization and monopoly control implied in new regimes of patenting (Brush 1999; Brown 1998 and this volume). The defense of the public domain is a powerful and important argument, and one that is shared by activists and intellectuals in a wide range of contexts, from open-source software to efforts to keep data generated by the human-genome project open for public access.[5]

Yet, as Habermas's legions of critics have reminded us, the question, *whose public?* is not an incidental one (Fraser 1992; Warner 1992). Certainly, the creation and protection of the public is not without its complications where indigenous rights are concerned. In the Americas as elsewhere, "the public domain" has long been a crucial axis through which nation-states have denied and expropriated indigenous holdings in resources and territory.

The position of the nation-state as the guardian of and claimant to "the public" is reinforced significantly in the Convention on Biological Diversity; as such, it powerfully marks the politics of benefit-sharing. Among the most dramatic shifts embodied in the CBD has been the transformation of resources once (not unproblematically) characterized as part of the international commons – such as wild plants, microbes, and cultural knowledge – into resources under national sovereignty (see Brush 1999). While granting southern nations a new kind of sovereignty vis-à-vis transnational corporations, the CBD hedges a bit on the question of "traditional knowledge," mandating that it shall be "respected and maintained" (Article 8j). In redrawing the commons in the shape of nation-states, the CBD highlights and arguably exacerbates long-standing conflicts between indigenous peoples and national governments. While some indigenous coalitions and activists have succeeded in using this provision as an entrée into UN-level discussions, the lines are nonetheless (re)drawn here between "source nations" and "source communities" as competing publics to whom benefits may be returned. This division, as we shall see, is powerfully produced and reproduced in many prospectors' assessments of better and worse places to bio-prospect.

If the question of *whose* public is a fraught one in the context of nation-indigenous relations, the instability of "the public" and its various foils (private, communal, corporate) is also a matter of much critical comment. Here, critical legal theorists have taken on the public domain as something that may be worth defending, as long as it is not idealized as a stable "place" with self-evident boundaries (see Aoki 1998; Coombe 1998; Boyle 1996). James Boyle, in his discussion of information and intellectual property, aims to dispense outright with the modernist geography of private and public as discrete, stable, and identifiable spatial units. Reminding us that "the market," for example, is considered "private" for some purposes but "public" for others, Boyle asserts that there is "no intelligible geography of private and public" (Boyle 1996: 27–8; see also Fraser 1992: 128).[6] If these concepts are constantly doubling back on themselves, then we might also, following Rosemary Coombe, suggest that the contested processes of delineating publics and privates are themselves generative of categories of social difference (Coombe 1998).

These two questions – Who can lay claim to the public? What contingent and complex processes define the public and the non-public? – are absolutely crucial to understanding how rights and obligations to or over biodiversity are being partitioned. Nowhere are these questions more evident than in the context of recent and stunning transformations in intellectual property, land tenure, and indigenous rights in Mexico.

Renegotiating Sovereignties

The impetus to discipline new forms of nature and potential forms of revenue derived from them comes not just from the incitement of the CBD to enable or ensure equitable "returns." The heavy-handed "community" of the GATT/WTO and NAFTA provides a competing set of imperatives, organized around the question of whether things formerly considered part of Mexico's national public domain shall be made privatizable. Mexico's entry into these trade accords has entailed radical changes in relationships among the public and the private, the national and the indigenous.

In Mexico as elsewhere, membership in regional and global trade agreements has demanded wholesale restructurings of national intellectual property legislation.[7] In the context of bioprospecting, this means, then, that while Mexico may gain some royalties from plant-derived drug profits, the nation must also recognize the patents on those drugs and allow them to be sold in the domestic market. (Until the "harmoniza-tion" of these property regimes in the early 1990s, drug patents were not recognized.[8]) These changes sit side by side with powerful restruc-turings of land tenure – another significant element of the question of access to and control over biological resources. NAFTA-oriented amend-ments to Article 27 of the Constitution ended Mexico's legendary constitutional commitment to land redistribution and communal-property stewardship. The changes to Article 27 signal a material and symbolic shift of seismic proportions for notions of land and property in Mexico. As the ideological and juridical centerpiece of the post-revolutionary state, the article established the basis for the state's expropriation of haciendas and the redistribution of these lands in the form of *ejidos*: communally worked lands that would make access to productive land a fundamental right. In the mid-1990s, *ejidos* had dominion over a remarkable 50 percent of Mexico's croplands and 80 percent of forest lands. In order to enter NAFTA, Mexican President Carlos Salinas de Gortari shepherded through congress the hotly contested 1992 Agrarian Law, which allowed for the transformation of communal *ejidos* into individually titled parcels that could be bought and sold. By allowing *ejidos* to enter the land market, a great deal of formerly unavailable terrain now has the potential to be acquired by private parties, a move geared toward encouraging large agribusinesses to invest in the Mexican countryside.[9]

Alongside fundamental changes to the very definition of the *ejido* (previously inalienable, now conceivably up for titling and selling) simmer contentious discussions over the place of indigenous communi-ties and peoples in the nation, many of whom live on *ejidal* lands.[10] Following the Zapatista uprising in 1994, negotiations between the Zapatistas and the administration of President Ernesto Zedillo generated a series of proposals and counterproposals (the San Andrés accords) regarding guarantees of indigenous self-determination. President Vicente Fox (former CEO of Coca-Cola-México and, with his election in 2000, the first opposition president to hold office in 71 years) promised to resolve the stalled negotiations of the San Andrés accords – a task which he famously promised to dispatch within fifteen minutes. More than two years later, the resolution of the Zapatista crisis, and with it, the question of the place of indigenous peoples within the national body politic, remained elusive.

Bioprospecting contracts are pointed sites for the negotiation of competing sovereignties in the midst of these refigurings of the nature of property, and of properties in nature. The making and unmaking of

bioprospecting's publics is one of the key arenas in which we can trace
the articulation of these newly vigorous neoliberal regulatory regimes,
their associated notions of entitlement and obligation, and oppositional
efforts to call these models to account.

Markets: The Business of Collection

Suggestively calling up yet another dimension to our concern with
prospecting's publics, among the most active supporters/funders of
international prospecting collaborations has been the US public sector
– specifically, the US government's International Cooperative Biodiversity Groups (ICBG) program (see Hayden 2003b). The ICBG began
in 1993 as essentially a publicly subsidized drug-discovery initiative. It
is, in this sense, a broader version of the US National Institute of Health
(NIH)'s long-standing support for plant and microbe screening for
cancer and AIDS drugs. In the early 1990s, the NIH added a few more
dimensions (and collaborators) to its interest in plant-based drug
discovery, linking such efforts now to conservation and rural economic
development. Like many "market-mediated" sustainable-development
initiatives that took shape in the early 1990s (Zerner 2000), the goal of
the ICBG program is to call on the pharmaceutical and biotechnology
industries to generate biodiversity-derived profits, while using contractual mechanisms to redistribute some of these profits back to the
"stewards" of biodiversity in the south (Grifo 1996; Rosenthal 1997).

It was this program that funded the ill-fated Chiapas project with
which I opened this chapter. That was not, however, the first ICBG
program in Mexico. The "Latin America ICBG" was funded in the first
round of this initiative, in 1993, and it has continued through a second
round (1998–2003). Based at the University of Arizona, this project
involves three source countries – Chile, Argentina, and Mexico – along
with the United States – based drug company Wyeth-Ayerst and,
initially, the agrochemical company American Cyanamid, as "industrial
outlets." In Mexico, the participating researchers are based at the
National University (UNAM); these ethnobotanists and chemists are
charged with collecting and sending Mexican medicinal plants directly
to Arizona's industrial partners in the United States. In exchange, they
receive minimal research funds each year and promises of a percentage
of royalties, ten to twenty years in the future, should those companies
develop a drug or pesticide based on these collections.[11] The project is
also designed to collect "ethnobotanical knowledge" about plant uses,
and to direct royalties back to the people or communities from which

this intellectual resource is culled (Timmermann 1997; Rosenthal 1997; see also Greene 2002).

In the ICBG program, developing-country collectors are supposed to sign contracts with each individual who provides them with plants and information. Benefits shared are figured in this agreement, as they are in many other prospecting programs, both as reward (a recognition that people have a rightful claim in their knowledge and plants) and as incentive (people must be encouraged, through the promise of dividends, to value their resources). "Communities" in the ICBG framework stand both as privileged sites of resources-provided and as the destination for benefits-returned (Hayden 2003a).

Significantly, the collecting strategies chosen by the lead UNAM ethnobotanist take the NIH's proposed mode of benefit-sharing on a substantial detour. Drawing on well-established research methods within Mexican ethnobotany, Harvard-trained Robert Bye has, indeed, forged another mode altogether of collecting both plants and benefit-recipients. This alternative strategy begins not in "communities," but in urban market-places – sites from which the UNAM research team culled the majority of their plant samples in the early years of this contract. As I've discussed elsewhere, plants found in urban markets have long been full of appeal for ethnobotanical studies (Hayden 2003a, 2003b; see Bye and Linares 1983). If some of the appeal of market plants is unabashedly logistical, this strategy does have its biochemical rationales.[12] Bye and his partners in the Arizona prospecting agreement, UNAM chemists Rachel Mata and Rogelio Pereda, have worked together for years analyzing Mexican plants, both picked and purchased. They point out that, given generations of use by urban consumers, market plants are particularly important sources of potential bioactivity.

But the relative merits of market research take some new turns when this research method intersects with a prospecting project that promises future royalty payments for "local resource providers." Bye has explicitly posed market studies as a tool for redefining the relationship between plants-collected and participants-enrolled: these studies are meant to help circumvent the potentially conflictual questions of "authorship" and bounded community dominion over well-traveled plants and knowledges, and to forge relationships with local interlocutors on markedly different terms.[13] As such, this strategy suggests very vividly some of the processes through which prospecting's publics take shape.

Bye has explained to me and other interested researchers, first of all, that one of the key characteristics of market plants in the current context is that they are part of the national public domain. This is so in large part because they circulate in a very particular kind of public sphere: that of commerce and the marketplace. (We might recall James Boyle's argument that publics and privates double back on themselves all the time: while "the market" is seen as the site of privatization in relation to the state, it can also be the sphere of the public, and the freely circulating [Boyle 1996].) And here, this notion of the market is invoked not as a site of knowledge-production but, rather, as a site of knowledge-distribution. As one Mexican ethnobotanist explained the situation to me, "Plant vendors are merely vectors of transmission of information – they're not sources, so they don't merit part of the royalty benefits." Another researcher told me, "It doesn't make sense to treat vendors as sources of knowledge who deserve compensation: when you buy the plants, you buy the information, and no further obligations are involved."

If not in the market, where are proper benefit recipients to be found? Consider a second dimension of this ostensible national public domain – emphasis, this time, on the "national." The public-ness at issue in market research is conveyed not just through appeals to a familiar notion of the market as a site of truncated social obligations (see Carrier 1997; Callon 1998); it is also construed with reference to Mexico's post-revolutionary, national public sphere – a place and an identity marked by notions of hybridity and *mestizaje*. The national-origin story cultivated in the aftermath of the Mexican revolution (1910–1917) reserves a characteristically ambivalent role for indigenous peoples: they may be the nobler half of the "cosmic race" but, even in progressive visions of the future of Mexico as a modern nation, indigenous people have been imagined as assimilating into a *mestizo* culture. Medicinal plants are vivid material symbols of this widespread official and popular narrative: though having identifiable roots in the indigenous "past," traditional herbal medicine now, the popular story tells us, reflects, and thus belongs to, the nation. Markets, in fact, do important service in this public-ization of medicinal plants in Mexico: many descriptions and invocations of the national *herbolaria* begin precisely with the extraordinary market systems through which medicinal plants (among many other things) have traveled since the height of the Aztec empire, and certainly well before (Hayden 2003b).

Such nationalizations in turn provide the warrant for the UNAM research team's vision of an alternate relationship between plants-collected and benefits-promised. Arguing that the character of this *herbolaria* makes it impossible to trace folk medicine to particular individuals and communities, Bye has effectively separated plant- and information-gathering from the process of enrolling local participants. His interlocutors were found instead in tentative alliances (forged in part with ICBG funds) with, for example, NGOs working in Tarahumara communities, indigenous artisans' cooperatives, and groups of traditional healers associated with the government's National Indigenista Institute. These forms of alliance are forged on the premise of shared goals (local-level, community-based sustainable development projects, or efforts to protect and encourage "traditional knowledge"). They are resolutely *not* "compensation" arrangements for plants and knowledge provided.

While Bye argues that this strategy allows him to channel project benefits where they are most appropriate and indeed most likely to take root, ICBG funders in the United States have not been entirely convinced. For one project director, this strategy has always seemed troublesome, precisely because it "breaks the link" between people, plants, and future benefits that this prospecting agreement is meant to reward – and arguably, to *create*. If ICBG authorities have remained wary of prospecting in the public sphere of the marketplace, two biodiversity policy-makers in Mexico City have also conveyed their doubts to me. Using market studies, they each argued (in separate interviews), allows the participating pharmaceutical companies to "have it both ways:" receiving plant extracts that are "preselected for [biochemical] activity" without the responsibility of negotiating with *campesinos* and *indígenas*.

For Bye and his research team, the material viabilities of market plants are indeed (and explicitly) inseparable from the liabilities that these objects promise to help them avoid. The combination of natural and social properties that Bye identifies and inscribes in these market plants (logistical ease, biochemical richness, national public-ness) points to a "solution" to the problem of benefit-sharing in Mexico at a moment when land rights, indigenous sovereignty, and dominion over biological resources and traditional knowledge lie at the center of volatile public debate and international activist mobilizations. The political and military conflict in Chiapas, and its reverberations both nationwide and internationally, certainly loom large here. Even before the Maya ICBG debacle, Bye repeatedly noted to me and other observers that his strategy has been predicated very much on a desire not to bring *this* project into *that* fray.

The decision to prospect in public has not, we should recall, been an argument that "communities" or community organizations deserve no benefits at all. Rather, these market-mediated travels through the "national" public domain – a mediating zone between community claims and drug-derived profits – have been a politically complex, quasi-nationalizing effort of their own, meant to collect both plants and people outside the logics of territorially-bounded, property-like claims to authorship and dominion.

Has the rapid demise of the Maya ICBG confirmed these researchers' preoccupations about the potential costs of trafficking in community-derived biological and intellectual resources? Provisionally, it would certainly seem that this decision of how (and how not) to be a bio-prospector in Mexico may have helped spare the UNAM team a similar fate. In the midst of an increasingly outraged public debate over bioprospecting that began in Mexico in 1997 and 1998 and continues today, Bye's ICBG project has remained relatively unscathed.

Public by Design: Microbes

Where Bye's invocation of publicness has been in effect a complex rewriting of a benefit-sharing mandate handed down by the US government, other prospecting contracts explicitly and hopefully attempt to engineer such safety-nets directly into their project design. In the 1990s, changes in the terms governing corporations' access to biological resources in the south lent new dimensions to the appeal of microbes as potential repositories of value (see Helmreich this volume, Helmreich 2003). They do so, again, by making (hopeful) recourse to the inherent public-ness of their objects of desire.

If plants are of interest to the pharmaceutical industry as sources of bioactive chemical compounds, microbes are this and a great deal more. The annals of biomedicine and biotechnology are teeming with microbes – yeasts, bacteria, fungi, and, of late, the recently named king-dom of "Archaea" (Helmreich 2003). These creatures have been amply metaphorized, as ubiquitous living agents, quasi-mechanical entities, unparalleled sources of chemical compounds. And, to adapt an apposite phrase from Bruno Latour, micro-organisms have happened to the biotechnology industry (and to myriad "societies") on more than one crucial occasion.[14]

In the 1990s, changes in the terms governing corporations' access to biological resources in the south have lent new dimensions to the appeal of microbes as potential repositories of value. On the one hand (and not entirely unlike "market plants"), this appeal continues to be guided by their much-touted natural richness, generativity, and potential as highly lucrative laboratory instruments. But some bioprospecting pioneers have also suggested that micro-organisms carry significantly fewer "cultural" associations than do medicinal plants, making them easier to extract from thorny political landscapes. More nature, less culture – it is a stunning formulation, an assessment of nature's sociality that can only make sense in a new political and regulatory climate in which nature now comes with new kinds of "stakeholders" attached.

The idea of microbes as culture-free resources is a narrative I first heard from Ana Sittenfeld, the former director of prospecting activities at Costa Rica's infamous national biodiversity institute, INBio (an institution set up with a great deal of northern investment, in part to help pioneer the new concept of benefit-sharing prospecting collaborations). At a forum on bioprospecting in the Mexican Senate in May 1997, Sittenfeld told her audience of policy makers and academics that it is a matter of common sense that micro-organisms and even insects are denizens of the national public domain, outside the boundaries of community or "cultural" management. It is on these kinds of "culture-free" nature, culled from government-protected lands, that INBio's prospecting activities have been focused.

Many Latin American biodiversity scientists and policy-makers bristle at the suggestion that Costa Rica should provide a model for anyone else in the region. Turning Costa Rica's notorious exceptionalism back on itself, researchers from Mexico, Chile, Colombia, and elsewhere point to the enormous amount of that nation's lands ostensibly under government protection, as well as to its "distinctive demographic" (very few indigenous peoples), to suggest that Costa Rican prospecting models are far from exportable and that, worse, they set a bad example. Costa Rica's publics are distinctive, we might argue – not translatable to other Latin American nations. His own reservations notwithstanding, the director of Mexico's National Biodiversity Commission (CONABIO) in 1997 supported a very INBio-like strategy for yet another prospecting collaboration in Mexico. The attraction was the idea of a streamlined and efficient exchange, with the enticing figure of culture-free nature at its core.

With CONABIO's support, UNAM's Biotechnology Institute in Cuernavaca (50 miles south of Mexico City) signed a microbe-screening contract with the San Diego, California-based biotechnology company Diversa in 1997. (Diversa also has microbe-prospecting projects in Costa Rica and in the United States's Yellowstone National Park, where geysers, mud bogs, and other extreme environments promise particularly hardy and distinctive microbial treasures.) The Mexico contract was conceived of as a strict technology-transfer agreement between northern and southern research institutions, with the hope of making irrelevant the thorny questions of community and traditional knowledge. While participating scientists and government officials hoped that working with microbes – on federally protected biosphere reserves, no less – would insulate them from "politics," the ensuing events have confirmed once again that public domains have politics too. This microbe-screening project *preceded* the Maya ICBG as the center of a political firestorm around the shape that national sovereignty shall take in the shadow of the WTO, NAFTA, and the kind of neoliberalism promoted by Mexican administrations since the mid-1980s.

Problems began, not surprisingly, when one of the biosphere reserves deemed a safe collecting space turned out to be coterminous with a large *ejido*. While this would have been a complicating factor in any event for questions of dominion and benefit-sharing, the post-NAFTA land "reforms" allowing *ejidatarios* to divide up their stakes in collective lands and sell them further complicates the picture here: the public, the communal, and the potentially private collide here, as they do in disputed territories across the nation (see Stephen 1998).

This question of *whose public* was also taken up in a larger sense by a group of concerned academics and activists in Mexico. Starting in 1997, a loose coalition of journalists and intellectuals (led in large part by Mexican economist Alejandro Nadal) mobilized a great deal of opposition to this agreement on myriad fronts: articles in the Mexico City daily *La Jornada*, activist gatherings and public meetings in Mexico City, and finally a formal complaint lodged with the Attorney General for Environmental Affairs, Profepa. These critiques invoked a broad notion of public accountability that has, in some ways, trumped UNAM's attempts to name these resources as part of a bio-legal public domain. Pointedly invoking yet another register of public-ness, the vaunted notion of an inalienable national patrimony – a sensitive term for our senators, Nadal quips in *La Jornada* – these critics question UNAM's legitimacy as the broker of corporate access to "Mexican" resources (Nadal 2000; Hernández 2000; González 2000). Nadal and his allies argue that UNAM may be a public university, and the contract may well have been approved by several controlling federal agencies, but neither of these things constitutes the consent or participation of the "Federation" – the nation, in its broadest juridical and conceptual sense. Moreover, they argue that such consent is definitionally impossible without a national law regulating access to genetic resources. Such a law has been in the works in Mexico since 1997, but has still not been approved. They thus demanded that public hearings (a series of *consultas populares*) be held before any further prospecting projects are approved, and as a central condition of the drafting of national legislation. The office of the attorney general, Profepa, did indeed end up granting a temporary moratorium on prospecting; the Diversa contract is now limping along, moribund. Congress meanwhile pointedly refrains from touching the prospecting question, in a sense leaving the matter of governance and regulation up to the actors who have brought these projects into the very sphere of debate and controversy which their architects hoped to engineer out of their research objects and collecting sites.

Alejandro Nadal's deliberately pointed reference to microbes as a kind of national patrimony alerts us to the many strategic domaining moves that are being made and contested in struggles over prospecting, and the nationalist histories that are at stake – ones which resonate with, though taking a form slightly different from, those in which medicinal plants have been named a form of national patrimony as well. The post-revolutionary state was founded on the expropriation and nationalization of mining, petroleum, and large haciendas. As such, land, subsoil resources, and petroleum have long held sway as potent symbols of national sovereignty. Elizabeth Ferry (2002) argues that the notion of patrimony backing these expropriations was defined explicitly as an alternative to nineteenth-century liberal models of property relations. To name a resource as national patrimony was to name it as a particular kind of property – a direct inheritance from the Spanish kings, and thus inalienable, standing outside market-oriented notions of value and commodification. At the same time, she notes that, especially in her area of research, mining, "patrimony always had to operate alongside and within the market." (Nobody, she reminds us, engages in subsistence mining.)

These always contradictory articulations between national patrimony and "the market" have become extraordinarily contentious in the wake of the neoliberal policies that have taken root in Mexico since the early 1980s. Vociferous debates now rage over the potential privatization of the petroleum industry and of *ejidos*, at the same time that bioprospecting agreements have given fuel to "domestic" conflicts over whose sovereignty is at stake when national patrimony is invoked. Bioprospecting in this sense indexes profound questions of governance that are inseparable from questions of dominion: microbes on government-protected lands proved high-profile targets for Mexico City activists and intellectuals concerned with questions of accountability, rights, and democratic decision-making in yet another sphere in which the privatization of (a newly designated) "national patrimony" irritates highly charged public and political sensitivities.

Governance, Risk, and Refuge

The instances of public prospecting I have discussed here might be understood, each in its own way, as efforts to steer clear of specimens that have "too many" claims attached to them, or that might be rooted in overly thorny political landscapes. It's worth emphasizing how deliberately and sometimes self-consciously the researchers I know invoke such public-ness – this is not a hidden strategy. Rather, researchers loudly proclaim that they are collecting in public precisely as a defense against the anticipated charge that, as bioprospectors, they are involved in the theft of traditional knowledge and community resources. The fear and threat of public censure are striking in their efficacy. Indeed, in the continued absence of binding regulation in Mexico on prospecting, and in light of the notoriously "soft" efficacy of UN conventions, activist pressure (feared or felt) has become one of the most important de facto forms of monitoring and accountability at work in the domain of bioprospecting.[15]

Prospectors' efforts to anticipate and circumvent such activist wrath have sparked the animation of some remarkable notions of public-ness, as a site of refuge. In the case of market plants, the prophylactic "safety" of the public domain leans on invocations of a Mexican national public sphere, defined as much by idealized market relations as by the appeal to *mestizaje* and the historical (and ideologically charged) assimilation of indigenous peoples into a "nation of mixtures." In the Diversa case, participating researchers and government agencies draw on the juridically inflected notion of public-ness that designated not just particular objects (microbes) but particular spaces (government lands) as sitting outside the physical or intellectual domain of "community." In both instances, the publics invoked were simultaneously "freely accessible" but also, in line with the Convention on Biological Diversity, beholden to "the nation" and its institutions.

These characterizations of the public as a safety zone clash intensely with classic liberal notions of the public sphere, in which the public is precisely the domain of conflict, debate, and contest. Certainly, as has become clear above, such sites of refuge do not always keep conflict at bay. As we saw in the Diversa case, microbes on government-protected lands proved to be magnets for, rather than immunizations against, public protest. But so too does prospecting in public markets, the strategy employed by the first UNAM prospecting effort I discussed, also come with its own potential "safety" breaches.

Recently, in the United States and Europe, two corporate patents taken out on compounds derived from "folk knowledge" – the kind of knowledge circulating in Mexican markets – were overturned, precisely because of the public-ness of the compounds in question. In May 2000, the European Patent Office overturned W. R. Grace's patent on a fungicidal compound from the Indian neem tree, widely used by Indian farmers for this purpose among many others. In response to a lawsuit filed by several NGOs, the patent officers agreed that the neem patent was simply a repackaging of established knowledge – it was based on prior art, and not corporate innovation, as the company had argued (CSE 2000). On the same grounds, the United States Patent and Trade Office (PTO) overturned a United States seed company's patent on the vine used by *mestizo* and indigenous communities in the Amazon basin to prepare the hallucinogenic beverage *ayahuasca* (though the *ayahuasca* patent was later reinstated on appeal).[16]

These developments point to another aspect of the delicate balancing act of prospecting in the public domain. UNAM ethnobotanist Robert Bye's decision to use markets as collecting sites will only "work" as long as the "freely accessible" public domain of commerce remains separate from the public domain of corporate intellectual property. The moment in which these publics collapse into each other – that is, the moment the participating companies decide that their potential patent rights are short-circuited by the public-ness of market resources involved – is yet another moment when prospecting in public also becomes a liability or risk.

Properties of Nature, Property in Nature

Prospecting and its associated debates and controversies provide us an opportunity to revisit one of the key legacies of science studies: the argument that scientific knowledge does not simply represent (in the sense of depict) "nature," but that it also represents (in the political sense) the "social interests" of people and institutions that have become wrapped up in its production (Latour 1993). Weaving these two notions of representation back together – that is, showing how science *is* politics by other means – is at the core of much of what has been called the social studies of science. In the production of prospecting's myriad publics, these two forms of representation merge visibly and take another, enterprising twist: the citizenry-representational dimension of the public sphere is intimately tied not just to depictions of the properties of nature, but to highly charged questions about potential property in nature.

With these contests over rights and obligations in mind, I have tried to ask not just whose public is at stake, but how? How are myriad constructions of publics given life in the context of bioprospecting, by whom, and to what effect? As we've seen, plants and microbes are teeming with new kinds of debate over their associated publics, the social relations that are contained within them, the interests they do or should contain, the representational work that they do. As university researchers, drug companies, government agencies, and activists attempt to identify, attribute, claim, and avoid the rights and obligations, the goods and the bads of biological-resource appropriation, the practices through which publics are themselves made and remade themselves become visible. In many ways, we might argue that prospecting is implicated not just in the appropriation of public resources, but in the denomination of resources as public in the first place. These denominations are not cut from whole cloth, but they are, I argue, calibrated to new conditions of possibility and impossibility: particularly, the complicated multilateral assessment that biological collections now "come with" stakeholders attached. The practices through which such relations and claims are written into biological resources, and back out of them again, provide a suggestive topographical map not just of the machinations and effects of privatization, but of the contradictory and complex processes of public-ization as well.

Notes

1. For statements and to track this debate in detail, see the following organizations and websites: RAFI (now the ETC group), at http://www.etcgroup. org; in Mexico (in Spanish and English) see CIEPAC at http://www.ciepac.org; and http://www.ecosur.mx/icbg/boletin.html. For the Berlins' statement in defense of their efforts, see http://guallart.dac.uga.edu/ICBGreply.html. See also the site maintained by University of Chicago graduate student Michelle Day, at http://home.uchicago.edu/~mmday/Mayanmedicine.html.

2. This might come as a slightly unexpected formulation for those inclined to think that it is rural and indigenous communities who run the "risks" in business dealings with transnational companies.

3. At stake here are modes of resource acquisition, fused to a provisional form of redress, which are intimately tied to the production of corporate intellectual property. That is, bioprospecting contracts depend on patented biotechnological and pharmaceutical products to generate the profits that will create royalties to be returned.

4. For a very different set of debates about the "sociability" of places and resources, see Carol Rose's (1986) discussion of intriguing arguments in US jurisprudence over the designation of waterways and roadsides as "inherently public domains."

5. See for example the ongoing conversation on www.sarai.net (parts of which are published in the Sarai Reader 01: The Public Domain) about the nature and possibilities of publics in the urban environs of Delhi, in the communities of open source software engineers and users, and in postcolonial scholarship and activism.

6. We might note in this regard that the UN designation of certain resources or spaces (deep sea, outer space, crop germplasm) as "global commons" has always cut two ways. Seed and drug companies have interpreted common-ness to mean belonging to all, arguing that (and acting as if) raw materials designated as commons may be freely used – until they are patented. Many developing nations have set the threshold for common-ness at a significantly different point, holding that crop germplasm, among other things, cannot be claimed as, or transformed into, private property (see Juma 1989), precisely because they are common in the sense of belonging to no one.

7. These multilateral trade accords require, among other things, that Mexico include pharmaceutical patents, stronger copyright protection, and plant-variety protection as part of its IPR regime.

8. In 1976, nationalist-populist president Luís Echeverría, in an impressive show of third-worldism, decided that Mexico would no longer honor pharmaceutical patents; not only did he and Congress rescind patent protection, but they put measures in place to nationalize the foreign pharmaceutical companies present on Mexican soil. The goal was to jump-start a national pharmaceutical industry, based in some measure on "national" medicinal plants (Hayden 2003b).

9. The magnitude of this quake is not diminished by the important observation that, as a growing number of case studies demonstrate, many *ejidal* communities are electing *not* to register and title their lands at all. Lynn Stephen (1998) among many others has provided a fascinating account of how some *ejidal* communities are taking up the new possibility of registering their titles and selling parcels of land, while others are resolutely ignoring and in fact refusing these Constitutional shifts.

10. Another 1992 constitutional amendment (Article 4) asserted that the Mexican nation is a pluricultural one, in which indigenous peoples have the right to their own modes of governance and customs. The question of how this shall be put in practice, and its implications for territorial sovereignty, remain hotly contested.

11. The exact percentage of royalties to be shared remains confidential, but project administrators in the United States tell me it is between 2 percent and 15 percent – this sum would pass through the University of Arizona before heading south. In this agreement, Arizona will keep 45 percent of that 2–15 percent, directing the remaining 55 percent to the country that was the source of the plant material (Timmermann 1997). Bracketing for the moment the complex question of how benefits would be distributed within the source country itself, "Mexico" would receive roughly 2–5 percent of royalties on any product that emerged from a Mexican plant sample.

12. Not only can ethnobotanists walk into a marketplace and walk out in short order with kilos of ten or twenty different kinds of medicinal plants, but the samples are already dried and thus are less likely than freshly collected plants to rot on extended collecting trips. In the context of this project, this efficiency is particularly attractive given the quota of 100 extracts per year that the UNAM researchers must send to the United States in order to continue to receive project funding – and even more so, given that they began two years behind schedule and had to spend the first year-and-a-half catching up on their missed collections.

13. In other work on this topic, I discuss at greater length the complexities of market research and its articulation with benefit-sharing. Most importantly, perhaps, the use of markets in this project is not precisely as a *substitution* for "community" interlocutors, but rather as a somewhat circuitous *conduit to* community participants (Hayden 2003a).

14. Microbes did not just help organize the reorganization of socialities around the notion of "public health" (see Latour 1988 and Stepan 1991). Microbes were also the subject of a seismic shift in US patent law regarding the patenting of living organisms (Diamond v. Chakrabarty 1980) and the basis of the technologies (such as PCR) that are now foundational to genomics research. As such, they have been central to the biotechnological revolution's dramatic reorganization of the very terrain of public research and private industry in the United States and internationally (see Rabinow 1996).

15. Of course, given the complexity of questions of dominion at stake here, it would be a mistake to suggest that regulatory certainty would solve the questions raised/intensified by prospecting.

16. See the website of the Center for International Environmental Law (CIEL), the US organization which filed the ayahuasca patent challenge on

behalf of several Amazonian coalitions, at http://www.ciel.org/Bio-diversity/ayahuascapatentcase.html.

References

Aoki, Keith. 1998. "Neocolonialism, anti-commons property, and biopiracy in the (not-so-brave) new world order of international intellectual property protection." Part of the symposium, Sovereignty and the Globalization of Intellectual Property. *Indiana Journal of Global Legal Studies* 6: 11–58.

Boyle, James. 1996. *Shamans, software, and spleens: Law and the construction of the information society*. Cambridge, MA: Harvard University Press.

Brown, Michael. 1998. "Can culture be copyrighted?" *Current Anthropology* 39(2): 193–222.

Brush, Stephen B. 1999. "Bioprospecting the public domain." *Cultural Anthropology* 14: 535–55.

Bye, Robert A., Jr. and Edelmira Linares. 1983. "The role of plants found in the Mexican markets and their importance in ethnobotanical studies." *Journal of Ethnobiology* 3: 1–13.

Callon, Michel. 1998. *The laws of the markets*. Oxford: Sociological Review.

Carrier, James G. (ed.). 1997. *Meanings of the market: The free market in western culture*. Oxford: Berg.

Center for Science and the Environment (India). 2000. "Back where it belongs: India emerges victorious from a legal wrangle with the US over the patenting of neem." *Down to Earth* 9(2). Available at http://www.cseindia.org/html/dte/dte20000615/dte_news.htm.

Clarke, Adele, and Joan Fujimura (eds.). 1992. *The right tools for the job: At work in 20th century life sciences*. Princeton: Princeton University Press.

Coombe, Rosemary J. 1998. *The cultural life of intellectual properties: Authorship, appropriation, and the law*. Durham, NC: Duke University Press.

Ferry, Elizabeth. 2002. "Inalienable commodities: The production and circulation of silver and patrimony in a Mexican mining cooperative." *Cultural Anthropology* 17: 331–58.

Fraser, Nancy. 1992. "Re-thinking the public sphere: A contribution to the critique of actually existing democracy." In *Habermas and the public sphere*. Edited by Craig Calhoun, 109–42. Cambridge, MA: MIT Press.

González, Aldo. 2000. "Biopiratería o apoyo al desarrollo comunitario? La guerra por los microorganismos." *La Jornada* (Mexico City), 10 January.

Greene, Shane. 2002. "Intellectual property, resources, or territory? Reframing the debate over indigenous rights, traditional knowledge, and pharmaceutical bioprospection." In *Truth claims: Representation and human rights*. Edited by Mark Philip Bradley and Patrice Petro, 229–49. New Brunswick, NJ: Rutgers University Press.

Grifo, Francesca. 1996. "Chemical prospecting: A view from the International Cooperative Bio-diversity Groups Program." In *Biodiversity, biotechnology, and sustainable development in health and agriculture: Emerging connections*, 12–28. Washington, D.C.: Panamerican Health Organization.

Habermas, Jurgen. 1989. *The structural transformation of the public sphere: An inquiry into a category of bourgeois society*. Cambridge, MA: MIT Press.

Hayden, Cori. 2003a. "From market to market: Bioprospecting's idioms of inclusion." *American Ethnologist* 30(3): 359–71.

——. 2003b. *When nature goes public: The making and un-making of bioprospecting in Mexico*. Princeton: Princeton University Press.

Helmreich, Stefan. 2003. "Life@Sea: Networking marine biodiversity into biotech futures." In *Remaking life and death: Toward an anthropology of the biosciences*. Edited by Sara Franklin and Margaret Lock, 227–59. Santa Fe: School of American Research.

Hernández Navarro, Luís. 2000. "Piratas de la vida." *La Jornada* (Mexico City), 12 September, p. 19.

Juma, Calestous. 1989. *The gene hunters: Biotechnology and the scramble for seeds*. Princeton: Princeton University Press.

Latour, Bruno. 1987. *Science in action: How to follow scientists and engineers through society*. Cambridge, MA: Harvard University Press.

——. 1988. *The pasteurization of France*. Trans. Alan Sheridan and John Law. Cambridge, MA: Harvard University Press.

——. 1993. *We have never been modern*. Trans. Catherine Porter. Cambridge, MA: Harvard University Press.

Muelas Hurtado, Lorenzo. 2000. "Appeal to the indigenous peoples representatives at COP5." Submitted by the author to bio-ipr@cuenet. com, 7 February.

Nadal, Alejandro. 2000. "Biopiratería: el debate político." *La Jornada* (Mexico City). 13 September: 22.

Rabinow, Paul. 1996. *Making PCR: A story of biotechnology*. Chicago and London: University of Chicago Press.

RAFI (Rural Advancement Foundation International). 1999a. "Biopiracy project in Chiapas, Mexico, denounced by Mayan indigenous groups: University of Georgia refuses to halt project." News release, 1 December. http://www.etcgroup.org.

____. 1999b. "Messages from the Chiapas 'bioprospecting' dispute: An analysis of recent issues raised in the Chiapas 'bioprospecting' controversy with reflections on the message for BioPiracy." News release, 22 December. http://www.etcgroup.org.

Reid, Walter, et al. (eds.). 1993. *Biodiversity prospecting: Using genetic resources for sustainable development.* Washington, D.C.: World Resources Institute; Instituto Nacional de Bio-diversidad; Rainforest Alliance; African Centre for Technology Studies.

Rose, Carol. 1986. "The comedy of the commons: Custom, commerce, and inherently public property." *University of Chicago Law Review* 53: 711–781.

Rosenthal, Joshua. 1997. "Integrating drug discovery, biodiversity conservation, and economic development: early lessons from the International Cooperative Biodiversity Groups." In *Biodiversity and Human Health.* Edited by F. Grifo and J. Rosenthal, 281-301. Washington, D.C.: Island Press.

Stepan, Nancy Leys. 1991. *The hour of eugenics: Race, gender and nation in Latin America.* Ithaca: Cornell University Press.

Stephen, Lynn. 1998. "Between NAFTA and Zapata: Responses to restructuring the commons in Chiapas and Oaxaca, Mexico. In *Privatizing nature: Political struggles for the global commons.* Edited by M. Goldman, 76–101. New Brunswick, NJ: Rutgers University Press.

Timmermann, Barbara. 1997. "Biodiversity prospecting and models for collections resources: the NIH/NSF/USAID model." In *Global genetic resources: Access, ownership, and intellectual property rights.* Edited by K. E. Hoagland and A. Y. Rossman, 219–34. Association of Systematics Collections.

Warner, Michael. 1992. "The mass public and the mass subject." In *Habermas and the public sphere.* Edited by Craig Calhoun, 377–401. Cambridge, MA: MIT Press.

Zerner, Charles. 2000. "Introduction: Towards a broader vision of justice and nature conservation." In *People, plants, and justice: The politics of nature conservation.* Edited by Charles Zerner, 3–20. New York: Columbia University Press.

The Obligations of Ownership: Restoring Rights to Land in Postsocialist Transylvania

Katherine Verdery

The property concept, our Introduction claims, has significant effects. Nowhere have they been more powerfully felt than in the countries of the former Soviet bloc, where after 1989 the lives of countless millions of people were radically transformed by programs to make private property, in a process that transferred to individuals and corporations control over numerous values – houses, land, and the collective wealth embedded in socialist industries – once owned by the party-state. Behind these privatization programs lay a property concept that stressed assigning exclusive property rights to new owners as the way to dismantle collective ownership. In another publication (Verdery 2003), I have depicted privatization as a matter not of *creating new* ownership rights but of *transforming socialist* property relations. Here I concentrate on another facet of the process: the creation not only of rights but of debts, obligations, and liabilities. Although these are always part of property – as debtors know all too well – public discourse about property is saturated by talk of rights. A widespread definition sees it as a "bundle of rights," and in Honoré's celebrated list of the eleven basic incidents of a private property relation only two concern duties or liabilities rather than rights (Honoré 1961: 112–28). Because this ideological emphasis on rights dominated the privatization process in the former socialist bloc (and often elsewhere), it tended to mask their darker face.

In this chapter I show how land returned after 1989 to its former owners in Transylvania was revalued – made a negative asset, for many land recipients – through privatization that aimed to assign ownership rights but covertly assigned risks and obligations. To focus mainly on rights, I argue, distorts the processes at work, as well as obscuring the values that land represented for different kinds of people. A rights emphasis veils the exercise of power underlying their creation and is itself an element in the power of the property concept – my themes in this chapter. To focus on liability and risk means that we would now ask not about the social relations through which property claims are made, fulfilled, or resisted but about those through which liability and risk are distributed, mediated, and mitigated. This is to ask (in Lash and Wynne's felicitous phrase) about the distribution not simply of "goods" but of "bads" (in Beck 1992: 3). Privatization in the former socialist bloc distributed both. In addition, it created new *kinds of persons*, who would be economically responsible individuals bearing not just rights but risks and debts.

Values, Rights, and Liabilities in Privatization

Privatization is about not just liabilities and debt but how value is assessed (see Alexander's chapter). Values (in the broadest sense) and how to distribute them among persons are central to both property relations and property talk. A property regime generally presupposes a stable matrix of values (both monetary and normative), as well as relatively stable institutions for distributing them. In the formerly socialist countries after 1989, however, values were almost wholly up for grabs; the entire order within which they were assessed and under-stood was so compromised that no value could be taken for granted. In such cases, it may be less consequential to receive rights to things than to control the process of fixing their values, sometimes turning assets into debts.

This was the frequent outcome of privatization, as international accounting firms and development organizations transformed social-ism's assets into liabilities, thus devaluing them economically.[1] To encourage international investment, those organizations imposed budgetary rules that determined a firm's value in terms of the relation between liabilities and assets, costs and benefits. But they applied these practices to a class of societies for which such calculations were totally alien, the notion of liabilities being very weak. Socialist political economies operated according to *soft budget constraints*; the state bailed out rather than bankrupting firms that operated at a loss. Although enterprise directors had financial obligations, they could generally fudge these or maneuver around them in some way. State-fixed prices and state-guaranteed markets diminished the risk further. In short, risk was centralized in the state (something true to a lesser extent, of course, in countries like Japan and France).

Privatization, however, dispersed risk toward lower-level actors (see Sneath's chapter), hardening budget constraints and introducing new accounting systems that made liabilities binding and put teeth into the idea of risk. Aggravating such tendencies was a high level of uncertainty in the global environment, which magnified for *all* actors both the risks inherent in action and the prospect of assets losing ground to liabilities. The risks were not just the economic ones that new owners and firms had to face; they could have sociopolitical dimensions as well. Post-socialist states might continue to absorb risks in order to avoid popular unrest; cultivators might have difficulty obtaining credits, not for economic reasons but because they lacked the necessary connections to bank officials. As Hayden's chapter also shows, "risk" is thus a complex notion.

These general points about privatization apply equally to its agri-cultural variant, decollectivization, in which assigning property rights in land distributed bads as well as goods. Decollectivization made land a carrier of liabilities. It gave people land rights, producing owners who would then take on debts for the costs of machinery and other materi-als, of buildings they acquired, of irrigation works, levies, and drainage systems they repaired – and even, as I will show, for basic production costs (plowing, seed, fertilizer, etc.). Although this is true of all agri-culture, the difference here was the magnitude of the indebtedness the new owners faced. They would also bear new tax liabilities, based on their presumed income from land. In Romanian law, recipients of land received the further obligation to cultivate it or ensure its cultivation: anyone leaving land unworked for two years could lose rights to it.[2] Even if it cost more to work land than to buy the equivalent produce, they would have to work it or find someone else who could. This is hardly a matter of just "restoring ownership rights."[3]

Land in Romania after 1989

Before I present my argument, I offer two clarifications. One concerns the context for treating these phenomena under the rubric of *property* rather than something else; the second is a brief summary of Romania's decollectivization.

Why "Property"?

"Property" was a notion packed with meaning in the socialist period. As Marx and Engels put it in the *Communist Manifesto*, "The theory of the Communists may be summed up in the single sentence: abolition of private property." For this reason, private property and its transformation into socialist property became a central feature of the identity of communist party-states. Because in each country the abolition of private property in land had affected vast numbers of people, swelled further by the nationalization of housing and industry, the successors to these regimes after 1989 found property an excellent vehicle for signaling to both their own populations and the wider (capitalist) world that times had changed. In Romania, the phrase "private property" (*proprietate privată/particulară*) was ubiquitous in the media and the language of government. Global financial organizations, for their part, made privatization an important condition for loans and investments critical to the countries' futures. If the 1990s produced a great volume of property talk in Eastern Europe, it was overdetermined by both international actors and national politicians.

In this context, to think of "property" in a standard Western-textbook way – as having to do with "persons" and "things" understood as separate kinds of entities, brought into relation – made good sense. These were, after all, people for whom the earlier collectivization of land had objectified it, sundering their relation to fields many had considered virtually part of themselves; now that sundering was to be reversed. An object-relations view of property thus made sense, as did seeing it as a matter of scarce and finite resources (in contrast to other chapters here, such as Parry's, in which the resource at issue – information – is seen as abundant). The standard liberal paradigm of property as the relations among persons that provide access to and efficient use of scarce resources therefore seems well suited to this context, even though it may be unproductive in others.

Decollectivizing Socialist Agriculture

Following the ascendance of communist parties in the Soviet Union and Eastern Europe in 1917 and 1945–48, agriculture was collectivized everywhere except Poland and Yugoslavia. Two main forms emerged: "state farms" and "collective farms," which I will call "SFs" and "CFs."[4] They differed in a number of ways not only from one another but from country to country. In the Soviet Union, in particular, these farms were a major source of public support: members received meals, housing, health care, schooling, vacations, pensions, and other benefits directly through their farms, in an arrangement much more comprehensive and generally advantageous than that in Eastern Europe (Sneath's and Alexander's chapters show something of this). Soviet farm chairmen were therefore much more powerful and their members more favorably disposed to them than was true in Eastern Europe, leading to substantial differences between these regions.

After 1989/91, politicians chose to decollectivize – dismantle, transform, or otherwise modify – these socialist agricultural organizations. That process too varied considerably from one case to another, proceeding much more slowly in Russia than in Eastern Europe. For example, in Russia many people resisted decollectivization, and privatization had not fully taken place there as late as 2002, whereas in Eastern Europe there was far less resistance. Most of the latter countries adopted some form of *restituting* rights to previous owners, whereas in the former Soviet Union, rights to land were *distributed*, regardless of prior ownership (see Verdery 2000). In parts of Eastern Europe, prior owners received rights to their families' prior holdings; in others, they instead received vouchers or other values equivalent to the value of their land in the socialist farms.

Of the various solutions, the one that produced the most chaotic results was the former: direct restitution. This was the route taken in Romania, where the official dismantling of socialist agriculture began with a law passed in 1991. Known popularly as "Law 18," it liquidated collective farms and restored ownership rights to the households that had "donated" their land at collectivization (1948–1962). Importantly, Law 18 applied only to the land held in *collective* farms (74 percent of Romania's arable land), not that in *state* farms (21 percent). Returning CF land proved a lengthy, conflictual, and litigious process (see Verdery 2003), for most prior owners received rights to the very same parcels their families had given the collectives, in the exact same locations. This principle was so difficult to implement, however – with multiple claims to the same parcel, extreme fragmentation of holdings, complications in reestablishing former boundaries, and so on – that even as of 2003, many ownership rights remained unclear. Once people obtained land, they might give some or all of it to newly forming producers' cooperatives called "associations," which sprang up because few land recipients could assemble the other production factors necessary to farming. Those who did not join associations had to work their land themselves, give it in sharecropping to landless villagers, or lease it to emerging entrepreneurs, likely to be from the previous agrarian elite.

Privatizing the *state* farms, however, proceeded differently. At first the state retained control of the land in them; its former owners were declared shareholders and were to receive dividends, whose value the Ministry of Agriculture set as minimally the equivalent of 300 kg. of wheat for every hectare that a given family had owned within the farm's perimeter. That is, there was no suggestion, as with the CFs, of reindividualizing people's land. In 1994, however, a new law announced that in five years, these prior owners could receive property titles to their former land: they could then leave it under SF management or withdraw it altogether. Because this law signaled the eventual privatization of state farms, many SF directors now planned toward buying their farms. Meanwhile, they were expected to keep those running under ever less propitious conditions (still-centralized bookkeeping, irregular deliveries of inputs, accumulation of debt, problems finding markets), which in many cases resulted in immense devaluation of their assets over the decade.

All these processes were visible in the Transylvanian community of my research, Vlaicu, a village of 274 households totaling 820 people (known as Vlaiceni).[5] Its collective farm was disbanded, an association was formed, and, with a lot of friction, delay, and various sorts of chicanery, about half of village households received rights to more or less the very parcels their families had owned before collectivization. (The mean size of restored holdings was 2.7 ha.) The remaining half consisted of in-migrant families who, although they had owned no land, theoretically might have received some but in fact did not. Many new owners began working their land, a few turned it over to tenant-farmers, and over half gave some or all of it to the Vlaicu Association. Shareholders in Vlaicu's four state farms received dividends, varying by farm and gradually diminishing as the SFs decomposed over the decade.

Given this context, I illustrate how decollectivization produced land as a negative asset for many of its new owners, and I contrast different notions of what constitutes an asset and different ways of understanding and managing risk. To present this material I distinguish between two kinds of obligation: social and monetary.[6] Prior to 1989, reciprocity based in social obligation had been a vital practice, for both villagers and socialist elites. Although new village landowners hoped to use social obligation as a means of working their land, a number of things – the breadth of property-rights restitution, an ensuing labor shortage aggravated by the age of the rural population, and the necessity of moving toward very costly technologies (such as herbicides) that save labor – forced them to substitute money for social relations, one system of valuing for another. For smallholders, such financial costs of exercising ownership rose as the economic value of land declined, and this trend further undermined owners' social capital. Devaluation therefore occurred on two intersecting planes, as the unwelcome accumulation of abstract money obligations overwhelmed land's social value. For larger farmers renting land from these villagers, however, as well as for the local political elites in charge of decollectivizing, social and political relations of other kinds enabled finding a value in land that it was losing for small owners.

The Declining Economic Value of Landed Property

Jubilant Vlaiceni receiving land rights in 1991 could not have foreseen how quickly they would come to find owning it a tribulation, laden with risk. The chief problem was that they had received rights to land without having most of the remaining factors of production; those were in the hands of powerful others, including transnational chemical companies. Thus, all smallholders had the problem of securing these and other capital inputs – which grew ever more costly over the decade, relative to incomes. That is, the risk entailed in procuring them increased with time. The ever-rising cost of farm buildings and equipment such as tractors, seeders, and combines far exceeded the savings of nearly everyone – rapidly destroyed by inflation. Bank loans were difficult to obtain. So were the (theoretically available) state-subsidized credits, for which one had to pay a 10–20 percent "commission" (i.e., a bribe) and would need very well-placed connections. Even with the subsidy, one faced fluctuating interest rates, varying (for one borrower) from an initial 62 percent, to 42 percent, next to 75 percent, and then to 110 percent.

Meanwhile, the prices kept rising. A small tractor bought in 1992 cost about 900,000 lei, the same tractor in October 1993 was 3.4 million lei – a nearly four-fold increase in one year. A large tractor that in November 1994 cost 9.5 million was 75 million in June 1997 and 150 million in August 2000 – a 16-fold increase. Or, to phrase it relatively: whereas a tractor purchased in 1994 cost the equivalent of 50 ha of harvested wheat, the same purchase a year and a half later required the wheat harvest of 100 ha, reflecting both the ballooning cost of equipment and the stagnation of agricultural prices.

Inflation affected other production factors too. Between 1994 and 2000, for example, the price of gasoline increased 30- to 40-fold and the cost of chemical fertilizer and of hiring someone to plow, 20-fold.

Against this, incomes rose less rapidly: a top industrial pension increased 18-fold (other pensions considerably less), slightly behind the increment in most inputs; the sale price of wheat and of pigs increased 15- to 16-fold, lagging further behind. Pensions were important because they were the principal source of income that enabled many of these villagers to pay for inputs.[7] Those lacking such pensions fared much worse. In considering these figures, it is important to remember that for 40 years, villagers had experienced virtually zero inflation. Against that background, the perceived risk entailed in the inflation rates of the 1990s was far greater than it would be for someone accustomed to periodic increments.

Most Vlaiceni chose not to assume large financial burdens and concerned themselves instead with managing the perennial risks of agriculture within narrower parameters. If they farmed on their own, at first they reused old seed. (One man boasted to me that he had resurrected the seed his father used in the 1940s.) They mixed small amounts of expensive fertilizer with free manure and used no costly herbicides, instead weeding by hand. Together with avoiding bank loans, these means helped to reduce people's financial exposure somewhat. They also used the Association itself as a risk-spreading instrument – a common function of cooperatives. First, it pooled everyone's risk by paying its members according to the mean harvest, rather than the yield of their specific parcel. Therefore (and second), people usually gave it land of poorer quality, more vulnerable to flooding, or farther away from the village center. In this way they reduced both their labor input (in the form of travel time) and the uncertainty associated with farming land that was difficult or marginal. They also used the Association to cushion labor scarcity – a major problem – pulling land out when they had enough labor and putting it back in when they did not. While such practices were advantageous for individual households, they undermined the Association's general prospects, since it therefore worked inferior land, its tractors had to travel farther and use more fuel, and the uncertainty as to whose land it would control precluded long-term planning. Villagers seemed not to realize that their strategies for managing risk thus increased it for the Association's leaders – and that this naturally brought the risks back to themselves as Association members.

The greatest hazard that can afflict a property object is devaluation. Across the decade, government policies toward agriculture, the widening price scissors, and bank interest rates influenced by the International Monetary Fund's stabilization program contributed to precisely this. The risks of farming became so high for smallholders that fewer and fewer of them could manage. By 2000, some of my respondents were borrowing money to pay for plowing. Many others were leaving large portions of their land uncultivated, a practice that devalues land by making it much more costly to bring back into cultivation. Still others were trying to sell, even though the price of land was inordinately low and the money obtained would soon disappear in the continuing inflation unless converted into dollars. Repeated floods brought the Association to a standstill; by the summer of 2000, it too left three-fourths of its land uncultivated. Villagers were now telling me that it cost them far more to cultivate a hectare of land than to buy the same amount of wheat at the market. When the tax holiday was over, they would have to pay taxes on income they were not receiving. It would cost them more to be owners than to sell.

In short, their land was becoming a negative economic asset. The financial obligations people had to assume so as to work it exceeded their capacities. Clear evidence of its devaluation is the trend in the price of land over the decade: as against the 15- to 40-fold increases in production costs and incomes, the price of land increased only three- to five-fold. A parcel of land that sold for 1.5–2 million lei in 1994 cost 7–10 million six years later. We might compare this with the cost of a top-quality milk cow in autumn 2000: about 7 million lei. To sell land, then, amounted to trading away one's hectare for a cow.

It is therefore reasonable to ask whether land was a positive asset in some other sense, and for whom. This leads to the question of different modes of valuing.

Other Values of Land

For certain kinds of people – political elites in communes, and social elites in villages – the value of land was not chiefly economic but political and social. The local political elite consisted of commune mayors, their councilors and lesser administrative staff, and members of the land commissions set up by Law 18. The process of land-rights restitution brought windfall profits to these local elites: it handed them a resource everyone wanted and charged them with distributing and titling it. Most such officials preferred to delay rather than facilitate the titling process Law 18 mandated. By failing to give out titles or to resolve the myriad problems associated with restitution, commune mayors and land commissions could keep claimants in a petitionary and dependent posture. They stalled so as to offer at least temporary use of problem land to their cronies, friends, and potential clients – or to work it for their own enrichment – for a year, or two, or three, until the aggrieved claimant might give up altogether and sacrifice title. They encouraged others to occupy contested land or to sue, thereby drawing out the process even further.[8] Meanwhile, the mayor would have converted this political capital into a display of potency by building himself both a villa and a clientele, who might help to get him reelected – or would at least obscure the machinations behind his building and land-use projects. The delays also provided a resource for political challengers, whose electoral propaganda seized upon an existing mayor's failure to complete land titling. (In my research area, this was a major issue in the commune elections of both 1996 and 2000.) Although in Vlaicu the titling of collective farm land was more or less complete by 2000, as late as spring of 2001 one neighboring village had received no property titles at all, and the distribution of land from state farms was just beginning.

I believe the titling process was slower than expected all over Romania in part because locally, land was a political asset – but only as long as it was not given out to its owners. Why should commune elites give out titles, destroying their patronage base? By exploiting the absentee status of many recipients, people's ignorance about the procedures, and other ambiguities, politicians could make allies. In doing so, they were following the well-hewn path of "capital accumulation" so vital in the socialist political economy, in which cadres built their bureaucratic power base by accumulating clients and cultivating far-flung networks of equals, based in reciprocity. Socialism's power system rested heavily on social obligations and "rights in people" (see Humphrey 1983). Any "risks" to be overcome were of this kind, not economic ones.

So much for the perspective of commune political elites. Villagers who received land – especially if they received more than about four or five hectares, qualifying them to consider themselves village elites – behaved comparably, if on a smaller scale. For them, land was a form of social capital, and they tried to use it to collect people. This was especially necessary because households with this much land rarely had adequate labor to work it; therefore they sought to collect sharecroppers and day laborers from among their neighbors and the village landless. Additionally, they might solve some labor problems by renting out their land to tenants or the Association. All these kinds of labor arrangements were important in part because quarrels over land had jeopardized relations with both kin and neighbors – the usual sources of labor assistance.

The problem for village elites was to secure labor through social ties, as had been the norm in pre-socialist times, rather than having to pay for it when cash was so short. Toward this end, they hoped to (re)assert their claims to status, considering that they had recovered their families' earlier prestige. In other words, in reestablishing themselves as land-owners and worthy people, they used the idioms of the pre-socialist rural stratification system, by which groups of landed locals had maintained a superior position over landless and in-migrant families. Following prior practice, they would obligate these families through "work parties," through ties of ritual kinship, and through patronage in the form of land given in sharecropping. In the pre-socialist rural world, aside from basic subsistence, land's asset value for all but the poorest peasants had been chiefly social, not economic; the main form of "devaluation" one feared was loss of status, not the collapse of land values or a widening price scissors. In that older world, too, selling land had been unthinkable: not only did it expose one to much greater risks, but it was a source of shame, amounting to an admission of incompetence. For the new village proprietors, then, the land and agricultural infrastructure that were negative assets from a budgetary perspective could be significant positive assets in the old/new order of status valuation – as long as they didn't run out of money.

For land to remain this kind of asset, however, required that it not be sold and that it be cultivated, even if at an economic loss. This was the lesson I learned from the several people who told me, in the summer of 2000, that they were still working their land despite having calculated that it was a sorely losing proposition. When I asked why, they replied, "*De ruşinea oamenilor!*" – from shame before others. "What will people say if they pass my field and see it full of weeds, or with corn a half-meter high in September?" exclaimed one villager. "They'll say, 'Look! There's Sandu's field, and what a mess! He should be ashamed!'" Having a field of fine and well-weeded crops that all could see was a way of reasserting superior status over those with less or no land. Likewise having an outdoor storage loft bursting with corn: especially given the low grain prices, corn sold in the market was less of an asset than corn everyone in Vlaicu could see. Aside from the state's requirement that land be worked, its cultivation was important to keeping owners visible on the landscape.

In my travels through Vlaicu's fields during the 1990s, this visibility was a constant theme. Whoever was with me would be commenting on the fields we passed, "Oh, there's Sandu's wheat, look how beautiful it is!" or "See those ugly weeds? those stunted cornstalks? That's

Dumitru's lousy work." Families from whom I was trying to learn crop yields were disconcertingly vague on how many kilograms of corn or wheat they had harvested, instead emphasizing the number of cartloads they had brought home. When I asked how many kilograms a cart held, they became exasperated, as if I just didn't get it. (I didn't.) The matter of seeing, which includes not just surface areas but the work put into them, is key to thinking about status, and it has implications for their conception of property. The goal of village elites was not simply to *have* land but to have it *worked* (see also Lampland 1995). Land had to be concrete, particular, bounded, and recognizably distinct from everyone else's. It and its products had to be visible – and visibly linked to their particular holding. In short, land had to be property as a concrete physical object, not as abstract shares in some state farm.

More than this, visibly successful cultivation manifested a person's ability to be an effective farmer. What was important about ownership was not simply holding rights but showing that one was master (*stăpân*) of the soil – an idea central to these villagers' conception of owning. Consider Emil, telling me how he felt about getting his land back: "Very happy! because I thought, I'll be *stăpân* over it. But it hasn't worked out that way, I'm not *stăpân* over it . . . I have to pay these terrible prices. I'd be *stăpân* if I had my own implements and a tractor." Thus, the rising costs of production discussed earlier threatened people's sense of their efficacy as owners, and as human beings.[9]

To return to the relations between social status and obligating labor: the Vlaiceni whom village elites hoped chiefly to attract as labor were families who had migrated in during the 1970s. They had received no land in the restitution, and their hold on their unskilled urban jobs was precarious. These people, however, proved very difficult to obligate. Many accepted sharecropping or day-labor arrangements only until they could buy their own small parcel, after which they would cease to work for others. Revealing a high level of class consciousness, such people responded thus to my questions as to whether they sharecropped: "We don't want to be serfs for the local nobles!" "If we work for them, it will be just like the days of serfdom. No way!" "I'm not going to make *someone else* a squire!" They too used the idiom of seeing, this time for social criticism: "Just walk the fields! Wherever you see weeds, that's where the rich people are working! *Our* fields don't look like that!"

The attitude of these in-migrants sharpened the financial crisis smallholders faced, forcing them into labor alternatives that required cash. Some hired wage-workers by the day, and some began spending exorbitant amounts on herbicides, which would spare them the need for labor. Lacking skill in the use of such substances, however, they frequently found that weeds grew anyway, requiring them to spend even more money on day labor. All these expenses further swelled the costs I have described above for plowing, sowing, and harvesting. They pushed villagers to assume ever greater risk by increasing people's financial exposure. In part, this increased risk came from international forces far beyond their control – the global devaluation of agriculture in comparison with other sectors, the macro-economic stabilization programs of the IMF, the Romanian government's subsidies to industry. All these were making it ever more difficult for villagers to cultivate their land – the key to manifesting their status. Unless they could find someone to work it without requiring cash up front, it would become a negative asset and lose its status value. They would suffer, in other words, a double devaluation.

To work their land in the face of ongoing economic crisis, the disappearance of local labor, and the collapse of the Association, Vlaiceni turned to larger tenant-farmers. In this, however, they encountered a problem, for such tenants operated according to different values. They erased the land's individuality, pooling all parcels into a single field and all harvests into uniform piles from which owners received a fixed rent. If they worked your parcel as part of one large field, then you lost your source of pride: fields better worked than those around them, crops more resplendent, more carts piled high with the harvest. The move toward tenant farmers, then, was a move toward abstraction, something villagers had been fighting for most of the decade. Following 30 years of not being able to think of a specific parcel as "theirs," they now clutched tenaciously at "their" land, its concreteness being their recompense for the communists' having treated it as an abstraction. But unless they could work it, they could not maintain its concreteness. Here, then, was an unexpected source of devaluation, from their point of view: land lost its asset value as a status symbol when it lost its particularity.

The Rentier Society: Risk, Tenancy, and Ownership

If smallholders were suffering the devaluation of their land as both an economic and a social asset, the calculus of property values worked out differently for certain others, especially some of the directors of state farms. They did not own land but worked as administrators – for the state, officially, but also for the owners-turned-shareholders. In the early 1990s they faced virtually no risks, since the state covered their costs.

Changes in the price of inputs or even of land did not affect them – unless they intended to create their own private farms on the backs of their ever-more-decrepit SFs. To succeed in this would depend on their buying their farms' aged buildings and equipment. For that infrastructure to lose value might actually be beneficial – that is, the risk of economic loss was not necessarily a bad thing, for it would lower the price they would have to pay at auction.

In such circumstances, these people too had reason to create and maintain social obligations in hopes of surviving the change from state to private property forms. Here they enjoyed a significant edge over smallholders, for their exposure to risk was already cushioned by their having inherited from socialism a rich cultural and social capital, in the form of university-based farming expertise as well as numerous contacts among suppliers of inputs, bank directors, heads of new companies that might buy their products, and so on. This edge would enable them to find in land an economic value it was losing for other villagers. Becoming what I call "super-tenants," such people would rent owners' land from a position of advantage, thus differing from other kinds of tenants because they had so much more wealth in the expertise and contacts necessary to make a go of farming and because their social status was superior to that of their lessors. Their peculiar circumstances arose from the peculiar rentier society decollectivization created: instead of many small tenants seeking land from a few large owners, we have many small owners chasing fewer large tenants. As long as the situation was in flux, however, the tenants would have to ensure themselves of owners, and social obligation entered into this process.

For many years, one of the four state farms (SF4) with land belonging to Vlaiceni had been run by a woman I will call Lila, in close collaboration with her husband Dan, who had also held jobs in the state agricultural sector. Both had university training, tremendous energy, and a great deal of initiative. During the socialist period SF4 had been fairly successful; they were thus able to pay their shareholders reasonably well for the first three or four years after 1991 – double or even triple the Ministry of Agriculture's fixed minimum. Paying well was initially easy, for the size of the dividends given out did not affect either their income (fixed state salaries) or their farms' viability. Because the county state-farm center would provide the necessary inputs for cultivation, they saw no reason to stint on their dividends. By 1996, however, the center had completely ceased to provide the inputs their farms needed and had stopped finding them markets. Now they would have to make enough money to buy their own inputs, under the increasingly unfavorable conditions already presented above, and to pay the shareholders as well. The size of dividends gradually began to drop back toward the set minimum – well below the generous 1,000 kg/ha another super-tenant was offering.

This was distressing to Dan and Lila not just because they had lived just down the road from their farms' shareholders for years but because their shareholders were also their future source of land. When the land in SFs reverted to its former owners and the couple could buy the farm infrastructure, they hoped to persuade people to rent the land to the new farm instead of taking it out. Believing that shareholders would be more likely to do this if they had already been well paid, the couple struggled to keep producing so they would be able to pay dividends – even at the risk of assuming production costs that might reduce the economic value of their farm's infrastructure. This indicates the importance they gave to creating social ties with villagers as their future source of land.[10]

Dan and Lila found themselves competing, however, with other super-tenants who could pay much better.[11] Well aware that their strategy for collecting clients might fail, the couple diversified their activities. By dint of great effort and ingenuity, they made enough money to buy a tractor of their own and some land, benefiting from its low price. Owing to their skill at farming and use of advanced technology, each new hectare increased their income for subsequent ones. Then, as other super-tenants and the Association failed, villagers began to ask the couple to take their land. By 2000 the total area they worked for themselves was about 25 ha, with additional amounts ranging up to 75 ha or more for others – and they were still hoping to buy the moribund SF4.

All these activities implied taking on increased risk, given the high cost of inputs. How did Dan and Lila manage it? First, throughout the decade they drew two salaries from their state jobs. This greatly reduced the risk entailed in their private activities, for even if those failed they would still have income. While their two salaries helped them accumulate for further purchases of equipment and inputs at home, most other villagers had no such cushion. Second, they placed some of the risk squarely on their lessors. In agreeing to work other villagers' land, they set terms that were not generous, offering a fixed rent of 300 kg/ha – an amount Dan and Lila believed they would always be able to meet. In a word, by setting the rent so low they put all the risk of harvest fluctuation onto the owner, for if their yields were good, they kept the difference (which they could later use to buy these very same people's land when they gave up trying to own it), and even poor yields were unlikely to fall below the rent they had set. Although some villagers grumbled that the amount was too low, by this time their alternatives were few; some were just grateful to have the land worked at all. Another super-tenant in the area, Dora, had found other ways of throwing risk onto the owners: she took only parcels that made up sizable compact fields (thus, owners bore all the risk of field fragmentation), and she would rent only from those who would pay the full costs of cultivation up front (thus passing onto owners the burden of mobilizing large amounts of cash). She had promised them very good rent – 1,000–1,100 kg/ha – but if there were a calamity, she guaranteed them nothing.

Both these examples suggest that leasing might be safer than owning, for being the owner of a concrete individualized property object potentially made one more vulnerable to risk than being a tenant. In other words, objects whose materiality is essential to their value may attract more risk to the extent that they are individualized – but this is the very secret of their *having* value (social if not market value), in that particular system of evaluation. In a budgetary system of valuation, by contrast, the advantage may come from avoiding ownership and settling for tenancy. Leasing – as other papers in this volume show – enables shucking off liabilities that owners are forced to bear, liabilities that in this period of Romania's history were substantial.

In this light, Dan and Lila's decision to buy land is puzzling. Why did they load themselves up with all the risks of owning, rather than continuing to pass off most of the risk onto the smallholder? Why did they see ownership of land as diminishing risks that the partisan of use-rights would see them centralizing dangerously in themselves? This strategy runs counter to the rationale of capitalist corporations: obtain control and spread the risk among the shareholders who "own" the firm. Yet Lila and Dan were going in the opposite direction. His explanation (based on many conversations with him) would go something like this. First, private property, which people had been largely denied under socialism, had accrued a positive valence that no economist's reasoning could easily demolish. Second, in the context of high instability and uncertainty with respect to both values and risks, the couple saw their profits as surer the more production factors they brought under their control, and that was best done by owning. Owning their tractors freed them of usurious machinery rentals; given the ever-widening price scissors, if they did not buy their tractor today they might not be able to afford it tomorrow. Owning their land freed them of uncertainty about whether enough villagers would offer them leases. Given the ridiculously low price of land, if they bought now they could buy more than if they waited. From this viewpoint, ownership *reduced* risk – the risk of unmeetable financial obligation.

It also freed the couple of social obligation that was becoming uncomfortable. Being a tenant meant embedding themselves in contractual relationships with villagers. If the harvest were good, everyone would see it; then they would be upset that they received only 300 kg/ha, and if Lila tried to explain costs (which were enormous), they would not believe her.[12] Every time she distributed the rent in the fall, she had to listen to their complaints that she hadn't given them enough – that their land was better than this, that they're old, that they did her a favor twenty years back, and so on. Better to spring free of them; then she could avoid that kind of scene. Dan and Lila needed to "collect people" when their future as super-tenants was uppermost in their minds and they saw more competitors in their environment. By 2000, however, things had shaken down. At this point they could afford to shed owners whom they had initially cultivated, and who were becoming a social liability. The people Dan and Lila needed to cultivate lay elsewhere, in extra-village networks resting on a variety of connections: school ties, village ties, kinship, and – perhaps most significantly – those they developed decades earlier in socialist agriculture. These kinds of connections would help them secure high-quality inputs at low cost, possible contracts for their harvest, and the eventual bank loan, should they need it.

For super-tenants, ownership meant reducing their social embeddedness locally, enhancing it extra-locally, and maximizing their control over the few factors they could control, even at the expense of centralizing risk in themselves. But their resources for managing that risk were greater: expertise, connections, sometimes state salaries, and information the ordinary villager lacked, which enabled super-tenants to succeed economically at farming. Even though they may have suffered the complete devaluation of state assets they had hoped to buy (as happened to Dan and Lila), careful deployment of their other resources gave land continued value for them. Ownership for smallholders, by contrast, loaded them with risks they had trouble escaping. Pressed constantly toward assuming monetary obligations rather than social ones, they were having to confront the extent to which their land had become a liability. If they were dissatisfied with their pay from the super-tenants and unable to farm the land on their own, many would have to sell; if they could find buyers for it, the price would not provide them with many years' pension. Otherwise, after two or three years' noncultivation, they could see it confiscated by the state, this time for good. Their capital, both economic and social, would have been devalued, if not (from their standpoint) completely destroyed.

Conclusion

What does the material I have presented contribute to thinking about property? First, I believe it helps us to see how even land, that concrete and material thing, a property object firmly embedded in local social relations, gave way to greater abstraction as it was devalued – twice – by people's incorporation into imperfect markets and a global economy unfriendly to traditional agriculture. Land lost its particularity as it entered the large fields of super-tenants, whence its product returned to its owners as bits of "the average harvest" and the "standard rent," regardless of the quality of their parcel. For smallholders, land could no longer be a concrete bounded object and still retain its social value (a fate they share with other groups drawn into the process of commodification). In the hands of super-tenants it then underwent another abstraction, because of their use of complex and costly technology for raising yields. Agriculture worldwide has ceased to be an activity producing nearly all its necessary inputs; instead, genetic engineering has made land no more than a neutral medium for absorbing manufactured imports and exporting "manufactured" products. Its own qualities grow insignificant, as it becomes but a platform for special seeds that respond only to specific chemical fertilizers and herbicides; improper application of any of these can wreck the harvest, no matter how good the soil. Super-tenants "respected" (their word) this technology. They bought imported Pioneer seed, top-quality fertilizer, and herbicides at exorbitant cost, increasing the overall level of expense and risk they would spread among their lessors. This is not, of course, a process peculiar to postsocialism: it is the story of agriculture everywhere. Peculiar to East European postsocialism, with its history of the family-owned farm, is only the remarkable speed with which collective farmers were ensnared in that process.

Second, I believe that emphasizing property's obligations and risks has given me better purchase on my data than I would have if I emphasized primarily rights. For a certain class of people, assigning property rights to land was a way of assigning "bads," not "goods." The element of financial obligation overtook the element of rights, undermining both the social value of land for these people and also their ability to work it. Holding ownership rights, then, was less important than manipulating the context in which things had value. In connection with this, deemphasizing rights reveals more clearly the new kinds of person that property restitution created. They were, first, persons who could not experience their ownership as efficacious, as "mastery" of the soil. Second, they were persons who bore not just ownership rights to land but accountability for it. To assume those rights subjected them to processes that devalued the property object, generated risks of which they were unaware, and opened them to debt. This kind of personhood, I believe, is new only to them: it draws them into a much wider process in which responsibility is individualized as corporations appropriate the rewards.

Finally, my focus on risks and liabilities has afforded us a glimpse of the work that the property concept accomplishes. Although scholars of property know that rights are just part of the story, millions of people subject to privatization were told only about the rights they would receive, not the obligations. Therein lies the poignancy of their situation, for the myth of property rights created great joyful expectations, which the realities of risk-bearing ownership would crush.

Acknowledgments

The form of my argument in this chapter has been much influenced by conversations with Keebet von Benda-Beckmann, Elizabeth Dunn, Ashraf Ghani, Caroline Humphrey, Phyllis Mack, Herman Schwartz, and Marilyn Strathern. In addition, I thank colleagues at the Wissenschaftskolleg zu Berlin (2000–01), including Peter Bernholz, Richard Bernstein, Wang Hui, Francis Snyder, and Patricia Springborg, for helpful comment on an early draft. Participants in the Wenner-Gren conference contributed greatly with their very helpful reactions.

Notes

1. Such as the World Bank, International Monetary Fund, European Bank for Reconstruction and Development, and international accounting firms (Price Waterhouse, Arthur Andersen, etc.).

2. See Romania's Law 18/1991, articles 53–5.

3. In truth, it is difficult to find a perfect solution for decollectivizing. Had people been allowed to sell their land immediately, many would have done so, producing a pattern of highly concentrated landholding as open to criticism as the policy pursued.

4. These differed in (1) the way they were formed (confiscations vs. "donations" of land); (2) their property status (state vs. cooperative); (3) their relation to the state budget (high vs. low investment); and (4) their ways of remunerating workers (fixed wages vs. a share of the revenues). See Verdery 2003, chap. 1.

5. The community is VLY-koo, the residents vly-CHENi.

6. Thanks to Marilyn Strathern for provoking this line of thought.

7. This is the only instance I am aware of in which Romanian industry actually supported agriculture, rather than exploiting it.

8. For a different argument on the place of uncertainty in the strategies of the nomenklatura, see Stephen 1996. He makes the argument that institutionalized uncertainty creates (or perpetuates) power for that group. (Thanks to Herman Schwartz for this reference.)

9. James Ferguson makes a related argument in his chapter "The Bovine Mystique," in Ferguson 1994: having cattle for status purposes is so important that people will not sell them even when to keep them incurs serious financial loss.

10. We see here two contrasting organizations of value: Dan and Lila were using money to collect people so as to obtain *land*, while villagers used land to collect people so as to obtain *labor*.

11. See Verdery 2003, chapters 7 and 8, for greater detail on why this was possible.

12. In 2000 she estimated that each hectare of wheat cost her six to seven million lei, as against about three million for villagers using less expensive technology.

References

Beck, Ulrich. 1992. *Risk society: Towards a new modernity*. Introduction by Scott Lash and Brian Wynne. Newbury Park, CA: Sage.

Ferguson, James. 1994. *The anti-politics machine: "Development," depoliticization, and bureaucratic power in Lesotho*. Minneapolis: University of Minnesota Press.

Honoré, A. M. 1961. Ownership. *Oxford Essays in Jurisprudence* 107: 107–28.

Humphrey, Caroline. 1983. *Karl Marx Collective*. Cambridge: Cambridge University Press.

Lampland, Martha. 1995. *The object of labor: Commodification in socialist Hungary*. Chicago: University of Chicago Press.

Stephen, Paul. 1996. "Toward a positive theory of privatization: Lessons from Soviet-type economies." *International Review of Law and Economics* 16: 173–93.

Verdery, Katherine. 2000. "Ghosts on the landscape: Restoring private landownership in Eastern Europe." *Focaal* 36: 145–63.

——. 2003. *The vanishing hectare: Property and value in postsocialist Transylvania*. Ithaca, NY: Cornell University Press.

seven

Property Regimes and Sociotechnical Systems: Rights over Land in Mongolia's "Age of the Market"

David Sneath

In Mongolia the debate over the ownership of land has become one of the most controversial political issues in the recent history of this postsocialist state. The introduction of laws that would allow, for the first time, the private ownership of land provoked heated discussion in a nation that continues to construct its identity with reference to ancient traditions of mobile pastoralism.

In the early 1990s, in the wake of the collapse of Soviet-backed state socialism, the Mongolian state undertook wholesale political and economic reform. A multi-party electoral system was introduced, and although the old "communist" ruling party (the Mongolian People's Revolutionary Party, MPRP) was confirmed in office, the state nevertheless embraced a broadly liberal agenda. The government embarked on a series of radical reforms designed to create a market economy. In common with other Soviet-bloc countries, the Western economic advice given to Mongolia resembled the stabilization and structural reform packages that the IMF and the World Bank recommended for poor countries in the 1970s and 1980s (Nolan 1995: 75; see also the chapters by Verdery and Alexander in this volume). It included the privatization of public assets, price liberalization, cutting state subsidies and expenditure, currency convertibility, and the rapid introduction of markets. The recommendations reflected a neoliberal program in which the economy should be emancipated from the political structure and permitted to assume its latent "natural" form, composed of private property and the market.

In 1991 Mongolia began a huge program to privatize collective and state enterprises.[1] In rural districts the reforms included the dissolution of the pastoral collectives (*negdel*) and most of the state farms (*sangiin aj ahui*). The collective herds of sheep, goats, cattle, horses, and in some regions camels were divided among the former members, as were the other collective assets such as motor vehicles, machinery, and equipment.

The introduction of the new property regime had the effect of breaking up the concentrated herd ownership, the large-scale movement systems, and specialist support operations that the collectives had organized. Many of the workers in the rural settlements lost their jobs but gained some livestock instead. This trebled the number of workers directly reliant on pastoralism for their livelihood from less that 18 percent of the national workforce in 1989 to 50 percent of the working population in 1998.[2] Livestock numbers began to rise. Pastoralists valued herd-wealth in its own right and now relied upon their domestic animals for subsistence, so increasing herd size became a matter of food security. From 1990 to 1998 the national herd increased by over 20 percent to nearly 32 million head.[3] However, the efficiency of pastoralism declined. By 1998 survival rates of offspring had fallen by around 10 percent, and livestock totals were able to rise only because levels of marketing and consumption declined by about 20 percent.[4] The exports of livestock and livestock products collapsed, while incomes, public services, and living standards declined dramatically (World Bank 1994: 19, Griffen 1995: viii). The number of people living below the poverty line increased from almost zero in 1989 to over 33 percent in 1998.[5]

One of the reasons for Mongolia's economic crisis was the loss of Soviet aid, which was reduced in 1989 and stopped altogether in 1991. (Some estimates suggest this had amounted to a third of GDP or more.)[6] However, to some extent Western nations, Japan, and international financial institutions took the place of Russia as aid donors and economic advisors. These donors provided support that rose to 25 percent of GDP by 1996 (Bruun and Odgaard, 1996: 26). The loss of Soviet aid, then, can be held but partially responsible for Mongolia's crisis. As Griffin argues, one of the reasons for the severity of the economic collapse was the way in which a new regime of private ownership was rapidly and destructively introduced (Griffin 1995: 12–13). There have been some "winners" in this revolution, but all the rural Mongolians I know now stress the relative wealth, security, and convenience that the collective period offered, and contrast these with the low buying power and uncertain future of the "age of the market" (*zah zeeliin üye*). This was one of the reasons for the landslide electoral victory of the "old communist" MPRP, who won 72 out of 76 parliamentary seats in the July 2000 election.

The dissolution of the state socialist planned economy transformed the value and characteristics of the elements that had composed it. The once collectively-owned livestock, land, machinery, and other "assets" took on new values and potentials to the extent that they could be fitted into whatever new networks of production and distribution actors could establish (see Alexander, this volume). The dissolution of the collective farms made over a quarter of a million former collective and state workers directly dependent on small holdings of livestock. In the harsh winter and spring (*zud*) of 1999–2000, Mongolia as a whole lost some three million livestock, around 10 percent of the national herd; more than two thousand households saw their entire livestock holding wiped out. A second winter disaster in 2000–2001 pushed the total livestock losses up toward 6 million and destroyed the livelihood of thousands more pastoralists. The scale of these losses, and the underlying problem of barely viable herding households, reflected the weakness of the atomized and demechanized pastoral sector that emerged from the transformation of the property regime.

Property Regimes, Pastoralism, and Land

The collectives (*negdel*) had been largely introduced in the 1950s, and each one managed pastoralism in an entire local government district (*sum*). They typically included something on the order of a thousand households, about half of which were specialist mobile pastoralists living in encampments throughout the district, and the other half performed service jobs in a central settlement. Pastoral households were organized into small groups (often of close kin) called "bases" (*suur*), and these were grouped into production brigades (*brigad*) and sections (*heseg*). Households were assigned livestock to herd and received a regular income. The collectives owned the bulk of the livestock of the district, but herding households were allowed 50 or in some regions 75 head of their own to supply domestic needs. Pastoralists would move livestock to different seasonal pastures, and when necessary, collective managers would employ the pastoral technique of *otor*, by which livestock are repeatedly moved over distant and lesser-used pastures at times of fodder shortage, as a method of intensively feeding them (Humphrey and Sneath 1999: 233–64). The collectives also maintained machinery for transportation and hay-cutting services that were used to support the herding "bases." In general, pastoralists were moved on the longest legs of the annual migration by collective trucks, and hay was delivered to help feed livestock during the difficult months of winter and early spring. Herders largely viewed this coordination and support of pastoralism as a very positive aspect of the old system and have sorely missed it since the advent of the "age of the market."

Brigades and sections were allocated seasonal pastures. Land was ultimately "owned" by the state, use was managed by the collective's leaders, and pastoral households generally made use of a recognized area of pasture within the areas allocated to their group. Of these the use of winter pastures (*övöljöö*) was most exclusive and associated with given households and *suur* (bases), who usually had animal shelters and stockpiles of dried dung there for heating. The winter and spring are the most difficult times of the year for livestock, and someone grazing animals near another's winter site had to leave sufficient land untouched for the household(s) assigned to it to feed their animals over the winter months. In other seasons there was generally considerable flexibility as to exactly where families would camp within the seasonal pastures allocated to their group.

The *negdel*s were dissolved in 1991–93 by issuing share coupons (*tasalbar*), which employees could use to claim a share of the enterprise as their "private property." Livestock, machinery, and other agricultural resources were distributed among the members. The land, however, remained a public resource used by local pastoralists and was regulated, theoretically, by local government.

This was seen as anomalous by development economists of the Asian Development Bank (ADB) and other advisors to the Mongolian government. The registration and titling of land was thought to be a necessary precondition for an effective market in land, and such a market was assumed to be the best way of realizing productive potential. In this discourse private agricultural and pastoral producers are bound to maximize the returns on their investments and land is cast as another economic asset that producers must own in order to protect and invest in it. In 1994 the ADB (1994: 33), for example, complained: "Currently, there is no private ownership of land. As a consequence, land tenure insecurity causes disincentives to invest in land improvements." The ADB strongly advocated a new Land Law which would allow the private ownership of land "to provide positive incentives to herders, farmers and others to maximize production and to protect land from damage or degradation."[7]

However, the new legislation met with fierce resistance. Many Mongolian parliamentarians were unhappy with the notion of privatizing land, particularly those considered "conservative" in the context of the post-socialist political arena, including many members of the former ruling Mongolian People's Revolutionary Party (MPRP). In the early 1990s parliamentary opposition repeatedly delayed the new land legislation. In order to get the bill through the parliament (*Ulsyn Ih Hural*), in November 1994 the more contentious clauses concerning outright private ownership were dropped. But another piece of legislation, the Land Payments Law, was developed by which the state would lease to individuals the "possession" (*ezemshih*) of campsites and pastures. This sidestepped the issue of outright ownership but still allowed for exclusive private rights to land. "Certificates of possession" (*ezemshigchiin gerchilgee*) could be issued to individuals and companies, giving them long-term exclusive access to land.

In 1996 the Mongolian Democratic Union (MDU), a coalition of more economically liberal parties, defeated the MPRP in parliamentary elections. The new government began to implement the land-allocation provisions in 1998. But the bill remained controversial, and in May 1999 some MPs expressed fears that the best pasture land would be acquired by the rich, to the detriment of poorer herders. Others accused the government of pursuing the legislation at the bidding of the Asian Development Bank in return for large loans, and one MP declared that land privatization could result in "civil war."[8] While this was widely seen as exaggeration, it reflected genuine fears that privatizing land would precipitate disputes over land claims throughout the country.

In the late 1990s Mongolian public opinion swung heavily in support of socialist "conservatism," amid general disenchantment with the MDU. N. Bagabandi, the MPRP candidate, easily won the 1997 presidential elections with more than twice the popular vote of any other candidate, and the MPRP won a landslide victory in the 2000 parliamentary elections. Among pastoralists there was widespread unease at the notion of privately owned pasture land, and considerable support for the "conservative" line. But many had also become concerned with protecting their use-rights to pastures, since the tight control of land use that local officials used to exercise in the past had decayed since decollectivization. However, the notion that land could be bought up and owned outright by individuals, particularly outsiders, remained deeply unpopular.

Mongolian local administrations were slow to divide and allocate grazing land. Most districts (*sum*) issued certificates only for seasonal campsites (principally *övöljöö*, "winter" sites) (Fernandez-Gimenez and Batbuyan 2000: 8). These were point locations, rather than swathes of land, but they entailed an implicit right to the pasture within a radius of several kilometers around the site. Initially the certification tended to simply legitimate existing use-rights to the seasonal pastures that households had been allocated in the past. The law was designed, however, to go much further than this. What was emerging was a property regime in which pasture land was neither open-access public property nor in private ownership. Instead the state created private rights to locational elements of what was still conceived as a wider system of pastoral movement. Although movement between pastures generally declined and became more difficult to arrange after decollectivization, these *övöljöö* sites were still thought of as wintering places. The *ezemshigchiin gerchilgee* "certificates of possession" might themselves be considered a new form of property, but if so they clearly represented a set of prerogatives and liabilities with respect to one site within a wider system of land use. This may change, of course, if long-distance pastoral movements continue to decline and pastoralists switch to year-round use of winter pastures, as tended to happen in Inner Mongolia (China), where pasture was divided and allocated to individual households or small groups (Sneath 1998: 1147–8). Even so, however, Mongolian notions of land will not change overnight. I have shown that even a radical decision to change the property regime becomes entangled in the practices people employ to make a living in specific environments. My next section will show how these practices cannot be extricated from cultural-political notions, many of which are very long-lasting. These notions can exist in harmony with certain property regimes and come into conflict with others.

Notions of Land in Historical Perspective

When the new revolutionary government of Mongolia gained power in 1921–24, it inherited a society in which pastoralism and the political order were inextricably linked. Historically, extensive pastoralism in Inner Asia relied upon a particular configuration of rights over resources. Rather than absolute individual ownership, mobile pastoralists depended upon public access to resources under the jurisdiction of a local political authority that regulated their use. Indigenous Mongolian notions of land "ownership" can be described as custodial, in that agencies had conditional rights to use territory and always within a wider sociopolitical framework. Indeed, in the past, land, livestock, and people were constituent elements of sociopolitical domains ruled by district authorities.

From the seventeenth to the twentieth centuries Mongolia was part of the Manchu Qing empire. Territory was divided into administrative districts called "banners" (*hoshuu*) ruled by hereditary lords or, in some cases, Buddhist monasteries. In this period Mongolian society was composed of a ruling aristocracy and subordinate classes that roughly corresponded to "commoners," "freemen," and a category of personal servants. The common subjects were tied to the *hoshuu* politico-territorial units and were required to render corvée service to local authorities. Pastoral families generally moved to different seasonal pastures with their livestock in an annual cycle, and land use was regulated by banner officials. The Buddhist Church, nobility, imperial administration, and some very rich commoners owned large numbers of livestock which were herded for them by subjects and servants who generally received a share of the animal produce in return. Overall patterns of land use were managed by the noble or ecclesiastical district authorities. The operations organized by the wealthy herd-owners could be highly sophisticated and involve specialist herders moving large, single-species herds to selected pastures so as to make best use of the local ecological resources at given times of the year (Simukov 1936: 49–55, Bawden 1968: 181).

The property regime for land was complex and consisted of various prerogatives held by legal persons at different levels in the sociopolitical order. Authority over the use of land was ultimately vested in the Manchu emperor. The actual unit for pastoral land management was the *hoshuu*, ruled by the *Zasag noyan* ("banner prince" or lord). Although the emperor retained the formal right to allocate land, in everyday life the right to use pasture land was at the discretion of the banner prince and his officials, who acted as custodians of both people and land. Within the *hoshuu*, the herdsmen were assigned to smaller units (*sum*) and subunits (*bag*). The territory of the *hoshuu* generally contained a number of different areas of pasture used in winter, spring, summer, and autumn. These seasonal pastures were divided among the various *sum*s and *bag*s, and the exclusive use of the winter pasture (*övöljöö*) was the most strictly enforced. In many cases the summer pastures for all the *sum*s of the *hoshuu* were in the same general area, and the allocation of land was often very flexible, with few restrictions on exactly where families could camp. When necessary, herders would go on *otor* and this necessitated a good deal of flexibility in access to seasonal pastures. In adverse climatic conditions in one area, herders were allowed to use neighboring areas of pasture.

Rights to land use were described in terms of entitlements to move herds or stay with them in a given locality. What was being acquired in this way was in no sense the ownership of the land but rights to use territory at a certain time in the annual cycle. The *Jasag* (banner prince) and his officials could and did often reserve the best pastures for their own use, but there remained a notion that the land of the *hoshuu* was managed by the *Jasag* for the general welfare of its members. And there seem to have been some limits on the powers of the banner prince if he tried to challenge established practice of his subjects (Bawden 1968: 90–91).

Proprietary rights were not limited to human agents. Imperial and princely jurisdiction over land was subject to the approval of spiritual authorities. The *gazariin ezed* ("masters" or "owners" of the land) are spiritual entities considered to be in control of the weather and environmental conditions of each locality of the natural world. Such spirits were, and still are, propitiated in annual ceremonies held at ritual cairns, called *oboo*. These ceremonies reflect the notion that humans do not hold land as they do other mundane possessions, but must enter into relations with the spiritual powers of the locality to ensure favorable conditions.

The *oboo* ceremony embodied and enacted the relations between human and superhuman forces associated with the land. As such they were highly political acts, denoting those who were the legitimate representatives of the human community as they stood in relation to the supernatural world. Just as subjects had obligations toward the secular authorities, so they did toward the spiritual authorities of a locale. The goodwill of these authorities could not be taken for granted. There is an account of a local *gazariin ezen* becoming angered in the late nineteenth century, as a result of a dispute over the rights of foreigners to make use of Mongolian land. The result was adverse local conditions and livestock losses (Pozdneyev 1971: 412).

In fact "ownership" and "owner" are poor translations for the role that actors played in the network of prerogatives and liabilities surrounding land use. The term *ezen*, usually translated "owner," also means "head," "ruler," or "master/mistress." This is a concept that applies to asymmetrical relations entailing obligations and expectations at several different social scales. It is used at the level of the domestic group (where the *geriin ezen* is the head of the household); at the level of some large resource or enterprise (land, a herd of animals, or a factory may have an *ezen*); and in the past it was also applied at the scale of the whole polity – a common term for the Manchu emperor was Ezen

Khan. Rather than being an owner of land in the conventional English sense, an *ezen* is one with control of and responsibility for the resource, and as with a head of state or household, this has a custodial aspect.

These indigenous notions of land and the wider social order which framed them remained important throughout the twentieth century. The relation was transformed, but retained as the state built the centrally-planned command economy. The way that pastoralists were successfully integrated was through the introduction of large politico-economic territorial units – the collective and state farms. A new revolutionary political language replaced the earlier aristocratic and Buddhist discourses. However, many elements of the *habitus* of pastoralists and their masters remained. The everyday term used for collective or state animals was *alban mal* ("official" animals), and the root of this term translated as "official" is *alba* – the feudal obligation owed by pre-revolutionary subjects to their lord. Indeed, in the pre-revolutionary era the term for a common citizen or serf was *albat* – "one with duty." In both periods these related terms referred to the obligations that pastoralists had to their superiors.

As important as the conceptual continuities, many of the practices of pastoralism were retained. The collectives and state farms regulated and directed land use, owned most of the livestock in the district, organized specialist herds of livestock, and enforced movements between seasonal pastures. The introduction of state and collective property and control of land, then, was not a radical conceptual break with the past, but represented a new formulation of earlier political relations.

The political underpinnings of regimes of ownership are very clear when expressed in Mongolian terms. The Mongolian term for the "economy," for example, is *ediin zasag* – composed of the word *zasag* (prince, ruler, government) and the term *ed* – which means both "possessions" and "thing," "article," or "item." "Economy" in Mongolian could be literally translated as the "governance of possessions." It is rather a good parallel, then, with the notion of property regime itself. Here the definition of the economic sphere depends, quite literally, on a notion of political authority.

Even the term generally used to translate the English term "land" in Mongolian (*gazar*) has a perceptibly different meaning. A broader more inclusive term than land, *gazar* can also mean "place" or "office." (Government, *zasagiin gazar*, for example, is the place/office of *zasag*). Other terms describe types of land, classified by their use – *bilcher* for grazing land, *hadlan* for haymaking fields, and *zuslan, namarjaa, övöljöö,* and *havarjaa* for summer, autumn, winter, and spring pastures, respectively. This ideation emphasizes land use, rather than a common substance that can be owned and possessed; indeed, what the international development literature terms in English the "Land Law" is in fact the *"gazar edlengiin huul"* – the "land-use law." The most widely used term for private land is *huviin gazar*. *"Huv"* is the term used for the concept "private" and means a share, portion, or allotment, as well as personal or individual. The verb *huvaah* means to divide or apportion. So, items of personal property are explicitly part of wider fields – be they domestic, district, or state political economies.

Pastoralism as a Sociotechnical System

Property can be understood as part of the wider social and material networks that generate its value – in short, it is an element of a *sociotechnical system*. Following Pfaffenberger (1992) I use this term to mean a system of activity that links techniques and material objects to the social coordination of labor.[9] By recognizing that technology and resources are inextricably bound up with social form, work such as that by Lansing (1987) and Pfaffenberger (1992) on precolonial irrigation systems in Bali and Sri Lanka respectively have shown how efficient productive techniques were lost as a result of political changes to property relations.

This sociotechnical-systems approach is of heuristic value in understanding Inner Asian pastoralism. Mobile pastoral techniques can be seen as part of larger sociopolitical systems and require the integration of complex social and material systems, just as an agricultural irrigation system does. A series of specific techniques and instruments was developed by pastoralists working in the Inner Asian environment. These included a form of highly portable housing the *ger* (yurt) with its lightweight stove, techniques such as seasonal moves and *otor* foraging forays, a wide repertoire of specialist skills, and a host of other devices such as the *uurga* (pole-lasso) and concave wooden *emeel* (saddle).

The primary site of these skills, tools, and techniques was generally the *öröh* or *ail* (household, encampment), but a second and frequently more important context was the district political economy and the larger-scale pastoral activities in which households engaged. In the collective era, mechanized hay-making, delivery, transportation, marketing, and retail operations formed part of this complex. Even domestic-centered pastoral practices were part of wider sociotechnical systems that included the jural framework of rights and obligations, district authorities, institutions of land use, and associated concepts of land itself. Of course, these configurations were also hierarchical political formations, and there is no doubt that the religious and political ideologies of both the pre-revolutionary and the collective eras served the interests of the managers of the politico-economic structures. But these systems of knowledge were not merely instruments of domination; they reflected a much wider range of human experience, including the technical constraints on production imposed by an "environmental" externality – be that conceived in spiritual or in materialistic terms. Based as they were on pastoral mobility and general access to land, these sociotechnical systems tended to maintain and support those aspects of land use, and this seems to have provided very real benefits for pastoralists.

Large-scale systems of pastoral movement appear well suited to making optimum use of available forage resources and can provide useful economies of scale. By moving livestock to different seasonal pastures, pastoralists are able to make use of the different ecological and climatic conditions to get the best results from pastures in the different seasons. As in successful pastoral systems elsewhere, the ability to move livestock in response to changing climatic conditions is a key method of avoiding livestock losses and making the best use of available resources (Behnke and Scoones 1993).

Pastoral sociotechnical operations reflected the different orientations of the agencies engaged in them. Households need to provision themselves, i.e. operate in a "domestic subsistence" role. Many of these requirements could be met by each pastoral family herding relatively small numbers of several species of domestic livestock – sheep and goats for meat and winter clothing, cattle for milk, horses for riding, and camels for transportation.

But larger operations were conducted by various herd-owning agencies such as monasteries, nobles, government offices, Chinese shops, rich commoners in the pre-revolutionary period, and the collectives in the Soviet era. Such operations were based on control of large numbers of livestock and had different goals – usually to generate a good supply of produce and livestock for the owners. This "yield-focused" role made use of the economies of scale by which large herds could be herded with little more labor than small ones, and benefited from large-scale movement and other pastoral techniques enabled by coordinating labor – such as specialized care of large single-species herds. These operations were based upon particular relational modes. In the pre-collective period these could be either *alb*, the obligations that commoners owed district authorities, or *süreg tavih* (to "place herds"), a contractual arrangement in which herding households had obligations to supply a certain quota of produce but kept the surplus for themselves. In many ways these institutions were comparable to the way in which the collective assigned livestock to herding households. In both cases it engaged households in a wider system of operation and oriented them to producing surplus.

These larger systems could export large amounts of produce and support subsidiary economic activity in both the collective and earlier neo-feudal pastoral economies.[10] But domestic-subsistence operations are poor at exporting surplus outside local networks. The expansion of this aspect of pastoralism in the late 1990s led to a build-up of herd size instead. Exports of meat and livestock fell rapidly with the dissolution of the collectives – by 1992 the total had sunk to one-fifth of the 1985 figure and hardly improved thereafter.

The Transformation of Value

The change of ownership regimes from collective to private collapsed most of the larger sociotechnical systems that had been constructed under socialism. Many types of property held the particular characteristics and values they did because they were parts of these wider systems. Livestock gained from privatization could be relied upon to provide some sort of income even when divided into small herds owned by individual families. But mechanical devices such as tractors and welding equipment, on the other hand, saw their utility and value transformed. They had been supported and operated as part of the collective's economy, and their utility often became minimal in the new rural environment.

A typical example is the case of three brothers living in Renchinl-hümbe, a remote district in Northern Mongolia. As former technical support staff in the collective, the three brothers had obtained about 200 animals each in the decollectivization process, and had to turn to herding to make ends meet after they lost their jobs. The two elder brothers, Pürev and Bat-Erdene, used to be tractor drivers, while Batbayar, the youngest, was a welder who had learnt his trade in the army, before returning to work for the local collective until decollectivization in 1993.[11] In addition to their small herds of livestock, all three brothers managed to secure their equipment from the collective during the privatization process. Batbayar obtained his welding gear and his brothers a tractor each – a remarkable set of apparently expensive assets which, one would have thought, should make them relatively wealthy men.

But the character and value of this property were transformed with the changing economic regime (see also Alexander's chapter). The tractors stood idle outside their *gers* and were hardly ever used. When they were, it was to haul the family's possessions to new seasonal pastures. When I first got to know the brothers in August 1996, they were preparing to cut hay by hand, despite the fact that they also had the grass-cutting machinery needed to do this by tractor. The main obstacle, they explained, was the expense of diesel and spare parts (when they were obtainable at all). I asked why they did not cut enough hay to sell to local families and cover their costs, but the brothers found such a plan impractical. The really good hay fields were a long way from the pastures they relied on for subsistence herding; the haymaking areas that could be used by local families were smallish patches of rather sparse hay, spread out over a large area. This meant that it would be very expensive to cut significant quantities of hay by tractor and transport it, and the brothers couldn't afford sufficient inputs to do this. Even if they had, very few local families were wealthy enough to be able to afford such costly hay. Instead, local men would spend an exhausting fortnight or so in late August, working dawn to dusk to cut hay by hand. Some of this hand-cut hay would be sold by those families who most badly needed cash. A full truck-load of hay (around 2 tons) sold for about 30,000 tögrögs at that time (US$55), a considerable expense to most pastoral families, and one to be avoided if at all possible for domestic economies with cash shortages.

When property is considered as a constituent element of socio-technical systems, it becomes clear how a change of regime transforms the value of assets. In Mongolia the collective and state forms of property had been central components of an integrated complex of sociotechnical systems. When the collectives were dissolved, the larger systems collapsed, leaving only domestic systems, now atomized and operating with assets transformed in value and potential by the new economic conditions. This caused a whole series of problems for herding families, many of whom had difficulty marketing their produce, and who no longer had the support of hay or transportation that the collectives had provided. The organization of *otor* movement and the regulation of access to pasture, which had been overseen by collective and state farm officials, declined. Without mechanized transport and managerial imperatives, pastoral mobility diminished. The lack of hay reserves and collective motor pools that could have been used to deliver fodder and move livestock was one of the principal reasons for the disastrous losses of livestock in 1999–2001.

Distribution of Liabilities in the New Pastoral Sector

As Verdery argues (this volume), it is revealing to analyze new property regimes in terms of the distribution of liabilities, rather than simply goods and assets. In this case, property rights became stakes in a wider system or network of operations including objects, resources and the organization of labor. This also brought a share in the risk that the network might collapse or operate unsuccessfully.

The new pastoral sector proved to be extremely vulnerable to bad weather, as was made tragically clear in the winters of 1999–2001, when Mongolia lost some six million livestock, a fifth of the national total. These *zud* (disasters caused by sever weather) were the result of an unusually dry summer followed by a savagely cold winter, in which temperatures dropped as low as –46°C. Losses were concentrated in some regions – one province, Dundgov', was particularly badly affected, losing more than a quarter of its livestock. Across the country some two thousand households were left without any livestock whatever after the first winter, and many more were left with unviably small herds. These losses had a traumatic effect on the national mood. Newspapers described the spectacle, shocking for Mongolians, of herders going to find their livestock carrying axes and knives, rather than pole-lassoes, because all that was left for them to do was to hack meat from the piles of frozen carcasses.[12]

The sad reality is that although these two years saw unexpectedly harsh conditions, the crises were entirely predictable. Severe weather of this sort occurs periodically in Mongolia, and a number of measures had been developed to mitigate its effects. Mobility was an important technique; herds were moved from the worst-affected localities to areas where conditions were better. This could be done rapidly in the collective era as managers could use teams of trucks and coordinate movements centrally. The collectives and state farms also stockpiled hay, which could be used to provide extra fodder for exhausted animals, and this also relied upon the motor pools for distribution to pastoral encampments.

The livestock losses themselves are in fact less important than their differential effects on the livelihoods of pastoral households. Even in the hardest hit regions, total herd numbers could, under the collective system, be expected to recover in a few years. However, the postsocialist pattern of livestock ownership made half the Mongolian population directly dependent on their own herds for subsistence – a massive distribution of risk. Some herds were wiped out entirely, and the poorest households had so few livestock to begin with that they were vulnerable to any sort of loss. In the collective era even these dramatic levels of livestock loss, should they have somehow occurred, would not have threatened the basic food security of pastoralists. Risk, as well as property, had been centralized – first by the *negdel* and second by the state itself, which stood behind and ultimately underwrote the collective's operation. If livestock were lost they were generally accounted for as collective livestock rather than personal animals – one reason why "private" livestock raising appeared so efficient in the collective period. Although individual herding households might lose some income if livestock losses prevented them from fulfilling their plan, liability for losses was spread throughout the collective – and indeed, soft budget constraints meant that the collective's liabilities were shared to some degree by the entire centrally planned economy. But the tiny, independent pastoral producers created by the privatization of pastoralism now faced starvation should their livestock die. The Mongolian government, made acutely aware of this, began to develop systems for spreading risk that were compatible with the neoliberal economic reforms. In March 2001 the government opened debate on a new Livestock Insurance Law, in the hope of reducing the risks to pastoral producers.

Social networks have a powerful effect on the distribution of both opportunities and liabilities. Those with close kin in different sectors and regions are generally able to rely on them for help in times of trouble. Social networks also connect poor households to wealthier families, and this can provide a support network for many of the most vulnerable. However, such social resources are far from evenly distributed, and those without good networks are more vulnerable. In some remote districts shortages are region-wide, so that very few people have sufficiently widely extended networks to get what is needed.

Joint Property

New institutional settings for property emerged during decollectivization. For example, a form of joint property appeared in the early 1990s as the larger state and collective operations were dismantled. The government made provision for the formation of enterprises termed "cooperatives" (*horshoo* or *horshoolol*), to be formed by members pooling their shares of the collective to gain joint ownership of some section of the old *negdel*. Some of these were medium-sized productive opera-tions based on a former collective resource, such as a vegetable-growing or hay-cutting operation, or a small dairy. Together with what remained of the collectives, these represented all that was left of pastoral and agricultural productive institutions larger than the household. But the ability of these smaller operations to survive in the new economic conditions was limited.

An example of this type of enterprise was the Bayan Tsagaan *horshoolol* in Bayantumen *sum*, Dornod. Founded in April 1993, it was a relatively small organization – composed of ten families, all of whom were kin (Humphrey and Sneath 1999: 157–8). The cooperative was formed around former collective assets – some vehicles, a large winter animal enclosure, some haymaking and potato fields. The membership was based upon the kin network of the man central to forming it. The *horshoolol* was described as a temporary and experimental formation, which might be disbanded if it was not seen to be working well. By 1996 the Bayan Tsagaan had been disbanded. Indeed, after they were formed, the majority of productive enterprises of this type went bankrupt or ceased trading, and the average number of staff and livestock holdings of the surviving enterprises declined. Of the 370 established throughout the country by 1992, fewer than half (173) still existed in 1998.[13]

A second type of rural cooperative (*horshoo*) also emerged immediately after privatization. These were marketing cooperatives – small-scale voluntary associations of pastoral households, set up to sell their produce and deliver the consumer goods the members ordered in return. Several of these were established in almost every district in Mongolia, often one in each *bag* subdistrict. The joint property in this case consisted primarily of trading capital and in a few cases a vehicle or building. These fared even worse than the productive enterprises, however, and virtually all of them had collapsed within two or three years of their founding. In the pastoral districts of Renchinlhümbe and Hanh, for example, all of the *horshoo* that had been formed had ceased operating by 1994. They went under for a number of interrelated reasons: the collapse of state transport systems and consequently increased cost of providing transport themselves, lack of credit oppor-tunities, inability to pay up front, unwillingness of the local people to sell to them, and cash-flow problems that made it difficult to pay their staff.

The failure of the cooperatives indicates the importance of the institutional settings in which property exists – institutions that may form part of sociotechnical systems but that also extend beyond them.

In the case of the Bayan Tsagaan *horshoolol*, despite the fact that it was a formally constituted productive enterprise based on joint property, it nevertheless rested on the social institutions of kinship – all of the members were relatives of the founder. The primary institutional focus remained the household. The membership's commitment to the cooperative was mediated by their obligations toward their own immediate family and close kin. Members had little hesitation about withdrawing their investment if this ever seemed to be in the best interests of household, family, and friends. The cooperative joint property, then, was rather unstable; it tended to be converted into another form – in this case "private" household property – when it became clear that the cooperative sociotechnical operation was failing.

This illustrates the importance of institutional underwriting of such systems. Looking at the institutional frames of the various pastoral institutions that have operated successfully in Mongolian history, it is striking that they were all sociopolitical institutions as well as economic ones. It was not simply the narrowly economic functions of the old collectives or their predecessors that guaranteed their continued existence. Their depth in social and political dimensions provided them with the stability and the ability to command the labor they needed. Unlike the postsocialist cooperatives, membership was not voluntary or conditional on any short-term benefit. In an analogous way, membership of the household (*öröh*) was also largely unconditional, its miniature "citizenship regime" entailing a wealth of social obligations. These have remained secure institutional bases for sociotechnical operations and their associated forms of property.

In the postsocialist era the only pastoral institutions that have been increasing their livestock holdings have been certain pastoral households managing their "private" herds. This small stratum of wealthy pastoralists seems to be in a position to reestablish some larger pastoral operations and reap the benefits of economies of scale and extensive systems of pastoral movement. In 1992 seven households reportedly had more than 1,000 head of livestock. By 1999 this number had risen to 1,061, of which 41 had more than 2,000 animals.[14] Of course, these are still modest holdings in comparison with the rich operations of the pre-revolutionary period, and many are likely to have lost livestock in the winters of 2000 and 2001. However, the rapid increase of herd size these households were able to achieve is impressive. The richest of them, that of Henmedeh of Sergelen *sum* near Ulaanbaatar, had accumulated 2,358 animals by the end of 1995, and had over 2,800 in 1999. In 1996 Henmedeh employed four herdsmen, and by 1999 he had expanded his operation to include seven hired herders who worked for him under contractual arrangements very similar to the historical *süreg tavih* relations. Henmedeh owned a truck and jeep, and he and his employees maintained a wider system of pastoral movement than most of the other nearby households. It might be that in the future an increasing number of wealthy owners like Henmedeh will accumulate sufficiently large livestock holdings to establish intermediate-scale pastoral operations, drawing on the labor of poorer pastoral households.

However, it is likely to take a very long time for such operations to become large enough to include the bulk of pastoral households. Such wealthy and successful pastoralists represent a very small minority – in 1998 only 2 percent of herding households owned more than 500 livestock.[15] The bulk of the pastoral sector was composed of households with tiny herds. More than two-thirds of livestock-owning households owned fewer than 150 domestic animals – the sort of herd size needed to make a sustainable livelihood in pastoralism. These poor pastoralists are generally the most vulnerable to shocks such as *zud*, and after 1999 many thousands have had their livelihoods destroyed.

Conclusion

Particular technologies – industrial or pastoral – may be seen as crystallizing an associated property regime. In this chapter I have tried to show how forms of property and their value and character are constructed by wider sociotechnical networks and the citizenship regimes that permit their operation.

The first half of the twentieth century saw the Buddhist patrimonialism of pre-revolutionary Mongolian society displaced by Soviet modernism, and then in the 1990s, another major transformation as the state adopted policies inspired by market liberalism. Each of these programs entailed property and citizenship regimes within which rights to land were constructed in a particular way. In the pre-revolutionary period land was the subject of spiritual authorities and its use by herders was regulated as part of the sociopolitical system of the *hoshuu*. In the collective period "ownership" of, or rather jurisdiction over, land was identified with the secular Mongolian state and the virtually sacred Mongolian nation, and the use of land was regulated by local-collective and state-farm management. In both periods regimes of property and of citizenship were constituent elements of the pastoral sociotechnical systems that provided the productive base of the rural economy.

The postsocialist market-oriented reforms, however, can be seen to have disassembled an integrated pastoral system and created an atomized pastoral sector of subsistence-oriented pastoral producer households. The primary means for achieving this was the introduction of a new regime of ownership that transformed state and collective property into private property. The originally exogenous technological elements, such as trucks and hay-cutting machinery, which had been relatively well integrated into the collective structures, were detached and frequently unable to fulfill the function they had served. Large-scale systems of extensive land use decayed, and the results were a pastoral sector poorly adapted to the Mongolian environment – as the extent of livestock losses demonstrated.

The reform-era controversy over private rights to land reflects both the history of the region and the resilience of indigenous attitudes toward land. In pre-revolutionary and collective eras, property regimes for land reflected the requirements of mobile pastoral sociotechnical systems that were established by elites in both periods, and in the past these systems were antithetical to institutions of transactable private land ownership. Although most of Mongolia's steppe-land is unsuitable for agriculture, it is conceivable that land conversion from public to private ownership will again make agriculture as well as pastoralism profitable for a minority at the expense of the majority.[16] It is unsurprising that the Mongolian political debate has expressed these fears.

Decollectivization generated short-lived forms of joint property held by cooperatives and other enterprises, but these lacked the institutional and obligational depth of the domestic group. In the end the operations of the household were looked on as the primary site for both property and subsistence. Mongolia is in the process of developing a new relationship between public and private rights to land. The future form of the pastoral sector is likely to depend upon the degree to which this new property regime can be integrated into viable sociotechnical operations and strong institutional frames underwriting them.

Notes

1. Asian Development Bank 1992: 86–88. World Bank 1994: 9.

2. National Statistical Office of Mongolia 1999: 95, 45, Statistical Office of Mongolia 1993: 6.

3. Statistical Office of Mongolia 1993: 28; and Ministry of Agriculture and Industry of Mongolia, 1998: 2.

4. National Statistical Office of Mongolia 1999: 83–4.

5. The United Nations Systems in Mongolia 1999: 5, World Bank 1994: 41.

6. Bruun and Odgaard 1996: 26; United Nations Systems in Mongolia 1999: 6.

7. The idea that private ownership should be introduced to protect land from degradation is an old theme in the debate over public land. Garrett Hardin (1968) promoted this approach with his description of the "tragedy of the commons" – reviving an argument first made in nineteenth-century England. Hardin's argument was widely rejected by pastoral specialists who found that his model was a poor guide to understanding the public-access grazing systems found in most existing pastoral societies, in which land use is generally limited by a variety of social and environmental constraints. See Feemy, Fikret, McCay, and Acheson 1990; McCabe 1990.

8. The Prime Minister, J. Narantsatsralt, found it necessary to deny the charge publicly. "The ADB loan and the development, approval and implementation of the law are two separate things," he told *Ödriin Sonin* (Daily News). A. Delgermaa. *The UB Post*, 1 June 1999, No. 22 (159), p. 2.

9. For further discussion of pastoralism as a sociotechnical system see Sneath 1999.

10. By the end of the nineteenth century Outer Mongolia was probably exporting at least one million sheep units of livestock to China each year – about 5 percent of that total national herd. In the collective era the Mongolian state was also able to procure and export about 5 percent of the national herd, by my estimate. See Sanjdorj (1980: 91); State Statistical Office of Mongolia 1993: 45, 82; and State Statistical Office of the MPR 1981: 221).

11. The name and certain details of the informants have been changed to protect their anonymity.

12. D. Sainbayar, *Önöödör*, 13 February 2001, No. 36 (1193), p. 3.

13. Of these only 109 owned livestock, the average holding being a modest 1,780 head. Hödöö Aj Ahyin Horshoologchdyn Ündesnii Holboo (National Association of Agricultural Cooperative Members) Statistical Department, Pers. Comm. July, 1999.

14. *Zasagyn Gazar Medeel*, No 2(63) 1992; National Statistical Office of Mongolia 2002: 146.

15. 60 percent of herding households (165,000) had fewer than 100 animals, 37 percent (102,000) had fewer than 50, and about 12 percent (32,000) had fewer than ten. National Statistical Office of Mongolia 1999:96.

16. At the end of the Manchu Qing Dynasty, many Inner Mongolian princes sold land (illegitimately, according to Mongol views) to Chinese farmers, becoming rich on the proceeds.

References

Asian Development Bank. 1992. *Mongolia: A centrally planned economy in transition*. Oxford: Oxford University Press.

Asian Development Bank. "Agricultural Sector Study of Mongolia," Division 1, Agriculture Department, February 1994.

Bawden, C. R. 1968. *The modern history of Mongolia*. London: Weidenfeld and Nicolson.

Behnke, R., and I. Scoones. 1993. "Rethinking range ecology: implications for rangeland management in Africa." In *Range ecology at disequilibrium*. Edited by R. Behnke, I. Scoones, and C. Kerven. London: ODI, IIED and Commonwealth Secretariat.

Bruun, O. and O. Odgaard. 1996. "A society and economy in transition." In *Mongolia in transition: New patterns, new challenges*. Edited by O. Bruun and O. Odgaard. Nordic Institute of Asian Studies, Studies in Asian Topics, No. 22. Richmond, Surrey: Curzon Press.

Erdenijab, E. 1996. "An economic assessment of pasture degradation." In *Culture and environment in Inner Asia, Vol. 1*. Edited by C. Humphrey and D. Sneath. Cambridge: White Horse Press.

Feemy, D., B. Fikret, B. McCay, and J. Acheson. 1990. "Tragedy of the commons 22 years later." *Human Ecology* 18: 1–19.

Fernandez-Gimenez, M., and B. Batbuyan. 2000. "Law and disorder in Mongolia: Implementation of Mongolia's land law." Unpublished paper presented at the IASCP Biennial conference "Constituting the Commons: crafting sustainable commons in the New Millennium," Indiana University, May 31–June 4, 2000.

Griffin, K. 1995. "Economic strategy during the transition." In *Poverty and the transition to a market economy in Mongolia*. Edited by K. Griffin. New York: St Martin's.

Hardin, G. 1968. "The tragedy of the commons." *Science* 162: 1243–8.

Humphrey, C., and D. Sneath. 1995. "Pastoralism and institutional change in Inner Asia: comparative perspectives from the MECCIA research project." *Pastoral Development Network*, 39 (b), ODI.

Humphrey, C. and D. Smeath. 1999. *The end of nomadism? Society, state and the environment in Inner Asia*, Durham, NC: Duke University Press.

Lansing, S. 1987. "Balinese 'Water Temples' and the management of irrigation." *American Anthropologist* 89: 326–41.

McCabe, T. 1990. "Turkana pastoralism: A case against the tragedy of the commons." *Human Ecology* 18: 81–103.

Ministry of Agriculture and Industry of Mongolia, 1998, " Mongolian agriculture and agro-industry," Report available at http://www.agriculture.mn/agroindustry.htm#2.

National Statistical Office of Mongolia. 1999. *Mongol Ülsyn Statistikiin Emhtgel (Mongolian Statistical Yearbook), 1998*. Ulaanbaatar.

National Statistical Office of Mongolia. 2002. *Mongol Ülysn Statistikiin Emhtgel (Mongolian Statistical Yearbook) 2001*. Ulaanbaatar.

Natsagdorj, S. H. 1967. "The economic basis of feudalism in Mongolia." *Modern Asian Studies* 1: 3.

Nolan, P. 1995. *China's rise, Russia's fall: Politics, economics and planning in the transition from Stalinism*. London and Basingstoke: Macmillan.

Pfaffenberger, B. 1992. "Technology and social change." *Annual Review of Anthropology* 21: 491–516.

Pozdneyev, A. M. 1971 [1892]. *Mongolia and the Mongols*. Volume 1. Edited by J. Krueger. Bloomington: Indiana University Press.

Sanjdorj, M. 1980. *Manchu Chinese colonial rule in Northern Mongolia*. London: C. Hurst.

Simukov, A. D. 1936. "Materialy po kochevomu bytu naseleniya MNR." [Materials concerning the nomadic life of the population of Mongolia]. *Sovremennaya Mongoliya* [Contemporary Mongolia] 2: 49–57.

Sneath, D. 1998. "State policy and pasture degradation in Inner Asia." *Science* 281 (5380): 1147–8.

_____. 1999. "Mobility, technology and decollectivisation of pastoralism in Mongolia." In *Mongolia in the twentieth century: Landlocked cosmopolitan*. Edited by S. Kotkin and B. Elleman. Armonk, NY: M. E. Sharpe.

State Statistical Office of the MPR. 1981. *National economy of the MPR for 60 years 1921–81*. Ulaanbaatar: State Publishing House.

State Statistical Office of Mongolia. 1993. *Mongolyn Ediin Zasag, Niigem 1992* (Mongolian Economy and Society in 1992). Ulaanbaatar: J. L. D. Gurval.

United Nations Systems in Mongolia, 1999. *Annual Report 1998*. Report published on the Internet (http://www.un-mongolia.mn/publications/anrep98.pdf).

World Bank, 1994. *Mongolia: Country economic memorandum; priorities in macroeconomic management*. Report No. 13612-MOG. Country Operations Division, China and Mongolia Department, Asia and Pacific Regional Office, Manila.

Part III

Cultural Recognition

eight

At Home in the Violence of Recognition

Elizabeth A. Povinelli

I In the Australian spring of 1989, I found myself under a brilliant Northern Territory night sky face to face with a two-barrel shotgun. I was driving on a back road in the middle of the Daly River Aboriginal Land Trust to an outstation, Banagula, located on the southern coast of Anson Bay. With me was a group of older and younger women and men from Belyuen and the Daly River Mission, two small indigenous communities in the Northern Territory. Banagula is one of a series of indigenous named sites and territories stretching along that Territory's northwestern coast. The people in my truck considered this coastal region part of the country of their parents and grandparents. Even without the wayward shotgun, traveling to Banagula from Belyuen or the Daly River Mission is always difficult. The only way to reach Banagula and other southern coastal Anson Bay sites from the north is to travel across the Anson Bay by boat or to drive inland to the Daly River Crossing (bridge) and then back north across a vast wetland plain. This plain does not significantly dry until late November, if it dries at all. Without a boat, or the motor and petrol to run it, those who wish to visit Banagula must attempt to drive across this rugged, bone-jarring landscape, crisscrossed with soft mud that bogs down even four-wheel-drive vehicles, with deadly king brown snakes and pigs and pig wallows.

Pigs, or the possibility of them, started our problems. As we approached the Banagula flood plain, everyone in the truck began discussing how many pigs could be found there and how nice it would be to roast one at Banagula. To that end, we began, albeit at the last moment, to assess our ammunition situation. I had my shotgun. One of the men from the Daly River Mission had his. But between the two of us we had only a few cartridges. The man from Daly River suggested we divert from the main road and travel back inland to an Indigenous outstation. There, he thought, we would find a man he knew from whom he could borrow a few extra shotgun cartridges. Several older women protested. They noted the long and rough nature of the road to this outstation, the "different languages" spoken by inland Indigenous groups as opposed to coastal groups, and the lateness of the day. Persuaded by the man from Daly River, I went ahead anyway. And, indeed, before long the sun had set and the road had become virtually impassable in spots. It was at one of these spots that we saw another vehicle driving in the opposite direction toward us. Everyone got scared; we were not in "our" country. Some people in the truck urged me to turn around and speed away, not really an option given the condition of the road. I followed the advice of others who urged me to stop and wait to see what the other truck would do. It pulled up slowly alongside my right-side window. I rolled down my window, they theirs. Out of their window came a shotgun and two questions, "Who are you?" and "What are you doing here?"

"Say something, somebody, please," I whispered. But no one did, so I replied, "I am just driving these old people to their coastal country." "No coast around here." The gun inched closer to my temple. "Come on, somebody say something," I again whispered. The man from Daly River Mission stretched out of the darkness of my truck and, pointing to one of the older women, said to the men in the other truck, "You mob were at Wadeye last year? This old lady came and sat down for that young boy business last year." I relaxed. The Daly River man had found what is referred to locally as a "road" (also, "track") between our truck and their truck. These men pointing the gun at my temple had joined in this ceremony. For the next few minutes we engaged in a common local genre of talk, talk in which social relations are entailed by sketching verbally and non-verbally the various connections that exist among people. This was colloquially described as "joining up" people. Some aspects of this genre of talk are explicitly referential in the sense that they refer to some instance of shared practice: joint ceremonies, camps, language, and ancestral relations; such was the case when the man from Daly River noted the common ceremonial practice that existed between members of our truck and members of theirs. Other aspects are more purely performative in the sense that a speaker uses a linguistic code or register to demonstrate his or her status as an insider to a speech, ritual, or kinship community. All these speech acts were performative in a broader sense – they entailed the road we were driving on as "passable" by entailing the social relations that undergird human physical circulation in the region. Finally the gun was lowered and withdrawn into the cab of the truck, and we continued on our way. In the end we collected only three or four shotgun cartridges, shot no pigs, and never made it across the black-soil plain. The ground was still too soft. But we did construct, in the effort to pass through the region, some of the Indigenous social relations and circulatory conditions on which territoriality is built, renewed, and renegotiated. Some of these practices, I should note, are against the law of the Australian state.

This short anecdote could easily serve as an example of the types of conflict that arise when different indigenous groups make competing claims over the control and use of the same stretch of territory – that is, conflicts over the social organization of property. Recent debates among indigenous people in the north of Australia and among scholars in Australian Aboriginal Studies have focused on exactly this type of conflict, debating whether indigenous ownership of land and cultural materials should rest exclusively on principles of collateral kinship, ceremonial association, birth, residence, patrilineal and matrilineal descent, or some combination of these and other forms of social relationship. But this anecdote also serves to highlight a strong and fundamental contrast between liberal democratic stances toward what Michael Warner (2002) has called "stranger sociality" and northwest coast stances toward the same. And, by extension, it illustrates how even the modern state's authority over the life and death of its citizens and subjects is challenged in strongly multicultural societies, and how a new balance is negotiated between the state and the local over who should live and who should die, and on what basis. In this case, the conflict over what constitutes trespass – what makes trespass an intelligible violation of the social order in a place like Australia, where, from the perspective of federal law, there is no death penalty. There is a lot of state death, if one considers the state to be the locus of decisions affecting the wealth and health of the nation. And a lot of this state death is focused on rural Indigenous communities where the life expectancy is about twenty years lower for indigenous Australians than it is for non-indigenes.

Most discussions of Australian Indigenous property rights have focused on the first set of concerns, that is, on the social organization of traditional Indigenous land tenure and cultural property; the diversity of social organization among precolonial Indigenous groups; the transformation of this social organization under the pressure of settler colonialism; and the fit between traditional forms of property and the current content of land-claim and cultural-heritage legislation. Thus, a long-standing discussion has focused on whether, and how, major pieces of federal land-claim legislation were modeled on the social organization of land ownership in Arnhem Land, and whether this local model can be generalized to the entire continent. For the most part, "social organization" has referred to contextually abstractable principles of kinship, marriage, and descent, such as the principles of patrilineality or matrilineality. These so-called abstract principles are often contrasted to historical, or contextual, relations such as birth and residence in a place, or ceremonial associations to a place.

These debates have had an important intellectual and political impact on the state recognition of indigenous land rights and cultural property. And yet, those who debate have been somewhat reluctant to confront how a liberal state politics of recognition has provided the enabling matrix for contemporary indigenous property regimes and what liberal principles this matrix installs as indigenous men and women navigate through space – as they go about their ordinary tasks, as well as how they navigate the space of liberal multicultural sentiment when they engage in the more extraordinary task of suing for the return of their land. It is these regimes of liberal sentiment that interest me in this chapter. Thus I am less interested in the social organization of property – indeed I am less interested in property per se – than in how, through using or claiming property, an entire regime of liberal social relations is installed in Indigenous social life; and in how, through these regimes, a struggle between people is recast as a struggle among cultural abstractions. In order to do this, I first provide a quick review of the history of land-claim legislation in the Northern Territory of Australia. I then discuss how these pieces of legislation presuppose, and demand, a social and cultural form abstracted from the given time of social life, and through these presuppositions and demands transform a conflict between specific indigenous persons and particular state and capital interests in their land into a struggle between cultural rights and human rights. I close the chapter with a discussion of a possible counter-ethics of social space that veers off the matrix of liberal humanism.

A caveat. I am not proposing that the practices of Northwest coast indigenous men and women described above and below represent an authentic if diluted indigenous "custom," or that they do not. The quick recourse to a shotgun to settle the minor dispute over right of way on the Daly River road could as easily be an example of how the notion of common lands has been infected by the notion of private property, as an example of precolonial forms of dispute management. Men and women on the northwest coast do recount violent fights among the ancestors that arose out of "jealousy" over land and spouses. But, for the purposes of my argument, it matters very little whether these are new or old social imaginaries, newly concocted from the present burlesque of postmodernity or purely distilled from the true past.

I

Many people have discussed at length the history of indigenous land rights as they emerged in the context of an increasingly self-identified multicultural Australia (for a longer and still excellent review see Keen 1984). A standard version of that history goes something like this. In the 1960s a coalition of Indigenous and non-Indigenous activists gained limited state and public recognition of indigenous cultural property and land and social rights after nearly two hundred years of indigenous resistance to European settlement (Reynolds 1983; Lippman 1981; Lyons and Parsons 1989; Trigger 1992; Day 1994; Wright 1998). The first major piece of land legislation in modern Australia was the *Aboriginal Land Rights (Northern Territory) Act, 1976* (henceforth the LRA), which provided a legal mechanism for indigenous groups to seek the return of the traditional lands. The LRA established a number of regional Land Councils charged with administering these indigenous land claims, disputes that might arise from them, and financial dealings with private companies seeking to do business in Indigenous territory. In the Daly River Aboriginal Land Trust, for instance, the Northern Land Council helps to settle land disputes, administers visitor permits, and negotiates with private companies on behalf of its indigenous clients. Since 1976, when the federal parliament passed the first significant piece of legislation aimed at indigenous land rights, a significant percentage of land in the Northern Territory has been designated "Aboriginal land," most under a strong form of title (nearly 40 percent of land in the Northern Territory is now held under Aboriginal unalienable freehold; see Neate 1989).

The LRA took its central definition of the "traditional Aboriginal owner" from the dominant emphasis that British and Australian social anthropology placed on the social generativity of structures of kinship and descent. A structuring structure composed of two principles, sexual difference and heterosexual reproduction, provided the primitive dualities out of which the organization of all other social practices such as religion, property, and economics were built. The explicit influence of social anthropology on land-claim legislation has changed over time.

Most obviously, land-claim and native-title legislation state that an anthropological report must accompany a claim. Anthropology also initially provided the key interpretive background to the concept of the "local descent group." In his very first land-claim report, the first land commissioner Mr. Toohey accepted the argument of W. E. H. Stanner, a student of the "father" of British social anthropology, A. R. Radcliffe-Brown, that all traditional Indigenous societies reckoned the descent of territorial rights through the father and father's father (patrilineally) and that an indigenous person could belong in a full sense only to one local descent group and thus to only one territory. The descent of territorial rights was based on principles of human patrilineal descent; and territory was conceptualized as a set of bounded land units. In so accepting this academically mediated model of indigenous social organization, Toohey instantaneously cast all other means by which "traditional" Aborigines associate identifiable groups of people with particular countries, and all other means by which Indigenous men and women circulate through various countries, as distortions or supplements to the heterosexual machinery of human descent. The spiritual and material relationship that Indigenous men and women had to land, to the dead, and to the unborn were reduced *in the last instance* to the heterosexual reproduction of blood, *symbolically* narrowed and demarcated by the patrilineal totem. And circulatory practices were separated out from property relations on the basis of the difference between politics and economy or, in the classic language of social anthropology, on the basis of the difference between the clan and the horde.

Though continuing to restrict descent to heterosexual reproduction (and its symbolic equivalent, adoption), since 1979 land commissioners have moved significantly away from viewing the "local descent group" as a strict anthropological concept to viewing it as an ordinary concept and phrase.[1] Toohey himself would reverse paths in his 1981 *Finniss River* report, stating that the land commissioner should base his understanding of recruitment into a local descent group "on a principle of descent deemed relevant by the claimants," not on anthropological theory or debate (Finniss River Land Claim 1985, para. 161). The third land commissioner, Michael Maurice, also argued that legal judgment should be oriented to local beliefs when he stated in his 1985 *Timber Creek* report, "It is [a] religious bond with the world . . . that the Parliament has endeavored to recognize by its definition of traditional Aboriginal owner with its three elements: family ties to land; religious ties; and economic rights, i.e., to forage" (Timber Creek Land Claim 1985, para 92). The most generous reading of this legal genealogy of the local would understand these land commissioners to be attempting to liberate indigenous understandings and practices of local descent from the vice-grip of anthropological theory. And yet, the common-sense family of land-claim legislation remains the classical lineage model developed and refined during the heyday of British structural functionalism. This lineage model has not been displaced but merely expanded to include a more diverse set of filial and lineal principles – one- or two-step matrifiliation, ambilineality, cognation. And, more importantly, although the Australian parliament and courts do not demand any specific principle of descent, they still demand it. In other words, making the meaning of the "local descent group" local does not relieve locals from the demand that they give these terms meaning.

The *Native Title Act* was passed by the federal parliament in 1993 and significantly amended in 1995, as a response to the High Court decision *Eddie Mabo v State of Queensland*, which recognized native titles having existed in Australia when it was first colonized. The court had found that where the Australian state had not explicitly extinguished native title, Indigenous Australians had and still held that title if they maintained the traditional customs, beliefs, and practices that created the substance of its difference (see Povinelli 1998). The 1995 amendment made the *Native Title Act* a less effective vehicle for land redistribution. At the end of the day it provides a weaker form of title than the LRA, and a more protracted form of negotiation and litigation (Athanasiou 1998). Although a weaker form of title than the LRA, the *Native Title Act* and most other regimes of indigenous cultural recognition absorbed from the LRA the core social assumptions about what indigenous traditional social organization consisted of, even as they broke the horizon of previous legal assumptions about common-law perspectives on indigenous property. The *Native Title Act* acknowledged the validity of native title in Australia and rooted the difference of native title in the difference of indigenous cultural traditions. Perhaps not surprisingly, then, the law demanded, as the condition for recognizing the ongoing vitality of native title, that indigenous claimants establish their descent from the original inhabitants of the land under claim; the nature of the customary law for that land; their continued allegiance to that law; and their continued occupancy of the land. The charge of native tribunals, as with land commissioners, is merely to adjudicate at the level of primary fact whether or not title has disappeared "by reason of the washing away by 'the tide of history' any real acknowledgment of traditional law and real observation of traditional customs."[2]

These are the main statutory conditions scholars usually point to when discussing the conditions that the state imposes on indigenous social groups in exchange for various forms of title over their traditional lands. But there are other "forms" of social life that are less discussed, and it is to these that I now turn.

II

The LRA and Native Title Act do not merely demand a social form in the sense of a specific model of kinship, marriage, and descent. They demand that indigenous persons, or their legal and anthropological counsel, produce their social practices as ruled, and rule-able, by a set of social abstractions. Take for instance the LRA, which defines the traditional Aboriginal owner not as an individual but as a "local descent group" which has "common spiritual affiliations" to a site on the land that place *it* under "primary spiritual responsibility for the site" and for the land.[3] It is the descent group – a hybrid being part abstraction and part social fact – that "owns" the land, not any one or several persons. Likewise, the Native Title Act places procedural demands on indigenous applicants that necessitate their producing a form of social life that can break any and all contexts. The following guidelines for the application of a native-title claim, for example, mandate that, no matter how the descent character of the group is characterized, it be presented in such a way that it can break the horizon of context.

> The description [of the claimant group must be] clear enough to allow someone else to see whether any particular person is a member of the group. The basic principle is that there should be some objective way of verifying the identity of members of the group. The following are *examples only* of what may be an acceptable description:
>
> - biological relations of a person named in the native title claim group (and relations by adoption, or according to traditional laws and customs);
> - relations or descendents of a person named in the native title claim group, and people related by marriage to those relations or descendents, including people in de facto or multiple partnerships, where such relationships are recognized by that group's traditional laws and customs;
> - relations or descendents of a person named in the native title group, and people who have been adopted by those relations or descendents;

- people who belong to the group, according to its laws and customs
  Note: a description of the group's laws and customs may be required.[4]

These guidelines are an excellent example of the extension into indigenous social life of what Marx understood to be a critical feature of liberal capitalism, the social abstraction. They demand that the real-time nature of social negotiation be abstracted into a social form that can break the horizon of social space and time. Indigenous persons and their legal and anthropological counsel must abstract out of the ongoing diachronic unfolding of social relationality an objective, synchronic structure. And they must not only present a synchronic structure, but also characterize that structure as determining ongoing social life. The principles of descent cannot be based on local subjective arguments about what contextualizing conditions do or do not matter to the value of pure heterosexual descent.

The Marxist critic of language, V. N. Volosinov, outlined the social implications of this tendency to treat ongoing social practices (negotiations and conflicts about "proper" social identities, roles, and relations) as governed by socially divorced abstractions. In the Saussurean legacy, including the post-structuralist heresy, the possibility of linguistic (and social) meaning is seen to rest on the agency of relational abstraction. And yet, these "abstractions" are the product of social labor. (Note, I am not suggesting that they are the product of social agents in the usual sense of the term "agent," see Povinelli 2001.) We can begin by remembering that Saussure referred to structure as virtual in nature – all that exists in any actual world is instances of usage, of the remains of social activity. The analyst must abstract some structure from instances of usage (that is, engage in a specific socially informed textual activity). To make an abstraction abstract – removed from its conditions of production – the analyst must erase his or her acts of abstraction such that the "diagram" (the structure of a kinship diagram, for instance) appears to exist prior to and independent of both of these orders of practice. And more, the analyst must construct the diagram in such a way as to make it appear to determine these orders of practice. Thus, not only does the law of recognition mandate a social and affective (spiritualized kinship and descent) content of Indigenous territoriality; it mandates a specific ideological form of those social relations – agential, abstract, universalizing, context-breaking. Note, abstraction from context provides a way that people who are not involved, not local, can adjudicate a local scene. How would a state official judge a scene if he or she could not refer to a set of common principles? Well, perhaps he or she couldn't. And that is the point: without the ability of someone else to see it, cultural difference would detach from the conditioning of state evaluation.

These specific requirements of abstraction are mimetic to a more general dynamic informing the politics of recognition. Postcolonial critics have sketched out the dynamics of recognition in colonial regimes (Fanon 1967; Bhabha 1994; Spivak 1999). Strongly influenced by Alexander Kojeve's reading of Hegel, some of these French- and Italian-influenced scholars saw the problem of colonial recognition as grounded in the problem of identity, the agony of the subject's confrontation with an other. But unlike the culturally deracinated referent of Kojeve's metropolitan struggle for identity, the naked I and the naked you, the struggle for recognition in colonial worlds was always already marked by a civilizational (and later cultural) difference. To put it simply, the condition of livability for colonized people depended on the colonized subject's ability to mimic the civilizational structures of the colonizer, central to which was the assumption of the human I as necessary to the enunciation of the sovereign subject – or for that matter any subject, split or whole. The discourse of cultural imperialism not only said to the colonized "you (culture) be me (civilization)" but "you (culture) must be me (civilization) in order to secure the object of value." Now this object of value could be anything – wealth, personal worth, or life itself. And, as Homi Bhabha and others have observed, this call for the full introjection of the colonizer's civilizational achievement could not be realized because it depended on the evaluative recognition of the colonizer himself. The more accurate form of the colonial proposition would be something like this: "you (culture) be me (civilization) in such a way that I (civilization) can recognize myself (civilization) in you (culture)." But the emergence of the "must," the marker of force in this scene of desire, was itself a historical achievement of those persons struggling against imperialism and colonization. Through social struggle, critics of colonialism and imperialism denaturalized the orientation of recognition ("you, of course, desire to be me; desire to have, or be, the things I desire") and they made explicit the cultural condition of this recognition. That is, they helped to show that, if this was a Hegelian struggle, it was an unfair struggle from the start, and not just at the end. It was not that the Master won because he was willing to put his life (civilization) on the line, but because he never was willing to, nor had to.

The form of address in multicultural societies has a genealogical resemblance to the form of address in colonial societies, even as the form of the variables has altered. In multicultural societies the condition of livability for minority and subaltern people depends on the colonized subject's ability to mimic a purified and abstracted form, but this time his or her own cultural past. "You be (traditionally) yourself." "Be yourself (traditionally)." Elsewhere I have discussed the impossibility of achieving this form of identity. Here I note simply that this new form of "recognition" is as much a demand as the older form. And further, it is a demand whose achievement continues to depend on evaluative recognition by an other. Again, the more accurate forms of the multi-cultural proposition would be: "you be yourself for me" and "you be yourself in such a way that I can recognize you without being undone." This is to say little more than what all liberal advocates and critics of multiculturalism note: cultural difference has its limits and these limits are defined as lying outside the evaluating culture. As the guidelines for preparing a native title application note, "someone else [must be able] to see." The "for me" of the demand "you be yourself" breaks open Indigenous social life to a dynamic of evaluative tension outside itself – it turns the truth of the local outside itself.

These statutes, and the public discourse surrounding them, recast the struggle between settler and indigenous social life and territorial associations, practices, and movements as a struggle between contempo-rary indigenous persons and their traditional customs. The social struggle between settler and indigenous territorial practices is abstracted and projected, first, onto an interpretative battle between the abstrac-tions of common law and customary law and, second, onto a "simple" comparison between a corrupt version of a people's here-and-now social practices and their own ideal version of their historical selves. State law is characterized and made to behave as a neutral referee, establishing as a matter of fact the contemporary relationship between a people and their own abstract traditional orders and mediating the limit of tolerance. But the limit of tolerance returns us to the opening scene and to the deepest and most difficult form of imposed liberal humanism – the concept of the human as a mode of liberal power. Claiming property within this regime of recognition installs not merely the agency of abstraction but the agency of the human as a neutral point that lies outside all claims on, or by, culture.

III

There we sat on a rutted dirt road under a sharp dark sky. No one was happy, though excitement was as clearly in the air as the stars overhead.

In the ensuing conversation, no one appealed to the potential shooter on the basis of his or my humanity, nor did anyone evoke the principles of cultural and social tolerance. Indeed, if an "appeal" to anything occurred, it was to a specific shared past. The value of our lives rested not on their abstract unity through a common concept, but their specific unity through a common practice. The value being recognized, if recognition is the appropriate term here, was the value of specific activities and the principles for connecting people through these activities. Some of these activities could be said to be intentional forms of association and contiguity (the decision to participate in a ceremony), some nonintentional (the place where one was born). Thus we can say that the people within my truck and within the other truck shared minimal but sufficient interactional stances even though their life experiences were very different. No one later questioned the legitimacy of the gunman's actions, or the legitimacy of what he might have done, although some people thought he was acting too quickly.

But in what sense is recognition the appropriate term, or concept, to apply to what we were doing that night? We could begin with the dehumanizing gesture of the gun threat (and what general principles of stranger sociability we can draw from it). But characterizing the gesture of the gunman in this way would be wrong, I think, because the human was not necessarily present in such a way that it could be reduced or removed (dehumanized). It can be hard to imagine social life without the social presuppositionality of the "human" or of "humanity." And, after one hundred thirty-three years of settlement in north Australia, it would be somewhat absurd to suggest that the concept of the human is absent in the indigenous Daly River. Indeed, indigenous men and women I know well do sometimes refer to something like a shared humanity that grounds the differences between social groups. However most of these conversations refer to the dehumanizing attitudes that racialized and racist policies and attitudes create. Young people and old people will say in these contexts that underneath white and black skin is "alla same person," often pinching their skin as they do so.

Be this as it may, when it comes to other indigenous persons, especially indigenous strangers, reference to a common humanity, or personhood, are rarely if ever heard, and even with non-indigenous people they are not necessarily relevant. The sudden appearance of a stranger in human form could signal the presence of a *nyuidj* (an ancestral being) or *munggul* (a sorcerer), or more mundanely, the presence of a human difference so great that no commonality with it exists. What is present in this form of difference is the absence of known "roads." What I mean by this might be clarified if we think of a set of points that have yet to be connected into any diagram. What that diagram might be holds promise and peril, but in the first instance, the diagram is simply absent. This type of absence is quite different from the absence of a humanity, posited as that without which fair treatment is suspended. In humanist recognition, the human (and the dehumanized and the unhuman) is always already haunting the as-of-yet diagrammed space. The question addressing the people connecting the dots, so to speak, is whether after they do so something recognizable as human will emerge. In other words, the ethics of humanist recognition is already determined in the last instance. A mandate hovers over a practice – construct social connectivity as you will, according to your customs, but construct it so that a human being is apparent or risk the consequences of being inscribed in humanism's internal contradiction, dehumanization. Thus the violence of dehumanization is internal to the scene of humanism. But it is not to the scene in which I was a participant.

What we did in that truck, that night, was not premised on the value of cultural difference and cultural tolerance any more than it was premised on the notion of a shared humanity or inhumanity. This is certainly not to say that what we did was posited on cultural intolerance and imperialism. It is to claim a discursive space not already defined by a particular history of discourse. It is to suggest that we should, and how we might, throw the ethics and practices of recognition off the humanist matrix without triggering the dehumanizing reflex of that same matrix. But if neither a human (nor an inhuman) nor a tolerant (nor an intolerant) recognition organized our activities that night, what were some of the positive features of what we were doing? How might these relate to local practices of territoriality? I answer this by way of detour, returning to the statutory mandate that to be recognized as the Indigenous owners of land, claimants must be a local descent group.

IV

Land claims and native title claims assume and mandate a specific form of heterosexual reproduction as that without which property is not transferred. But, for the older men and women in my truck on that night in 1989, a local descent group was not a taken for natural fact, nor an abstraction they applied to other social relations such as marriage, ceremony, and economy. It was unclear at the time what mechanisms of connectivity held more value, and in what contexts. Then, older men and women would emphasize the "chain relation" of "family" members rather than their descent relation. Chains between persons and places could be established on the basis of affinity, descent, birth, ceremonial knowledge and rank, language association, friendship, and history. The emphasis, in other words, was on the connectivity that allowed for circulation through regions, the inclusive use of landscapes, ceremony, economy, and sociality. So, for example, we could understand the social group these men and women describe as having been "joined up" between 1850 and 1950 to be the result of sexual difference and heterosexual reproduction. If we did we would see marriage as occurring first between proximate countries within a linguistically defined territory; then between proximate language territories; and, finally, between the two ends and middles of this coastal landscape. It is a mistake, however, to view representations of social groups as regimented by heterosexuality or *that which the diagram diagrams* to be heterosexual descent – though it is perfectly reasonable to describe the entire group and specific subsections as a local descent group. Before the sexual, however, was a geo-textuality debate about how social space should be composed. A complex of economic, personal, and ceremonial relations and practices is figured out of local notions of spatial proximity, directionality, and seriality (Povinelli 2002).

Even if heterosexual reproduction (kinship and descent) is a natural fact found in every society, that fact says very little about the specific value it has relative to other modes of social connectivity and circulation. To see what is at stake we must shift from viewing kinship and descent as a universal of *human* life on the basis of its presence in all *human* societies to treating it as one concrete member in a complex and concrete set of social relations. Once kinship and descent have been reconcretized and reembedded in the specific social lives of specific persons, a very different series of questions can be asked: Which has more value in a given context, a ceremonial or descent tie to a person or a place? Does a certain density of types of connections to a person or a place become more valuable than the sheer fact of being born into the abstract order of a descent group? Moreover, what are the contexts in which any of these modes of relationality (or connectivity) matter? Here I return to the question of whether recognition is the appropriate term, or concept, to apply to what we were doing that night or whether some other concept, such as connectivity, might be more useful. And this is exactly why studying indigenous property rights in strongly multicultural societies like Australia so important. They demand that local practices and conceptions of space and sociality be re-figured for "Western" courts in two ways: (1) local practices and concepts must be compatible with abstract humanism; and (2) local attempts to make them compatible must be erased.

The notion of connectivity provides a more positive sense to the territorial practices of indigenous men and women that I have known over the last seventeen years. The territories they traverse, use, and take care of are built on a set of negotiated roads into and out of social groups and social places. These roads provide movement through places as well as the use of places. Social cohesion, social groupness, is a contextually sensitive effect of the density of these roads between people and places. Different, potentially dangerous, people and places, and thus social and territorial impenetrability, appear when the known roads between a person (or persons) and other persons or places become exceedingly thin, absent, or impossible to enact performatively. No social group is simply "the same" – simply positable or actionable on the basis of a "we" or "our" form which abstracts out all difference. The abstraction does not "hold" property. A group of people may approach an exclusive form of "our," as in our place, our country, and our ceremony. But they never exactly reach this form of identity because they come into a world already layered with preexisting connectivities and circulations and because not everyone in the group has exactly the same social history to these connectivities. Children have different places of birth, cere-monial allegiances, moieties, and sentiments than one or more of their parents. Nor do the people I know try to overcome this difference, to seek a social state without reserve. Difference is. And it is used to negotiate new social facts. Negotiations over what is the language of a country, where the country begins and ends, whether the country is defined by its borders or radiates out from specific Dreaming sites, what are the relevant and most valuable sites of connectivity – these are not taken to be cultural failures or signs of a lost tradition, but the very nature and possibility of social life.

The ethics of constructing a social diagram out of social parts is surprisingly neutral among the people I know. They certainly view the ability to "join-up" people and social lives as a talent (*djewalabag*, a cleverness, or intellectual brilliance). They even claim that this ability is a social necessity, especially in the shadow of the often violent colonization of the north, in which the settler government rounded up and interned disparate indigenous social groups in small Indigenous compounds. They celebrate their parents' cleverness in "joining up" (fitting together) the disparate, often disputing groups that local desires and the bureaucratic state had thrust together. And yet no one says, or otherwise indicates, that in the presence of difference (in the absence of a known road) someone should or ought to make a road between themselves and the stranger. The ethics of difference might be said to be an acknowledgment of the necessity of overcoming difference without an imperative of doing so.

But roads in the north are paved and unpaved, recognized as public or private by the state, and remembered by Indigenous men and women as having been cut by their ancestors. State law provides new roads Indigenous people exploit into and out of land in two ways worth mentioning. First, land-claim legislation abstracts and elevates one mode of relationality (descent) over all others. This demand is not without consequence. The expectation that indigenous claimants and their advocates must present a social group in such a way that someone who knew nothing about the group could specify it, runs smack against the practices of negotiated connectivity seen in our interaction. And yet, in many parts of Indigenous Australia, certainly in the north, the principle (or road) of descent is now a vital part of intra-indigenous social negotiations. Whether this is considered a positive or negative development depends on where you sit and how well your truck works. If an indigenous person, or group of persons, has only one form of connectivity to a place, and that form is membership in a descent group, then they are wise to cite, and insert, the full weight of the law in their struggles for recognition and legitimation. Of course, the opposite is equally true. Those indigenous groups having dense birth, ceremonial, economic, and social ties to each other and a place but who do not constitute a descent group find no solace in this law of recognition.

Second, to understand the disjuncture between ideologies of recognition and practices of territoriality, property forms need to be situated in two broader contexts: namely, law as a more general juridical field and the public as an orientation of legitimation. These two broader contexts help illuminate how "indigenous property" is the misrecognized relation that settlers have to their own ideological impasses projected into their struggle with indigenous subjects, rather than the state's recognition of the relation between an indigenous group and their spiritualized ideals. Let us return once again to the Daly River, this time unpacking why some of the women were afraid of the approaching truck.

In Daly River indigenous communities, as in many communities in settler and indigenous Australia, people debate how to alleviate high rates of substance abuse, suicide, and the more general malaise arising from extreme structural poverty. In the Northern Territory, in the mid-1990s, 60 percent of Indigenous Australians earned between $1,000 and $9,000. Nationally, indigenous unemployment hovered around 35 percent. Not only is economic space fragmented, based on a person's race and settlement history, national generational time is out of joint also, a disjunction which has significant ramifications for a culturally-based law of recognition. In the mid-1980s, government agencies reported that the average life expectancy of indigenous Australians was only 52 years. By 1998 it had inched up to 57 years for men and 62 years for women. As startling are the imprisonment rates of indigenous men. Who then, or what, is responsible for these gruesome statistics?

Many settler and indigenous leaders have called for the resumption of customary forms of ritualized punishment as a means of "settling down black youth." For instance, in 1996 the Queensland Minister of Aboriginal and Islander Affairs, Mr. Lingard, proposed "a radical scheme" that would make "customary law – including the use of corporal punishment – compulsory in isolated black communities." The legislation was intended to police juvenile crime in remote communities through the policed agency of traditional culture, thereby unburdening state resources.

State support of customary law in criminal cases would seem to reinforce the High Court's recognition of customary law as the foundation of native title. Many members of indigenous communities have directly encountered this latter rhetoric of support. Several women riding in the truck to Banagula had participated in, exchanged gossip about, or watched relatives testify in numerous land claims for country in and around the Daly River and Belyuen – or would soon do so. In addition, they and their male relatives had participated in numerous discussions with Aboriginal Land Councils, mining companies, and tourism outfits about the relationship between customary beliefs and development schemes; all these groups emphasize, in the company of indigenous persons, the respect they feel for indigenous customs. Finally, most indigenous people have a more diffused sense that public opinion now "respects" and "recognizes" the worth of Indigenous culture – within limits. But note, although the Australia High Court argued that customary law provided native title with its foundation, as I mentioned above, neither the Australian state nor the judicial branch has ever recognized the validity of indigenous customary law. Customary law is not relevant in charging persons under criminal law. (Many courts do allow customary law to influence the sentencing of an indigenous defendant.)

Moreover, the state-backed, compulsory return of customary law is mediated by majoritarian commonsense standards of corporeality. Even while calling for the resumption of customary forms of punishment, the Queensland minister stated that "extreme punishments such as spearing would be ruled out" though "other forms of corporal punishment would be acceptable but would have to be monitored" (Emerson 1996). Everyone in our trucks understood this discursive disjuncture and the impasse it presented in ever realizing the native title conditions imposed upon them, even realizing the autonomous condition of their own social practices. Though the recognition of native title rests on Indigenous persons demonstrating a continued adherence to their customary law, criminal law may well sanction aspects of it. In *Barnes v the Queen, 1997*, for instance, the court refused bail to an Indigenous applicant charged with the manslaughter of another Indigenous man. The Indigenous man had requested, through his counsel, to be released on bond in order to return to the indigenous community, Lajamanu, to receive traditional punishment. The applicant's counsel described to the court the content of traditional punishment for murder in terms not foreign to Curr's own description of the Bangarang: "spearing of both of the applicant's legs four or five times, using sharp and shovel-nose spears; punches with fists to the applicant's face and chest; blows to the applicant's head and back with the use of large heavy wood boomerangs; and similar boomerangs being thrown at the applicant, who would have a small shield with which to protect himself" (McGrath 1997/1998). The court found that bail in this case would be unlawful – the tacit authorization of an assault intended to kill or cause grievous harm to the victim. As Max Weber and others have noted, intentional acts of grievous bodily harm remain the legally sanctioned privilege of the state. Practices that provide robust evidence of the existence of traditional laws so vital to native title and land-rights cases may not be the grounds for an efficacious argument in criminal law courts.

Critical reflection on indigenous law does not merely occur within the juridical field, to borrow a phrase of Pierre Bourdieu. These cases do, however, provide critical discursive grounds and language for public debate about cultural difference and cultural evil. Cases like the above two circulate in the mass-mediated public sphere, reanimating already existing archives of public memory, prejudice, and sensibility, inciting public debates about what indigenous law, ceremony, and culture are really all about and whether the nation and its institutional bodies should protect, enhance, or support them.[5] They continually reopen the question of who and what "we" are as a nation, where "their" customs, beliefs, and practices fit in, and on what basis and in what contexts "we" can judge "them." And they divert attention from potentially radical challenges to the nation and the status of its core values such as "democracy" and the "common law." Moreover, they change the vector of who is responsible for these conditions of Indigenous social life: Indigenous people themselves or the Indigenous bureaucracies like the Northern Land Council. After all, public pundits note, a significant amount of land has been returned to Indigenous groups and their culture has been recognized as having worth. In High Court decision, *Wik v. the State of Queensland (1996)*, the majority decision put it this way, "To the extent that the tide of history has not washed away traditional laws and real observance of traditional customs, their legitimacy and content rest upon the activities and will of the indigenous people themselves."[6] After such a radical change of commonsense notions of social responsibility, there can be little surprise over the anti-multiculturalism backlash in the mid-1990s.

As I have noted elsewhere, relatives of some of the men and women in our trucks would make headlines several years after this event. Several men from the Peppimenarti Community, a small Indigenous community located south of the Daly River, went on trial for, and were eventually found guilty of, manslaughter. The public spectacle of the trial primarily revolved around the defense argument that the death was an accidental result of men's customary ritual business and thus not subject to the Australian penal code (Watt 1992a, 1992b). Long before this public trial and its circulation in the press, indeed, during the same time we were making our way to Banagula, indigenous men were debating the implications of resuming certain modified forms of ritual practice. A charge of murder or manslaughter might be one implication if the person holding the gun to my temple had argued successfully that I should be shot according to "customary law." But there are more insidious re-articulations of indigenous practices than the translation of certain territorial practices into criminal acts. At stake is the subject of action, her relation to herself, and her practices of community under the moral rather than abstract criminal signatures of Justice, Fairness, Repugnance, and Right.

Notes

1. In one of his reports Toohey stated, "The words 'local', 'descent' and 'group' are ordinary English words to which a meaning can be attached, given a context which in this case is the Land Rights Act. The matter should not be approached with some preconceived model in mind to which the evidence must accommodate itself. Rather it is a matter of the conclusions to be drawn from the evidence. A local descent group may be 'recruited on a principle of descent deemed relevant by claimants.'" (See Lander, Warlpiri, Anmatjirra Land Claim, para 89.)

2. *The Wik People v. the State of Queensland, 1996. Australian Law Review* 141: 46.

3. The *Aboriginal Land Rights (Northern Territory) Act 1976* also stipulates the traditional Aboriginal owner must be entitled to forage as of right, but this entitlement has never been the basis of a decision.

4. National Native Title Tribunal, "Guidelines to Applicants, Registration test information sheet, No 2," October 1998.

5. *Barnes v Queen* was reported in the *Sydney Morning Herald*, as, periodically, are other cases which strain the easy reconciliation of the law of cultural recognition and the "real" of Aboriginal customary law.

6. *Wik v. the State of Queensland, (1996).* In *Wik*, the High Court was asked to decide the status of native title on pastoral lands. Did native title survive the granting of a pastoral lease, or was it diminished or extinguished? The High Court ruled that native title was not necessarily extinguished by pastoral leases, but that pastoral rights were superior rights to native title where there was a conflict between them. The ruling was important because a large portion of land available to native-title claims lies on current or former pastoral lands.

Refernces

Agamben, Giorgio. 1998. *Homo Sacer: Sovereign power and bare life.* Trans. Daniel Heller-Roazen. Stanford, CA: Stanford University Press.

Athanasiou, C. 1998. "Land rights or native title?" *Indigenous Law Review* 4: 14–15.

Bhabha, Homi. 1994. "The Other question: Stereotype, discrimination and the discourse of colonialism." In *The Location of Culture*, 66–84. London: Routledge.

Day, Bill. 1994. *Bunji: A story of the Gwalwa Daraniki movement.* Canberra: Aboriginal Studies Press.

Emerson, Scott. 1996. "Tribal law plan for black youth." *The Australian* 8 August, p. 4.

Fanon, Franz. 1967. *Black face, white mask.* New York: Grove.

Finniss River Land Council. 1981. *Report by the Aboriginal Land Commissioner, Mr. Justice Toohey.* Canberra: Australian Publishing Service.

Keen, Ian. 1984. "A question of interpretation: The definition of 'traditional Aboriginal owners' in the Aboriginal Land Rights (NT) Act." In *Aboriginal land-owners: Contemporary issues in the determination of traditional Aboriginal land ownership.* Edited by L. R. Hiatt, 24–45. Sydney: University of Sydney Press.

Klymicka, Will. 1995. *Multicultural citizenship.* Oxford: Oxford University Press.

Lander, Warlpiri, Anmatjirra Land Claim, *Report by the Aboriginal Land Commissioner, Mr. Justice Toohey.* Canberra: Australian Government Printing Service.

The Law Reform Commission. 1986. *The recognition of Aboriginal customary laws.* Vol. 1, Report no. 31. Canberra: Australian Government Printing Service.

Lippman, L. 1981. *Generations of resistance: The Aboriginals' struggles for justice.* Melbourne: Longman.

Lyons, Pamela, and Michael Parsons. 1989. *We are staying: The Alyawarre struggle for land at Lake Nash.* Alice Springs: IAD Press.

McGrath, Shane. 1997/1998. "Traditional punishment prevented: Barnes v The Queen." *Indigenous Law Bulletin* 4.8: 18.

Neate, Graham. 1989. *Aboriginal land rights law in the Northern Territory.* Chippendale, NSW: Alternative Publishing Cooperative.

Peirce, Charles Sanders. 1998. "What is a sign?" In *The essential Peirce:* Selected philosophical writings, volume 2 (1893–1913). Edited by the Peirce Edition Project, 4–10. Bloomington, IN: Indiana University Press.

Povinelli, E. A. 1994. *Labor's lot: The history, culture and power of Aboriginal action.* Chicago: University of Chicago Press.

——. 1998. "The state of shame: Australian multiculturalism and the crisis of Indigenous citizenship." *Critical Inquiry* 24: 575–610. Special Issue: *Intimacy.* Edited by Lauren Berlant.

——. 2001. "Sexuality at risk: psychoanalysis (meta)pragmatically." In *Homosexuality and psychoanalysis.* Edited by Tim Dean and Christopher Lane, 387–411. Chicago: University of Chicago Press.

——. 2002. *The cunning of recognition: Indigenous alterities and the making of Australian multiculturalism.* Durham, NC: Duke University Press.

Reynolds, Henry. 1983. *The other side of the frontier: Aboriginal resistance to the European invasion of Australia.* Sydney: Penguin Books Australia, Ltd.

Spivak, Gayatri. 1999. *The Critique of Colonial Reason: Toward a History of the Vanishing Present.* Cambridge, MA: Harvard University Press.

Timber Creek Land Claim. 1985. *Report by the Aboriginal Land Commissioner, Mr. Justice Maurice.* Canberra: Australian Government Publishing Service.

Trigger, David. *Whitefella comin': aboriginal responses to colonialism in Australia.* Cambridge: Cambridge University Press.

Warner, Michael. 2002. *Publics and counter-publics.* New York: Zone Books.

Watt, Bob. 1992a. "Flogging a custom, a court told." *Northern Territory News*, 28 July, p.3;

——. 1992b. "Flogging outside law." *Northern Territory News*, 6 August, p. 3.

Weber, Max. 1994. *Weber, political writings.* Edited by Peter Lassman and Ronal Speirs. Cambridge: Cambridge University Press.

Wright, A., (ed.). 1998. *Take power like this old man here: An anthology celebrating twenty years of land rights in Central Australia, 1977–1997.* Alice Springs: Jukurrpa Books.

Cultural Rights and Wrongs: Uses of the Concept of Property

Michael Rowlands

A n aspect of cultural rights is the protection of "cultural property." Cultural property requires protection to the extent to which it forms the objectification of a right to collective expression and identity (cf. Niec 1998). Unlike human rights, which are rights of the individual, cultural rights are claimed collectively by those who identify themselves as of common descent, ethnic origin, or shared religion. Moreover, such claims are justified by the argument that cultural property is not a matter of individual creativity but rather of inheritance through collective transmission from the past into the future. This would sum up the argument that there is a special relationship between cultural rights and cultural property, one that stands in a certain paradoxical relationship to that between human rights and personal rights in property. The purpose of this chapter is to explore the extent to which there is a conflict between individual and collective rights and, if so, what implications are to be drawn from it.

The potential conflict that might exist is embedded in notions of property and, in particular, in the well-known distinction, formulated by Maine in *Ancient Law,* between "movable" and "immovable" goods (Maine 1986 [1963]: 264). Cultural rights legislation is influenced by the evolutionary notion that the ownership of movable goods was encouraged by the development of market economies and the freeing of personal property from collective controls. Because of this assumption about the association of cultural rights with premodern property relations, cultural property has suffered from imprecise definition and sometimes downright hostility, from being characterized as a "backward" form of collective ownership. As Posey and others have argued, cultural rights are seen to restrict individual ownership and the alienation of goods, thus "threatening such basic tools of international industry and trade as Intellectual Property Rights" (Posey 1998: 42). The notion of "inalienability," which was opposed to "modern" forms of exchange and value production, had therefore to be reappropriated and reconfigured by anthropologists into forms of proprietary claim that, rather than being remnant or peripheral, could instead be recognized as constituted within modern market relations (cf. Gell 1992, Carrier 1997). Annette Weiner pointed out, citing Maine, that by imitating the distinction between immovable and movable goods, inalienability requires that goods inherited through time should not at the same time be freely exchanged. The "paradox of keeping-while-giving" is the reconciliation of exchange with the ideal that "what makes an object inalienable is its exclusive and cumulative identity with a particular series of owners through time" (Weiner 1992: 32). But this argument did not resolve the conflict between collective and individual rights except by reasserting not only the primacy of the former over the latter but also the priority of inheritance over exchange, i.e., the primacy of "keeping-while-giving."

Several recent studies using Weiner's argument have shown the variable nature of alienable/inalienable categories and the ways in which both forms of property may coexist (Kopytoff 1986; Godelier 1999; Strathern 1988; Thomas 1991). If cultural property is not some evolutionary remnant or the consequence of a lack of exchange value, then we need to conceive of cultural rights as a means of defining a distinct form of property, which can share with more individualized notions of property the potential for the creation of value. The obvious example of this is the exchange value of an image. However singular or unique an item of cultural property might be, not only can one pay to see it in a museum and gallery but also it can have an exchange value realized through the sale of copies of images and their copyright. In this case it scarcely matters whether "control of one's own culture" is really about keeping cultural knowledge to oneself alone or is a means of claiming a form of property that can generate a unique form of exchange value. It is the inalienable and collective quality of cultural property that makes this a different form of value and orders social relations as a collective right to lay claim to its possession and to profit from this.

Moreover, significant changes have been recognized in the conditions for making such claims. The moral rights dimension of intellectual property may account in part for this since it is technologically easier than ever to lay claim to an original and sell a copy (cf. Brown, this volume). But besides the value question, there is also a wider political context, which asserts that cultural property, defined as heritage, now plays a much larger role in defining the right to exist. In an influential article on the rise of cultural fundamentalism in Europe, Verena Stolcke mentions that "cultural difference is now understood increasingly in terms of the possession of distinct cultural heritage rather than idioms of race and ethnicity" (Stolcke 1995: 5). By drawing our attention to a perceived need for a discrete cultural identity, she highlights a point made by others: namely, that a shift has occurred from a politics of redistribution to a politics of recognition. Both Charles Taylor (1994) and Nancy Frazer (1995) have argued that gaining cultural recognition has displaced socioeconomic redistribution as the remedy for injustice and the goal for political struggle (the redistribution-recognition dilemma). The notion that cultural difference is simply a strategic response to the need to control and redistribute resources seems quite antithetical to the essentializing claim of a politics of recognition. The right to exist asserts instead a claim to a unique identity supported and identified with an objectified notion of culture that may be gained or lost but not exchanged. What this means is that in order for injustice to be recognized, it is necessary not only to deal with the conditions that erode identity but also to arouse feelings of loss and the need of redemption.

In Stolcke's argument we can recognize a trend toward basing identities on claims to essentialist pasts and the purification of cultural origins. Cultural heritage, by claiming to justify the possession of a distinct cultural property as a right, objectifies these identities. More-over, there seems to be no problem in defining heritage as a unique cultural property and also treating it as a form of exchange value realized through tourism, sale of souvenirs, theme parks, and the "Disneyfica-tion" of the past. The growth of the heritage industry is one example of a politics of recognition, which attaches value to monuments, objects, and intangible heritage so as to define identity through the possession of cultural property. Instead of a universalist notion of property through which rights of legal ownership can be assured, a gray area of moral/ethical accessibility opens up, based on the creative power of reuniting people with their pasts. Separation and grievance for a loss unfulfilled, whether of people or cultural things, also entails demands for recognition (cf. Feuchtwang 2003). It can be argued that what makes particular forms of cultural property the objects of hatred and violence is precisely the conditions which transform grief into unresolved grievance, loss as suffering whose resolution can only be anticipated in a future act that holds the "community of suffering" together.

Cultural Property and Rights

On 6 December 1992 at Ayodha in Northern India, the Babri Masjida, a 450-year-old mosque, was attacked and demolished by Hindu fundamentalists. They claimed that the mosque stood on the foundations of a Hindu temple marking the birthplace of the legendary Hindu hero-king Rama. The mosque had been built by Babur, the first Mughal emperor in 1528–29 AD, and the site became an object of dispute between Hindus and Muslims during the nineteenth century, reaching a climax in 1949 when the Indian government ordered that it be closed. Although the background to Hindu and Muslim politics has been extensively discussed, the role of archaeologists in the dispute is less well known (cf Layton, Stone, and Thomas 2001). B. J. Lal, the head of the Indian Archaeological Service, had excavated the site fifteen years before and written a credible report that produced no evidence of an earlier Hindu temple destroyed by the first Mogul Emperor. But leading up to the attack on the mosque, material evidence was produced based on site plans that not only had such a temple existed but also fragments of wall decoration and ornamented pillars had been found earlier and reburied on the site. These pieces were "found again" by activists during the pillaging of the site and put on display to demonstrate the veracity of the case against allowing the mosque to remain standing on the birth site of Rama. No doubt the activities of archaeological experts may in the long run be found to be less than professional in this context. But that is not really my point, which is that all concerned now operate with conceptions of cultural heritage which see it as rightfully belonging to named groups, acting as indigenous systems of collective allegiance. The facts that have led Hindu nationalists to attribute value to a set of objects can be seen to have nothing much to do with the intrinsic value of the objects per se, but rather with a meaningful narrative created in interaction with these objects over a long period and activated at a specific moment of perceived crisis. The destruction of mosques in Bosnia has a similar interpretative frame, stretching for over a hundred years but made active only in special circumstances of the collapse of the former Yugoslavia (Layton, Stone, and Richards 2001).

Anthropologists have recently been considering indigenous conceptions of the "ownership" of cultural practices. "Copyrighted cultures" are clearly of significance for local peoples in a variety of contexts but they also seem to be accompanied by a "ring fencing" of authenticity as some kind of culturally irreplaceable core (Brown 1998). Spivak has described this "right to culture" as strategic essentialism (Spivak 1999: 230), in order to overcome the opposition between constructionist and essentialist or relativist views in the literature on ethnicity. There is nothing surprising in the fact that people can be strategic and politicized about a sense of identity nor that this impulse precedes and certainly continues long after the control of a resource has been accomplished. Increasingly, we find that the objectification of culture as a possession can be recognized as constitutive of a "long-term identity," an identity that is not a colonial or postcolonial invention. This suggests that in objectifying their "culture," people not only claim to possess it but do so in a self-conscious and self-reflexive manner. In other words, people do "live" their cultural practices but also reflect upon, evaluate, discuss, modify, and dispute them, and this has taken specifically politicized forms in both earlier and more recent contexts (Harrison 2000: 663). We end up with a growing consensus that the objectification of culture as something possessed is a fairly constant if not universal condition with long-term historical antecedents, as well as more recent modernist trends. But at the same time the processes of such objectification have changed and are changing, which in turn relates to altered conceptions of the nature of property.

Richard Handler has been particularly influential in reorienting anthropology back to viewing culture as a form of property. The significance of an object, he claims, lies not in any intrinsic value per se but in the moment and act of its completion. The museum quality of an object may, he argues, be summed up as representing a sense of closeness between the observer and the moment when "the craftsman finished and use began" (Handler 1988: 23). Handler describes this as an example of modern "possessive individualism," wherein value is generated when human beings inscribe labor on a part of the natural world. There are clearly other ways to imagine human creativity and the relation of humans to material objects, which does not privilege this particular view of individual agency.

The notion of authenticity as an original state that should be preserved at all costs has also been challenged by those who would see a contested and dynamic nature in the meaning of cultural heritage (Kopytoff 1986; Gosden and Marshall 1999; Holtdorf 2001). Nevertheless, the values attached to cultural property encompass a whole range of claims, from those of Zuni for their war gods, which, once returned, are meant to disintegrate back into the earth to do their work, to Maori who wish to keep written records of their achievements and history. In this respect, the practices of conservation and museums have never been immutable. The idea that there is a dominant mode of preserving or conserving cultural heritage, which basically privileges material longevity as an assumed goal, is now widely questioned. The "test for authenticity" in the World Heritage Convention guidelines was effectively challenged for its lack of attention to cultural values when a Shinto shrine in Japan was turned down for the World Heritage list because it was traditionally dismantled and renovated every twenty years (quoted in Wharton 2002). The Nara document on Authenticity was effectively a turning point, which shifted the focus in World Heritage legislation from conservation based on "universal value" to "local interpretation."

What these shifts also connote is that if value is not an intrinsic aspect of objects but a function of our conceptual and social interactions with them, culture and property are aspects of the same field, are indivisible and broadly speaking inseparable. In this way, Handler argues against attributing objective reality to "things" since it claims to provide an authentic experience by connecting an audience to an objective past, i.e., a view of value and the meaning of objects that is intrinsic rather than relational to that past. But if we follow Stolcke's observation, we are faced by a number of issues, which suggest that the objectification of culture as patented possession bestows intrinsic qualities to things as part of the right to control culture as property. Many cases can be cited in which culture is owned as a kind of patented possession, a right based on some form of purchasing or licensing (e.g., Harrison 2000). Moreover, like modern copyright, rights act as a means of authorizing circulation and distribution of access to property, rather than positing diffusion through uncontrolled instances of "cultural contact." Harrison argues for a certain kind of cultural self-objectification developing in Melanesia, as a response to the need to protect threatened identity and the assertion of rights to commonly held cultural property. But notions of rights also permit the separation of culture from property in creative ways precisely because of the fact that this can be used strategically to exclude others from possession, i.e., in terms more compatible with international property law.

This is why we can discern several novel assertions about the nature of culture in a number of international conventions on cultural rights. One is the value of self-awareness about belonging to a particular culture and of acting upon it. Practices which were "taken for granted" in the past now become acts of self-awareness and the foci for political action. This can of course be symptomatic of a certain decline in confidence about "having a culture," much as you gasp when you can't breathe. The second, for example in repatriation debates, is the acceptance that participation in political life requires the possession of a culture. But the extension of a rights terminology into the right to "have a culture" creates ambiguity precisely through the modification of the legal definition of rights with the term "cultural." What Michael Lambek (1998) rather disparagingly has called the "contents and container view of culture" is alive and well in the discourse of international conventions on cultural rights. Both these assertions are not new in themselves, but in the 1990s they gained a certain salience – and, in particular, considerable attention from specialists attempting to turn moral rights into legal rights in order to find a way of transcending this dualism.

Attaching Value to Cultural Property

The turn in academic discourse toward discussing objectification of culture, of knowledge as intellectual and cultural property, has been linked to recognition of cultural rights in the public sphere (c.f. Brown 1998, and this volume; Povinelli, this volume; Strathern 1996) and in turn to the political implications of the rise of a "heritage culture" (Lowenthal 1998). Both these trends support the right to preserve "a traditional way of life," as enunciated in the 1948 UN Convention on Human Rights.

Cultural Rights legislation stems from the 1948 UN Convention, which vaguely recognized that besides the killing of people, destroying a people's way of life as "traditional" denied them the right to exist (Schmidt 1995; Prott 1998). It was vague because international legislation was and to large extent still is directed to preserving the rights of individuals, which has meant that the idea of preserving a group exists as a moral issue rather than a legal right. The 1990s having been declared the decade of cultural development, and the World Commission having produced the report *Our Creative Diversity,* attempts were made to basically turn this vague notion of tradition into a legally enforceable right. Worries about overconfident assertions of cultural rights have since then generated a dialogue about how to qualify the language of rights with the meaning of culture, i.e., is it rights over creativity, or rights to preserve or have access to "a culture," or the right to save "a culture" or sustain cultural diversity analogous to biodiversity?

Confusion also occurs in the variety of terms used Terms such as *multi-culturalism, cultural diversity, cultural pluralism, cultural fusion, hybridity* are used almost as if they are interchangeable instead of denoting significantly different concepts. Cultural diversity, for example, is used with increasing frequency in preference to multi-culturalism because the term better implies diversity in unity rather than a broad acceptance of cultural difference. Cultural fusion is disliked because of its implications of erosion and loss, and hybridity is preferred because of the possibility of choice. Because of these difficulties, there has been a tendency to avoid overgeneralized legal definitions, e.g., in the reaction to the UNIDROIT convention on illegally stolen and exported cultural objects, whose implementation has required very specific limitations to applying it. Moreover, there has been a reluctance to appear to be imposing universalized "rights culture" on the bearers of "traditional cultures," driven, in the case of cultural rights, by the strong input of indigenous-peoples movements. The reburial issue, for instance, highlights the strain between indigenous peoples who, feeling themselves under threat, need to "control their culture" and those who believe that through NAGPRA legislation, objects of scientific interest are being destroyed. Ironically, making "indigenous peoples" the repository of cultural knowledge transmitted from the past – as if this has had nothing to do with contemporary issues – is equally resented: "I am tired of going to international conferences and being relegated to the 'beads and feathers' group as though I cannot be expected to know anything about medical or botanical resources and their management" (an indigenous representative quoted in Prott 1998: 171).

Activists' use of the language of rights to push a case may give several meanings to "traditional culture." The Hindmarsh Island affair, however, demonstrates the problems that arise when the presence of statute law to define tradition is paramount in a claim. In this case, the definition of authentic tradition, supported by an anthropologist, was used by a group of Aboriginal women to prevent building a bridge to the mainland from an island associated with their secret knowledge. When another group of Aboriginal women came forward denying the claim made by the original group of women about the nature of secret knowledge (that knowledge of fertility was secret and should not be disclosed in the case), the issue of what constitutes "traditional culture" was raised. Also, if this meant that "traditional culture" could change or be dynamic in adapting to contemporary political questions, then the fidelity of culture itself would be brought into question (Weiner 1999). Joyce Linnekin summed up the dilemma thus: "writing about the contemporary construction or the 'invention of culture' undercuts the cultural authority of indigenous peoples by calling into question their authenticity" (Linnekin 1991: 446).

Disputes over rights of access to cultural property, which involve debates over authorization and legitimation (i.e., who has the right to possess it, display it, use it as part of a "politics of belonging"), make the concept of ownership problematic, not necessarily because of the assumption that such claims can be assessed by using the same universal standards but from the idea that such assessments can be made only through a critical framework giving primacy to local interpretations. But who gives voice to these claims is negotiated around the way terms like heritage or cultural property become identified with a highly reduced language of indigenous rights.

Legal Fictions and Cultural Property

Since much of the experience of indigenous rights is derived from debates in conservation, in particular the rapid globalization of disputes around rainforest conservation over the last fifteen years, it is worth drawing upon some of the general issues these cases raise. Up to now the debate has been dominated by northern environmentalist interests, agencies of donor governments, and international financial institutions such as the World Bank. As research is carried out on the bureaucratic operations underlying the environmentalist discourse, it has been increasingly recognized that debate is dominated by a short-term language that facilitates rapid decision-making. Ferguson, in an influential study of such organizational logics, has argued that "the thoughts and actions of 'development' bureaucrats are powerfully shaped by the world of acceptable statements and utterances within which they live" (1994: 18). Burnham, writing on forest conservation in Cameroon, describes how by managing to define their interventions in narrow technicist terms, external agencies are able to speed project approvals, strengthen confidence in achieving definable goals, and argue for budget increments (Burnham 2000). Contributing to this simplification of complex realities is the deployment of a language of cultural rights as a means of justifying the attachment of resources to local communities, particularly if defined as indigenous, because they are thought to have special knowledge or skills in managing the environment. He describes how within development and conservation policy discourses, certain "key terms" like "community," "indigenous peoples," "common property," "sustainable management," and "biodiversity" become associated with securing a coherent sense of policy and obscuring areas of fundamental contradiction (Burnham 2000).

Such tendencies toward simplification and reductionism are well known to anthropologists familiar with colonial administrations. The 1990s saw a revival of many of these criticisms, as powerful institutions such as the World Bank espouse neoliberal and neo-Malthusian policies to favor privatization of land and forest-resource tenure. This has encouraged a trend towards the creation of a "common property" constituency that would argue for "traditional" rights in common property as an effective way of managing natural resources at the local level, by encouraging people to agitate for the defense of their local resources. At the same time, this has been accompanied by attacks on state ownership of land and a general aversion to the role of the state as harbinger of corruption and bureaucratization inimical to an entrepreneurial spirit. In West Africa, for example, where a British colonial administration recognized customary land law through setting up native authorities, this has promoted strong local incentives for the revival of "traditional claims," with the additional tendencies for "customary law" to freeze history and create fictions of what constitutes a traditional community, based on the unrealistic expectations of an earlier generation of functionalist ethnographers about what consti-tuted a tribal community. By contrast, in formerly French colonies, where the colonial administrations refused to recognize traditional land-tenure systems and instead adopted the role of "guardian of all the lands" (i.e., that at colonial contact land in Africa was vacant and without possession), there remains an incentive to ignore both "tradi-tional" and current local land-tenure systems and to impose supra-local legal contracts as the only way to deal with intractable conflicts. In consequence, much of the painstaking ethnography on land tenure and indigenous concepts of ownership is blithely ignored.

Into this broadly drawn situation, a discourse on cultural rights and property has recently been introduced through the activities of external donors and other institutions, to justify devolutionary policies and the empowerment of local communities. In Cameroon, for instance, the emphasis on "traditional communities," or the use of language such as "participatory forest management" as a means of establishing local sustainable management of forests espoused by expatriate donors, bears little relation to how such "communities" are constituted and defined in practice (cf. Burnham 2000). However, in many cases this doesn't seem to matter and there is a quite explicit sense that if "communities" do not exist now, they will in the near future and it will be the job of suitable development-oriented NGOs to create them. So if history repeats itself, it does so through the use of a more charged language drawn from the right of a group to exist and to hold cultural property in common. In Cameroon, for example, since the 1994 Forestry law, community forest projects can be established based on claiming access to manage and exploit forests within the immediate vicinity of a local community. A community project proposal has to be made to the government, which inevitably means that either an NGO or a local elite association will act as the broker. They have to demonstrate that "traditional" rights pertain through use to a particular tract of forest and that a traditional structure exists in order to manage it as a resource (cf. Povinelli's chapter 8).

Probably the most widely used justification for the recognition of a community in these circumstances is the notion of "indigenous peoples." Principle 22 of the Rio Declaration on Environment and Development asserts, "Indigenous people and their communities have a vital role in environmental management and development because of their knowledge and traditional practices. States should recognize and duly support their identity, culture and interest and enable their effective participation in the achievement of sustainable development." According to this view, indigenous forest peoples live in harmony with the rainforest, causing little long-term damage because of simple subsistence technologies and low population densities. Defining indigenous usually means identifying people by their long-term residence and common ancestry, common language and culture, a first-comer status, and a minority relationship to the state. They are also said to have indigenous knowledge of the rainforest both as a potential economic resource and for harboring skills in sustaining a manageable environment. The World Bank has been particularly active in incorporating "indigenous peoples" into its development policies. A 1982 "Tribal Peoples Operational Directive" was superseded in 1991 by an "Operational Directive 4.20 on Indigenous Peoples." A key feature of this directive was to press for the identification of local indigenous peoples and their informed participation through direct consultation in the development process. The use of terms such as indigenism and participatory development has become synonymous with the ability of development agencies to operate at a truly grassroots level. It can be safely said that most of these initiatives have not met with any great enthusiasm. In Africa and India, this is due to the rejection of the notion of "indigenous peoples," on the basis that it is a concept relevant only to states with a history of dominant white-settler colonialism. If all African peoples are indigenous, it is difficult to define "the right to belong" on the basis of origin, since such a claim will always be politicized and used situationally to claim resources. By linking rights of community to cultural and natural heritage as a Latour type of hybrid identity, participation in the development process becomes a matter of social exclusion rather than of democratic principle, and the promotion of indigenous rights can lay the basis for a "politics of belonging" (Nyamnjoh and Rowlands 1998).

A rhetoric of indigenes versus strangers has become a prevalent feature of politics in Cameroon, where the attachment of political conditionalities to development encouraged multipartyism in the early 1990s (Geschiere and Nyamnjoh 2000). To be indigenous in Cameroon in the twenty-first century means to claim primary origin, to vote by ethnic origin, to assert rights according to heritage and residence, and to exclude others as later migrants (regardless of the fact that recent history of many such areas shows complex patterns of population movement that would make it practically impossible to define any one pristine group). Instead, the past can be ransacked for suitable evidences of local origins or of lost cultural traits that would justify indigenous claims. While this naturalizing of identity removes the question of responsibility from the realm of political discourse, access to whatever resources might be available changes from a responsibility of state allocation to a right of recognition, which becomes more or less synonymous with co-residence within an ethnic homeland.

Transmission of Grievance

While a rights discourse can be deployed for strategic purposes, its attachment to heritage and cultural property can also imply, at least in one sense of injustice, grievance about some past hurt or trauma that has been inadequately transmitted and recognized. Repatriation claims on cultural property are instances where grief over loss transmits into a grievance due to lack of recognition. Mourning is transmitted to living descendants as grievance, well beyond the immediate victims who suffered loss. Instances of politically radicalized transmission of grievance over long periods of time, such as those of Palestinian refugees or the descendants of Holocaust survivors, have led to developing ways to encourage survivors to deal with loss, e.g., ranging from constructing memory-books to human-rights lawyers pressing for state-level apologies and compensation. Acknowledging grievance has become therefore a generalized feature and demand of much recent human and cultural-rights legislation; it is perhaps most sensitive to the recognition that the forms grievance takes differ within a range of modern situations (cf. Feuchtwang's [2000, 2003] seminal work on this).

Blame, vengeance, compensation, or an apology are all possible ways of satisfying the need for recognition; empirically, this is clearly the right focus for many studies concerned with examining forms and reconciliation of grievance. Which, if any, of these options is likely to be chosen, however, does seem to depend on the nature of the original sense of loss and divestment. As Feuchtwang (2003) has observed, grief becomes grievance through the idealization of loss, when the original sense cannot be resolved through adequate mourning and where the conditions do not exist to help people forget. Monuments, for instance, are in one sense responses to the demand for recognition of loss, an attempt by the nation or other group to prevent grief from turning into grievance by giving adequate and continuous recognition of loss and, at the same time, intermittent periods of forgetting and being able to get on with one's life. The cultural transmission of loss is essentially, therefore, a collective endeavour, whether based on constructive forgetting or on the transmission of grievance; both tend to be objectified in monuments or sites of the original loss and in objects and images that revive and convey to others the emotional pang of loss and grievance (Rowlands 1999).

Freud saw the work of mourning as recalling a lost object, and when feelings are most acute and unresolved, idealizing the object can be accompanied by self-denigration. Feelings ranging from paranoid anxiety to acute idealization of lost objects can therefore accompany fantasies of being attacked, rejected, or humiliated and are lived as real experiences – as things, not words. It is not surprising therefore that the energies of grievance should be externalized in the recovery of lost objects as a way of retelling past events, of collecting and transmitting grievance, and thereby of seeking some sense of completeness and final resolution in a court of recognition. Graves, ancestral cults, memorials, archives, and museums are all potential sites for doing this, associated as they are with the essential process of turning bad into good deaths.

Several authors have remarked (e.g., Gellner 1983; Nora 1989) that nations are recognizably self-conscious in their appropriation of myths of origins and in commemorating sites of collective memory. The documentation of national loss and grievance includes not only archives and documentation but, in recent cases of mass killing, the techniques of forensic science, forensic archaeology, and museum curation in order to induce dramas of recognition and grievance. Renan made his famous remark that history was for the nationalist as poppies were for the opium addict in order to allude to this propensity for the state and the nation to be in contradiction over the adequate recognition of past acts of violence and genocide that surrounded their foundation. Any "enquiry" brings to light deeds of violence which took place at the origin of all political formations, even of those whose consequences have been altogether beneficial. Unity is always effected by means of brutality (Thom transl. of Renan 1990: 11). It is also often the case that states formed through the violence of conquest and massacre will insist on repressing such representations of the national past. The expulsion of minorities or indigenous peoples, of religious and linguistic minorities, is such a feature of the modern state built on collective violence that the encouragement of selective remembering, the mutuality of silence, and the exclusion of minority voices is constitutive of the foundation myth. From town planning, or modes of hygiene and public welfare, to heritage tourism and biographical writing, immense efforts are made to secure a certain admission of the past within an overall strategy of looking to the future as a positive outcome of a collective unity.

It is not surprising therefore that a feature of minority indigenous movements has been espousal of cultural rights to revive the past and relocate a sense of grievance within a personalized sense of recovery from hatred and rage. The modern state has by and large run out of options for silencing the revitalization of the past and, in order to keep the peace, has had to turn to or be coerced to turn to alternative forms of authority. Hence, state encouragement of Aboriginal art as an authentic cross-cultural product, or representing the authentic in architecture and town planning, in heritage, and in re-planned museums helps to forge new traditions and to apologize somehow for the past. The tendency for this to freeze the past; to institutionalize an original sense of creativity which was otherwise variable and dynamic, has been a source of both complaint and recognition, e.g., in the right to convert an original creation into an object for sale, which has been both empowering and enriching for many indigenous peoples and an unwelcome sign of commodification. But it has opened up the divide between original "ownership" as part of a universalized notion of cultural property, which tends to simplify and preserve culture as a static entity, alongside the relationships embedded in culture, which must be protected and retained as fluid and creative. It is this revitalizing of "local culture" in the face of forces of reification and commodification that it seems is opening up a silenced world of grief/grievance formerly kept under control.

The return and reburial of human remains deposited in their hundred of thousands in Museums and Anatomy departments all over the world, often in the aftermath of past acts of genocide, exemplifies the growing recognition in cultural rights legislation of the moral and ethical ties that bind. In the majority of cases where human remains are of recent (often nineteenth-century) origin, the argument for the removal of such remains from display in Museums and/or their return to original communities for reburial has been widely accepted. But the event which suggests that there may be limits to the moral case was the discovery in 1996 of a more or less complete skeleton known as "Kennewick Man" in Washington State, which is thought to be 8,400 years old, the oldest remains yet found in the Americas. The remains have subsequently been claimed under the NAGPRA legislation by four Native American groups, evoking a rebuttal by archaeologists wanting to study them. The Hastings amendment, new legislation that has been enacted, would require establishing evidence of the cultural origins of remains before allowing their repatriation. The case is still unresolved, but a striking feature is the degree of ill feeling generated, with accusations of racism and careerism made against archaeologists belonging to the American Committee for the Preservation of Archaeological Collections. A sense of grievance among impoverished minorities may be displaced into many aspects of contemporary injustice, but what is unusual is that resolution is achieved not through anti-racist legislation or better welfare but through insistence on the return of bones for reburial. Popular cults that commemorate the dead revitalize the past through a form of re-telling or revision, so that their grievance and those of living descendants can be assuaged. The restitution of cultural property can, I suggest, be interpreted as a form of revitalization cult, which attempts to assuage grief that became grievance through the belief that the other afflictions of being indigenous in pluralistic settings (alcoholism, high infant-mortality rates, prostitution, and poverty) may finally be resolved by according the remains of ancestors "a good death."

While resolving the transmission of grievance can obviously take many forms, what these cases share is that recognition of injustice should lead to retrieval of dignity and respect. In turn, this affects notions of possession and in particular of cultural property. Legal ownership is not in doubt in any of the cases mentioned, but everyone involved is, broadly speaking, concerned to put this aside – to operate on a liberal consensual base that moral ownership should be the principal issue. But moral ownership is here based on a principle of priority, i.e., that the creative property of having originated a cultural product transcends any later claim based on legality. That, in turn, raises the question that priority is claimed as a higher *value*, which along with economic notions can also be seen to be a product of moral virtue and the right to belong. The tendency for bodies like UNESCO to assert moral ownership as a higher value than legal ownership is therefore consistent with the recognition that the value of humanity itself is at stake and, in these circumstances, the needs of science or the market should take second place.

Heritage, Politics, and Memory

The demand for recognition has been made more explicit recently because it has been accompanied by the self-knowledge that we are formed by it. In Charles Taylor's terms, "Due recognition is not just a courtesy we owe people. It is a vital human need" (26). What has emerged, he would argue, as the key need is the recognition of cultural difference and the struggles of subjugated peoples against homogenization. But this is closely linked to western notions of authenticity that involve concepts of creativity, fundamentally at variance with such a discussion. Moreover, recognizing the unique identity of this individual or that group rests on the assumption that their distinctiveness has been suppressed or submerged in the past. The sin committed by assimilation policies is the assault it mounts on authenticity. As seen in the case of indigenism, a politics of difference can be full of denunciations and discrimination against others, which are hard to accept as justified simply on the basis of asserting the right for a traditional way of life or to preserve unique identities against external influences. Much of this could be seen as consistent anyway with a neoliberal "strong discourse" that not only constructs cultural difference as respect for the dignity of others but also orients alternate identities as options consistent with a form of governmentality that encourages choice. UNESCO, for instance, in the 1970 convention, defines cultural property as "an essential element in the personality of the peoples of the world, diminishment of which seriously undermines their right to a distinct way of life. People have rights to cultural property consistent with the need to gain a consciousness of their cultural creativity and therefore of their own dignity" (UNESCO 1970). In addition to this recognition of cultural choice, UNESCO from early on was concerned not to imply some cultural imperializing world order and to recognize that each state has the right to define cultural property consistent with what guarantees the preservation of its own creativity. Japanese legislation, taken as a model by other South East Asian states, includes tangible and intangible cultural properties, folk culture, and monuments. The UNESCO inter-governmental committee for the recognition of cultural property defined it as anything that could be said to be "highly charged with cultural significance" for a particular member state. Implicit is the contradiction between the universalist notion of the right to protect anything as world heritage that sustains human dignity and the rights of individual states to define their own cultural property consistent with their own needs. The individualizing of authenticity as something to be revealed in the personality writ large has therefore been disseminated as a universal right that must at the same time be accredited with local manifestations. The uneasy balance between these two individualizing tendencies can be seen in many cases where "authentic culture," implying culture as possession, something one can have more or less of and in particular which may be under threat through histories of migration and ethnic pluralism, is being reasserted as a right to be recognized and enforced through control and safeguards of cultural property.

My purpose has been to point out that a politics of recognition has now dissolved the difference between a sense of authentic, local, dynamic process of creativity and worries about loss of culture, as a reified property or possession that is under external threat. We can no longer see the latter as a figment of nineteenth-century imaginary, or of the outmoded paradigm of international agencies and cultural institutions prone to defend cultural identities against the individualizing forces of the market. Academic paradigms can be accused of lacking a sense of the public sphere in which policy is formed and of rather blithely disregarding such issues as outmoded or naive. Yet the right–recognition–cultural-property nexus embedded in neoliberal discourse is enormously influential and widely seen as the current basis for an important sphere of public policy. At one level, the contrast between rainforest conservation, indigeneity, and the transmission of grievance could not be greater, but at another more abstract level, these shade into each other as part of the struggle for existence in the twenty-first century.

Acknowledgments

I owe a great debt of gratitude to Beverley Butler and Stephan Feuchtwang for discussions which clarified many of the points made in this chapter.

References

Brown, Michael. 1998. "Can culture be copyrighted?" *Current Anthropology* 39: 193–222.

Burnham, Philip. 2000. "Whose forest, whose myth?" In *Land, law and environment: Mythical land, legal boundaries.* Edited by Alan Abramson and Dmitri Theodossopoulos. London: Pluto.

Carrier, James. 1997. *Meanings of the market: The free market in western culture.* Oxford: Berg.

Ferguson, James. 1994. *The anti-politics machine.* Minneapolis: University of Minnesota Press.

Feuchtwang, Stephan. 2000. "Reinscriptions: Commemoration, restoration and the Interpersonal transmission of histories and memories." In *Memory and methodology.* Edited by Susannah Radstone. Oxford: Berg.

Feuchtwang, Stephan. 2003. "The transmission of loss and the demand for recognition." In *Regimes of Memory.* Edited by Katie Hodgkin and Susannah Radstone. London: Routledge.

Fraser, Nancy. 1995. "From redistribution to recognition? Dilemmas of justice in a 'post-socialist' age." *New Left Review* 212: 68–93.

Gell, Afred. 1992. "Inter-tribal commodity barter and reproductive gift-exchange in old Melanesia." In *Barter, exchange and value.* Edited by C. Humphrey and S. Hugh-Jones. Cambridge: Cambridge University Press.

Gellner, Ernest. 1983. *Nations and nationalism.* Cambridge: Cambridge University Press.

Geschiere, P., and F. Nyamnjoh. 2000. "Capitalism and autochthony: the seesaw of mobility and belonging. *Public Culture* 12: 423–52.

Godelier, Maurice. 1999. *The enigma of the gift.* Cambridge: Polity.

Gosden, Chris, and Yvonne Marshall. 1999. "The cultural biography of objects." *World Archaeology* 31: 169–78.

Handler, Richard. 1988. *Nationalism and the politics of culture in Quebec.* Madison: University of Wisconsin Press.

Harrison, Simon. 2000. "From prestige goods to legacies: Property and the objectification of culture in Melanesia." *Comparative Studies in Society and History* 42: 662–79.

Holtdorf, Cornelius. 2001. "Is the past a non-renewable resource?" In *Destruction and conservation of cultural property.* Edited by Robert Layton, Peter Stone, and Julian Thomas. London: Routledge.

Kopytoff, Igor. 1986. "The cultural biography of things. In *The social life of things.* Edited by Arjun Appadurai. Cambridge: Cambridge University press.

Lambek, Michael. 1998. "The past imperfect: remembering as a moral practice." In *Tease past: Cultural essays in trauma and memory.* Edited by P. Antze and M. Lambek. London: Routledge.

Layton, Robert, Peter Stone, and Julian Thomas (eds.). 2001. *Destruction and conservation of cultural property*. London: Routledge.

Linnekin, J. 1990. "The politics of culture in the Pacific." In *Cultural identity in the Pacific*. Edited by J. Linnekin and L. Poyer. Honolulu: University of Hawaii Press.

Lowenthal, David. 1998. *The heritage crusade and the spoils of history*. Cambridge: Cambridge University Press.

Maine, Henry Sumner. 1986 [1963]. *Ancient law*. Tucson: University of Arizona Press.

Nyamnjoh, F., and M. Rowlands. 1998. "Elite associations and the politics of belonging in Cameroon." *Africa* 68: 321–37.

Niec, Halina (ed.). 1998. *Cultural rights and wrongs*. Paris: UNESCO.

Nora, Pierre. 1989. "Between memory and history." *Representations* 26: 7–25.

Posey, Darrell. 1998. "Can cultural rights protect traditional cultural knowledge and biodiversity?" In *Cultural rights and wrongs*. Edited by Halina Niec. Paris: UNESCO.

Povinelli, Elizabeth. 2001. "Radical worlds: The anthropology of incommensurability and inconceivability." In *Annual Review of Anthropology* 30: 319–35.

Prott, Lyndel. 1998. "Understanding one another on cultural rights." In *Cultural rights and wrongs*. Edited by Halina Niec. Paris: UNESCO.

Renan, Ernest. 1990. "What is a nation?" In *Nation and narration*. Edited by Homi K. Bhabha. London: Routledge.

Rowlands, Michael. 1999. "Remembering to forget: Sublimation as sacrifice in war memorials." In *The art of forgetting*. Edited by Adrian Forty and Susanne Kuechler. Oxford: Berg.

Schmidt, Peter. 1995. *Plundering Africa's past*. Bloomington: Indiana University Press.

Spivak, Givatry. 1999. *A critique of postcolonial reason*. Cambridge: Harvard University Press.

Stolcke, Verena. 1995. "Talking culture: New boundaries, new rhetorics of exclusion in Europe." *Current Anthropology* 36: 1–24.

Strathern, Marilyn. 1988. *The gender of the gift*. Cambridge: Cambridge University Press.

——. 1996. "Potential property: Intellectual rights and property in persons." *Social Anthropology* 4: 17–32.

Taylor, Charles. 1994. "The politics of recognition." In *Multiculturalism: Examining the politics of recognition*. Edited by Amy Gutman. Princeton: Princeton University Press

Thomas, Nicholas. 1991. *Entangled objects*. Cambridge, MA: Harvard University Press.

Weiner, Annette. 1992. *Inalienable possessions*. Berkeley: University of California Press.

Weiner, James. 1999. "Culture in a sealed envelope." *Journal of the Royal Anthropological Institute* 5: 193–210.

Wharton, Glenn. 2002. "Can conservation respond to indigenous demands?" *Public Archaeology* 3: 24–35.

The Menace of Hawkers: Property Forms and the Politics of Market Liberalization in Mumbai

Arvind Rajagopal

"Why do you people keep coming into the city? Why do you clog the streets and harass people?" The questions were directed at Sandeep Yeole, secretary of the Ghatkopar (West) *Pheriwala* committee. A former *pheriwala*, or street vendor, himself, Sandeep was now an activist organizing street vendors in his locality in Mumbai. That morning he was concluding a presentation to a group of city professionals on the problems facing pheriwalas. He answered with another question: "If I had a *crore* of rupees [ten million rupees] and were to come into the city, I would be welcomed with open arms. I would be offered my choice of bungalows to buy. Why is it that the pheriwala, who struggles to survive and works hard for his living, is rejected?"[1] Sandeep put his finger on a point of discrimination. His interlocutors saw hawkers as an assault on the public, implicitly construed as people like themselves. But an illiberal property qualification united their community of interests: only the well-to-do were assured entry. Sandeep was using a master-key to the doors of their imagination, bypassing their objections to pheriwalas. Who today would object to a *crorepati* (someone with a crore or more of rupees) after all? The truth is that, in the spate of demolition raids launched on street vendors, even the rich ones with armies of municipal officials in their pay are not spared. "The menace of hawkers" described in the dailies is not the menace of their poverty; it is that they exist at all. That is, they become a mirror for all kinds of doubts and ills attending the transition from state-led development to market liberalization.

227

It is ironic that in a time of market ascendancy, these most tenacious of entrepreneurs, operating in subhuman conditions and yet an integral and growing part of the economy, should be demonized and victimized. Pheriwalas (literally, those who move around), or hawkers, roam the streets of Indian cities, bearing baskets on their heads or pushing handcarts and calling out their wares, offering goods and produce cheaper than in the stores. They are a part of the economy that spurs consumption, but are understood as vagrant figures to be disciplined. Pheriwalas are real figures, seen as illegal in relation to the formal economy, but are also metaphorical in that they symbolize disorder. They unsettle the clear boundary between categories: proletarian and bourgeois; person and commodity. Pheriwalas are entrepreneurs, not wage slaves, but the condition of their survival is that they depreciate their own human capital while underselling those not obliged to do so. They generate millions in revenue but are denounced as hurting "legitimate" business. They are accused of encroaching on "public" land, and of dirtying and jamming the streets, that is, of occupying space that is not theirs. They are denied the rights accorded to private citizens, of immunity from violence, or from destruction of their property. In an earlier era of state-led development, they could be seen as vulnerable citizens requiring a measure of protection. With deregulation and privatization, they are seen as the cause rather than as the symptom of market forces out of control. If, as Sandeep Yeole indicated, property is assumed as a kind of natural right generating its own legitimacy, pheriwalas appear on the borderline of those of who hold such rights; violence is directed against them as a way of affirming the distinction between legitimate and illegitimate property rights. Property emerges as a political category underwritten by the law, and inseparable from the violence through which a given state regime enforces the law.

This chapter explores recent debates on Mumbai pheriwalas to illuminate shifts in the cultural politics of property rights accompanying globalization in India. Although pheriwalas have for decades thronged the streets and sidewalks of Mumbai, a series of court battles won by middle-class activists in recent years has focused media attention on them. Media sympathy is with the middle-class activists. Pheriwalas survive at the margins of city spaces by the unquenchable and ever-growing demand for their services. But they must raise capital at exorbitant costs, and pay large bribes or fines (the distinction is unclear to pheriwalas) to police, municipal, and ward-level officers.

With increasing city population, they have preferred to remain stationary rather than be roving vendors, as the name pheriwala dictates. In the prevailing climate of market liberalization, new corporate investment in mini-malls and trendy department stores has sought to create a consumption aesthetic and a shopping environment appropriate for the times. Hawkers, who juxtapose their goods for sale alongside refuse for disposal, draw a mushrooming question mark around the new consumption aesthetic. Against the sophisticated sales techniques on display in the stores, hawkers disclose the exuberant survival of the most elemental form of markets. Indeed, their efficiency in cutting costs threatens to lure customers away from most established stores. In this context, the scandal created around the issue of pheriwalas, and the increased ferocity of demolition raids, long a means of controlling the pheriwala population, is revealing. It indicates not merely an escalating battle to beautify the city. In fact, different conceptions of the market are at war with each other, and the "legitimate violence" of the state is used to defend an embattled, corporate version of the market against its more successful, if anarchic, alternative.

In my encounters with middle-class activists against pheriwalas, I was impressed with their sincerity and commitment. What was striking, however, was their insistence on the letter of the law. In a city where 60 percent of the population are squatters and provide the bulk of its labor force, to insist on legality in the abstract is impractical, to say the least. Indeed, in conversation, many would give vent to views that were anything but abstract. "These people are not from Maharashtra. They are outsiders," declared a local social scientist, reflecting a widely held view.[2] "We are not saying, 'Throw them into the Arabian Sea.' We just don't want them to come here, that's all," one activist explained to me.[3]

Mumbai's middle classes appear to have come of political age, but in a distinct way. Disenchanted by the failed promises of Nehruvian secularism and developmentalism, and more recently, of Hindu nationalism, they now seek political goals modeled closely on those of the West – clean streets and sidewalks, unobstructed movement for pedestrians and motorists, slum-free environments, and so on. In doing so, they champion the idea of public space on which, as they point out, no one ought to claim exclusive rights. The overwhelming majority of public-interest cases now are filed by middle-class residential associations and urban-beautification committees.

Market liberalization arrived in India following more than four decades of state-led economic development. Its proponents claimed it was the cure for the problems developmentalism could not solve (Bhagwati and Srinivasan 1993; Byres 1997). It indexes a new political rhetoric, moving away from state protection and entitlements for the poor and vulnerable classes to a model of empowerment based implicitly or explicitly on property rights. Market liberalization triumphs, in its supporters' accounts, by infusing and transforming despotic state regimes with the spirit of liberty and equality. In fact, it deepens the divide between haves and have-nots; there is, as Sandeep Yeole pointed out, a property qualification for admission to the Elysium of liberty and equality. Markets have become the latest vehicle of these enlightenment values; as such they represent an elite cause. But the forms in which they are subjectified and embraced as popular causes have an older provenance.

Although demands for liberty and equality are considered equivalent in modern societies, the claims are contradictory, not identical. The values themselves are abstract, but the decisions about which freedom is compared to which equality, for whom and under what conditions, are practical ones and point to more concrete historical arrangements. Modern individuals may understand themselves as both free and equal, but how do they make sense of their actual situation, which is neither free nor equal? Etienne Balibar (1994: 50–51) has argued that it is through the categories of "property" and "fraternity," or community, that the contradictions between liberty and equality are mediated. Dominant forms of property socialize individuals into the actual ways the values of liberty and equality are practiced and regulated. Alongside the leading forms safeguarded by law are older and newer forms of property which tend to lack the same degree of protection, for example common lands or intellectual property.[4] Extant understandings of property are constantly being repoliticized, and new forms eventually mutate and develop to express conflicts unresolvable through older property forms. An inventory of different kinds of property could be used to trace a historical outline of capitalist development itself: e.g., landed property, mercantile and industrial property, labor-property, and intellectual property. A given state regime gives rise to historically determinate property forms, and in turn provides the crucible for the elaboration and refinement of different types of property, which then demand new modes of regulation and generate new kinds of political contestation.

Tracking the changing forms of property thus discloses the import-ance of the category in mediating the devolution and distribution of power, in the departure from state absolutism and the shift to modern governmentality. Postcolonial societies, however, demonstrate a more complex and convoluted relationship between state regime and prop-erty form. For example, in India, the colonial state sharply limited the forms private property could take, favoring British over indigenous capitalism. (The social manifestation of this rule of colonial difference was a proliferation of indigenous communities based on religion and caste, enumerated and sanctified by the colonial census. "Community" is Balibar's second category of mediation, we may recall.) The independent state widened the social basis of governance and oriented itself to indigenous economic development. But strict controls over the economy were retained. Public and private industrial sectors were both granted protection from indigenous and foreign competition through a "license-permit raj." In effect, a small, salaried middle class was created under state protection, tacitly entrusted with the task of building the national economy.[5] But there was no system of accountability by which it could be judged, nor could the terms of its treatment be revised according to its performance. The postcolonial state applied its controls in the name of the national community. But the basic form and substance of the state, in terms of the civil service, the police, the courts, and the army, remained from the colonial period with little change, for reasons usually ascribed to political constraints.[6] The shift from colonial to postcolonial rule was accordingly more a political than a cultural shift. In governmental procedure and elite mindset, it is the continuity with colonial rule that is more striking. The outcomes of development empowered new social groups who challenged this legacy, to be sure. But the cultural forms in which such contestations were posed usually rendered them marginal.

In retrospect, there was an overly optimistic reliance on economic growth and its trickle-down effects, and on the middle class's own responsibility to the nation at large. Protection nurtured economic inefficiency as much as it did competitiveness, unfortunately, and the reluctance to challenge inherited wealth (for example via land reform) meant that the middle class was allowed to imagine state-sponsored privileges as its own achievement. State-led development meant that modernization was a top-down process, intended to emulate results already achieved elsewhere, even if the imitation was to be, somehow, uniquely Indian. In effect, the form of property through which the Indian middle class was socialized itself assumed a pedagogical relationship between itself and the population at large. Far from acting as a force for democratization or as an incubator of universalist values, property rights as endowed by the state here staged an illiberal attitude of privilege that could not be separated from the developmentalist mission.[7]

The dominant culture of the market under the developmental state reproduced this class difference in its own way. With economic planning and the accompanying constraints on consumption, marketers addressed a relatively small, urban audience identified by the acronym PLUS, People Like Us. It was to this upmarket consumer base that corporations devoted the bulk of their advertising and marketing expenditure. This was the fraction of the population that could be cultivated and "grown," in terms of psychological aspiration and, importantly, in terms of the value they could deliver to marketers. According to the reigning models of Indian marketing based on Maslow's hierarchy of needs, the majority of the population were fixed at a consumption level close to subsistence and would not (or could not) seek new forms of consumption to express their needs. Broadly, utilitarian appeals were deemed sufficient for the majority population; a consumer aesthetic was developed for the upmarket segment alone. This stratified approach was the counterpart of developmentalist state culture, whereby a Nehruvian secular technocracy was held above the masses. The failure to develop a popular aesthetic in the political sphere was, therefore, mirrored in the consumer market (see Rajagopal 1998–99).

Market liberalization and the roughly concomitant growth of nationwide television pointed to the *terra incognita* of the majority society, whose political allegiance had been assumed in benevolent or not-so-benevolent forms of clientelism, and whose cultural allegiance hardly figured at all, given the disconnect between elite and popular spheres. The changes wrought by markets and media together led, over time, to popular pressures increasing on established domains of politics. In fact, I would argue, the notoriety acquired by hawkers itself points to the politicization of previously more passive and acquiescent sections of society.[8] It indicates that areas and forms of experience formerly excluded from mainstream media may now be publicized. This provides a kind of affirmation for those who identify with the images shown and potentially emboldens their presence in the public sphere, as I will indicate in greater detail below.

The Growth of Media and New Forms of Politics

The evolution of communications has been highly compressed in India. For example, the internet arrived little more than a decade after nationwide television in most parts of India, and many public telephones only arrived when television did. In a short time, an explosion of communicative possibilities swept across a society of deep linguistic and regional divides and a small, albeit expanding, middle class. The uneven character of the resulting development has provoked new forms of social imagination that cannot be understood simply as delayed manifestations of events already seen elsewhere. A range of new practices is seen – for example, more individualized and flamboyant modes of comportment, alongside increasingly public and aggressive definition of singular identities that were earlier more recessed, fluid, and fuzzy. A distinctive ensemble of commodity aesthetics is diffusing across not only the stores and bazaars, but other old and new urban spaces as well as more intimate settings, displacing and transforming earlier understandings of harmony and balance.

The media reorder perceptions and precipitate new ways of seeing and thinking, but they do not emerge in isolation. They arise as part of a far-reaching change in social relations due to the growth and spread of markets. A provisional way of describing them is in terms of the increasing centrality of consumption to the formation of social identities. Previously identified as strictly private, consumption has become a new and unpredictable form of civic participation, distinct from those prevailing in the era of the developmental state. At one level, this is banal, but it deserves more examination. It indexes not simply the market behavior that economists have taught us to recognize, but the accompanying circulation of images and information via the media as well.

One way of characterizing the shift is in terms of the exponentially increased circulation of non-material forms of property. Take the example of advertising images. While such images must circulate freely for potential customers to learn about the product advertised, they remain the private property of their original owners: anyone else publicly using an advertising logo, for example of Coke, has to compensate the corporation for the privilege of doing so. To take another example, the distribution of free software has been recognized not only as a good in itself, but also as a way of building a consumer base that can later be charged in one way or another. Linux, the operating system distributed freely as an alternative to Microsoft's proprietary code and now enjoying over a tenth of the market, is an example. These non-material forms of property are non-rivalrous: they are not diminished when there are additional users; they are essentially inexhaustible (cf. Parry, this volume). Arguments about property tend to rest on the centrality of *scarcity* in theories of the economy. Intellectual property, although relatively new, is paradoxical in that it is in some important ways better understood using much older, indeed "primitive" conceptions of the economy, rather than those derived entirely from capitalism. As Marshall Sahlins has pointed out, like Georges Bataille before him, *abundance* rather than scarcity is the premise of primitive economies, pointing to different social mediations of needs (Sahlins 1972; Bataille 1988). The media, in circulating images and information that can theoretically be shared by everyone, indicate the possibility of such abundance, through what Balibar has called "universal property" (Balibar 1994: 52–3). Modern communications can, therefore, sustain modes of participation distinct from the competitive, zero-sum activity of markets. These new forms of solidarity are already being mobilized and require more accurate understanding. I suggest that they cast light on the explosive salience of the imagination and the resulting importance of identity politics in recent times (Appadurai 1996; Rajagopal 2001).

The institutionalization of television in India (nationwide broadcasting beginning as recently as the 1980s) has in fact worked to illuminate hitherto-excluded life-forms such as those of the pheriwala, while rendering them vulnerable to absorption in a new visual economy. I can offer several examples of pheriwalas appearing in street scenes in news or feature films shown on television. However, I will begin by considering an example from advertising, since it is the genre making the closest connections between culture, the economy, and the new visual regime instanced in television.[9] With the establishment of national television, it has begun to be considered viable to address large consumer markets not only as a business proposition, but also as an aesthetic one. In the ad discussed below, conceived for a more "downmarket" product, we can glimpse the traces of the stratification and reorientation of sense perceptions and their enfolding into a new commodity aesthetics.

A Scene of Consumption: The Cup that Cheers

The ad is for Brooke Bond A-1 *kadak chaap* tea. Kadak chaap indicates that this is strong tea (lit., the stamp of strength; kadak means strong, vigorous), and in India, the kind of tea favored by working and rural classes.[10] Tea stalls operating on city sidewalks would vend it. Staged in a melodramatic and characteristically Bollywood style, the ad shows a bulldozer, flanked by sinister-looking figures, demolishing undefined shanty structures on the street. The soundtrack is suggestive of a warzone, with helicopters and air-raid sirens loud in the background. A swarthy, bearded man wearing dark glasses sits in the shadowy interior of a white car, peering intermittently at his lawyer (i.e., a man in lawyer's costume) and his henchmen as they direct the demolition. Facing the bulldozer is a young woman in a white sari, drinking tea. Her costume suggests she is a social worker or an activist. The camera pauses a moment to focus on the glass of tea in the woman's hand. On the street, tea is drunk in glasses, and at home, it is drunk in cups. A roadside tea stall is being demolished, and the woman has decided to resist it. Sitting in front of the bulldozer, the woman challenges the man at its wheel to run over her. A sharp exchange of words results in the bulldozer operator taking to his heels, while the crowd lies down prone all around the machine. Brooke Bond A-1 kadak chaap works its magic, and an unarmed woman triumphs over a gang of toughs.[11]

The ad stages a typical scene in Mumbai and other cities in India, of the confrontation between the majority who dwell and make their livelihood on the street, and the minority who view the streets as but the circuitry of the formal economy in which they themselves work. The ad offers symbolic redemption for the sidewalk residents and vendors who are invariably vanquished in such confrontations, but through the image of a consumer brand and the rhetoric of a young, female consumer.

Now, everyday scenes of demolition are accompanied by police squads and city workers, as representatives of the only institution with usufruct rights in public space, namely the state. The ad boldly dramatizes the popular belief that the state is ruled by a class fraction partial to itself, or that it is hand-in-glove with criminals. The conundrum of a state undertaking illegal action is answered, appropriately enough, by a charismatic figure, a pretty heroine matching the goons' tough talk with her own fluent, idiomatic slang. Gendering the confrontation lowers the political threshold for its reception, we may note, bringing as it does aspects other than the class contradiction central to this conflict. For the ad to feature real pheriwalas might perhaps distract from its aesthetic. Indeed the life and work of pheriwalas themselves are nowhere to be seen here; their existence has to be inferred from the image of the bulldozer, the glass of tea, and Brooke Bond A-1 kadak chaap. Characteristically, the growing market for national and global consumer brands, which in part replaces the informal economy of roadside stalls, seeks to absorb the image of that which it replaces. But the audio track, shifting from a melodramatic announcement of the brand, to the soundscape of a battlefield and the snappy repartee of street-talk, invokes the rhythms and lexical repertoire of popular cinema. The arcs of the visual and audio narratives both culminate in a global brand gone local, but in the ways they traverse the lexicon of popular culture, their moral economies overlap but do not coincide.

The ad acknowledges the violence involved in the control over urban space and the spectacular forms through which it takes effect. The violence is not simply epiphenomenal to a project of political control: it is itself productive, linking its audience in a shared sense of fear and fascination. If in precapitalist society sumptuary expenditure flowed to poorer classes, in contemporary capitalism such expenditure is nested within the elaboration of an aesthetic whereby consumption styles are rendered normative. The demolitions are perhaps a sign of the devolution of sumptuary expenditure and its transformation into a spectacle for general enjoyment.[12] With economic liberalization, more concerted attempts to entice foreign investment, and the growth of a consuming middle class whose mode of asserting their citizenship rights now typically occurs by refiguring their relationship to the poor, such forms of violence have gained prominence, albeit with a rhetoric that denies their illiberal nature.

The Pheriwala as a Contested Figure of Indian Modernity

That an economy seeking to advance itself should retain ancient means of circulating goods suggests many things about it, but interestingly, what becomes controversial is not the inhuman treatment of pheriwalas or the grotesque form of modernization this represents. The most prominent part of the criticisms is in fact aesthetic and political: street vendors are seen as offensive, inconvenient, and illegitimate. Attempts to impose order on city spaces are also about the value of the real estate involved; order and value are recurring themes in the aesthetic, economic, and political arguments waged here. Given the ability of the pheriwala to weave through the heterogeneous zones of the city without necessarily having the right to reside in them, it is perhaps not surprising that in a time of unregulated global flows of capital and images, pheriwalas become a symbol of dreams of liberalization gone awry, and, as such, the negative image of an unattainable disciplinary project. A climate of terror is instilled through demolition and destruction, illuminating the despotic character of state power under market liberalization.[13]

The hawker belongs to the informal economy – and indeed provoked the concept itself (Hart 1973; *Seminar* 2000). In India, at least, the distinction between formal and informal economies is an invidious one, since the economy would collapse without its innumerable "informal" components; "informality" refers mainly to the lack of protection against exploitative conditions of work, and indicates the different rhetoric of state power operative in this segment. As a whole the formal economy excludes the majority of the population. This highlights the prominence of political power over economic relations in Indian capitalism; the law must sanction violence in order to protect the salaried classes' privileges and deny the rest their rights. What then brings the otherwise unremarkable exercise of violence against this segment of the informal economy into the news?

If the majority of the city's population in Mumbai are squatters, occupying less than 2 percent of the city's land, encroachment is not only a problem that diminishes public space, it is also a solution to a larger problem of maldistributed resources. But the juristic climate today is less sympathetic to the poor, with a new generation of judges in court who view older, more inclusive ideals of Nehruvian development partly responsible for the country's failure to become a world power. If during an earlier wave of public interest litigation, the right to life included the right to earn a livelihood, today it is rights to "unrestricted" public space that pheriwalas are seen to threaten.[14] If campaigns for pheriwala rights partake in the general, all-around increase in public assertiveness, they are more than matched by a wave of middle-class activism championing varieties of nimbyism.

The informal sector was supposed to provide the reserve labor force that fed the formal economy as it expanded. Precisely the opposite has happened, interestingly. In 1961, 65 percent of Mumbai's workforce was employed in the organized sector and the remainder in the unorganized sector; thirty years later the proportion was reversed. By 1991, 65 percent of employment was in the unorganized sector.[15] Although middle classes are fond of claiming that pheriwalas are well-to-do freeloaders (see below), most vendors are poor and marginal.[16] Nevertheless, these figures suggest that the dynamics of this segment of the economy might illuminate the changing forms of state regulation that have accompanied liberalization, as well as the differentiated political capacities now being made available to citizens.

Working at the bottom end of the market, *pheriwalas perform a socializing function*, exposing consumers to products, allowing them to assess the fair value of goods and establish civil relations with strangers on the basis of mutually acknowledged but differing interests. The forms of display at a pheriwala's stall facilitate better interaction than is usually available to consumers at department stores or malls. Transactions with pheriwalas, in all their nakedness, enact the most fundamental form of market exchange. The market, Braudel reminds us, brings the arenas of production and consumption into contact with each other. It thus acts as the interface with the outside world for each of these realms, with the unknown and unpredictable. The market, he writes, is like coming up for air, bringing one face to face with the other (Braudel 1982: 26). Here we have the unruly energy of the bazaars, the assault of different sensations, and varieties of costume and countenance. Commodities lie available for inspection and comparison across competing stalls, mediated only by the typically fluid, dialogical encounter over pricing and payment. It is here more than in any other market environment, we may remind ourselves, that the customer is truly king. For a new consumption regime to be instituted in the process of metamorphosing a pheriwala economy into a store-and-mall-based one is no simple matter, however, especially if the hope of transcending pheriwalas is destined to be in vain. The attempt to delegitimate an older consumption aesthetic in Mumbai is a spectacular one, occurring through a series of demolition raids conducted in public.

Demolitions: A Glimpse of "Field Action"

At the helm of the demolitions in Mumbai in 2000–2001 was G. R. Khairnar, former deputy Municipal Commissioner and for a period Officer on Special Duty, in charge of demolitions. He became famous for his fearless targeting of affluent builders violating zoning rules, and for his public accusations that the Chief Minister was associated with criminals, a charge he continues to make against successive governments. He is considered both incorruptible and ruthless.

Khairnar is a man with a soft voice and a hard stare. A nexus between bureaucrats, the political mafia and business has replaced the rule of law, he argues, and ordinary people do anything they can to survive, compounding the lawlessness. Hawkers, and many others, ignore or defy the law, and Khairnar's contribution is to teach them the value of discipline, as he sees it.[17] But he invited me to accompany him on "field action" and see for myself, smiling as he invited me. Without his saying anything further, I felt a certain exhilaration at the prospect.

On the appointed day, I boarded a van with Khairnar and a French documentary team doing a TV series on global cities. In Mumbai, Khairnar was their first stop. The convoy that accompanied us was an impressive one: a bulldozer, two jeeps with policemen, two trucks to carry away confiscated goods, and Khairnar's van. As we arrived at an open-air vegetable market, the halt of the convoy had an impressive effect. Baskets of vegetables began to be hoisted on the heads of their anxious owners, as they fled the scene. Those vendors who had invested most in their produce were in for the greatest loss, as it was not possible to remove everything from the advancing crew in time. Brilliant red tomatoes rolled in every direction. In seconds, scores of people gathered from all around to watch, and the whole street was suddenly crowded. Khairnar strode in briskly, pointing here and there, and the bulldozer went into action, here clawing off a gunny awning with its slender bamboo supports, and there crumpling up patchwork roofs. The Municipal Corporation staff darted around to grab produce to deposit in their goods trucks. The spectacle of destruction is riveting: the abrupt obliteration of carefully gathered and nurtured matter, of accumulated time and energy. That such devastation can be wrought without reprisal deepens this fascination, since it confirms the sense of the extent of the power at work.

What must it feel like to have demolition victims at your mercy? One woman whose roadside shack was being torn down at the same time was weeping and begging Khairnar with folded hands to save her home. Her child was crying too. Addressing the girl, Khairnar asked, "Who taught you to weep like that?" His sympathies had hardened over time. But the child's tears were genuine; for some reason the roadside shack, miserable as it was, ought not to have been demolished, although the task was already half-finished. The crew departed, assuring the poor woman that she should come to "Sir's office" for compensation.

When I described the events I'd seen to friends who lived in Mumbai, I expected to hear sympathetic cries of indignation. Although each of them was left of center, in each case I was given a talking-to. Some friends saw it as an attempt to clean up public space, to restore pedestrians their long-denied rights. Everyone formulated it in terms of an attempt to restore rationality, to overcome illegality, and to assert the law. This was itself interesting. In fact, newspapers report that bulldozers are regularly sent to destroy vendors' stalls without warning.[18] Although Khairnar claimed always to issue a preliminary signal, the president of the Hawkers' Union, Sharad Rao, accused politicians of turning a blind eye to the "rampage" being carried on in Khairnar's name. "For the past two months, the indiscriminate eviction of hawkers and destruction of their goods has been going on, but not a single MLA or MLC [Member of the Legislative Assembly or Member of the Legislative Council] has spoken against it," he said (*Times of India*, 22 June

2000). K. Pocker, general secretary of the Bombay Hawkers Association, was careful to specify his objection: "We are not challenging the demolition action, but destruction of goods is not permitted by law" (*Times of India*, 22 June 2000).

But the issue of encroachment, whether by hawkers or slum-dwellers, could not even arise if it was not sanctioned by local political bosses and ward officers, who operate to deliver votes to Members of the Legislative Assembly or of the Legislative Council and receive favors from the organized building trades that erect shanties. Builders violate zoning and other laws with impunity, encroaching on public space, protected by politicians who draw on their votes at election time – and, in some cases, provide free utility services to the residents in return. Many problems arise and persist because of the inadequacies of urban planning and the connivance of politicians and bureaucrats, but in 2000–2001 pheriwalas became the scapegoats for a range of them, being the most visible links in the chain, and the least protected.

The wave of attacks on encroachment began, curiously enough, with Operation Sunshine in December 1996, a drive launched by the Left Front-ruled West Bengal government. In it, nearly 100,000 pheriwalas from Calcutta's streets were uprooted. The drive was allegedly launched to make the city look attractive for foreign investment on the eve of the visit of the then British Prime Minister, John Major. A few weeks later, the West Bengal Legislative Assembly passed a bill making hawking a cognizable and non-bailable offence punishable with rigorous imprisonment up to three months, a fine of 250 rupees, or both (*Times of India*, 17 September 1999). The general secretary of the Communist Party (Marxist)-affiliated Calcutta Street Hawkers Union, Mohammed Nizammeddin, demanded of a reporter, "What is going on? Are hawkers our new class enemy?" (*Telegraph*, 1 December 1996).

In Mumbai, however, the discourse focused on issues of appearance and hygiene, although it was dismissive rather than hortatory. Here for instance is an account of a roadside food stall:

> After the lunch hour, the vendors pull out plastic tubs filled with used steel plates and soak them in dirty water. The plates are dried with a soiled rag and reused. Water meant for cooking is stored in rusted tins to be used later. For these and other reasons, those who eat in roadside stalls are exposing themselves daily to gastroenteritis, jaundice, typhoid and a host of other diseases. (*Times of India*, 1 August 1999)

Perhaps it was this reporter whose eye was jaundiced, but often the problems of urban space devolved entirely onto street vendors.[19] Thus: "The plight of pedestrians in Mumbai is pitiable. Most roads in Mumbai (including newly laid Development Plan roads) do not have footpaths. And footpaths, wherever they exist, are encroached upon by hawkers" (*Indian Express*, 19 September 1998). "[W]here they are reinstalled is not our problem," said M. S. Vaidya, president of Sion (East) Residents' Forum, one of several associations against the drive to create hawking zones in their neighborhood (*Times of India*, 15 September 1998). "Clearly, we are not interested in throwing hawkers into the Arabian Sea," a member of one citizen's group assured a reporter (*Times of India*, 8 March 1999). This could have been only partially reassuring to hawkers, at best, but then the statement was not directed at them.

How indeed could dialogue be imagined with such a population? Complaints about hawkers suggested that only force could remedy the problems "citizens" perceived. For example, a residents' association in Churchgate complained to the ward authorities that hawkers "had left practically no space for pedestrians and customers and made it convenient for small-time thieves and shop-lifters to indulge in pickpocketing, misbehavior with ladies, etc." (*Afternoon Despatch & Courier*, 5 May 1999). Many shopkeepers, for their part, claimed hawkers diverted business from their stores. "Legitimate business of shops is being robbed specially on the D. N. Road area where several hawkers sell smuggled luxury goods," according to Gerson Da Cunha, convener of the solid-waste management committee of Bombay First. A convener of the Citizens' Forum for Protection of Public Spaces, a voluntary movement to deal with "the hawking woes," declared, "By patronizing such hawkers we are giving rise to a cancer in the society and abetting crime." The hotel industry claims it loses at least Rs 5 million daily due to hawkers. "They are snatching away business from right under our nose," according to Association of Hotels and Restaurants Vice President Ravi Gandhi. "On days when hawkers are on strike, our business goes up by 30 to 40 percent" (*Times of India*, 8 February 1999). Hawkers are thus described as unfair competition and as a drain on the legitimate economy.

Conclusion

"Pheriwalas will always be with us," pronounced Munna Seth, who controls the handcart rental business in Ghatkopar (West), in Mumbai. "If the BMC tear down our stalls, we will use hand carts. If they confiscate the handcarts, then we will spread our goods on the footpaths. If they push us off the footpaths, then we will be walking the streets with headloads. If they send us off to Bhayander or Dahisar, we will still board the train and come back into town every day. We will keep coming back. Nothing will stop us, because our survival is at stake."[20]

Sobha Singh, who runs the handcart business with his brother Munna Seth, explained:

> The pheriwala is the cause of trouble. The pheriwala is a very poor and small person. A poor man has to learn to behave himself. If the public says that the cart is in the way he should say yes and move his cart. But today's pheriwala says *Gandu tum bolne wala kaon hai*. [(Expletive) who are you to tell me?] The road is of the public and he has the right to say that. But he does not respect the public.

Today's pheriwala fights back, Sobha Singh points out, and doesn't take violations of his rights quietly. Indeed, despite being marginal, hawkers find means of fighting back, using a range of strategies and tactics. For instance, *paotis*, receipts issued for refuse-collection charges, are the street vendors' equivalent of traffic tickets and a proof of civil transgression. In the absence of any other form of official acknowledgement such as vending licenses, which few vendors have, paotis nevertheless constitute a sign that the state has noticed their existence. Paotis have thus become de facto licenses, akin to state-issued identity cards, that vendors use when they move courts and seek injunctions against civic authorities. In a sign of the escalating war against pheriwalas, even paotis are no longer officially issued (*Indian Express*, 21 April 1999). This has merely diverted revenue to "private" hands in public servants' own informal economy, and hawkers' payments have now become bribes. To take another example, when pheriwalas seek representation by political leaders, these leaders are dubbed criminal elements whose goals are to thwart urban order.

In its rudimentary form, the market will always be with us, because, as Braudel writes, "in its robust simplicity it is unbeatable . . . the primitive market is the most direct and transparent form of exchange, the most closely supervised and the least open to deception" (Braudel 1982: 29). Even if air-conditioned stores are seen as the destiny of Indian markets, and the pheriwala is thought to be either a relic from the past or a symptom of corruption and regulatory laxity, "[t]here is no simple linear history of the development of markets" (ibid., 26). We can extend

Braudel's observation then to the forms of property as well, when he writes: "In this area, the traditional, the archaic and the modern or ultra-modern exist side by side, even today" (ibid.). New forms of property do not necessarily erase older ones. The maturation of intellectual property causes us to revisit theories of the primitive economy, and to re-examine our assumption that admirable as the poor may be, oppression is their lot in a capitalist economy. The abundance of intellectual property, however, for example, in the shape of advertising images, can offer symbolic leverage for marginal elements in modern society. Similarly, the development of city spaces must require us to reflect on how markets grow. There is no linear movement from the bazaar and the souk to the department store and the mall; rather, all of these may evolve in parallel. Without doubt this leads to the exercise of and demand for rights by more people, leading to a political and regulatory crisis when outdated conceptions continue to guide politics and policy-making.

Over time, there has been an interesting shift in the judiciary's response to the plight of those living on the footpaths. In the year 2000, the Indian Supreme Court emphatically rejected the idea that street vendors and others displaced from public lands required any state protection. Its decision has gained notoriety for its harsh language: "The promise of free land, at the taxpayers' cost . . . is a proposal which attracts more land grabbers. Rewarding an encroacher on public land with a free alternative site is like giving a reward to a pickpocket."[21]

In the landmark Olga Tellis case in 1985, the judges had expressed qualified sympathy for those who lived and worked on the footpaths, defending in principle their right to do so, while going on to set the precedent for their legal evictability in practice.[22] The later judgment, however, places a question mark against that earlier view. Those who occupy public land have no rights requiring restitution if they are evicted, according to this decision. The state is the provider, in such a view, and since its resources are finite, it cannot be expected to answer to all claims on it. The relation conceived here between the state and its subjects is that between giver and receiver. Hawkers are of course anything but passive recipients of the state's mercy; their sophistication in dealing with the bureaucracy has enabled survival amidst the most inhospitable circumstances. Here, corruption and criminality are indices of incomprehension as well as of disorder, signals of new combinations of property forms taking shape. It is improbable that the forces being generated in this process could long be contained within the kind of neoliberal climate we have been witnessing.

Acknowledgments

My thanks to Maharukh Adenwalla, Darryl D'Monte, Colin Gonsalves, Nayana Kathpalia, Sandeep Yeole, and the archivists at the Centre for Education and Documentation in Mumbai. I am also grateful to the participants at the Wenner-Gren symposium in April 2001, to the editors Caroline Humphrey and Katherine Verdery for their patient and illuminating suggestions, and to the editorial comments of an anonymous reviewer. A short-term senior fellowship from the American Institute of Indian Studies assisted in the conduct of this research. A conversation with M. S. S. Pandian in Chennai was important in an early stage of conceptualizing my argument. A different version of this chapter appeared in *Social Text*, No. 68, 2001, pp. 91–113.

Notes

1. I.e., ten million rupees. A crorepati (below, in main text) is someone with a crore or more of rupees. At the time of writing, 45 rupees equaled one US dollar. A crore of rupees would purchase a modest apartment in South Mumbai today, but a bungalow would cost much more.

2. Remark made by participant at Mumbai Study Group meeting, 17 June 2001.

3. Interview with activist, name withheld, July 2000, Mumbai. This very image recurs in news interviews with activists as well. See below, p. 241.

4. For an elegant argument on the relational character of property, see Myers 1988. On common lands as common property, see Chakravarty-Kaul 1996. She shows that as the institutions responsible for common property lands declined over time, defending them became matters of championing community identity rather than economic government, and the emphasis shifted from governing to *policing* these lands (Chakravarty-Kaul 1996: 256–7, 262–75).

5. Most scholars agree that the middle class in India is small, although they may differ on just how small it is. But middle-classness as an *identity* extends far beyond any definition that has been proposed. The idea of the middle class has a contradictory appeal, simultaneously avowing class and disavowing inequality. My use of the term here indicates a grey area, rather than a precisely definable position in the relations of production, since the real and imagined aspects of middle-classness clearly operate in tandem. See Rajagopal 1998–99.

6. This is not any longer a controversial argument. For an influential statement, see, for example Chatterjee 1997: 278 and *passim*.

7. The emergence of Hindu nationalism in the mid-1990s represented, in a limited and problematic way, an indigenization of dominant political forms, but its predominant thrust was more against the substance of Nehruvian developmentalism than against its form. See Rajagopal 2001.

8. See the interview with Sobha Singh, below, and *passim*.

9. I draw from Claude Lefort the idea that one society can be distinguished from another in terms of its *regime*, i.e., the manner of shaping of human coexistence. The institution of a new visual regime thus involves a process of the reconfiguration of politics and the reshaping of the public; it simultaneously presents a technology for the perception of social relations and for *staging* them before society at large. See Claude Lefort 1988: 217.

10. The ad was scripted by Piyush Pandey, and was made by Ogilvy & Mather. Thanks to Ashok Sarath for this information.

11. I thank Santosh Desai of McCann-Erickson for making a copy of the ad available to me.

12. Georges Bataille has argued that a society is determined not so much by its mode of production as by the mode of expenditure of its surplus. See Bataille 1988: 167–81. In this formulation, consumption and destruction can be equally accommodated.

13. Since the 1980s, state-led economic development formulated under Prime Minister Jawaharlal Nehru is being abandoned in favor of market liberalization. Although the state retains enormous power, its class biases are sharper, and the forms of its legitimation reflect this shift in interesting ways. See Rajagopal 2001.

14. The landmark judgment in this respect is Olga Tellis and Ors. v. Bombay Municipal Corporation and Others (1985) 2 Bom CR 434 1985 (3) SCC 545. AIR 1986, 180.

15. Bombay Metropolitan Development Authority, *Draft Plan for 1995-2005*, Mumbai 1997. Cited in Sharit Bhowmick, "A raw deal?" *Seminar* (New Delhi), 21.

16. A study of hawkers determined that one-fourth of them could not read or write, and that the cost of their wares ranged from Rs 500 to Rs 2000. See Sharit Bhowmik, "Hawkers' study: some preliminary findings." Unpublished ms., n.d. For more general discussions, see Breman 1996; de Soto 1990.

17. G. R. Khairnar, personal interview, 15 August 2000, Mumbai.

18. Suresh Kapile, general secretary, Mumbai Hawkers' Union, quoted in *Times of India*, 8 March 2000.

19. However, one study in Pune showed that the cheapest street food was equally or less bacteria-laden than restaurant food. See Tinker 1997. Cited in Tiwari 2000: 31.

20. Munna Seth, handcart supplier, Ghatkopar (W), Mumbai. Interview, August 2000.

21. Almitra H. Patel v. Union of India. (2000) 2 SCC 679.

22. Olga Tellis and Ors. v. Bombay Municipal Corporation and Others (1985) 2 Bom CR 434 1985 (3) SCC 545. AIR 1986, 180.

References

Newspapers and Periodicals

Afternoon Despatch & Courier, "Hawker's Paradise," 5 May 1999.

Indian Express, Raju Z. Moray, "Trampling Over Footpaths," 19 September 1998.

Indian Express, Express News Service, "Scrap paoti system, High Court orders BMC," 21 April 1999.

The Telegraph, Sujan Dutta, "City Lights," 1 December 1996.

Times of India, Namita Devidayal, "Impasse over hawking zones continues," 15 September 1998.

Times of India, Namita Devidayal, "As frustration levels increase, a citizens' movement takes shape," 8 March 1999.

Times of India, Vidyadhar Date, "Hawkers come together to form national union," 17 September 1999.

Times of India, "Sold out: Hawkers at Nariman Point," *Bombay Times,* 8 March 2000.

Times of India, "Hawkers threaten to demonstrate outside legislators' homes," 22 June 2000.

Times of India, Himanshi Dhawan, "Roadside stalls 'offer' more than a meal," 1 August 1999.

Times of India, Tina Chopra, "Vested interests hold-up solution to hawkers impasse," 8 February 1999.

Court cases

Almitra H. Patel v. Union of India. (2000) 2 SCC 679.

Olga Tellis and Ors. v. Bombay Municipal Corporation and Others (1985) 2 Bom CR 434 1985 (3) SCC 545. AIR 1986, 180.

Books and Scholarly Articles

Appadurai, Arjun. 1996. *Modernity at large.* Minneapolis: University of Minnesota Press.

Balibar, Etienne. 1994. "'Rights of Man' and 'Rights of the Citizen': The modern dialectic of equality and freedom." In *Masses, classes, ideas*. Trans. James Swenson. New York: Routledge.

Bataille, Georges. 1988. *The accursed share, vol. 1: Consumption*. Trans. H. Robert Hurley. New York: Zone Books.

Bhagwati, J., and T. N. Srinivasan. 1993. *India's economic reforms*, New Delhi: Ministry of Finance, Government of India.

Bhowmik, Sharit. n.d. "Hawkers' study: Some preliminary findings." Unpublished ms.

——. 2000. "A raw deal?" In *Seminar* (New Delhi). Street Vendors. Special Issue. No. 491.

Bombay Metropolitan Development Authority. 1997. *Draft plan for 1995–2005*. Mumbai.

Braudel, Fernand. 1982. Trans. Sian Reynolds. New York: Harper and Row.

Breman, Jan. 1996. *Footloose labour: Working in India's informal economy*. Cambridge: Cambridge University Press.

Byres, T. J. (ed.). 1997. *The state, development planning and lberalisation in India*. Delhi: Oxford University Press.

Chakravarty-Kaul, Minoti. 1996. *Common lands and customary law: Institutional change in North India over the past two centuries*. Delhi: Oxford.

Chatterjee, Partha. 1997. "Development planning and the Indian state." In *State and politics in India*. Edited by Partha Chatterjee. New Delhi: Oxford.

de Soto, Hernan. 1990. *The other path*. New York: Harper and Row.

Hart, Keith. 1973. "Informal income opportunities and urban employment in Ghana." *Journal of Modern African Studies* 11.

Lefort, Claude. 1988. "The permanence of the theologico-political?" In *Democracy and political theory*. Trans. David Macey. Minneapolis: University of Minnesota Press.

Myers, Fred. 1988. "Burning the Truck and Holding the Country: Pintupi Forms of Property and Identity." In *We are here: Politics of Aboriginal land tenure*. Edited by N. Wilmsen. Berkeley: University of California Press.

Rajagopal, Arvind. 1998–99. "Advertising, politics and the sentimental education of the Indian consumer." *Visual Anthropology Review* 14: 14–31.

——. 1999. "Thinking about the new Indian middle class: gender, advertising and politics in an age of globalization." In *Signposts: Gender issues in post-independence India*. Edited by Rajeswari Sunder Rajan. New Delhi: Kali for Women Press.

———. 2001. *Politics after television: Hindu nationalism and the reshaping of the public in India.* Cambridge: Cambridge University Press.

Sahlins, Marshall. 1972. *Stone age economics.* Chicago: Aldine Atherton.

Seminar (New Delhi). 2000. Street Vendors. Special Issue. No. 491.

Tinker, Irene. 1997. *Street foods: Urban food and employment in developing countries.* New York: Oxford University Press.

Tiwari, Geetam. 2000. "Encroachers or service providers?" *Seminar* (New Delhi) No. 491.

Part IV

Critiquing Property

Value, Relations, and Changing Bodies: Privatization and Property Rights in Kazakhstan

Catherine Alexander

Snares, tricks, plots come hurrying
Out of their dens . . .
Now comes the love of gain – a new god
Made out of the shadow
Of all the others . . .

Meanwhile the ground, formerly free to all
As the air or sunlight,
Was portioned by surveyors into patches,
Between boundary markers, fences, ditches . . .

Now I am ready to tell
How bodies are changed into other bodies.

(Ovid, *Metamorphoses*)

In *Metamorphoses*, Ovid recounts the coming of the Age of Iron after the Golden and Silver Ages when gods and heroes walked the earth and the fullness of the land was open to all. What characterizes this Iron Age are the claims men now make upon the earth, an abrupt transformation marked by a shift in social relations. Plowed, mined, and ransacked for its riches, the ground is newly quantified and made the object of exclusive claims by men against men. In this chapter, I examine the move from state- to privately owned property and concomitant modifications in the form and substance of objects, persons, and the relations

251

between them – a process Ovid's poem captures perfectly. My focus is the process of privatization in the 1990s in Kazakhstan, one of the Central Asian Republics of the former Soviet Union.

As Hann (1998: 1) suggests, anthropologists' core understanding of property is based on social relations between persons as mediated by things, whether material or intangible. That definition is itself rooted in Henry Maine's dictum that "property" is essentially a bundle of rights (1905). Traditionally, anthropologists' concerns in respect to property have been to unpick that bundle, examining, for instance, how membership in kinship groups may give a person particular rights of access, or the means by which different rights to, and relations through, an object are determined and managed (Scott 1988).

But suddenly, with the fall of the Soviet Union in 1991, a seam of new questions about the nature of property was exposed. Encouraged by foreign aid agencies (Harloe 1996: 4–5), the Newly Independent States embraced capitalism and what was seen as its foundational plank – private property – in a series of mass privatization programs that swept through much of the former Soviet Union and the eastern bloc countries. A series of unanticipated problems arose through these privatization processes, problems that in turn revealed previously unexplored aspects of property. One immediate point was that the temporal context of property mattered. Many eastern European states had a history of private property before collectivization, even if the precise form was different in each country. Returning to old claims scarcely proved straightforward, as Verdery shows for Transylvanian land reforms (1994, 1998, 1999, 2003); spatially, too, the land to which claims were made proved surprisingly elastic. Other states such as Kazakhstan, freshly emerged from the Soviet Union, had virtually no pre-Soviet history of private property. In the main, industry and cities were Soviet, or were traceable only to the nineteenth-century Russian colonial presence, since the pre-Soviet form of social organization in Kazakhstan was nomadic (see also Sneath, this volume). This, then, raised specific challenges, ignored in the largely generic approach used to transfer property from state ownership to individuals. Apartment blocks, factories, and the infrastructure skeining together the Central Asian Soviet Republics arose in the absence of private ownership, and, as Verdery indicates, under a regime that evaluated cost and worth quite differently from a market-based model of value.

In such a fraught setting, privatization offers an opportunity to analyze and question the definition of property offered above. In particular, the process of privatization described here problematizes the very definitions of "person," 'thing," and "relation," bringing to the fore the polyvalent nature of value implicit in any property relation. The state too appears as a crucial element in the way people talk about the reconfiguring of persons, things, and relations. A sense of abandonment by an overarching structure that had meshed persons and objects together appeared repeatedly in informants' accounts under the rubric of "theft." In the conclusion, I return to the notion of theft as relational absence, the dark mirror of property relations.

With this in mind, I explore three themes: the move away from state ownership that had to be effected before reconnection to different forms of property could take place; the reconstitution of the objects and persons between which new forms of relations are developing; and the idea of "value" in its many guises. There is the search for value when trying to cost an item in the absence of a market and competition; value as the different moral accounts placed upon the same process of privatization; and value as the essence of a thing, produced by the difference that is demanded by the act and form of relation.

At the center of the discussion are two case studies of factories in Almaty, Kazakhstan's former capital, that were moved from state ownership to joint- and finally open-stock companies. The undoing of workplaces provides poignant examples of the unravelling of the previously entwined character of Soviet work, domestic life, and the person. In one sense, it could be said that these enterprises changed from one form of collective property to another – what Stark, in his research on Hungary (1996), terms recombinant property forms. The appearance and enactment of such forms is very different in Kazakhstan and Hungary, however, due to differences in each country's recent economic and political histories. We should consider the moment of privatization separately from what happened thereafter. Within that moment, so readily glossed as the legal transfer of rights from the state to the private sphere, a number of implicit processes were also occurring that account for the confusion over exactly what was happening.

Talking to city officials and residents of recently-privatized apartment blocks in Almaty about the state's changing role revealed a range of perceptions. Multiple constructions of the relation between people and state meant that understandings of the movement from state to private ownership were far from straightforward. In the first place, what did "the state" *mean*? Some informants spoke of the state *as* the people: that which is state-owned is therefore owned by the people – a Hegelian-Marxist conception. At the same time, another key model of the relationship between people and state posited the state as representative *of* the people, managing and owning assets on their behalf – essentially a paternalistic model. The third idea of this relationship saw the state as other, which encompassed a range of constructions. There was the state as enemy of the people, something to be negotiated around. At the other end of the continuum, the state was nothing and nobody, for its complete diffusion into all realms of life meant that it effectively disappeared; being everywhere it was also nowhere.

As people tried to come to terms with the new economic and political environment and its effect on their own socioeconomic position, they continued to use these old models of the state and its relationship to the people in exegeses of what had happened to former structures within which the person was suspended. What is notable about these various models is both that officials and citizens alike drew upon a similar categorical arsenal, and that one person might refer to several models to make a range of points even if, when stacked together as above, they suggest fundamentally different resonances and relationships. As a last observation on this variety of portrayals of the state, it should be noted that each version implicitly also acts as a description or exegesis of the person, since each model refers to "the people" in one form or another. What follows from this is that representations of the state are essentially relational, and that they often emerge from shifting understandings of the condition of the person (see also Alexander 2002).

The initial movement of privatization, the first, careless rupture, logically necessary at an ideological level but muted in its performance, was the separation of persons and things from the state. Thus the notion of the state in this construction as wholly incorporative had first to be decomposed into constituent parts before the parts could be reconnected – indeed, before they could be connected at all. "How can we own again what we already own!" was a constant, exasperated cry by informants, citizens, and city officials alike. The legal processes that followed produced a double disjuncture between form and content. Apparent continuities of form masked abrupt changes in the internal constitution of both things and persons; meanwhile, scratching a changed outer form often revealed that the substance of relations, things, and persons had remained constant. Gasché (1999) argues that the notion of relation exists prior to and independently of the properties of things; thus the very act of changing relations through law in and of itself alters the characteristics or value, in all senses, of the linked things.

In the case of industrial enterprises, the objects with which people were to have changed relations were internally reconstituted while their outside forms were maintained. Considering objects separately from their environment, as was done for the purpose of privatization, also reveals that the attributes of an object are, in part, relational. Through the semantic legerdemain of the law, elements that had fitted into a holistic system were isolated and stripped of their contextual characteristics. Without transport, supply, and distribution networks, an industrial enterprise is only a bloodless pound of flesh. Kazakhstan is now littered with dead factories and steppe cities built around huge processing complexes that have become half-abandoned urban disaster zones.[1]

Persons' attributes were legally recast, allowing them to make such relations in the first place. The change could perhaps be summarized as the movement from entitlement to eligibility – that is, from rights embedded in the very notion of citizenship to a more individualized conception of possibility. Eligibility for share ownership was repeatedly changed. Within the new politico-legal framing of eligibility, individual enterprises worked out their own ideas of qualification for share ownership. This change thus affected understandings of rights of personhood, citizenship, and property on the one hand and, on the other, the relationship *between* "being," "belonging," and "things."

The story, then, is one of bodies and their changing characteristics, whether property objects or people: of apparently changed forms where the content remains constant; and of the sapping of industry by hollowing out the form, leaving factories in name alone. Richard Pipes notes that "the word property evokes in our minds the idea of physical objects: real estate, bank accounts, stocks and bonds. But . . . increasingly in the modern world it has come to apply to incorporeal assets such as credit, patents and property rights" (1999: xii). The temporal and spatial context in which property exists may not be so readily evoked, but is as much part of real estate and patents as the objects that are more neatly tied up into legal categories.

Privatization

The Economist suggests that more than fifty methods of privatization exist (1993: 20). This kind of analysis highlights the fact that simple definitions of privatization are embedded in a wider environment of competing ideologies, world markets, previous political structures, and hidden configurations of relations that cut across open legal structures of entitlement. Understandings of the market and private ownership are necessarily context-dependent and multi-functional (Lane 1995: xv); they also rest on a series of assumptions about the legitimate control of assets and economic efficiency. Nonetheless, we can begin with some general assumptions. Lavigne (1999: 162), for example, proposes as a definition of privatization "the legal transfer of property rights from the state to private agents," state property here being taken to include assets belonging to the state and to socialist co-operatives. The implication is that rights are transferred in their entirety rather than being reallocated (Brabant 1998: 212). Ownership, for example, may simply be divorced from the exercise of ownership rights (ibid.). But the supposition for both Lavigne and Brabant is that (particularly in postsocialist jurisdictions) the process of privatization introduced this moment of reallocation, yet in fact, ownership rights within the Soviet Union always were a focus of negotiation through practice.

So, more granularity is required. Maine's "bundle of rights" definition of property can be decomposed into a consideration of rights temporal and spatial. Multiple rights may coexist as present interests, each contingent upon others' temporal claim. Agricultural land in Kazakhstan has been transferred to private ownership with a limited time period of ninety-nine years and, as yet, no provision has been made for lease extension. Technically, then, both state and citizen enjoy current interests. In this sense, rights to a thing can be imagined as being temporally stacked up behind the thing itself, stretching as far as patience and legal clauses will allow. The temporal context of property relations has also shifted in the experience of the person for whom work formerly meant little immediate cash return, but confidence in pensions and future welfare. A common "before and now" construction was the change from such long-term certainty, to short-term anxiety as to how ownership could be transmuted into security and reliability. "With privatization," it was often said, "our future has been given away." This future in part was accounted for by the potentiality of the land's rich natural resources as yet undrilled or uncovered but sold off in terms of extractive rights to foreign firms.

Privatization in Kazakhstan officially began with the establishment of the State Property Committee in January 1991. However, the process differed markedly from that which was initially promoted. The first stage was housing privatization. Housing coupons were distributed according to the length of time citizens had worked, based on a formula for a nominal citizen who had worked for 21 years. Entitlement here was simply through labor and being a Kazakhstani citizen. The advertised idea for those who had more coupons than necessary was that the surplus could be used for the second stage of privatization: mass privatization of small enterprises. In fact, in the second stage, the government decided that excess housing coupons could not be used for exchange and they simply became worthless. This abrupt and blatant change from the advertised program resulted in widespread mistrust in governmental promises (Kalyuzhnova 1999: 28), which subsequent actions would compound.

Late in 1993, the second stage began. New coupons were issued that could be invested in any of the newly established Investment Privatization Funds within a government-approved list. These funds then participated in sell-offs and auctions of government-owned stock and small enterprises. By January 1994, 169 Funds had been formed. However, coupons could be neither traded nor used to buy equity directly (Kaser 1997: 33) and, by November 1994, the public had placed only 15 percent of the issued points into Funds. This wave of privatization was not a great success for several reasons. The Funds were run by inexperienced managers with no clear restructuring strategy who often flouted the few regulations in existence – giving, for example, exaggerated estimates of early profits or seeking to "evade the legal provisions on a 37 per cent maximum holding in any one enterprise (by creating a multiplicity of subsidiaries to buy into an enterprise)" (Kaser 1997). Where Funds were not rival groups, they often formed themselves into cartels to control the supposedly open auctions. Fund managers rapidly moved shares between Funds, so that it became impossible to distinguish precisely who had invested in what. Lacking capital for future investment, enterprises could not buy raw materials for processing, and many jobs were "frozen:" staff were "given unpaid leave" or simply not paid, patterns that continued.

Consequently, the material base of many small businesses deteriorated, sometimes irrevocably. People left employment that used their professional training to find what money they could, usually buying and selling in markets. The Funds themselves came to be regarded as something of a joke. Many merged, many more vanished entirely. One couple showed me all the certificates and documents they had received, now carefully kept by the husband in an old shoe box. The wife commented that she kept asking him to throw the whole lot away, as they had so little room in their apartment and it was pointless to hang onto a pile of junk. He agreed that the papers were worthless, but saw them as a souvenir of a particular time. "Somewhere out there," he said, "there is a business or an enterprise that I have shares in, that I partially own. But where is it? Who knows? I have no idea. Maybe it has closed. Maybe I am a rich man. But I will never know."

The third phase (1996–1998) was the individual sale of large enterprises, defined in the State Committee for Privatization's guidelines as over 5,000 employees. The *Financial Times* called this the "Kazakh sale of the century" (25 October 1996). Enterprises were sold at extraordinary speed. Barely had the legally requisite public advertisement appeared than a notice of sale would be published, giving rise to speculation about who had prior information about forthcoming sales and from whom. Enterprises that were not remotely viable were offered at auction, purchasers taking on debts along with assets. Again, for a bureaucracy that might find the path of probity a little too restrictive at times, there were many opportunities here for declaring enterprises bankrupt and allowing their purchase at extremely low prices. Indeed, in December 1996, there were demonstrations by several thousand trade unionists "in protest against unpaid wages and pensions and irregular ('wild') privatization" (Kaser 1997: 51).

Recalling this period, people speak first of the lack of information. Sometimes no-one knew that an enterprise was being offered for purchase until its sale was reported in the newspapers. Sometimes acquisitions were settled through bribes before the official tender was even advertised, then ratified legally after the charade of public tender. "In effect," an ex-engineer commented, "it was all done legally, but the lawyers were on the side of the big businessmen. The legal experts were bought up by the people who wanted the enterprises. You could say the law was bought by these people – after all, most of it hadn't been written yet." Those directly involved with the early days of privatization describe the utter confusion as public administrators struggled to formulate and enact the move away from communal property. Three things emerged from this: lack of trust in the government and the law, lack of trust in the bureaucracy who managed the process, and a fear that the future of the country has been sold for short-term gain to a limited number of officials. The governmental credibility crucial for such a major economic shift is almost entirely absent.

Case Studies

The following section describes two industrial enterprises in Almaty, before considering factors of prime concern to both in the change from state-owned to open-stock companies: valuation, share allocation, decision-making, credibility, and residual control by public institutions.

The Sweet Factory

During the Second World War, the Soviet government moved several factories from the Ukrainian frontline to their territorial hinterlands. In 1942, four sweet factories were relocated from Kharkov as part of this transfer, each to a different city in Kazakhstan. As was standard Soviet practice, each factory manufactured the same full range of products with the same machinery and staffing structure. In September 1991, state subsidies were cut and the factories' workforces decided to opt not only for privatization, but to make each factory an independent enterprise. Almost immediately the factory in Shymkent in southeast Kazakhstan failed. This case study focuses on Almaty's factory, where workers and management reached a formal Agreement to privatize its assets in February 1992. At this juncture, the economy was still relatively stable and production levels of 9,000 tons per annum continued.

In 1995, reflecting the general economic crisis, production levels dropped to 10 percent. At this point, the management board decided to send all workers on "unpaid leave" until they could justify bringing them back. But these decisions were rejected by the workers, who instead proposed that the two operating shifts would each work one week in five, taking the rest as unpaid leave, each shift working half a day. That same year, the factory recorded a loss of one million dollars. During this time, workers sought other ways of earning money, whether selling homemade cakes in local markets or (for the mechanics) carrying out repairs in exchange for goods or money. Some found their side employment more lucrative and reliable than the factory wavering on the edge of collapse, and never returned. The experience and understanding of privatization within this factory therefore varied hugely for different actors according to their position.

The very capacity of each factory to manufacture all possible confectionary goods also meant that it was hard to achieve economies of scale since each product required a different process and specialized machinery. The additional significance of this Soviet tendency for each factory to incorporate all related processes and products first emerged when the sweet factories decided to operate independently of each other. All the recipes had been used in common. There were no patents simply because rights to use were inclusive rather than exclusive. Following privatization, some of the factories tried to claim intellectual property rights to recipes that had previously been used by all. In the end, the problem was solved by maintaining previously common recipes in collective ownership by the three surviving factories, while subsequent innovations by any one factory would belong exclusively to it. Suddenly the race was on to be the first to marry the flavor of new nationalism to a unique brand of Kazakhstan chocolate. At this time, the main novelty was creating a marketing agency to replace the collapsed Soviet distribution network. Each sweet factory developed its own strategy separately and was therefore in competition not only with foreign suppliers but also, for the first time, with the others. Value qua monetary worth was now derived from a sense of value as difference.

In 1997, for the first time since privatization, Almaty's factory showed a small profit, and by the following year the losses of 1995 had been wiped out. Dividends were paid for the first time in 1999. However, this rosy picture of the factory was undermined by whispers that capital was still so low that, in order to pay dividends at all, twelve million tenge had been borrowed.[2] There were insufficient funds left to pay for raw materials and necessary capital investments, which partly explained why so many departments were still running well below capacity and, apparently, demand.

The Textile Kombinat

The Textile Kombinat was built between 1965 and 1971.[3] Almaty was chosen as the site of this enterprise to provide employment, then in short supply, for women. In its heyday, it was the largest textile enterprise in Soviet Central Asia and one of the ten largest in the entire Soviet Union. Again, like the sweet factory, the Kombinat brought all associated manufacturing processes under one roof, so that cotton from Tajikistan and Uzbekistan was dyed, spun, and woven into different fabrics in workshops within the Kombinat, which spanned several neighborhoods in size. A few clothes were also produced. The supporting social infrastructure was breathtaking. More than 9,000 people were housed in factory hostels and apartment blocks built for workers. There were kindergartens, holiday resorts, hospitals, pioneer camps, and a colossal Palace of Culture. Approximately 6,000 people were directly employed by the factory, about 10,000 when supporting facilities were taken into account. Equally significant, as one of the most prestigious industrial enterprises it was a frequent point of reference in constructions of a happy, successful Soviet past, not only by former employees but by people who still lived in the immediate neighborhood, and indeed farther afield in Almaty.

Immediately after Independence in 1991, the Textile Kombinat continued to produce the same range of goods, but the break-up of the

Soviet supply and distribution network had devastating effects. With little capital in hand, the management team of the Textile Kombinat was unable to match prices offered to Tajik and Uzbek cotton growers on the world market. Supplies rapidly dried up, while the Kombinat limped on using up old stock. Again, the principal market in Russia suddenly vanished and the factory found itself producing goods with neither sales outlets nor the knowledge to compensate for the loss. Previously, whatever had been produced had been taken from the Kombinat and redistributed elsewhere; now cheap textiles and modern designs flooded into Kazakhstan from China and the Middle East. It took several years before the Kombinat was able to modify what it produced to meet altered tastes and fashions.

The Kombinat was privatized in the mid-1990s. The immediate consequence was the rapid divestment of the social facilities and the gradual closure of one department after another. Now vast production floors stood empty, their windows smashed, the machinery that survived nightly pillaging silent. A spinner who had spent her working life in the Kombinat but lost her job in 1997 cited the current state of the peeling Kombinat as a marker of the sad decline of Soviet industry, the loss of pride in Kazakhstan's products. No social facilities remained; the hospitals, apartment blocks, and pioneer camps were either sold or handed over to the city council (Akimat). No buyer could be found for the Palace of Culture, which lay forlornly empty when it was not housing the occasional art display or children's ballet class. One-tenth of the productive workforce, about 1,200, remained in the single working department.

Valuation: The Naming of Parts

As indicated above, there are many ways through which to transfer collective rights into private ownership. The singularity of the industrial sector in Kazakhstan is that rights did not just move from the many to the one but, so to speak, from the many to the many. "The many," however, was differently constituted in each case. Not only did various criteria for eligibility replace one entitlement through citizenship, but the nature and exercise of rights also changed. Before rights in the enterprise could be allocated, or even considered, an agreement had to be reached as to exactly what the thing *was* to which different categories of people were now to have a different legal relationship. Hastily formed privatization departments were scratching their collective heads over how to parcel up state-owned industrial enterprises for, just as ownership can be singular or corporate, so too does an enterprise represent an aggregate of machines and buildings, of stock and fuel and much else besides.

What really brought home the problem of identifying the enterprises was the first step in the "process of privatization": placing a nominal value upon the enterprise. The notion of "value" holds not only the sense of cost, or equivalence, but also connotations of a thing's worth, its essence – quite simply, what it is. In keeping with these two meanings of value, sometimes incompatible, the difficulty was twofold. First there had to be the naming of parts, and then a means of locating a price where there were no equivalents in the absence of a market. In the first stage of privatization, similar parts of different State Owned Enterprises (SOEs) were sometimes sold off together but, in the realization that this resulted in monopolistic advantage that was deemed detrimental to the great drive to the free market, these new enterprises were split up again and reconstructed. Thereafter, the first agreement was that the land upon which factories were built belonged to the state and was not included in the valuation. This decision was rescinded in May 2000, so the internal constitution of legally defined entities continued to be fluid. The second key decision was to examine the founding charter of each enterprise to determine whether or not the "social buildings" were to be included in the valuation. In effect, this decided whether or not the enterprise was to be stripped of the social infrastructure that had formed such an important part of Soviet working life.

Fashions in production techniques oscillate the world over; a Fordist emphasis on holism, however, continued in the USSR long after it had been superseded by management techniques bent on specialization elsewhere in the world. In this sense, holism, as Kotkin's *Magnetic Mountain* shows so clearly, incorporates not only the mechanical nuts and bolts but also the manufacture of workers and consumers, regulating both work and social environment (see also Harvey 1989: 126; Beynon and Hedges 1982). Until the moment of valuation, it was assumed by workers and citizens alike that these social buildings belonged to the factory. Workers were entitled to enjoy these facilities, subject to internal regulations and, of course, availability. Entitlement came either from working at the factory or from belonging to a family with a factory worker. With privatization, however, remuneration for work was generally filleted back to a salary. Citizens spoke of a loss of rights, of confusion over what had happened to the buildings that epitomized the glory days of work and materialized the high prestige of some factories.

The physical disintegration of sites of work can be seen as part and parcel of the disintegration of the Soviet worker. As a citizen, the person was entitled to work and, through that work, to the social and material benefits with which it was interwoven. With privatization, the social infrastructure vanished, along with the implicit contract that the world of work embraced provision of a whole living environment. Labor became commodified, just exchanged for money. The person then has become fragmented, as has the site of work. Part now meets part.

The sweet factory's charter included only the factory building: control of social facilities was swiftly handed over to the city council (the Akimat). The Textile Kombinat, however, was transferred to the workers with its social buildings intact, since they were designated in its founding charter. For the management this was something of a poisoned chalice, since there was simply no capital to pay for these facilities that had always been heavily subsidized. Almost immediately the new management board divided the enterprise into two operations, one functioning, the other asset-holding, although the latter was effectively a liability.[4] Such capital as existed was located in the operational arm until the Akimat agreed to take over the capital-draining social infrastructure. Most workers did not clearly understand this first stage and saw it as an instance of bureaucratic dark dealings. Informants urged me to ask Akimat officials what had happened to these buildings. "One minute they were there and the next they were gone. They should belong to us, but nobody knows what happened, who has them, and why they went." For many, this sudden disappearance of the holistic place of work was just another instance of political shenanigans removing rights and selling off public, and therefore collectively owned, assets.

Another common misconception of the privatization process is thrown up here. The people who asked me to find out who had snatched the social buildings from the factories understood that privatization had entailed the transfer of assets from one party (the state) to another (a private individual). What was so hard to grasp was that in the "transfer," many of these buildings had just been left to rot, too expensive to maintain in the absence of state subsidies. Privatization therefore frequently translated as tearing off profitable elements, abandoning the rest to wind and rain. But this was not the common understanding, which was simply that the state had sold these assets, so someone must have them, and the state (the people) should have, but had not, received money for them. The effects of removing the social infrastructure from these enterprises were huge, and not only in economic terms. An ex-nurse who lived in the vicinity of the Textile Kombinat said, "Now the factory has virtually gone, and with it the cultural life of this area. Everything has just been thrown out in the street."

Nonetheless, the ethos of the workplace providing more than just cash payment for labor prevailed in some enterprises that managed to weather the late 1990s. The sweet factory still maintained an impressive clinic on site and helped with funeral costs so that, even though highly reduced, there was still a sense of cradle-to-grave paternalism. The state-owned Kazakh Oil company was generous to its employees to the extent that a government official complained that its wealth remained within the company. An unemployed engineer commented, "Everyone knows that the head of Kazakh Oil has 150 million tenge. Where does the money come from? From us! It's stolen from us."

Placing a valuation on what remained of the enterprises proved a headache. As the deputy chief of privatization said, "When the first privatization law was passed no-one had any experience. It was very difficult to value enterprises that were to be sold. Of course, there was no market at that time, so how were we to know what price something could be bought and sold for?" The special commission set up to determine value decided to start with the initial cost of setting up the enterprise in question (remember the sweet factory was established under wartime conditions), essentially applying the standard Marxist labor theory of value to pricing. The amortization of these assets was then estimated at 1–5 percent p.a., depending on the quality of the construction materials. The conversion from roubles to tenge was then factored in by dividing the total by 500, before different inflation rates were applied.[5] This figure was further modified by adding in all the expenditures deemed necessary to bring the basic buildings up to standard, before future profits were estimated to give the full current worth. Again, in the absence of a market, estimations of future profit were as speculative as the original cost of establishing the enterprise.[6] The privatization chief admitted that quite a few enterprises ended up with a negative value before future profits were calculated – leading one to wonder about profit estimations, since surprisingly few enterprises officially ended up with a negative value.

The valuation method was later refined by including the *location* and *purpose* of the enterprise in the initial price. Thus, a centrally-positioned restaurant would now be worth more per square foot than one located in the distant city suburbs. In effect, the internal constitution of the enterprise was once again being, in all senses, reevaluated. Or, to put it another way, the properties of the property object to which rights were to be sold or allocated were redefined and reconstituted while the external form remained constant. Rights through shares now included a notion of context and not just enclosed space and tangible contents. Nonetheless, the idea that context was an essential part of an enterprise went no further. Constructed simply as a transfer of ownership, the whole process of privatization side-stepped the issue of precisely what was being transferred. When people were apparently given the rights to have shares in state-owned enterprises, or to own collectively the enterprise for which they had previously worked, this is not exactly what happened. The enterprise was a conglomeration of buildings and services, of equipment and social infrastructure; it was the land on which the buildings stood and it was, perhaps most importantly, a node in a network of training schemes, supply, distribution, and subsidy. Enterprises were offered up for collective ownership shorn of many properties that had allowed them to function – had allowed them, in fact, to be characterized as an enterprise at all. It is hardly surprising that many failed after an initial period of using up stock and paying employees in kind. Lacking the social infrastructure that had been such a defining feature of Soviet working life, capital or stocks to process, enterprises were often akin to an organ severed from a body.[7]

Share Allocation: The Properties of People

At an informal level, another set of characteristics, or properties, came into play, enabling officials to take advantage of insider knowledge when lucrative assets were to be sold off. These were generally connections built up during the Soviet period. Common background, education, workplace, and party membership: all of these are elements of the person, and a means of connection to a shared point. The true value or constitution of the person then, like the enterprise, is also located in position and context.

At the moment of independence, cities and the industrial sector were dominated by Russians, collective farms by Kazakhs. One reason for privatizing enterprises through universal issue of vouchers was to avoid granting de facto ownership privileges to state enterprises that would have resulted in the non-Kazakh population gaining wealth out of proportion to their political weight (Smith, et al. 1998: 149). Smith et al. (ibid.) claim that this gave the Kazakh nomenklatura[8] an edge in the privatization process, yet few non-Kazakh factory directors were replaced, and there is considerable circumstantial evidence that share apportionment was so reshuffled that control now rested with the directors.

Privatization of these two enterprises took at least two stages to complete. The first was to move from full state-ownership to closed joint-stock companies in which the state still had a 90 percent controlling share. "The state" in this context could be either the local Akimat or the republic itself. Other enterprises, such as those in the defense sector, that continued to be controlled by the state, usually for strategic purposes, were not valued in the sense of having a price attached. Nonetheless, they were also subject to a long period of reclassification. This did not affect the companies themselves so much as the organizational level that had rights to control them. Non-strategic enterprises moved to a closed joint-stock position where the controlling share was not owned by the state. Some enterprises remained in this position, some went on to become open joint-stock or wholly privately owned.

The initial moment of privatization illuminated and briefly brought to the fore a range of models of relationality and entitlement. The following years saw a rapid reconfiguring of ownership before the question of access and entitlement sank again. Common understandings of entitlement bumped up against legal definitions in all their bewildering multiplicity and, all the while, elite networks of connection and information permitted another category of people, the nomenklatura, to dart into the maelstrom of rights transfer and pick out successful enterprises.

The government's first set of eligibility criteria was to have been through house-ownership coupons allocated on the basis of labor. This prerequisite was abandoned in favor of a new coupon allocation on the basis of location: town or country. Underlying this division was the premise that ethnic difference conforms to geography, since cities are dominated by non-Kazakhs. Ownership rights were therefore now partly understood through a model of ethnic belonging. For internal transfers, the law dictated that 75 percent of shares should go to the factory's labor force. Within this 75 percent, however, there was some room for maneuver at a local level.

In the sweet factory, eligibility was assessed by length of service from a minimum of two years, later extended to include pensioners and to take rank into account. The management board, therefore, by their own definition of eligibility, ended up with a greater proportion of the shares within the 75 percent overall allocation. This was a touchy subject. Apparently there was no mechanism to monitor the changing profile of ownership, so the share holders came to be "all mixed up now," as the finance director remarked rather frostily, and no means existed of verifying the proportion owned by management staff. After the initial sales to the workforce, there were three more share issues, although these were open.

At first, the Textile Kombinat approached the question of share allocation quite differently. A senior member of the Textile Kombinat staff said of the initial allocation:

> Everyone got together, workers and management, and we set our own terms for who was eligible to receive shares out of the factory's pool of 75%. We decided that not just factory workers, but also suppliers from collective farms should have a share, and people who used to distribute our goods and so on. The only limit we set was that no one person should have more that 10%. We behaved differently then. Now it doesn't matter how many shares one person has, but then we thought it did. People are different now and if one person has more than 50% of shares – that's just normal. Maybe that's because now we're in a market economy, or maybe it's because now most people just don't have any money to buy shares.

The Kombinat was now run by a Board of Directors, which owned more than 50 percent of the shares. Unofficially, the chairman and President of the Board, a married couple, were described as the factory's owners. They were said to have amassed well over 90 percent of the shares after the first distribution. I could not formally confirm this, but the chairman grinned when I asked, and did not deny it either. In both cases, there was a rapid rearrangement of the share-ownership profile after initial allocation.

Share allotment had another effect. The proportion owned by different categories led to different legal and informal rights and obligations. Remaining enterprises came under direct state control. This was not always an advantage, as ministries tended to merge and re-form at quite an alarming rate, so that enterprises or lesser committees subordinate to one ministry might suddenly find themselves masterless, lacking any status whatsoever. On the other hand, some managers said they felt that government had cast off business to make its own way in the world, whereas state-sponsored enterprises still attracted ministers' attention. Unwelcome as such rapacious attention could be for the remaining profitable enterprises, it still allowed direct access to government. As described above, a range of categories existed between state and private ownership. In the move from joint to private closed-stock company, a miscalculation was made over the transfer of Textile

Kombinat shares, leaving the state with 0.3 percent. The director, an extremely canny woman, was delighted to discover this mistake, as it gave her the opportunity to claim the privileges of both a publicly-controlled *and* a private company, as she chose: the obligations that the state owed her company through the rights they had in it (essentially access to ministers), and the rights that she could practise as de facto owner of the enterprise.

It was extremely difficult to get people to talk about what had happened to share allocation after the initial distribution. Workers knew that in most cases the management had succeeded in securing at least 51 percent of the shares; in many cases one or two individuals had gathered over 90 percent of the shares. Senior management of the sweet factory, the Textile Kombinat, and indeed the state administration, were apt to cast such a reshuffling of ownership as a rational change in the basic philosophy underlying privatization, as an Akimat official observed:

> In the first stage of privatization a regulation stated that the labor force of an enterprise would get 10% of the shares free of charge, so there could be up to 2000 people with this 10%. But other people come along and buy shares for money and they find that they are being bothered by these people with the 10% who maybe want them to do things differently. So, after 1996, the law changed and ownership was sold to one to three people at auction. This way people know who owns the enterprise and who is responsible. If a collective gets something without paying for it they won't bother about it. They're not interested.

In a situation where many workers were being sent on unpaid leave, or simply not being paid, a strongly worded offer to sell shares in return for receiving wages was unlikely to be turned down. Similarly, selling shares enabled many to realize cash to meet immediate needs. In the sweet factory I was told one story of an engineer (in the biscuits department) who sold his shares to pay for his mother's funeral in Moscow. Another worker (in toffees) sold her shares to repair a drain leaking into her kitchen. By borrowing, the factory was able to pay dividends in 1999, but so many shares had been issued by this point that this only amounted to 5 tenge per share. Watching the factory stumbling through lean times, many thought it better to cash in what they could at 50 tenge a share, the official price. This was a huge drop from the initial nominal issue price of 250 tenge, but it was cash in hand, and considerably more than dividends yielded. These sales also indicated a range of share values. Most workers said that the financial director told them the buying and selling price, and arranged for share transactions. A nascent stock market exists but is almost exclusively used for block sales to organizations. In factory corridors, shares were also sold "from hand to hand." Through such private unofficial sales it was generally estimated that 60–80 tenge per transaction could be raised; the change in ownership would be ratified later.

These movements emphasized the fact that property relations were understood within a thin temporal context governed by risk and uncertainty. Hann notes that property may be understood as rights over things that guarantee a future income stream (1998: 4). This view of property necessarily includes the legal and customary climate that will ensure the enjoyment of such rights. In Kazakhstan, the institutional credibility underlying property relations was increasingly whittled away (see also Litwack 1991). Investors had a strong sense of unease over what legal move the government might make next. Credibility, and confidence in the source of legitimacy for upholding new property regimes, play a significant role in the temporal aspect of property relations, and here they were lacking.

Within the command economy, the collectivity (represented by the state) mediated relations between people and industrial enterprises. In the case of share ownership, relations were more immediate but rights were limited. The single right granted by mass privatization – that to dividends or a share of the enterprise's profit – was a meaningless right with the collapse of the Investment Funds, for the investment certificates became nothing more than empty signs lacking a referent. With internal transfers of undertakings, decisions were usually restricted to an executive body acting on behalf of the share ownership. In Kazakhstan, the internal workings of enterprises became largely invisible; the occasional facts that surfaced suggested that the controlling power remained in the same hands as before privatization. Prior to April 1993, factory directors were political appointees. After that, a coordinating council was set up for each factory with local state representatives; this body then chose the factory director. More than 75 percent of existing directors remained in their posts. Being allocated shares therefore carried with it no measure of decision-making or control over the enterprise; these rights remained with the management. In terms of rights over return, dividend payouts became limited or non-existent.

Property is also embedded in law. The residual control that rests with public authority is an important element in determining the precise nature of rights and relations to property, in terms of both use and ownership. In transition economies, such as Kazakhstan, however, the legal framework defining regulatory controls was often lacking, incomplete, or contradictory, leaving the way open for arbitrary local decisions on implementation by regulatory bodies. Where legislation did exist the most frequently cited problems were that the law could be circumvented through bribery, and firms unable or unwilling to participate in bribing officials were regulated out of business. This latter problem beset operations in the private sphere from small shops to large-scale enterprises.

"Like all such things," a Kombinat executive commented on legislation passed nominally to protect domestic industry, "it was just words in the end. All these things are political games, just words."

Conclusion

Theft has been a recurrent motif in this chapter: the future has been stolen, the factories' social buildings (index of a social contract) have been stolen, the sealed-off wealth of the state-owned Kazakh Oil has been stolen. In each case, the speaker identified the victim as him- or herself or the people, "it has been stolen from us." The perpetrators are not so clearly identified. Investment Fund managers seemingly vanished, banks collapsed with people's savings, the sale of state assets was often announced after the event. One informant observed how frequently the passive voice was used in such narratives, whether in newspapers or conversation. The circumspection of the passive is more politic when people speak, in the same breath, of fear; but it also foregrounds and animates the action and effect, while eradicating the actor: "snares, tricks, and plots come hurrying out of their dens," to recall the epigraph from Ovid. These idioms of swindling and plundering, which frame so many stories of changing property relations in Kazakhstan, can be seen in the light of negative property relations. If property represents social relations, then theft is the absolute denial of those relations. Abstracting and depersonalizing the action accentuates the perceived absence of relations. This lack of connection expresses first the gap between current political promises and experienced exclusion and desolation, and secondly the leap between cognitive models of property relations of "then" and "now."

The theft talked about here indicates a loss of social relations, just as property "stands for" those relations. Theft speaks of the removal of rights to collective property through *belonging*, as much as the property of rights. The relations of property and theft here then spin around understandings of the relation of persons to the state. In the official, public narrative of this connection, the communist state could be seen as the Absolute, achieving relation to itself in indivisible unity – thereby excluding any movement toward relation, including that of negation; indeed movement itself was thus excluded. Mass privatization entailed a fracturing of unity, a multiplying of difference and an introduction of instability, mobility, and a new short-term temporality. Private transactions always occupied this space of separation, but *within* an over-arching structure of connection; it was this web that fell away. For those who felt they were part of the state, it is hard to understand this new relation *to* the state that presupposes separation *from* it and all that this form of belonging entails. Admitting even the possibility of this separation and a new relation between people and state was the necessary precondition for privatization.

Shifts in conceptual paradigms mark the abrupt end of an era. Bodies, persons, and things metamorphose into different legal categories, or keep their outer shape while changing substance. Relations – which at once secure the difference of things, make things, and indicate corres-pondences between things – change and transform. In the passage below, Ted Hughes (1997: xi) describes the time in which Ovid wrote *Metamorphoses*. Beneath the smooth confidence of the Augustan Age lurked ideological turmoil; if one did not know the context, it might easily stand for Kazakhstan at the turn of the millennium.

> The obsolete paraphernalia of the old official religion were lying in heaps, like old masks in the lumber room of a theatre, and new ones had not yet arrived. The mythic plane, so to speak, had been defrocked. At the same time, perhaps . . . as a result, the Empire was flooded with ecstatic cults . . . it was at sea in hysteria and despair . . . These tales . . . establish a rough register of what it feels like to live in the psychological gulf that opens at the end of an era.

Notes

1. The World Bank Report (1998) listed 57 such collapsed industrial towns.
2. In 2000, $1 was the equivalent of 180 tenge.
3. "*Kombinat*" as opposed to "*fabrika*" (factory) implies a large-scale operation, or industrial complex integrating several related processes.

4. See Verdery's chapter in this collection for further discussion of liability transfer.

5. Inflation figures were taken from the statistics institutions. It is fair to say that historical series are extremely unreliable (Lavigne 1999: 44–50). In December 1991 and October 1992 higher inflation series were adopted by Presidential decree, raising the final value significantly.

6. The valuation of profits did not take into account the higher qualitative value placed on internally-produced goods (see Humphrey 1999) as opposed to the lower price of most imported goods (usually from China and Turkey), nor the much higher value in all senses of Euro-American goods.

7. The organic metaphor trailing through this chapter to describe the effects of industrial privatization in Kazakhstan is vivified in Parry's chapter in this book.

8. The nomenklatura were the political and economic elite of the Soviet period, who were privileged in the system's transformation.

References

Alexander, C., 2002. *Personal states: Making connections between people and bureaucracy in Turkey*. Oxford: Oxford University Press.

Beynon H., and N. Hedges. 1982. *Born to work: Images of factory life*. London: Pluto.

Brabant van, J.M. 1998. *The political economy of transition: Coming to grips with history and methodology*. London: Routledge.

The Economist. 1993. "Privatization: Selling the state." 21 August. 328(7825): 18–20.

Firlit, E., and J. Chlopecki. 1992. "When theft is not theft." In *The Unplanned Society*. Edited by J. Wedel. New York: Columbia University Press.

Gasché, R. 1999. *Of minimal things: Studies on the notion of relations*. Stanford: Stanford University Press.

Hann, C.M. 1998. "Introduction: the embeddedness of property." In *Property relations: Renewing the anthropological tradition*. Edited by C.M. Hann, 1–47. Cambridge: Cambridge University Press.

Harloe, M. 1996. "Cities in the transition." In *Cities after socialism: Urban and regional change and conflict in post-socialist societies*. Edited by G. Andrusz, M. Harloe, and I. Szelényi. Oxford: Blackwell.

Harvey, D. 1989. *The condition of post-modernity: An enquiry into the origins of cultural change*. Oxford: Blackwell.

Hughes, T. 1997. *Ovid's Metamorphoses*. Harmondsworth: Penguin.

Humphrey, C. 1999. "Traders, 'disorder,' and citizenship regimes in provincial Russia." In *Uncertain Transition: Ethnographies of Change in the Postsocialist World*. Edited by Michael Burawoy and Katherine Verdery. Lanham, MD: Rowman and Littlefield.

Kalyuzhnova, Yelena. 1999. "Privatization in Kazakhstan – an overview." *Kazakhstan Economic Trends*. pp. 34–5.

Kaser, M. 1997. *The Economies of Kazakhstan and Uzbekistan*. London: The Royal Institute of International Affairs.

Kotkin, S. 1995. *Magnetic mountain: Stalinism as civilisation*. Berkeley: University of California Press.

Lane, David. 1995. *Russia in transition: Politics, privatization and inequality*. London: Longman.

Lavigne, M. 1999. *The economics of transition. From socialist economy to market economy*. New York: St. Martin's.

Litwack, J. 1991. "Legality and market reform in Soviet-type economies." *Journal of Economic Perspectives* 5: 77–9.

Maine, Henry. 1905 [1861]. *Ancient law*. London: John Murray.

Pipes, Richard. 1999. *Property and freedom*. London: Harvill.

Scott, Colin. 1988. "Property, practice, and aboriginal rights among Quebec Cree hunters." In *Hunters and gatherers: Property, power and ideology*. Edited by T. Ingold, D. Riches, and J. C. Woodburn, 35–51. Oxford: Berg.

Smith, G. V., A. Wilson Law, A. Bohr, and A. Allworth. 1998. *Nation-building in the post-Soviet borderlands: The politics of national identities*. Cambridge: Cambridge University Press.

Stark, D. 1996. "Recombinant property in East European capitalism." *American Journal of Sociology* 101: 993–1027.

Verdery, K. 1994. "The elasticity of land: Problems of property restitution in Transylvania." *Slavic Review* 53: 1071–1109.

——. 1998. "Disambiguating ownership: Rights and power in Transylvania's decollectivation." In *Property relations: Renewing the anthropological tradition*. Edited by C. M. Hann. Cambridge: Cambridge University Press.

——. 1999. "Fuzzy property: rights, power and identity in Transylvania's decollectivization. In *Uncertain transition ethnographies of change in the postsocialist world*. Edited by Michael Burawoy and Katherine Verdery. Lanham MD: Rowman and Littlefield.

——. 2003. *The vanishing hectare: Property and value in postsocialist Transylvania*. Ithaca, NY: Cornell University Press.

Economic Claims and the Challenges of New Property

Carol M. Rose

The news is full of strange and wondrous new forms of property. Ownership disputes now erupt out over such novelties as internet domain names, frozen reproductive tissue, and tradeable pollution allowances. But changes in what counts as "property" are nothing new. Over two hundred years ago, Blackstone's Commentaries (1765–69) discussed then-normal categories of property – "advowsons," "dignities," "corodies" etc. – that would mystify a modern lawyer. As old property categories submerge, new ones surface and demonstrate how dynamic a subject property really is.

What process drives changes in the things that people call "property"? It is a truism in property theory that property is not concerned with things as such, but rather with relationships between people with respect to things. New classes of property, then, should have some connection to the changing work that people want property to do for them with respect to other people. One very old argument for property, for example, is that property promotes political independence. This view was once deployed to support aristocrats' landholding vis-à-vis kings (Allen 1957), but more recently people have used it to bolster welfare benefits as "the new property" (Reich 1964). Some have argued that property allows a person to project his or her personality into the world (Radin 1982); if so, it's no wonder that with modern photography and recording technology, celebrities now claim property-like rights in their images and "styles" (Coombe 1998).

In this chapter, however, I focus on an explanation long given by economically minded commentators: the force that creates property, it is said, is *scarcity*, or sometimes put differently, increased demand for some given resource (Blackstone 1765–69; Posner 1998). If there are plenty of berries for everyone, the argument goes, the issue of mine and thine just doesn't arise, about either the berries or the bush on which they grow. And it is much the same for any other resource. But either gradually or due to some shock like new technology or new demand, the users start to deplete the berries, and conflicts ensue as all vie for the increasingly scarce berry bushes. Now some begin to separate out and husband portions of the berry-fields, marking off their sequestered portions while respecting the signals of others who do likewise. At the end of the story, the once-common resource is divided into property rights, with all participating owners peacefully and carefully managing their respective portions of lands and bushes, to the collective benefit of all (Blackstone 1765–69; Demsetz 1967).

This optimistic just-so story has taken some hits in the last decades (Krier 1992; Rose 1994), a point to which I will return. Yet it is continually retold, probably because in fact we often do see people creating new forms of property when goods become scarce. The newly minted property system in internet domain names gives an example, but so does every informal queue that theater-goers form at the box office, where participants recognize temporary entitlements to the point of admonishing line-breakers.

What good is property under conditions of scarcity? Two constant answers run through the economic thinking about property. One answer is that property encourages labor and investment; the other is that property identifies who has what.

The first refrain – that property encourages effort and good management – is fairly intuitive, and it is also very old, dating back at least to Aristotle. This argument became the central theme of classical and neoclassical economic theories of property. On this view, property showers the benefits of hard work, investment, and good husbandry on the owner of the worked-upon property – while property also stings that same owner for sloth and poor planning. Hence property brings home to the owner the effects of his or her acts – or in the economists' language, "internalizes" those effects – encouraging good management and punishing slackness. For lack of a better word I call this the "internalizing" role of property (Bentham 1802; Posner 1998; Demsetz 1967).

The second refrain is that property simply serves to identify authoritatively the claims that any given person has to any given resource. This answer is also enormously important, if perhaps less highly touted. Property's "identifying" role obviously reduces conflict, at least insofar as all recognize one another's property. But beyond that, property's "identifying" role logically precedes its "internalizing" role: because property rights identify the person in control of any given thing, they assure the person that he or she can take the fruits of his or her efforts. Particularly important, property's identifying role makes trade possible. When owners are known, all parties can negotiate for resources instead of fighting over them. In turn, trade encourages specialization and makes property all the more valuable by bringing new customers. Thus newly opened transport routes make land values rise, whereas – as old Soviet enterprises learned to their chagrin – the collapse of state-run trading networks made their assets' value plummet (see Verdery, Alexander, and Sneath, this volume).

One feature of property's "identifying" role should be flagged: its moral neutrality. Perhaps it would be nice to give the first claim to property to those who, as Locke said, "mix their labor" with a thing, as the "internalizing" role would suggest. But it may not really matter who gets the initial entitlement, a point that Ronald Coase (1960) made some years ago in a very important article. As long as the parties can trade, Coase argued, resources will generally gravitate to those who value them most highly, no matter who has the initial entitlement. Thus for the society as a whole (though not for the individuals involved) the important matter is not who gets the initial claim, but rather that claims be well-defined, secure and tradeable. If they are, then individuals will lubricate the economy by bargaining for the things they want and that they can improve and trade anew.

Indeed, in the initial allocation of property rights in law, property's identifying function often does take precedence over reward to effort. "First possession" is a very widespread claim for ownership, but it often has little to do with deservingness, as anyone who has claimed an adjacent bus seat or library chair for baggage should understand. In international law, national claims to ocean fisheries and undersea minerals often have no more elevated basis than sheer proximity: shoreline countries get the bordering ocean resources (Sugden 1986). In the common law as well, simple proximity often leads to ownership. For example, wildlife that appears on someone's land is "constructively owned" by the landowner. Would-be hunters can seek out the landowner and ask permission, whereas the landowner who wants peace and quiet could hardly track down all the potential hunters and pay them to stay away. Hence the initial property right goes not to the hunter-worker but to the person who is *easiest to locate*, and who can set priorities and reduce conflicts among those who might want the animals. Indeed, the same "identifying" idea appears in a modern judicial decision giving a right of informed consent to patients whose tissues might be used in medical research. Though not formally designated as a "property" right, the function is similar: the patient does no research, but he or she is easy to identify; researchers who want to use his or her cells can ask him or her, and his or her consent can order claims to the subsequent development of research work.[1]

Finally, there is more than a trace of property's identifying role in the disposition of formerly state-owned assets in the countries of the former Soviet Union, whose mammoth problems are discussed in several chapters in this volume. Some must have thought it better to establish a property regime rapidly, even if the old bad guys got first crack at the goodies, than to wait until arguments about "deservingness" sorted themselves out (Alexander, Sneath, Verdery, all this volume). The hope is simply that if some set of persons can be identified as "owners," then normal market trades can develop, and over time the more rational and industrious resource users can purchase mismanaged properties from incompetents and thugs. The justification, if any, lies not in the deservingness of the initial claimants – quite the contrary – but rather in the idea that simply getting property *started* will bring more general benefits to society by encouraging labor and trade over the long run. These long-term rewards supposedly dwarf the moral unattractiveness of the early phase.

Thus while the "internalizing" claims for property have a certain moral ring (property rewards hard work), the "identifying" role of property is more morally indifferent to claims of justice or fair distribution. Even Blackstone (1765–69) implicitly queried the morality of property's identifying role when he asked why property should pass through inheritance. He never answered the question, but instead adroitly turned to the benefits that property can bring by encouraging labor – that is, the internalizing role. In his mind, these benefits must have drowned out the troubling questions about just why this person or that had this resource or that.

This indeed is a common move in privatization and globalization arguments – ducking questions about distribution, and instead turning to the hopes for property's internalizing, wealth-producing role. Supposedly globalization will lead to greater overall wealth in the long run, and that wealth must make up for the moral ambiguities in initial entitlements. For whatever reasons, there is enormous optimism in the current era that this institutional justification is warranted.

In the remainder of this chapter, I will explore some arguments that challenge this set of economic understandings – that is, arguments that the wealth-producing claims for private property are overstated or incomplete on their own terms. This by no means exhausts the list of the complaints about property – there are, for example, important complaints that misplaced property concepts "commodify" matters that do not belong in markets (Radin 1996). But I will confine this chapter to several arguments that confront precisely the *economic* claims for private property, the very economic claims that globalization adherents hope will drown out quibbles about justice and fairness in the distribution of entitlements.

Contra Property 1: It May Not Emerge At All

One important fact about property is that specific entitlements only have content within property *regimes*. You can claim that something is yours until you are blue in the face, but unless others recognize your claims, it does you little good. Consider your behavior in staking out a spot at an outdoor concert. You put down a blanket on the ground. This works while few have arrived, but when the crowds come, you need to be on the spot to keep others from encroaching on your blanket. Sociobiological accounts cite animal territoriality – birds tweeting in the trees – as a kind of proto-property, but this is not really property at all. Property is making a claim *that others recognize*. Having to guard your blanket, or to tweet all day, is the antithesis of property. What makes property so useful an institution is that you can signal your claims to others who recognize them, without the expense and annoyance of having to maintain a guard.

When, then, is property part of a property *regime*? Legal scholars frequently claim that government creates property, and indeed it often does. But another pervasive source of the necessary rules of recognition is simply custom, as in those queues at the theater. Customs can even defy the law: after shoveling snow from a parking space in front of the house, a Chicagoan will place a chair to mark "his" or "her" cleared spot, and though it is not legal to make such private claims on formally public spaces, other Chicagoans generally recognize them anyway. (Rose 1994).

But what if there are no preexisting laws or customs for property rights in some given resource? Will people create a property regime? The optimistic story described above says yes, but Garrett Hardin told another famous story to the contrary in his "Tragedy of the Commons" (1968), whose title has become a metaphor for pessimism about the human ability to manage large but finite resources. Like the optimists, Hardin began with a resource that people use in common, in his case a grazing field. He reasoned that anyone who ran his or her livestock freely would take the full gain from feeding his or her animals while letting most of the overgrazing costs fall on the other stockpersons. Hence each stockperson would choose to graze as many animals as possible – to the ultimate decimation of the field. No happy ending here; resources go from plenty to penury without passing property.

Which is right, the optimistic or the pessimistic story? As a matter of neoclassical economic theory, where persons are assumed to act from self-interest, Hardin's Tragedy is considerably more convincing. In modern game-theory language, the commons graziers are in a Prisoner's Dilemma (or rather more technically an N-Person Prisoner's Dilemma), a situation in which the optimal joint outcome of the participants would be to cooperate – here "stinting" and allowing the field to renew itself – but the best move of each individual participant is to cheat. Not only does each grazier give his or her stock free run, but he or she also shirks on fertilizing the grass; after all, the other graziers will all share the benefits. Better to shirk, and hope someone else fertilizes – which of course no one does.

Could custom restrain this unproductive behavior? Unfortunately, cooperative customs can scarcely arise where everyone is cheating. Anyone who sets a good example will just wind up the patsy. What about law and government? As the property scholar James Krier notes (1992), government is simply the Tragedy of the Commons Part II: someone has to plan and organize government and then enforce its laws, but why would any rational actor do all that committee work? Why won't everyone shirk again, in the hopes that someone else will do the organizing and enforcing?

In fact, customs and government do support viable property regimes. But on a self-interested rational-actor model, it is hard to say why. I have argued elsewhere that this is why such models fall back on just-so stories when it comes to the invention of property (Rose 1994). And in fact, while we do often create property regimes through law or custom, we sometimes fail. Some things are relatively easy to turn into property, for example land. Land stands still, and it can bear markers like fences that can become recognizable cultural signals; thus while not all people treat land as property, many do. But other things are much harder to turn into property, especially large and diffuse resources like air or water or wildlife stocks.

Indeed, as Hardin pointed out, his pessimistic story is particularly salient for environmental resources. An earlier version of the commons tragedy was written about fisheries, a type of resource that is classically over-exploited, and that is in deep trouble across the face of the earth (Gordon 1954). A global economy must face other equally serious environmental problems: coal smoke has fouled the air for centuries; other combustibles pour out the greenhouse gases that warm the globe and apparently cause storms, rising seas, and perhaps new diseases; sewage and mining wastes poison the world's rivers; hunters and fishers capture dwindling endangered species, siphoning them into an illegal trade that is second only to narcotics. Where are the property rights that should manage these diffuse resources? These resources are too big, too uncontrollable, too easily left as a wide-open common where the rational move is to take while you can, and where only the patsies exercise restraint. Intellectual matters – expressions, inventions – are still harder to turn into property, and even when they are, they are regularly pirated (Rose 1998).

Hence the actual fact of property in some resources does not erase the equal fact that we lack property regimes to deal with other critical global economic issues. There are efforts to bring property to bear on some of these problems – and I will describe some shortly – but no one should think that the "tragedy" is passé, or irrelevant to modern economies. More generally, the tragedy teaches us that property regimes differ in difficulty and expense for different resources and under different social conditions. Where it is difficult and expensive to create property, property is slow in coming, and in the meantime valuable resources can collapse.

Contra Property 2: You Can't Get Away From Government

Garrett Hardin suggested several examples in which property can overcome the Tragedy of the Commons, but in an extensive embellish-ment of Hardin's work, William Ophuls (1977) argued that the real solution to the Tragedy is Leviathan, that is, government. Socialist regimes represent Leviathan in direct action, but even in capitalist regimes, Leviathan sometimes issues direct command-and-control regulation. In a sense, Leviathan and private property can be seen simply as alternative resource-management regimes. Private-property enthusiasts, however, are by no means neutral in the choice between these two alternative solutions to the commons problem. Some, notably

Milton Friedman (1962), have roundly criticized Leviathan's direct control for its adverse effect on political liberty. Many others criticize the statist, command-and-control approach for its *economic* consequences.

Direct command-and-control regimes tend to deploy negative incentives, taking the form, "do this and do that, or we will punish you." Property regimes, on the other hand, generally deploy positive incentives: "do this and do that, and we (or someone) will reward you." Which of these regimes is more economically efficient? The answer is, it depends. Take two extreme examples, galley rowing and flower arranging: Threat of punishment might well induce a galley hand to row, because rowing requires sheer effort that a boss can monitor relatively easily. Flower arranging, on the other hand, requires care rather than effort. Here it is much more difficult to elicit good work by threat of punishment; one gets better results by looking at several arrangements, and paying for the arrangement one most likes.

While by no means an airtight distinction, some commentators think that the effort/care dichotomy explains why slavery historically gravitated to jobs requiring monitorable effort, and why even slaves were compensated when they performed skilled labor (Fenoaltea 1984). Attempting to use force to get someone to make, say, a nice piece of furniture would have elicited too much shirking and nowhere near enough ingenuity. An even more striking example is the creativity that is encouraged by intellectual property regimes. To the best of my knowledge, no nation attempts to force artistic or scientific creativity by threat of punishment; even in the old Soviet Union, scientists got special rewards for their endeavors.

Now, what counts more in modern economies, sheer effort or ingenuity/creativity? Sheer effort still does matter, and where it matters most, we should expect the most command-and-control organization, as in factory lines. But where inventiveness and planning count for more – as in the entrepreneurial ownership of the factory itself – property and positive incentives predominate, enhanced by competition. This idea runs through the privatization of the formerly socialist economies: governments sell off previously nationalized industries in the hopes that a less *dirigiste* command structure may add to economic nimbleness. Leviathan, it seems, is clumsy and expensive.

This same idea of deregulation has arrived in environmental law, particularly in the United States. We have already tried Leviathan in the form of command-and-control regimes, prescribing specific pollution-control devices for autos and factories and even deodorant containers; the results, while preferable to no regulation at all, have been costly and inflexible. Hence some environmental cognoscenti are eager to replace command-and-control with property, especially in the form of what I will call "tradable environmental allowances" (TEAs), that is, portions of a given environmental resource that are treated as individual property (Rose 2000a).

One of the most successful of these programs is the United State's 1990 legislation to control sulfur dioxide (SO_2) emissions, which are precursors to acid rain. This legislation capped the total SO_2 emissions that would be allowed throughout the country, divided the total into 1-ton TEAs, allocated the TEAs to existing industries, and then permitted the TEA holders to trade to anyone who wanted to purchase them. The idea is that when a polluter has to purchase TEAs for every scrap of pollution, he or she will figure out the most cost-effective methods to reduce the gunk, and if that producer reduces it enough he or she even can make some money by selling his or her excess TEAs. A TEA regime thus cuts back on overall pollution, while decentralizing decisions and encouraging innovative and cheaper prevention methods – just the advantages claimed for property regimes over Leviathan. And in fact, the cost of acid-rain TEAs has dropped far below anyone's expectations in 1990, suggesting that with a bit of ingenuity, it was far cheaper to control these emissions than anyone thought. The acid-rain program's success has spun off TEA ideas in other environmental domains. Fisheries are a major example, particularly in Australia and New Zealand, and TEAs have been proposed for subjects ranging from endangered-species habitat to wetlands preservation to the greenhouse gases that cause global warming (Rose 2000a).

With all this euphoria, why are there not more TEA regimes? One answer comes from moral objections: in connection with global warming, for example, US business interests argued for a TEA system in which they could buy greenhouse-gas allowances abroad instead of reducing pollution at home, but European commentators long objected that such trades would amount to shirking a moral duty to clean up one's own messes.[2] A second reason for the lagging emergence of TEA regimes arises from objections to their distributional consequences, a point that has a familiar ring in privatization controversies more generally. Entrenched interest groups under an earlier regime often fear they will not prosper under a more privatized trading system involving TEAs, and their recalcitrance can stall any regime change, no matter how beneficial it might be for environmental conservation generally (Libecap 1989). Sometimes the only way to get past this resistance is to pay off the old-timers – a method reminiscent of privatization in the former Soviet Union, where the old nomenklatura resisted until they got the bulk of the shares in many newly privatized enterprises. Similarly, in the few TEA regimes that have been instituted to date, most of the newly created tradeable allowances have been handed over directly to the entities that were most favored under the status quo ante.

Under the US acid-rain legislation, for example, the very industrial plants that emitted the most pollutants received most of the initial allocations of TEAs, and any new plants had to buy TEAs from them to cover any new pollution (Merrill 2000). But this kind of distributional favoritism to the old "winners" does not sit well with newcomers. In the debates over global warming, for example, less-developed countries (LDCs) categorically reject the idea that in order to advance their new industries they will have to offset new pollution by purchasing TEAs from the already-developed North. Instead, they insist on a distribution of rights wherein the LDCs are favored, and the large industrial producers in the North have to take responsibility for greenhouse-gas reduction, either by reducing their own pollutants or buying TEAs from the LDCs (Rose 2000a).

And finally, there are real questions about the efficiency gains from property-like rights in environmental resources. No property regime can work unless entitlements can be monitored; otherwise, cheaters can exceed their quotas or not even bother to buy entitlements, unraveling the entire scheme. But environmental substances – for example greenhouse gases – are exceedingly difficult and costly to monitor, and trading them only adds to the monitoring problem. Another efficiency problem is that environmental trades may not deal in genuinely interchangeable "goods." Pollution traded upwind causes more damage than it would if it stayed downwind; a newly created wetland, built to compensate for filling another wetland elsewhere, may differ from the old one dramatically in flood control and habitat characteristics (Salzman and Ruhl 2000). Still another problem is substitution: when faced with the prospect of paying for TEAs in one species, for example, a fisherman may switch to another species that is still an unpropertized "common." In this he resembles the biological prospectors that Cori Hayden and Bronwyn Parry describe elsewhere in this volume. When faced with the need to pay for specific biological sources, these prospectors instead search for substitutes in the "public domain."

In short, like other privatization projects, TEAs raise many political, distributional, and economic issues, suggesting that TEAs for the moment cannot be seen as a total cure for environmental ailments. Still, the idea behind TEAs – that is, governmental creation of new private property rights as an engine for environmental protection – is currently very popular in global environmental circles. For example, international wildlife preservation organizations now think it critically important to enlist local communities, who normally would attempt to get rid of the wildlife that intrudes on their farms. If they have a kind of property-like share in wildlife-park revenue, they might be more inclined to safeguard the animals and report poachers rather than encouraging them. Notice that the hope here, as with TEAs, is the classic "internalizing" function of property: that ownership in newly minted environmental rights will give the communal owners an interest in careful management of the wildlife resources (Rose 2000a).

One very important point, however, is that TEAs and their analogs are *not* pure private property. They are rather state-created entitlements to control some portion of a given resource. Many more conventional property rights also depend on governmental policing, but TEAs represent a particularly striking concession to the pro-Leviathan view: this kind of property could not exist unless created and enforced by the state. One could say, then, that for all the talk of TEAs as private-property concepts in environmental management, these devices are very much the top-down creatures of Leviathan. And beyond this, these Leviathan-created property rights share some of the difficulties that can arise in other quests for privatization of formerly governmentally controlled resources; distributional issues, monitoring problems and questions of comparability suggest that Leviathan cannot so easily extricate itself.

Contra (Private) Property 3: There Are *Good* Commons-es Out There

Generally TEAs (and similar schemes) represent a vision of *private property* created by *Leviathan* to solve the *tragedy of the commons*. But are property, government, or tragedy the only available options? Not according to the political scientist Elinor Ostrom and her school. According to Ostrom, there is no "tragedy of the *commons*," and we don't need either Leviathan or private property to solve it. Ostrom argues that Hardin's tragedy was not the "commons," but rather a situation of "open access." The real commons – including the very livestock-grazing commons that Hardin used as an example – tells a story of conservation and sustainable-resource use, since communities in Europe and elsewhere used common-field agriculture for almost a thousand years. Some still do. To be sure, vis-à-vis the outside world, these limited common-property regimes (which I will call LCPs) are indeed *property*, in the sense that insiders can exclude outsiders. But on the inside they are *common*, and they are governed neither as private property nor by Leviathan's command and control, but by their own well-worked-out community customs and practices (Ostrom 1990, Seabright 1993).

Ostrom and her colleagues have scoured the world for sustainable customary LCPs, and they have found them in plenty – grazing areas in Switzerland and Japan, communal forests in India and Indonesia, irrigation works in Tibet and Spain, fisheries in Turkey and Malasia and Brazil. Even in the United States, the lobstermen of Monhegan Island informally manage the surrounding waters as a LCP, excluding outsiders by cutting their traplines, and policing insiders through a variety of well-understood norms about the times and locations for fishing. As a result, the Monheganers capture nice, fat lobsters, and they do so with less effort than other nearby lobstermen fishing in open-access grounds (Acheson 1975).

Ostrom's work has coincided with a broader burst of academic interest in LCPs and their customs and norms (for example Ellickson 1991). Environmentalists too have become interested, arguing that governmental programs can recreate LCPs' sustainable practices by nurturing community co-management of environmental resources. The idea of community participation in wildlife-park management mentioned above is a part of this line of thinking. But an even more basic plan is simply to recognize local peoples as formal owners of the resources that they have effectively managed over the years.

An unfortunate pattern in many parts of the world is that traditional peoples are not considered *owners*, no matter how long and how sustainably they have managed their fisheries or forests. Indeed, states are often at best indifferent and at worst hostile to these peoples. All too often state officials open up traditional peoples' home locations to commerce, and thereafter these places are treated as fair game for outside miners, ranchers, and farmers (Brosius 2001, Kimerling 2001). Not surprisingly, modern calls for the recognition of traditional people's customary claims come not only from environmentalists but also from human-rights organizations (Breckenridge 1992).

Intellectual property (IP) scholars too have noticed this problem, claiming that IP has a Western individualistic bias that effectively robs communities of what should be their common intellectual products. Somewhat like TEAs, IP rights are state-created private-property rights in "public goods" that are difficult to turn into conventional property and that would otherwise be open to any taker – there diffuse environ-mental resources, here expressions and inventions. IP acts as an alterna-tive to secrecy in protecting the creator, and in so doing, IP supposedly encourages more creativity while also encouraging disclosure and the dissemination of ideas.

IP is indeed individualistic insofar as it favors particular authors or inventors who are easily identifiable, and who get rights for making distinctive changes or additions to the existing fund of knowledge. This pattern has been described as a "romantic" bias in IP law (Boyle 1996). But such a pattern is in fact a standard feature of all of Western property law: all other things being equal, the most easily identifiable claimants tend to get recognized as "owners," and individuals with distinct contributions, being most readily identifiable, are the easiest candidates for property rights (Rose 1998).

As Michael Brown points out in this volume, "traditional" people themselves often recognize individuals as owners of certain kinds of knowledge, even if racism and ethnocentrism block some Westerners from noticing them. But Western IP's favoring easy identification also plays a role in leaving unprotected many products of traditional agriculture and folk creations, particularly where knowledge has accreted over long periods time through blended successive efforts of unknown contributors. Where no individual creator or distinctive contribution is easily identifiable, it is difficult to fit any creative product into standard IP forms.

The upshot is that developed countries' laboratories and publishers can raid the intellectual storehouses of traditional peoples, treating plants and songs and stories as public goods (that is, "products of nature" or the "common heritage of mankind"). These commercial interests tweak the traditional lore, then copyright or patent the results, and finally claim property in the ensuing pharmaceuticals or seed plants or stories or music, even claiming the right to sell them back to the very peoples who first created the prototypes (Brown, this volume; Seeger, this volume; Farley 1997; Rose 1998).

Less-developed countries have complained about this pattern, and some efforts are underway to recognize folk tales and traditional agricultural genetic products as property of the nation in which they were produced. Notice, however, that this still diverges from a full recognition of property rights in the producing communities, especially given the very uneasy relationships of many central governments to their own traditional peoples. Moreover, there is some question whether any modern IP form is appropriate for the local knowledge of some traditional peoples; whereas a major goal of most IP is the ultimate dissemination of information, some traditional peoples may have the opposite goal of preserving sacred secrets (Farley 1997; Brown, this volume)

One caveat is in order about communal-property regimes, both ancient and modern. Despite the attractiveness of many custom-based, sustainable community-resource management practices, there are some important political reasons why more modern democratic governments have been uneasy about "custom" as a basis for property law (Rose 1994). Custom-dominated communities can be rigidly hierarchical, xenophobic, deeply conservative, and misogynist. On the last point, one finds very few lobster fisher*women* among the Monhegan Islanders, and few women in the councils of community irrigation systems around the world. Customary law denying independent property to women has been cited as a factor in their vulnerability to spousal abuse and even to AIDS (Rose 1994; Crosette 2001). Such customary-property rules make more individualistic property look comparatively appealing. It is not an accident that women have looked to outside commercial interests, like the Grameen Bank or even multinational employers, for relief from local hierarchies (Lim 1990). Interestingly enough, mavens of internet culture often cite the LCP literature to show the workability of community norms (as opposed to formal law) as an appropriate means for governing the Net (Rose 1998). Yet the internet too can slip into hierarchy, as when all-powerful webmasters act as the autocrats of their sites.

Contra Property 4: Too *Much* Property Ruins the Economy

Individual property, Leviathan, common-property regimes – all are supposedly answers to the Tragedy of the Commons, inducing careful management into resources that would otherwise be squandered. But a few years ago, the property scholar Michael Heller argued that a specter quite the opposite from Hardin's also haunts property: this is the "Tragedy of the *Anti*commons." If the Tragedy of the Commons consists of universal use rights with no powers to exclude, then the Anticommons is universal exclusion rights that prevent any use. Heller's example was the empty storefront buildings in Moscow just after the breakup of the Soviet Union. Why, he asked, did flimsy kiosks on the sidewalks sell everything from shoes to appliances, directly in front of empty retail buildings? His answer was that there was not too *little* property in the empty buildings, but too *much* property. In spite of its anti-property rhetoric, Soviet law had created so many overlapping claims to the buildings that they froze into legal paralysis: no potential user of the building could collect all the necessary agreements to make actual use of the buildings. And so they sat empty, their sullen windows looking out on the kiosks' bustling business (Heller 1998).

Thus the Anticommons complaint is that too many overlapping entitlements can petrify productive resource uses, undermining both the "identifying" and the "internalizing" functions of property: no one has clear control of the resource, and hence no one is encouraged to manage it prudently. Inheritance sometimes creates an Anticommons, as larger units are divided into increasingly small ones (Heller 1998). A proliferation of deed restrictions, or multiple patents in related technologies, might create others. It has even been argued that environmental or land-use regulations may create an Anticommons (Buchanan and Yoon, 2000).

Although Heller did not make the point, the Tragedy of the Commons is usually a problem of *under*developed legal or customary regimes, whereas the Tragedy of the Anticommons is a product of *over*developed legal or customary regimes. But students of more traditionalist informal property regimes might point out something else that Heller did not mention: that the Anticommons is no more uniformly tragic than the Commons is. Traditional customary regimes often include complex and overlapping rights. Medieval European communities scattered individuals farmers' fields (Smith 2000). Among the pre-encounter Maori in New Zealand, a single shrub might be split into multiple rights, with different persons entitled to birds, leaves, and bark (Banner 1999). Such complicated rights baffle outsiders and limit commerce, but they may actually serve a non-obvious protective function, insulating a community's resources against commercial encroachment from the outside world. Outsiders cannot figure out how to buy in, and insiders cannot sell out. In that sense, complexity limits commodification and safeguards at least some continuity in the membership in a common-property regime (Rose 2000a).

Property-law scholars' analysis of the Anticommons has focused not on these traditionalist understandings of property, however, but rather on modern commercial property, where it is taken for granted that trade and commerce in property is desirable. This scholarship has taken two rather subtly different directions, the first toward simplifying property into usable and tradeable bundles, and the second toward a much more radical rejection of property altogether.

The first of these, the simplifying strategy, has been a topic of great interest in property scholarship since the 1990s, although it proceeds from relatively conventional commercial views of property. Behind a new formalism in property law is the realization that usable commercial-property rights must fall into relatively simple packages of entitlements. In contractual relations, by contrast with property, people can specify extremely detailed rights and obligations; after all, they are the ones who negotiate the contract, and they should know what it says. But property is different: durable property, notably land, may pass from one person to the next to the next indefinitely, and in commercial societies, those persons are very likely to be strangers to one another. Remote takers of the property may have not the faintest notion of conditions imposed by long-dead former owners. Since people will only know what they are getting if property rights take one of a limited number of reasonably well-defined shapes, the law of property has evolved in a particularly formalistic manner. Both courts and legislature thus routinely strip away any odd or unexpected arrangements when property changes hands, negating purported property interests that are too complex or too difficult for third parties to understand (Merrill and Smith 2000; Rose 1999).

Formalism is attractive for a number of reasons, some of them sheerly aesthetic (Riles 2000). The "simplifying" version of property's formalism is at bottom a standard version of an economic function, resting on the premise that property is most valuable when it can be freely used and traded. Nevertheless, there is a radical wrinkle in this supposed functionalism. If legal institutions must keep property relatively simple, then claims-clearing practices are central to a functioning commercial-property regime. This means that courts and legislatures occasionally remove some people's perfectly good title for the sake of simplification and legibility. Unrecorded titles may be lost forever to the true owner; perfectly legal claims that are unguarded, such that others squat on the property and use it, may also be lost forever in favor of the squatters. By the operation of simplifying and claims-clearing measures, the law effectively vindicates latecomers and trespassers, showing a bit of expropriation at the core of commercial property law (Rose 2000b).

Vastly more radical, however, is the second direction of Anticommons property scholarship: the suggestion is that perhaps property itself is a poor idea, at least for certain kinds of resources; perhaps the wide-open commons is not tragic after all, but comedic, in the sense of leading to happy outcomes. There is a limited but very old European (and more recently American) legal tradition that certain kinds of physical location

– notably roads and waterways and sometimes town squares – should always be open to the public for purposes of commerce and communication. This tradition implicitly rests on the idea that such locations are at their most valuable when open to all, because in such locations, the back-and-forth exchange of commerce, information, and ideas overwhelmingly outweighs any "tragedies of the commons" that might arise from physical overuse of the underlying land (Rose 1994).

In current debates, the chief proponents of the open commons focus not on roadways and such, but rather on intellectual property. For example, Heller and his colleague Rebecca Eisenberg (1998) roundly criticize the overblown "propertization" of knowledge about genes. They point out that most scientists need to build on the work of others. If researchers have to collect multiple owners' permissions, they say, their administrative costs will be much higher, and this fact will discourage inventive people from extending the work of their predecessors. Similarly, other IP scholars raised storms of opposition to the Clinton Administration's "White Paper" on information technology, a foray that would have extended a quite restrictive set of property rights into the Internet. Opponents argued that this "propertization" would misuse current IP law and impede the very kind of communication that leads to inventiveness (Samuelson 1996).

Intellectual property is undoubtedly a particularly salient subject for this strand of anti-property thinking. The subjects of IP – expressions and inventions – are not scarce in the sense that finite resources are scarce; what is scarce is the creativity that IP attempts to protect and to encourage. But the problem is that creativity does not just come from the internalization that property rights provide, that is, rewarding the creator by allowing him or her to own and charge for the results of his or her inventiveness. Creativity also comes from give and take with others, from the synergies in brainstorming, from the sharpening and expansion of ideas through networking (Merges 1996). Indeed, as some IP scholars have pointed out, there is a great artificiality in the IP conceit that a single author or inventor can be named as the creator of any intellectual product at all; even Shakespeare, so often lionized as the great Romantic example of the creator, produced his work in a profoundly collaborative environment (M. Rose 1993). One sees this even more explicitly in the "chain art" and "story trees" that have blossomed on the Internet.

Current IP law in fact does implicitly recognize that creativity comes from the wide-open commons as well as the internalization of property rights. Copyright has a limited duration, and patent an even more limited one; copyright in particular has exceptions to permit commentary and satire and other forms of "fair use." All these qualifications in effect slip elements of the commons into IP. But there is much concern among liberalizing IP scholars that those concessions to the commons may be closed off, through over-patenting of genetic findings, through privatization of the Internet, and through contractual constraints – the "shrinkwrap permissions" – that require software consumers to waive use and exchange rights that IP law, taken alone, would have granted (Lemley 1999).

Thus, at a minimum, the Anticommons and related literatures suggest that private property cannot be a universal solution, and that economic well-being itself requires some constraint on the proliferation of private property, some balance between it and commons.

Summing It All Up

Many of the moral qualms about property – and about globalization as well – may spring from the seeming moral indifference of property's central function of identifying owners. In its identifying role, property may be completely unconcerned about claims of distribution and justice; no matter who owns what initially, it seems, property and trade can make societies wealthier. But to many, those distributional claims do matter very much indeed. Private-property proponents tend to paper over such claims with arguments about property's general enhancement of wealth. These economic arguments for private property, while persistent and powerful, are clearly subject to some qualifications, and this chapter has recounted some of the important ones: many significant resources remain outside property regimes and subject to the "tragedy of the commons;" government continues to be an essential element in new forms of property; informal common-property regimes still play a role in resource management; and some new economic concerns show that too much property can discourage inventiveness and creativity. None of these qualifications completely undermines the very forceful economic arguments for property. But they should make us realize that "more property" may not always be a complete solution even to economic problems. For private property to work, we need customs, government, and a relaxed attitude – and even some attention to the distributional ideals that might make private property's formidable wealth-producing potential become morally acceptable as well.

Notes

1. Moore v. Regents of the University of California, 793 P.2d 479 (Cal. 1990).

2. Europeans, however, have become more favorable to the TEA concept since the Kyoto agreements on global warming.

References

Acheson, James M. 1975. *The lobster gangs of Maine*. Hanover, NH: University Press of New England.

Allen, J. W. 1957. *A history of political thought in the sixteenth century*. London: Methuen.

Banner, Stuart. 1999. "Two properties, one land: Law and space in nineteenth-century New Zealand." *Law and Social Inquiry* 24: 807–52.

Bentham, Jeremy. 1931 [1802]. "Principles of the civil code." In *Theory of legislation*. Edited by C. K. Ogden. London: Kegan Paul, Trench, Trubner & Co.

Blackstone, William. 1979 [1765–69] *Commentaries on the Laws of England*. 4 vols. Chicago: University of Chicago Press.

Boyle, James. 1996. *Shamans, software, and spleens: Law and the construction of the information society*. Cambridge, MA: Harvard University Press.

Breckenridge, Lee. 1992. "Protection of biological and cultural diversity: Emerging recognition of local community rights in ecosystems under international environmental law." *Tennessee Law Review* 59: 735–85.

Brosius, J. Peter. 2001. "Between politics and poetics: Narratives of dispossession in Sarawak, East Malaysia." Paper delivered at the Yale Seminar in Agrarian Studies, New Haven, CT.

Buchanan, James M., and Yong J. Yoon. 2000. "Symmetric tragedies: Commons and anticommons." *Journal of Law and Economics* 43: 1–13.

Coase, Ronald H. 1960. "The Problem of social cost." *Journal of Law and Economics* 3: 1–44.

Coombe, Rosemary J. 1998. *The Cultural life of intellectual properties: Authorship, appropriation, and the law*. Durham, NC and London: Duke University Press.

Crosette, Barbara. 2001. "In India and Africa, women's low status worsens their risk of AIDS." *New York Times*, 26 February 2001, p. 9, col. 1.

Demsetz, Harold. 1967. "Toward a theory of property rights." *American Economic Review* 57: 347–59.

Ellickson, Robert C. 1991. *Order without law: How neighbors settle disputes.* Cambridge, MA: Harvard University Press.

Farley, Christine Haight. 1997. "Protecting folklore of indigenous peoples: Is intellectual property the answer?" *Connecticut Law Review* 30(1): 1–57.

Fenoaltea, Stefano. 1984. "Slavery and supervision in comparative perspective: A model." *Journal of Economic History* 44: 635–68.

Friedman, Milton. 1962. *Capitalism and freedom.* Chicago: University of Chicago Press.

Gordon, H. Scott. 1954. "The economic theory of a common-property resource: The fishery." *Journal of Political Economy* 62: 24–42.

Hardin, Garrett. 1968. "The tragedy of the commons." *Science* 162: 1243–8.

Heller, Michael A. 1998. "The tragedy of the anticommons: property in the transition from Marx to markets." *Harvard Law Review* 111: 621–88.

Heller, Michael A. and Rebecca Eisenberg. 1998. "Can patents deter innovation? The anticommons in biomedical research." *Science* 280: 698–701.

Kimerling, Judith. 2001. "'The human face of petroleum': Sustainable development in Amazonia?" *Review of European Community and International Environmental Law* 10: 65–81.

Krier, James E. 1992. "The tragedy of the commons, part two." *Harvard Journal of Law and Public Policy* 15: 325–47.

Lemley, Mark A. 1999. "Beyond preemption: The law and policy of intellectual property licensing." *California Law Review* 87: 111–72.

Libecap, Gary D. 1989. *Contracting for property rights.* Cambridge: Cambridge University Press.

Lim, Linda Y. C. 1990. "Women's work in export factories: The politics of a cause." In *Persistent inequalities: Women and world development.* Edited by Irene Tinker, 101–19. New York and Oxford: Oxford University Press.

Merges, Robert P. 1996. "Property rights theory and the theory of the commons: The case of scientific research." *Social Philosophy and Policy* 13: 145–67.

Merrill, Thomas W. 2000. "Explaining market mechanisms." *University of Illinois Law Review* 2000: 275–98.

Merrill, Thomas W., and Henry E. Smith. 2000. "Optimal standardization in the law of property: the *numerus clausus* principle." *Yale Law Journal* 110: 1–70.

Ophuls, William. 1977. *Ecology and the politics of scarcity*. San Francisco: W.H. Freeman.

Ostrom, Elinor. 1990. *Governing the commons*. Cambridge: Cambridge University Press.

Posner, Richard A. 1998. *Economic analysis of law*. 5th edn. New York: Aspen Law and Business.

Radin, Margaret Jane. 1982. "Property and personhood." *Stanford Law Review* 34: 957–1015.

——. 1996. *Contested commodities*. Cambridge, MA: Harvard University Press.

Reich, Charles A. 1964. "The new property." *Yale Law Journal* 73: 733–87.

Riles, Annelise. 2000. "The transnational appeal of formalism: The case of Japan's netting law." Available at www.ssrn.com.

Rose, Carol M. 1994. *Property and persuasion: Essays on the history, theory and rhetoric of ownership*. Boulder, CO: Westview.

——. 1998. "The several futures of property: of cyberspace and folk tales, emission trades and ecosystems." *Minnesota Law Review* 83: 129–82.

——. 1999. "What government can do for property (and vice versa)." In *The fundamental interrelationships between government and property*. Edited by N. Mercuro and W. J. Samuels, 209–22. Stamford, CT: JAI Press.

——. 2000a. "Expanding the choices for the global commons: Comparing newfangled tradable emission allowance schemes to old-fashioned common property regimes." *Duke Environmental Law and Policy Review* 10: 45–72.

——. 2000b. "Property and expropriation: Themes and variations in American law." *Utah Law Review* 2000: 1–38.

Rose, Mark. 1993. *Authors and owners: The invention of copyright*. Cambridge, MA: Harvard University Press.

Salzman, James and J. B. Ruhl. 2000. "Currencies and the commodification of environmental law." *Stanford Law Review* 53: 607–94.

Samuelson, Pamela. 1996. "The copyright grab." *Wired Magazine*. January issue, 134–8, 188–91.

Seabright, Paul. 1993. "Managing local commons: Theoretical issues in incentive design." *Journal of Economic Perspectives* 7: 113–34.

Smith, Henry E. 2000. "Semicommon property rights and scattering in the open fields." *Journal of Legal Studies* 29: 131–69.

Sugden, Robert. 1986. *The economics of rights, cooperation, and welfare*. Oxford and New York: Blackwell.

Cyberspatial Properties: Taxing Questions about Proprietary Regimes

Bill Maurer

> When I considered what people generally want in calculating, I found that it is always a number.
>
> (Muhammad ibn al-Khuwarizmi, *Compendium on Calculating by Completion and Reduction*)

Internet-based banking products, electronic commerce transactions, and internet-based offshore financial services are new objects of proprietary and regulatory concern. Each seems to circumvent state apparatuses such as community investment and taxation regimes designed, at least in principle, to serve the public weal. In this chapter I ask whether these new objects of property necessitate a rethinking of property's moral form. They are not merely challenging regulatory frameworks; they are challenging moral obligations involved in territorial state jurisdictionality. If property always entails moral claims, then new kinds of proprietary objects that trouble legal and regulatory obligations unsettle the moral orders in which property is constituted. Cyberspatial properties, by unsettling these moral orders, make visible the contours and the limits of liberal and critical theories of property, themselves bound up with its moral orderings.

If cyberspatial properties call forth the limit of both liberalism and liberalism's critique, they also demand a re-working of the conceptual apparatus of criticism and an accounting of the tight relation between languages of critique and languages of property. For example, it will not do to simply reverse the upside-down images of ideology to which Marx and Engels referred ("in all ideology men and their circumstances appear

297

upside-down as in a *camera obscura*," 1977: 164). The answer to Marx's question, "what is the secret of the commodity?" will not necessarily further analysis here. Marx discovered labor underneath value, and sought to restore to workers the value they owned because of their inherent ownership of their labor, which had been alienated by the wage relation. The answer to Marx's question, then, was itself an element of liberal property-form, for the person as owner of its body and capabilities is at the center of the labor theory of value.

As in algebra, so in liberal and critical theory there are givens and there are unknowns. The algebraic process involves conducting identical operations with mathematical equivalencies on either side of the equation to "solve for" the unknowns. What is the value of x around which the equation rotates? For Marx, it was abstract labor, material conditions, and "actual life-processes." Solving for x, however, does not explain why the mystifications of capital take the form of commodity fetishism, or the property-form itself. This form consists of the separation of persons from things, owners from owned, and the abstraction and objectification of property despite the relations inhering in it. As Diane Nelson poses the dilemma, "[p]laying detective and getting down to how the fetish 'really' works completely misses the magic act" (1999: 77). The limits of Marxian critique thus compel another, more nuanced look at the object of its critique: liberalism. In this chapter, Margaret Radin's writings on property will help me to delineate certain liberal views of property in order to demonstrate their formal elements and pragmatic operations. The mathematical operation of algebra will function as an analogy to the work of critique, just as it has functioned as an analogy for efforts to find solutions to all manner of mysteries.

Consider mystery movies, for example. If the analysis of property takes the form of a "whodunit," it reproduces the conditions of its own possibility by holding steady all the old oppositions of liberal theory: object and subject, emotion and reason, property and person – to name but a few. The detective in the whodunit plays the role of the analyst. Agatha Christie's Miss Marple is a good empiricist; she gathers clues and reconstructs the crime, and thereby deduces the identity of the murderer. The "facts" on which her reconstruction rests are themselves beyond question. They are there for anyone to see – all it takes is a trained eye and a quick mind, and all the pieces of the puzzle fall into place: we solve for x. In a whodunit, we "coldly and without emotion await the end to learn who committed the murder. The whole interest is concentrated in the ending" (Zupancic 1992: 83).

Some of Hitchcock's mysteries function very differently. Here, the audience knows from the start who committed the murder. There is no *x* demanding solution. The dramatic tension does not build up through the gathering of clues but rather through the staging – or restaging – of the crime itself. This restaging, in Hitchcock, is quite literal: it occurs in a moment where a fictional scene is portrayed within the fictional narrative of the film itself. We wait for the time when the murderer is on a stage where we expect the murderer's guilt to be reenacted. As Zupancic writes, "The fascinating point is not the revelation of the murderer's identity, the reconstruction of the crime and the deduction of the truth, *but the manner in which the truth is displayed* – or is gazing at us, if we can put it that way, in the glint of the murderer's eye" (ibid., p.84, my emphasis). This narrative device, the play-within-the-play, also reveals the conditions of possibility of fictionality itself. That which is excluded from the film in order for it to function as narrative, all the background assumptions and prediscursive elements that are the conditions of possibility of narrativity and performance, are condensed into the moment of the fictionality *within* the film. The conditions of possibility (for example the camera-operator) cannot be shown in the main fiction or they would dissolve the narrative. But they *can* be shown – through a process of doubling or duplication – in the fiction-within-fiction. In Hitchcock, this doubling reveals the "sign of guilt" of the murderer, as well as the signs of guilt of the originary fictional act. The effect is that of a set-up (for the murderer). Zupancic terms this device a "mousetrap:" with a mouse, we already know the identity of the cupboard thief, so we set a trap for it by constructing a miniature cupboard and enticing it with cheese to duplicate its original crime, a cupboard from which it cannot escape.

In what follows, I treat internet banking and electronic commerce taxation together with Margaret Radin's "pragmatist" account of property. This allows me to foreground the limits of liberalism and the forms of algebraic critique that accompany liberal theory. Next, I turn to a new phenomenon in offshore financial services. In 1999 and 2000, the Caribbean country of St. Lucia brought into existence a new form of International Business Company (IBC) for international investors seeking to avoid taxation in their home jurisdictions. St. Lucia's IBC legislation co-occurred with and was explicitly linked to the opening of a free port for Chinese goods on the island's southern tip and a gated luxury-housing development on the island's northern tip. The legislation allows IBCs incorporated there to be listed on the Hong Kong Stock Exchange – simultaneously troubling the "here" and "there" of what analysts inappropriately gloss as financial "flows."

The concluding section sets a sort of mousetrap for critical analysis. It returns to the algebraic reasoning of critique via the medieval Islamic philosophies that inaugurated algebra, and the misinterpretations of these philosophies by European mathematicians. In the Islamic texts, reading between the lines of the translations, one finds a very different account of the relation between reason and the real. The foundational text for European algebraic reason, it turns out, was a treatise on the inheritance of property in land. It hinged on the moral forms animating property that escaped its English translator because they were at right angles to his own moral assumptions about property.

Internet Banking, Electronic Commerce, and Specters of Communities Past

In introducing the bill that became the Community Reinvestment Act of 1977 (CRA), U.S. Senator William Proxmire argued that granting a bank a public charter and federally insuring its deposits implied the bank's acceptance of certain obligations. "A public charter conveys numerous economic benefits," Proxmire stated, "and, in return, it is legitimate for public policy and regulatory practice to require some public purpose" (Proxmire, 123 Cong. Rec. 1958). Specifically, the CRA required that banks meet the credit needs of the communities in which they built their physical establishments (12 USC section 2901ff; 12 CFR section 25.41; see Overby 1995). The CRA sought to eliminate "redlining," by which banks would refuse to lend within regions coterminous with racial and ethnic minorities and/or a high proportion of residents living in or near poverty.

The anti-redlining mission of the CRA did not take the form of negative proscriptions so much as positive affirmation of the obligations incumbent upon a bank to serve the public. The CRA is framed by a discourse of duty. In a statement that becomes increasingly explicit about the duty a bank is supposed to uphold – a duty, ultimately, to provide *credit* – the US Congress issued a finding that:

> (1) regulated financial institutions are required by law to demonstrate that their deposit facilities serve the convenience and needs of the communities in which they are chartered to do business; (2) the convenience and needs of communities include the need for credit services as well as deposit services; and (3) regulated financial institutions have a continuing and affirmative obligation to help meet the credit needs of the local communities in which they are chartered (12 USC 2901).

The CRA stresses community connection and community development through credit. Money, here, is not the universal solvent flattening social relationships into variations of the same but, in its guise as credit, becomes the materialization of belief and faith, the glue of society, the obligations that bind and underwrite the world (cf. Simmel 1990).

In the CRA vision, banks promote what William H. Simon (1991) calls "social-republican property." Social-republican property is distinguished from other forms of property in that those party to such property rights must "bear a relation of potential active participation in a group or community constituted by the property," and "inequality among the members of the group or community" must actively be limited (Simon 1991: 1336). Coming very close to asserting a "right to credit," but deferring right through the language of need, the 1977 Congress nearly equated access to credit with political entitlements like voting. Redlining, then, would not simply be unfair but both anti-communitarian and anti-democratic.

Internet banking has generated a flurry of opinion and debate about the translation of such communitarian and democratic obligations into cyberspace (see, for example, Beetham 1998; Keyser 2000). If an internet bank accepts deposits from people living around the country, and if the banking activity itself occurs in "cyberspace," and not at a teller window located in physical space, then how can a bank's "community" be defined for the purposes of the CRA? And how will the social glue that credit supposedly instantiates stick if the "social" is not immediately, geographically evident?

In a practical sense, the question is moot because the CRA has transformed since 1977, especially with the passage of the Financial Services Modernization Act (FSMA) of 1999, and large-scale consolidations in the banking industry that have transformed banking from a local affair into an increasingly national one. The FSMA diminished the sanctions against lenders who fail to comply with CRA guidelines, reduced the frequency of CRA examinations, and put new regulatory burdens on non-profits and other organizations that would seek to benefit from a lender's CRA-based provisions of credit (for example a non-profit mortgage provider serving low-income home-buyers). One of the purposes of the FSMA was to permit the creation of "financial holding companies" (FHCs) that offer investment banking, consumer banking, and insurance services all under one roof – one-stop financial shopping. In effect, the FSMA merely served to authorize mergers and acquisitions that had already been taking place in the financial services industry since the 1990s.[1] Brick-and-mortar banks already choose their "assessment areas" for the purposes of CRA compliance. National banks can select an assessment area that is "less poor" or "less risky" than others, meet CRA guidelines, and possibly even earn an "Outstanding" rating for doing so, since CRA regulations also reward lending "innovations" (Cocheo 1999).

But it is the question of how an internet-based bank will meet its CRA obligations, not the question of poor people's (continuing lack of) access to credit, that generates and moves the debate. In a law-review article on the topic, Thomas W. Beetham writes, "The 'community' of a cyberbank is nowhere and everywhere at the same time . . . a bank's reach is as broad as the Internet itself. Without a 'brick-and-mortar' branch, the assessment area as defined by the existing regulations simply fails to make sense" (Beetham 1998: 924). The debate over internet banking focuses on determining what obligations an internet bank owes, and to whom, rather than assuring a "right to credit" or meeting everyone's credit "needs." In doing so, it tweaks definitions of "community" and reorients the conversation to the topic of "equality."

Those seeking to find a way to ensure internet banks' CRA compliance turn to a special definition of "community" set out in the CRA regulations themselves. A community's primary definition is geographic but can also be held to consist of "military personnel or their dependents who are not located within a defined geographic area" (Beetham 1998: 917; 12 CFR section 25.41(f)). This definition of community, based on military membership and a sort of military citizenship that devolves through bloodlines, has allowed the company USAA to offer financial products to this "community" while meeting its CRA obligations by granting access to credit to members of its own customer base. In effect, USAA has "delineate[d] its entire deposit customer base as its [CRA] assessment area" (ibid.).

Using the military model to create assessment areas for internet banks poses an "exclusivity" problem, however. As Beetham remarks, "The mere existence of a purely Internet bank is basically a form of redlining in and of itself – but income-based rather than geographic-based" (Beetham 1998: 930), and an "on-line customer based definition of 'community' [would be] antithetical to the principles of equality in access and opportunity – at least until on-line services are more freely available to low- and moderate-income groups" (1998: 930). For Beetham, overcoming the exclusivity of computer and internet access is prior to overcoming the exclusivity of wealth. To avoid the further exclusion of the poor from access to credit, then, he calls for equal access to computers and the internet: "'Equality' rather than 'community' should be the focus of regulatory scrutiny. Accordingly, the CRA should focus on encouraging banks to afford all customers equal access to their services and an equal opportunity to apply for loans that they would evaluate on a national basis" (1998: 928). In effect, Beetham redefines the obligations under the CRA as being owed to abstract individuals, not "communities" or other interest groups, and exemplifies the shift from community to individual in neoliberal discourse generally.

Debates over whether and how to tax electronic commerce – internet-based sales of goods and services – have taken similar turns. Electronic commerce poses the challenge of how to collect tax on sales conducted on-line. Regulators – and frantic and financially strapped local governments – fear that e-commerce will spell a loss of tax revenue. There are currently no accounting standards for electronic commerce, so determining how much tax an internet-based business might owe becomes a challenging task, especially if the business accepts payment in the form of the various electronic cash products that are specifically designed to eliminate paper-trails and ensure the same kind of anonymity as cash-only transactions. Local governments fear the potential loss of tax revenue from workers and businesses displaced by the new economy. The most immediately apparent example of the latter, for academics at least, is the internet bookseller Amazon.com's negative effect on independent and college bookstores. Organizations from the US National Retail Federation to the Organization for Economic Cooperation and Development have expressed the concern that not taxing electronic commerce lends a competitive advantage over "store-front" retailers (see Chan 2000, n.109).

The biggest problem, however, is that of jurisdiction: even if you can determine what taxes are owed, to whom are they owed? One lawyer puts forward the following hypothetical:

> A customer in Norway uses his computer to access a server located in India to purchase goods produced by a U.S. company. The U.S. company has no other presence in, or contact with, Norway or India. Under these circumstances, which country or countries may tax the U.S. company's business profits on its sale to the Norwegian customer? (Chan 2000: 252)

As with the debate over the CRA, the internet is presumed to dissolve the bonds tying people to place. As the US Department of Treasury summarizes,

> The concept of a U.S. trade or business was developed in the context of conventional types of commerce, which generally are conducted through identifiable physical locations. Electronic commerce, on the other hand, may be conducted without regard to national boundaries and may dissolve the link between an income-producing activity and a specific location. (US Department of Treasury 1996: 20)

This, in turn, immediately brings up the problem of sovereignty, for "no area of the law is closer to the subject of sovereignty than taxation" (Chan 2000: 254). Taxation is a pivot of governmental obligation, embodying the duty of citizens to pay taxes, and the duty of a government to serve the public weal. Taxation creates property akin to the social-republican model. It is derived from certain rights and duties, and it extends out into other rights and duties, animating the state itself in its expression as the collective will. Paying taxes is the corollary of voting. Since these rights find form within territorial nation-states, the apparent a-spatiality of cyberspace troubles their future application.[2]

Electronic commerce has in some debates taken on the character of a vampire, sucking the life-blood of the sovereign state. It is not surprising that electronic commerce is frequently brought up in the same discussions as offshore gambling and tax evasion, two other revenue-draining activities supposedly facilitated by the internet infrastructure that creates "cyberspace" (Maurer 1998). Unlike tax evasion and gambling, however, electronic commerce belongs to a set of putatively legitimate activities – business advanced in the pursuit of profit, which, by definition, is the paragon of the good and virtuous. Without quashing the entrepreneurial spirit or eroding state sovereignty as a territorial form, then, how can regulators deal with the challenges it poses?

One solution, proposed by the Clinton administration in the mid-1990s, assumed that the real risk posed by electronic commerce was offshore tax evasion, and then sought to provide a remedy that would mitigate it. The proposed remedy foregrounded *residence*, and the obligations incumbent on an individual vis-à-vis the state within which the individual resides. In the Clinton administration plan, electronic commerce would proceed using some form of electronic currency purchased from a local bank. The e-currency would identify the jurisdiction in which the purchaser resides. During an internet sale, tax would be calculated based on the buyer's "place of consumption," or legal residence. The seller would place the revenues collected "with a third-party escrow agent, who would funnel the money to the appropriate government" (Chan 2000: 262).

Home is where the heart is. A curious feature of the Clinton proposal is that it relied on brick-and-mortar banks and neighborhoods of homeowners. What would happen, under this plan, if people bought their e-cash using email aliases from internet banks? The proposal evokes the world of small towns populated by homeowners who bank at the local building and loan, and not a world of highly mobile transients with minimal attachments to their various places of residence who rely for their financial needs on either internet-only financial institutions or check-cashing outlets and pawn shops. What does the Clinton plan make explicit about the categories of liberal thought in its encounter with cyberspatial properties? As with the CRA, the debate over electronic commerce brushes against the social-republican community-cum-nation on the one hand, and the abstract individual proprietor of the free market on the other.

Cartesian Grids and the Metapragmatics of Property

We should not be surprised by how closely the framing of the "problems of" and the "solutions to" internet banking and electronic commerce map onto debates in liberal theory. Margaret Radin (for example 1993) has developed a liberal theory of property that begins from the assumption that certain forms of property are so deeply linked to personhood as to be constitutive of it. She uses this assumption to argue for things like the right of renters to redress under government "takings" jurisprudence, claiming that a tenant's home is just as constitutive of their personhood as a homeowners' home. Radin's conceptual apparatus hinges on a distinction between what she calls "personal" and "fungible" property, the former more deeply intertwined with subject-formation, the latter more deeply imbricated in the world of market values. Radin is clearly indebted to certain thinkers in the liberal and critical tradition like Locke, Kant, Hegel, and Marx. At the same time, she is at pains to defend herself against the charge that she offers a timeless and transcendent theory of property. She also defends herself against both orthodox market libertarians and communitarians or social republicans. What interests me, however, is how her personality theory of property at the same time incorporates both orthodox liberalism and communitarianism through a modal transformation of those theories and an infolding of some of their core elements.

First, take orthodox liberalism. By granting a domain of fungible property, Radin incorporates one core element of this doctrine: fungibility in terms of market values. By centering on the person as proprietor,

Radin incorporates another element. But she considerably expands the person's domain, to include ever-increasing concentric rings of personal possessions extending around the person. As she describes it:

> To visualize the problem about the scope of personhood, we can think of a dot surrounded by two concentric circles. The dot is the abstract self, the moral agent, in its barest possible version. The next circle takes in the self's endowments and its attributes. The outer circle takes in its products and possessions. (Radin 1993: 25–26).

Second, take communitarianism or social republicanism. What is the self in Radin's analysis of takings or residential rent control if not the self who inhabits a world in which things like rent and credit, far from mere market relations, are more importantly the glue binding members to one another in community? Rent, for Radin, not only creates a relation of possession that partially constitutes home and person, but organizes persons in collectivities of interest and sentiment, with visions of the good and just linked to mutual obligations and faith.

Distinguishing herself from both libertarians and communitarians, Radin uses the abstract "dot" of the moral agent and the social glue of property relations to develop what she calls a "thick" theory of the self. For Radin, the inner circle of attributes and qualities and much of the outer circle of products and possessions are assimilated to the core self. Thus, the self is both the abstract individual of liberalism – "its barest possible version" – and its associated domain of putatively inalienable possessions figured through relationships with objects and others. This "thick" theory of the self can be used to weave together two strands in liberal thought and, at the same time, to blur two perpendicular axes of oppositions: person and property, subject and object on one axis, and "dot" and relation, bare abstraction and lived experience on the other. Radin uses the term "blur" to describe what her theory of property does to the subject/object, subjective/objective, normative/empirical, and other such oppositions, and holds that this blurring is in keeping with her pragmatist project. But perhaps blur is not the best term. Taken to its limit, the thick theory of the self here (which is also a theory of "thickness") effects a modal transformation of the Cartesian coordinate system within which those oppositions make sense, rendering it nonlinear, infolding into itself.

This is not, however, what Radin does with it. Instead, she turns to pragmatism. She argues that it is *not* her interest to describe a transcendent reality in transcendent terms or to linger over moral questions, so as to arrive at an account of the kind of persons and property relations that *ought* to exist given certain initial conditions. Rather, she claims she is "starting from where we are" (Radin 1993: 6), by admitting "the existence of," and regulating "ourselves normatively by, the distinction between personal and fungible property" (ibid.). Doing this simply points up that the subject/object dichotomy, for example, is already blurred in the practical activity of social mediation. In effect, she writes, her project is one of "cultural description/critique of American institutions of property and the legal discourse in which they are couched" (p. 9). Radin argues that in order to understand the "culture" of property, one needs to grasp "a shared language and culture *before* property understandings can be conceivable" (ibid., my emphasis). If we take Radin's pragmatism seriously, such a before-time is a logical impossibility, since property only comes into being in its continual, practical becoming. Or, put another way, the "shared language and culture before property" makes property "both external and extra but also an essential condition of that which it supplements" (Rousseau, quoted in Strathern 1992: 205; see for example Derrida 1976: 271, 281).

How should we understand the contortions that transform the topography of the liberal, Cartesian grid on which oppositions like fact/value, object/subject, abstraction/relation are mapped out? I think of these contortions as a kind of de-rendering or desublimation that returns to liberalism all of the connective tissues that hold it together but that are deemed outside or prior to liberalism: agents and objects and their associated notions of abstraction and relation. I am interested not so much in Radin's pragmatics as in the implicit metapragmatics or moments of supplementarity that are both external to and an essential condition of the "shared logic and culture" of property. The contortions of the Cartesian grid and the metapragmatics of property, together, trouble holism and the notions of connection or relation that liberal and critical criticism depends upon, and make Radin's liberal world considerably messier than it first appears.

Radin, however, sublimates the messiness here into her pragmatics, her "starting from where we are" – an apparently neatly bounded and perceivable world, despite all the boundary-troubling entities like potentially commodifiable babies that Radin uses to advance her theory of personal property. This sublimation or straightening-up perpetuates the frameworks of fact/value, object/subject, and abstraction/relation. It does so, however, with considerable ambivalence; we are not quite sure, after reading Radin, whether that Cartesian world is as straightforward as it seems, whether the domains of persons and things, abstractions and relations, are as clear as we might have once thought. The effect is not simply to reinscribe the liberal *topos* so much as to produce a nostalgia for it, a nostalgia both "for the idea of the individual" and "for a relational view of the world" (Strathern 1992: 188–9).

What happens when we view regulatory responses to internet banking and electronic commerce as parallel nostalgic exercises that conjure an imaginary before-time, a time that itself demands the supplement of the crises or conundrums that supposedly follow it? The nostalgic move allows the regulatory debates to take the narrative form of the "whodunit" mystery movie: who subverted CRA? Who evaded taxes? How can we solve the crime and mete out the punishment? Asking these sorts of questions the way Miss Marple might merely mystifies the productions that made both community and (dis)investment, revenue-collection and tax evasion, inhere in each other in their founding moment. But the form of these phenomena is perhaps more like a mousetrap – a setting-out of the conditions for the larger fantasy of capitalism within the mini-fiction of cyberspatial properties.

Has Anybody Seen St. Lucia?

St. Lucy is the patron saint of the blind and those with eye trouble. Around 300 AD, in Syracuse, Lucy prayed at the tomb of St. Agatha for her mother's illness – a flux of the blood – to be cured. It was, and in return, her mother agreed to allow Lucy to give her life to God. Unfortunately, her betrothed, a pagan, betrayed Lucy's faith to the governor, who ordered her sold into prostitution. God made her immovable, however, like a mountain, and his guards were unable to carry her off, so they killed her. In another legend, St. Lucy either gouges out her own eyes to prevent her being recognized by the governor's men, or has them gouged out as part of her torture. God miraculously restores them, either in her head, or else on a plate from which they can see God's grace (see Thurston and Attwater 1956: IV, 548–9). St. Lucy's Day, 13 December, was, in the Julian calendar, the shortest day of the year in the Northern Hemisphere. In Scandinavian countries it became a festival of lights.

The island of St. Lucia in the eastern Caribbean was so named because it was sighted by Columbus during his fourth voyage on St. Lucy's Day in 1502, and/or because its dominating topographical feature is the twin peaks of the Pitons mountains, which rise straight out of the sea to a height of around a half mile, massive and immobile like St. Lucy. St. Lucia has been an independent commonwealth since 1979. It has been led by the St. Lucia Labor Party since 1997. In 1999, under Prime Minister Kenny Anthony, the government passed legislation that brought into being the St. Lucian version of the International Business Company (IBC), one of the most common offshore financial corporate frameworks in the Caribbean and elsewhere (Hampton 1996; Maurer 1997; Roberts 1994).

St. Lucia's offshore sector boasts three unique features. First, it is the product of a public-private collaboration between the Government of St. Lucia and Pinnacle, a private company named for the Pitons and whose trademark logo is the twin peaks. Second, the Pinnacle registry allows companies to be incorporated wholly on-line – you visit the website, record your company name, and pay (via credit card or on-line transfer) a registration and incorporation fee. Third, IBCs so incorporated may be listed on the Hong Kong Stock Exchange. The government's strategy for offshore finance development involves transforming the regionalisms that have defined the Eastern Caribbean since colonial times. A former British colony, St. Lucia had relied on banana exports since the 1950s. The consolidation of bananas had been encouraged by the Banana Protocols of the Lomé Convention, established in 1957, according to which European powers agreed to purchase a quota of bananas from their former colonial possessions until 1993. From the 1960s to the 1980s, the Lomé system, together with local civil-servant elites, helped "develop" banana farmers through patron-client relationships. It also inserted farmers into the state apparatus through agricultural schemes and the Windward Islands Banana Association (WINBAN), which set standards for production and organized the boxing, transport, and shipping of the product.

Neoliberal arguments and forces from the United States, the United Kingdom, and elsewhere have spelled the beginning of the end of this quasi-protectionist system and the politics of patronage associated with it. Rising debt-servicing ratios, structural-adjustment programs (SAPs), and the development of macro-regional free-trading blocs (the European Union, the North American Free Trade Agreement, and the looming Free Trade Area of the Americas) mean that the days of the banana economies of the Caribbean are numbered. St. Lucian systems of communal-land tenure, the informal sector, and labor-sharing may insulate farmers from the coming crisis (see for example Barrow 1992; Dujon 1997). In the meantime, however, St. Lucian political and business leaders have been pressing ahead with alternative measures, including tourism development, luxury gated-housing projects for expatriates, and the creation of the offshore financial-services sector.

As an index of the regional transformations effected by the Anthony administration, consider the presence of the two Chinas in the Caribbean. Prior to the Anthony government, Taiwan had maintained an embassy on the island, and the old United States military base on Vieux-Fort had languished as a little-used port. Now, the People's Republic of China maintains an embassy near a new, exclusive gated community, the Taiwanese have left, and Chinese capital is flowing into the new Vieux-Fort Goods Distribution Free Zone. The governments of China and St. Lucia envision the emergence of the zone as a transshipment and distribution node for Chinese goods to reach the Caribbean market, and for Caribbean goods to reach China. This, together with St. Lucia's form of on-line IBC, peculiarly re-centers St. Lucia and redefines the boundaries of its "region," making it a node for Chinese capital and simultaneously a part of China through the financial center of Hong Kong.[3]

Offshore finance is not merely one development strategy among others, nor is its foothold in the Caribbean merely an effect of island politics responding to global forces. Throughout the region, including St. Lucia, offshore finance has become a discursive tool for Caribbean elites to forge new visions of nationalism and criticize new quasi-colonial relationships with the United States and Europe. Caribbean jurisdictions marketing themselves as offshore financial-service centers muster images of trust, stability, respectability, and, paradoxically perhaps, colonial empire, in order to sell their product. Those images have also redounded into Caribbean nationalist discourses and self-perceptions.

Offshore finance becomes a "necessity," then: first, because these states see little other recourse given the demise of a model of development based on direct aid and trade preferences from former colonial powers. And second, because offshore finance empowers visions of national distinctiveness and modernity, which, in turn, find special purchase in an oddly oppositional "rights" discourse – in a "right to offshore finance" – that Caribbean leaders direct against international critics of offshore finance (including me and my colleagues).[4] The end of the former powers' obligations to the postcolonial Caribbean means that Caribbean countries must "diversify" their economies. The creation of distinctive "island identities" through image industries like tourism and offshore finance firmly connects that potential diversification to national pride. In the Caribbean, offshore finance also reflects a reterritorialization of regionalism. In St. Lucia, that reterritorialization co-occurs with the country's promotion as a cultural center of the

Caribbean. Local poet Derek Walcott's winning of the Nobel Prize for Literature, the internationally billed St. Lucian Jazz Festival, and recent academic and policy conferences, all speak to the country's strategy to re-center itself, culturally, in a Caribbean region that, via St. Lucia, is contorting toward China. Where, through various failed attempts at West Indian federation, St. Lucia had once been the political center of regional integration, it is now a cultural center of regional disjunction.

St. Lucia's offshore experience suggests questions about parts and wholes at different levels of scale: of what is St. Lucia a part: the Caribbean? a new China? the global economy? Of what is the Vieux-Fort Goods Distribution Free Zone a part: the island of St. Lucia? China? Of what is an IBC incorporated in St. Lucia but listed on the Hong Kong Stock Exchange a part: the St. Lucian economy? the Chinese economy? the Hong Kong Stock Exchange? These questions are answerable only under the sign of nostalgia for a before-time in which such place distinctions would have made sense.

Recall Radin's unwitting infolding of the lines of the Cartesian coordinate system, her innocent near-desublimation of liberalism's binaries. For St. Lucia the topography of difference folds in on itself, or falls back into its own disjunctions. It does so without negation but through the positive necessity for, and a positive lack that constitutes, offshore finance in the Caribbean. The positive necessity is assumption of the absence of any other alternative for the Caribbean under regimes of finance capital. The positive lack is the assumption that there is nothing "there," except a legislative framework and some technological infrastructure. That framework and infrastructure are not, by them-selves, determinate. If they were, then offshore finance would not "succeed," anywhere, because every place would be a tax haven for some other place. What is necessary for "offshoreness" is precisely to be an elsewhere that is a nowhere and an everywhere, rather like St. Lucy's eyes and her vision. So, where is St. Lucia's offshore "center?" It's hard to say, since it is not a place or a point on the Cartesian grid.

The problem of analysis becomes a problem of critical vision. What, after all, does St. Lucy "see?" Not the clear, enumerable facts of liberal inquiry, but facts on a more theological plane.

Algebraic Reason and Visions of Illiberal Property

Algebraic reason, the obsession with solving for x to find the hidden figure in the whodunit, dominates liberal and critical approaches to property. Algebraic reason does not provide a critical ground outside the discourses and practices of property under liberalism and capitalism so much as a "re-setting" of their insides (as Annelise Riles noted during the Wenner-Gren conference). Algebraic reason demands that the givens and unknowns be knowable things in the world: objects or persons, abstractions or relations. It demands that these be apprehensible to a knower who formulates the problem of the unknowns in linguistic utterances or sign systems that themselves undergird the apparatus of that which is to be known. For Marx, the unknown, the hidden term, was the labor that accounts for surplus value, and accounts for it in the mathematical sense of algebraic reckoning. He used equations to understand the ideology of the general equivalent, itself indexed through an equation of setting everything to the value of money. Yet labor as constitutive of value was already quite well known to liberal theory.

In the cases at hand, algebraic reason leads regulators and critics down well-worn paths. Discussions about cyberspatial properties turn on the no-space and the every-space of cyberspace. Yet the spatial referents within which these properties are framed remains some transfiguration of the nation-state, the community, the abstract individual, the market, and so on. We solve the problem of internet banks' community reinvestment requirements either by hypostasizing "community" or by elevating to new heights abstract individual "equality." We solve the problem of taxation on electronic commerce either by defending the state's territorial jurisdiction (to say nothing of its "right" to revenue and its "duty" to its citizens' commonwealth) or by reifying the consumer transaction into the ancient *oikos*, taxing transactions based on the home-space within which consumption is imagined to occur. For St. Lucian offshore finance, we are led to ask questions about what is where and recapitulate a nostalgia for a world of territorial sovereignty and jurisdictionality neatly spatialized.

As I see it, the task is not to conjure a critical metalanguage within which to stand outside and above property formations. The very call to something outside and above partakes of the depth ontologies charting the Cartesian grids about which Radin unwittingly reminds us. Instead, I want to set a mousetrap, a restaging of the larger fictionalities carrying with them the flow and the blurring of the objects and subjects in cyberspatial properties. Just as a mousetrap for Hitchcock was a play within the play, so I will now put forward an analysis within an analysis, and turn to the first popular text on algebra, Muhammad ibn al-Khuwarizmi's ninth-century *Compendium on Calculating by Completion and Reduction*. It is from al-Khuwarizmi that English and other European languages derive the term "algorithm," meaning a procedure for solving a problem that involves a repetition of an operation (a performative iteration). The text presents abstract principles of solving equations and then illustrates them with cases having to do with what, under contemporary capitalisms, would be glossed as property relations: divisions of an inheritance; payments of dowry; prices in a market; and transactions involving slaves and their debts.

There are moments of incommensurability in the translated text, however. The 1831 translator, Frederic Rosen, admires the "science" and clarity of logic he finds in this ninth-century Arabic tome, in contrast to "Hindu" mathematical treatises. The latter treatises, Rosen complains, have a tendency to espouse "dogmatical precepts, unsupported by argument, which, even by the metrical form in which they are expressed, seem to address themselves rather to the memory than to the reasoning faculty of the learner." He continues, "The Hindus give comparatively few examples, and are fond of investing the statement of their problems in rhetorical pomp" (in al-Khuwarizmi 1831: x).

At the same time Rosen is baffled by the set of examples that make up the final third of the book. The science seems to break down, and Rosen is forced to add footnotes to the effect that:

> The solutions which the author has given of the remaining problems of this treatise, are, mathematically considered, for the most part incorrect. It is not that the problems, when once reduced into equations, are incorrectly worked out; but that in reducing them to equations, arbitrary assumptions are made, which are foreign or contradictory to the data first enounced. (*sic*, in al-Khuwarizimi 1831: 133)

al-Khuwarizmi introduced numbers in what Rosen repeatedly calls an "arbitrary" manner, in order to solve the problems of inheritance that arise when men rescind their testaments on their deathbeds, or give slave-girls with dowries to their inheritors.

Rosen overlooked the theological implications of the text, however. Because of this, he misapprehends the function of number. Like all classical Islamic texts, this one begins "In the Name of God, Gracious and Merciful!" (p. 1) and concludes, "God is the Most Wise!" (p. 174). Rosen was misled by the apparent "simplicity of style" (p. xi) into thinking that numbers always reflected countable objects in the world. The "arbitrary" numbers in al-Khuwarizmi's text beg the question: What is the nature of the numbers, the countable items, the facts in the world that "people generally want?" For al-Khuwarizmi, they always emanate from and speak to the law. In this case, it is a divine law, although, as it is of a world before the (apparent) modern separation of "religion" from the rest of life, divine law is a misnomer, and "law" itself should suffice. Indeed, Rosen's only recourse in figuring out the problems that occupy the last third of the book is to "the law." Without adjudicating the very notion of "religion" here, however, my point is simply this: al-Khuwarizmi's facts do not so much index the spatiotemporal coordinates of things in the world, as operate on a level of divine knowledge flows. For al-Khuwarizmi, numbers were not transparent. Enumeration was not a natural act but a metaphysical one. Solving for x was not finding the "real" value of a slave or cost of a bride. It was, instead, partaking in, following along with, pointing toward the quintessence, the absolute. It follows that the kind of "property relations" recounted in al-Khuwarizmi's text were also a means of pointing toward the absolute.

The "arbitrary" numbers also beg the question of the implicit metaphysics of Rosen's footnotes, and, I am suggesting, our own liberal and critical inheritances. Not bracketed by divine call but written in the margins that escape it, Rosen's footnotes nevertheless are not objective (read secular, rational) commentary. This is not merely because Rosen fails to acknowledge the text as "religious." Rather, Rosen's commentary is itself enframed by liberal property and the Cartesian grid of subjects and objects, abstractions and relations. The key opposition for Rosen is number as an abstract principle, on the one hand, and things in the world that can be counted, on the other. It is an opposition that is incredibly productive, animating whole liberal worlds full of objects and subjects, things that can be possessed and people or other entities who can establish relations of ownership. It also animates the citizen/state, equality/community opposition, and the self-as-proprietor central to liberal capitalism. At the same time, the arbitrariness of the delineation of such oppositions must be sublimated for this self to take shape, and for rules of property transfer to appear as merely technical and morally ambivalent rather than morally charged affairs. This is precisely the issue in all three of the cases of cyberspatial properties explored in this chapter: the effort at sublimating the messy morality of property into clear and natural relations between subjects about objects.

Cyberspatial property, I am suggesting, like *all* property, is a "mobile locus of becoming commingling identities as it migrates" via imaginary lines of flight (undersea cables? satellite link-ups?) (Bogue 1996: 95, writing on Deleuze and Guattari 1996: 85). It constitutes "a disjunction that remains disjunctive, and that still affirms the disjoined terms, that affirms them throughout their entire distance, *without restricting one by the other or excluding the other from the one* (Deleuze and Guattari 1996: 76, original emphasis). Here, the disjunctions between fact and evidence, property-as-thing and property-as-relation, object and subject maintain their efficacy in liberal and critical analysis only if both terms of the dichotomies are kept disjointed and there difference affirmed. Yet, as Deleuze and Guattari suggest, that disjunction never fully purifies either term; hence, property, even in its mere invocation, is the necessary but failed work of purification. Cyberspatial properties make this failure explicit. Like St. Lucy's eyes on a plate, deterritorialized from the mountain that her body has become and reterritorialized out of the "quintessence" (the mysterious divine fifth element of medieval alchemy) to "see" (that is, to witness) the obligations of faith, property demands its own testimony. Our modes of facticity and analysis alike are preconditions for the emergence of property.[5] Here, those modes include our efforts to deduce the secret of the commodity, the limits of the liberal and critical theory of property, the mousetraps we continually set and are caught in when we mistakenly strike out to solve the whodunit.

Acknowledgments

I would like to thank Katherine Verdery, Caroline Humphrey and the Wenner-Gren Foundation for organizing an incredibly stimulating conference and for giving me the opportunity to develop the ideas expressed here. I would also like to thank the other participants for their critical and collegial engagement. Tom Boellstorff, Jane Collier, Cori Hayden, Diane Nelson, Hugh Raffles, Annelise Riles, Suzana Sawyer, and Marilyn Strathern provided helpful comments on various versions of this chapter. I would also like to thank my dauntless colleagues in Caribbean offshoreland, Sue Roberts and Mark Hampton, without whom I would have never ventured to St. Lucia. Research in St. Lucia was supported by a grant from the National Science Foundation (SES 9818258) as part of a larger project, and the School of Social Sciences, University of California at Irvine. Writing has been supported at various stages by UCI, the Australian National University's Centre for Women's Studies and the Research School of Pacific and Asian Studies. The opinions expressed here are my own and do not represent those of any other agency.

Notes

1. Even in advance of the FSMA's passage consolidation had *not* significantly changed patterns of lending in low-income neighborhoods (Avery et al. 1999). Consolidations allowed mega-banks to go national, and thus to choose which jurisdictions to lend to in order to meet their CRA obligations. If a bank only has to demonstrate a certain level of "effort," it can choose to lend to poor areas that are less poor than others.

2. This vision of the nation-state is not simply spatial, but social-republican. As with the debate over internet banking, structures from imagined capitalisms past crop up: "brick and mortar" banks, and "storefront" retailers, as opposed to mega-conglomerate financial holding companies and Walmart.

3. Offshore finance interdigitates with the merchant-capitalist fraction of Caribbean islands' elites, which may account for the degree of social acceptability that offshore finance has found in the region. "The 'hegemony' of circulation over production in the region from precolonial days had engendered a sophisticated legal and financial infrastructure to facilitate import-trading activities" (Marshall 1996: 209). And the resurgence of the merchant elite and decline of the agricultural-industrial-government sector elite during the 1990s reflected global shifts in governance from welfare statism to neoliberalism.

4. Roberts, Hampton and I were taken to task by Caribbean social scientists (especially the Marxists!) for our criticisms of offshore finance as a development strategy at a Caribbean studies conference in the spring of 2000.

5. I follow here some of Marilyn Strathern's conference comments.

References

Avery, Robert, Raphael Bostic, Paul Calem, Glenn Canner, Kelly Bryant and John Matson. 1999. "Trends in home purchase lending: consolidation and the Community Reinvestment Act." *Federal Reserve Bulletin* 85: 81.

Barrow, Christine. 1992. *Family land and development in St. Lucia.* Institute of Social and Economic Research, Monograph Series No.1. Cave Hill, Barbados: University of the West Indies.

Beetham, Thomas W. 1998. "The community reinvestment act and internet banks: Redefining the community." *Boston College Law Review* 39: 911–35.

Bogue, Ronald. 1996. *Deleuze and Guattari.* New York: Routledge.

Chan, Clayton. 2000. "Taxation of global e-commerce on the internet." *Minnesota Journal of Global Trade* 9: 233–68.

Cocheo, Steve. 1999. "What price 'Outstanding?" *ABA Banking Journal* 91(6): 43–53.

Deleuze, Gilles and Félix Guattari. 1996. *Anti-Oedipus: Capitalism and Schizophrenia*. Minneapolis: University of Minnesota Press.

Derrida, Jacques. 1976. *Of grammatology*. Trans. by Gayatri Chakravorty Spivak. Baltimore: Johns Hopkins University Press.

Dujon, Veronica. 1997. "Communal property and land markets: agricultural development policy in St. Lucia." *World Development* 25: 1529–40.

Hampton, Mark P. 1996. *The offshore interface: Tax havens in the global economy*. Basingstoke: Macmillan.

Keyser, William. 2000. "The 21st century CRA: How internet banks are causing regulators to rethink the Community Reinvestment Act." *North Carolina Banking Institute* 4: 545–67.

al-Khuwarizmi, Muhammad ibn Musa. 1831. *The Algebra of Mohammed ben Musa (Compendium on Calculating by Completion and Reduction)*. Trans. Frederic Rosen. London: Oriental Translation Fund.

Marshall, Don. 1996. "From the triangular trade to (N)AFTA: A neo-structuralist insight into missed Caribbean opportunities." *Third World Quarterly* 17(3): 427–53.

Marx, K. and F. Engels. 1977. "The German Ideology." In *Karl Marx: Selected Writings*. Edited by David McLellan, 159–91. Oxford: Oxford University Press.

Maurer, Bill. 1997. *Recharting the Caribbean: Land, law and citizenship in the British Virgin Islands*. Ann Arbor: University of Michigan Press.

——. 1998. "Cyberspatial sovereignties: Offshore finance, digital cash, and the limits of liberalism." *Indiana Journal of Global Legal Studies* 5: 493–519.

Nelson, Diane. 1999. *A finger in the wound: Body politics in quincentennial Guatemala*. Berkeley: University of California Press.

Overby, A. Brooke. 1995. "The Community Reinvestment Act reconsidered." *University of Pennsylvania Law Review* 143: 1431–1531.

Radin, Margaret. 1993. *Reinterpreting property*. Chicago: University of Chicago Press.

Roberts, Susan M. 1994. "Fictitious capital, Fictitious spaces: The geography of offshore financial flows." In *Money, power and space*. Edited by S. Corbridge, R. Martin, and N. Thrift. Oxford: Blackwell.

Simmel, Georg. 1990. *The philosophy of money*. London: Routledge.

Simon, William. 1991. "Social-republican property." *UCLA Law Review* 38(6): 1335–1413.

Strathern, Marilyn. 1992. *After nature: English kinship in the late twentieth century*. Cambridge: Cambridge University Press.

Thurston, Herbert and Donald Attwater (eds.). 1956. *Butler's lives of the saints*. 4 vols. London: Burns and Oates.

US Department of Treasury. 1996. "Selected Tax Policy Implications of Global Electronic Commerce." Washington, D.C.

Zupancic, Alenka. 1992. "A perfect place to die: theatre in Hitchcock's films." In *Everything you always wanted to know about Lacan but were afraid to ask Hitchcock*. Edited by Slavoj Zizek, 73–105. London: Verso.

Index